Estimation of the Time since Death

Estimation of the Time since Death

Current Research and Future Trends

Edited by

Jarvis Hayman

Marc Oxenham
School of Archaeology and Anthropology,
Australian National University, Canberra,
ACT, Australia

ELSEVIER

ACADEMIC PRESS

An imprint of Elsevier

Academic Press is an imprint of Elsevier
125 London Wall, London EC2Y 5AS, United Kingdom
525 B Street, Suite 1650, San Diego, CA 92101, United States
50 Hampshire Street, 5th Floor, Cambridge, MA 02139, United States
The Boulevard, Langford Lane, Kidlington, Oxford OX5 1GB, United Kingdom

Notices
Knowledge and best practice in this field are constantly changing. As new research and experience broaden our understanding, changes in research methods, professional practices, or medical treatment may become necessary.

Practitioners and researchers must always rely on their own experience and knowledge in evaluating and using any information, methods, compounds, or experiments described herein. In using such information or methods they should be mindful of their own safety and the safety of others, including parties for whom they have a professional responsibility.

To the fullest extent of the law, neither the Publisher nor the authors, contributors, or editors, assume any liability for any injury and/or damage to persons or property as a matter of products liability, negligence or otherwise, or from any use or operation of any methods, products, instructions, or ideas contained in the material herein.

Library of Congress Cataloging-in-Publication Data
A catalog record for this book is available from the Library of Congress

British Library Cataloguing-in-Publication Data
A catalogue record for this book is available from the British Library

ISBN: 978-0-12-815731-2

For information on all Academic Press publications visit our website at https://www.elsevier.com/books-and-journals

Publisher: Stacy Masucci
Acquisitions Editor: Elizabeth Brown
Editorial Project Manager: Xun Wang
Production Project Manager: Selvaraj Raviraj
Cover Designer: Christian J. Bilbow

Typeset by TNQ Technologies

Contents

3. Biochemical methods of estimating time since death

Lena M. Dubois and Katelynn A. Perrault

4. The application of insects to the estimation of the time since death

James F. Wallman and Melanie S. Archer

5. TSD estimation in the advanced stages of decomposition

Eline M.J. Schotsmans, Wim Van de Voorde and Shari L. Forbes

6. The importance of microbial communities in the estimation of the time since death

David O. Carter

9. Radiocarbon and amino acid racemization (AAR) and the time since death

Stewart J. Fallon and Colin V. Murray-Wallace

10. The development of grading systems to determine human decomposition: Total Body Scoring of decomposed human bodies in indoor settings

Jarvis Hayman and Marc Oxenham

Contributors

Melanie S. Archer, Victorian Institute of Forensic Medicine and Monash University, VIC, Australia

Melanie M. Beasley, Department of Anthropology, Purdue University, West Lafayette, IN, United States

Roger W. Byard, School of Medicine, The University of Adelaide, and Forensic Science South Australia (FSSA), Adelaide

Alyce Cameron, School of Archaeology and Anthropology, Australian National University, Canberra, ACT, Australia

David O. Carter, Laboratory of Forensic Taphonomy, Forensic Sciences Unit, Division of Natural Sciences and Mathematics, Chaminade University of Honolulu, Honolulu, HI, United States

Joanne Bennett Devlin, Forensic Anthropology Center, Department of Anthropology, University of Tennessee, Knoxville, TN, United States

Lena M. Dubois, Organic and Biological Analytical Chemistry Laboratory, MolSys, University of Liège, Liège, Belgium

Stewart J. Fallon, Research School of Earth Sciences, Australian National University, Canberra, ACT, Australia

Shari L. Forbes, Département de Chimie, Biochimie et Physique, Université du Québec à Trois-Rivières, Trois-Rivières, QC, Canada; Australian Facility for Taphonomic Experimental Research, University of Technology Sydney, Sydney, NSW, Australia

Felicity Gilbert, School of Archaeology and Anthropology, Australian National University, Canberra, ACT, Australia

Jarvis Hayman, School of Archaeology and Anthropology, Australian National University, Canberra, ACT, Australia

Lee Meadows Jantz, Forensic Anthropology Center, Department of Anthropology, University of Tennessee, Knoxville, TN, United States

Colin V. Murray-Wallace, School of Earth, Atmospheric & Life Sciences, Faculty of Science, Medicine and Health, University of Wollongong, Wollongong, NSW, Australia

Marc Oxenham, School of Archaeology and Anthropology, Australian National University, Canberra, ACT, Australia

Katelynn A. Perrault, Laboratory of Forensic and Bioanalytical Chemistry, Forensic Sciences Unit, Division of Natural Sciences and Mathematics, Chaminade University of Honolulu, Honolulu, HI, United States

Eline M.J. Schotsmans, Centre for Archaeological Science, University of Wollongong, Wollongong, NSW, Australia; PACEA De la Préhistoire à l'Actuel: Culture, Environnement et Anthropologie, UMR 5199, CNRS-Université de Bordeaux, Bordeaux, France

Dawnie Wolfe Steadman, Forensic Anthropology Center, Department of Anthropology, University of Tennessee, Knoxville, TN, United States

Wim Van de Voorde, Department of Imaging and Pathology, Forensic Biomedical Sciences, KU Leuven - University of Leuven, Leuven, Belgium; Department of Forensic Medicine, University Hospitals Leuven, Leuven, Belgium

Giovanna M. Vidoli, Forensic Anthropology Center, Department of Anthropology, University of Tennessee, Knoxville, TN, United States

James F. Wallman, School of Life Sciences, University of Technology Sydney, Sydney, Australia; Centre for Sustainable Ecosystem Solutions, School of Earth, Atmospheric and Life Sciences, University of Wollongong, Wollongong, Australia

About the editors

Jarvis Hayman is a retired surgeon who studied archaeology, completing a Master's degree at the Australian National University in Canberra with a thesis on the archaeology of the Scottish Highland Clearances. He then combined his medical and archaeological knowledge to complete a PhD on the estimation of the time since death in decomposed human bodies in Australian conditions. His research areas of interest are: historical archaeology and forensic archaeology/anthropology. He is a Visiting Fellow at the Australian National University and the co-author of Human Body Decomposition.

Marc Oxenham is a Professor in Bioarchaeology at the Australian National University, Canberra, Australia. His expertise in human skeletal biology has been recognized nationally through invitations to consult on a range of forensic cases for the Australian Federal Police, Australian Government Solicitor, The Australian Defense Forces (in particular Unrecovered War Casualties-Army) as well as the New South Wales Police Force. His main research has concentrated on exploring aspects of human palaeopathology and behavior by way of analyses of human skeletal and dental material. He has held teaching and research positions at Colorado College, USA, and the ANU. He was president of the Australasian Society of Human Biology (2012–14), an Australian Future Fellow (2013–17), elected a Fellow of the Society of Antiquaries of London in 2011 and elected a Fellow of the Australian Academy of the Humanities in 2016.

Chapter 1

Approaches to time since death estimation

Jarvis Hayman, Marc Oxenham
School of Archaeology and Anthropology, Australian National University, Canberra, ACT, Australia

How to develop a more accurate estimation of the time since death in human bodies found decomposed or decomposing has exercised the minds of criminal investigators and others interested in advancing scientific knowledge since the first forensic cases described by Sung Tz'u in 13th century China [1]. When more intense interest in the subject developed in the 19th century, research first focussed on the recognition that the fall in the temperature of a corpse could be of use in determining the time since death in the early stages of decomposition [2–4], but it was French Army Surgeon and entomologist Jean Pierre Mégnin who recognised that different groups and species of insects were attracted to a decomposing body during the various stages of decomposition [5]. Of necessity, this led him to describe the different stages of decomposition in order to match them with the various species of insects appearing on a corpse at varying stages during its decomposition. Unfortunately, this led to his descriptions being used to convict people, often wrongly, of unlawful killing. In 1897 Murray Galt Motter, after a study of 150 disinterred human bodies in and around the Washington DC area in the USA, commented, in relation to using insect succession to estimate the time since death, that it was not possible to make any universally applicable generalisations and indeed it was not safe to draw any conclusion at all [6]. Although the study of entomology and its value in estimating the time since death in bodies found decomposed has advanced greatly since that time, especially in the last 30 years, there is still an error rate that invites caution when it is employed in criminal cases.

Since the 1950s when researchers increased their efforts to match temperature with the time since death and especially after the studies of Thomas Marshall and F. E. Hoare in the 1960s in their attempts to determine a mathematical model, there has been increased interest and research into all aspects of human decomposition. As new technological innovations have been introduced into scientific research, they have been employed in attempting to more accurately estimate the time since death [7–10]. These have included

Estimation of the Time since Death. https://doi.org/10.1016/B978-0-12-815731-2.00001-7

attempts to find a linear relationship between changes in biochemical substances with the decomposition of the corpse not only in the early stages but also in the advanced stages of decomposition; the use of microscopy and physicochemical methods of dating skeletal material such as chemiluminescence, the citrate content of bone and in the last decade, the use of body scoring methods to quantify the stages of decomposition.

The research published by Mary Megyesi and others in 2005 on a method of quantifying the stages of body decomposition with a Total Body Score gave a significant boost to attempts to more precisely determine the time since death in human bodies found decomposed [11]. Many studies since then have attempted to refine quantifiable scoring of the decomposed remains and to produce models incorporating the many variable factors which affect the rate of decomposition but to date the number of these factors such as temperature, moisture, context, scavenging etc. as well as the subjectivity of body scoring methods have defied efforts to produce a more statistically precise model. Attempts have also been made to define a "universal model" applicable to all situations in which a decomposed body is found but so far this has not been proved to be possible because the contextual and climatic situations in which a corpse may be discovered are so numerous and so varied that it may never be possible with present technology although the hope is that it may become feasible in the future with the development of quantum computing [12,13].

The following section provides an overview of the chapters presented in this volume. As will be seen, some focus on very specific postmortem stages with the initial chapters following a progressively longer timeline after death. Subsequent chapters discuss a range of both new or developing approaches and techniques to estimating TSD, some of which will be quite novel to some readers. We have attempted to be as thorough in our coverage as possible, with some techniques, or versions thereof, being commonly employed in forensic case work, while others are much more experimental and largely untested in the courts.

Roger Byard, in Chapter 2, begins the substantive part of this volume by reviewing research on estimating TSD in the early postmortem period (or 24–48 h), although some of the techniques reviewed can be utilised within the first 24 h (e.g. algor mortis, or the more or less predictable decline in body temperature in the early postmortem period). Indeed, the Hensgge nomogram remains the preferred method. Livor mortis, generally used to identify body position after death, and rigor mortis changes over time are also discussed, both approaches to TSD estimation being dependent on a wealth of variables most of which will be difficult to control for. The process of autolysis and putrefaction are briefly described, with a detailed description of how 'stages' in this process can be utilised for TSD estimation dealt with in Chapters 5 and 10. Roger also notes the limited value of using gastric emptying (evaluation of stomach contents) in determining the time since a last meal. Also mentioned is the lesser known, in the West at least, use of mechanical and electrical muscle excitation techniques for TSD estimation, approaches that perhaps require more replicative research. Overall, Roger provides a wealth of techniques of varying levels of accuracy and precision in the estimation of TSD within the first two days postmortem.

In Chapter 3 Lena Dubois and Katelynn Perrault explore the value of biomarkers in estimating TSD, the core premise being that measurable biomarkers change (increase or decrease) in a predictable and relatively standardised manner during the postmortem interval. Perhaps one of the most well know of such approaches is analysis of the concentration of potassium in the vitreous humor of the eye, which is arguably useful up to 72 h postmortem. A wealth of other biomarkers have been analysed, both sourced from within the body itself (e.g. ammonia and nitrogen concentrations) and others from decomposition products that have seeped into the immediate environment (e.g. phosphorous and sodium) with varying degrees of value in TSD estimation. In terms of preservational durability, and thus the ability to be sampled, adipose tissue lipids and by-products have received considerable attention in recent years. Again, such biomarkers can be sampled from the body directly or from the surrounding burial matrix (generally soil). Proteins, including enzymes and protein metabolism by-products also appear to be of value in examining the postmortem interval (PMI). Some of this protein-focused research has revisited work on the vitreous humor with promising outcomes. The premise that DNA and RNA degrade in a regular and measurable manner postmortem has also received attention in recent years. It would seem that the rate of decay is dependent on various factors, including tissue type and temperature and despite a wealth of recent research, the approaches are still experimental rather than of practical use in case work. Decomposition odour (volatile organic compounds, VOC) is an important variable in insect colonisation succession patterns and it is not surprising that research into the measurement of VOCs released by the decomposing corpse has shown some promise in the estimation of the TSD. Practical approaches include recent work on trimethylamine concentrations in postmortem tissues. Lena and Katelynn finish their chapter with a consideration of the practical value of biomarker research to date, in as much as proposed methods can pass evidentiary standards. Their conclusions are sobering, because only a very few of the hundreds of biomarkers assessed to date consistently provide useful TSD estimates.

James Wallman and Melanie Archer review the role of insects in estimating TSD, an approach that can extend the assessable postmortem window substantively beyond the first 48 h. The underlying premise in forensic entomology is that particular species will colonise and utilise a corpse for a finite period of time and that the subsequent changes to the decomposition fluids and tissues will provide a more suitable ecosystem for subsequent colonisation by different species (whether insect or other factor-moderated): a process termed succession. James and Melanie begin by introducing the key insect players, those that have evolved to a point where they rely on locating and colonising decomposing animals in order to reproduce: for the most part certain fly and beetle species. It is important to note that it is a minimum PMI that is being estimated as it is often difficult or impossible to determine the lag period between death and subsequent initial insect colonisation. Apart from insect succession, James and Melanie discuss the role of specific species maturation (e.g. stage and size) in developing an estimate of the minPMI. A range of confounding factors are also discussed, including the issue of insect species identification which can have significant flow on effects in calculating the minPMI. Other issues include seasonality and weather, including retrospectively generated temperature estimates with temperature being a significant variable in insect activity and reproduction rates. A significant portion of James and Melanie's chapter is given to procedures, and associated issues, with insect collection methods and processes. This is particularly pertinent in cases where sampling is not being carried out by the forensic entomologist. The Chapter concludes with a series of forensic case studies that illustrate the role and value of forensic entomology.

In Chapter 5, Eline Schotsman, Wim Van de Voorde and Shari Forbes tackle the complex issue of estimating TSD when a body has reached an advanced state of decomposition. In noting the difficulties inherent in estimating TSD with advanced decomposition they stress the importance of context, not least of which is the effect of temperature (and humidity) in either accelerating (higher temperatures) or slowing (cooler temperatures) decomposition. The environmental context (e.g. soil) has a major influence on decomposition rates, and thus estimation of TSD, particularly in terms of its ability (or inability) to facilitate microbial action, gas exchange and moisture movement. Apart from faunal interference (e.g. vertebrate scavenging), human body disposal behaviours (e.g. by embalming or being confined in a coffin) will affect the rate and nature of decomposition. Moreover, individual characteristics such as sex, age, and body size will influence decomposition rates to varying degrees in different burial environments. Eline and colleagues also discuss the effects and predisposing conditions for preservation (e.g. mummification, freezing, saponification) of soft tissues and how such issues can be dealt with. The intriguing case of bog bodies, the context of which is generally well known among northern European archaeologists, is also mentioned. They discuss the important issue of differential decomposition (and preservation), which should be taken into consideration when assessing total body scores (TBS usually assumes uniform rates of decomposition throughout the entire body, including the external appearance) for the decomposition of the entire corpse. A significant portion of the chapter reviews and critiques current methods for estimating TSD using either formulae and/or a TBS with a substantive comparative test of such approaches using a complex case study. They conclude by suggesting more regional models of decomposition are better suited to TSD estimates and that specialists need as broad a knowledge base as possible to deal with this vexing problem.

David Carter's chapter departs from a focus on techniques with a particular or specific value at various periods postmortem when he examines the role and value of microorganisms in estimating TSD. David begins by looking at microorganisms and microbial communities and one way in which that can be of value in estimating TSD: microbial community succession (a concept of particular importance in forensic entomology). Unlike the case with insects, a body will harbour an antemortem microbial community that will change at death, clearly requiring an understanding of such communities prior to death. Microbes not only contribute to the processes of decomposition, but microbial succession tracks important stages in this process, one key event being the major microbial succession event following rupture of the body tissues caused by the production of putrefactive gas. Importantly, microbial action can continue significantly beyond the early postmortem period, well beyond the timeframe of traditional forensic entomological approaches. Indeed, microbial communities play a role in bone degradation with some promise of extending the window of TSD estimation significantly. An advantage of using microbes is that sampling can take place by way of standard swabs and species identification can be carried out using DNA identification techniques. The use of microbes in TSD estimation is perhaps one of the most exciting and promising areas of research at present in this discipline.

In Chapter 7 Alyce Cameron and Marc Oxenham explore the value and range of approaches to estimating TSD using skeletonised remains. In general, approaches focus on methods that seek to identify levels of organic remains preserved in skeletal material and those that examine the physical breakdown of the non-organic components of bone. For instance, UV fluorescence seeks to identify proteins that may still be preserved in bone, although the value of the approach lies more in being able to differentiate between recent and much older (>100 years) remains. Other tests, such as chemiluminescence which can identify iron in haemoglobin, has had varying success and clearly requires much more research as does work on citrate content of bone and rates of DNA degradation in bone. Other techniques, such as Infra-red and Raman spectroscopy, which can identify the molecular structure of bone, while having a significant role in other areas of medical and forensic science have yet to make a significant impact on the estimation of the TSD, although they certainly seem to be a promising area of further research. When considering the decomposition of bone structures, Alyce and Marc note that histological techniques exploring surface bone changes show some promise, particularly with respect to changes in surface pores over time. They note that weathering has received a considerable amount of attention, but a wealth of variables (not least climate and general environmental factors) may play a significant role in the development of a general model of weathering and TSD estimation. Clearly, estimating TSD in skeletonised remains is fraught with difficulty, but current research appears promising.

The next chapter, by Felicity Gilbert and Marc Oxenham, explores current research into estimating TSD in aquatic environments. The first point made is that, in contrast to conventional wisdom, decomposition in aquatic environments does not necessarily follow terrestrial decomposition stages, notwithstanding the corpse will often follow the same basic processes while one unique factor is the relatively early loss of the skin (or gloving as it is referred to). They note that during the early postmortem period algor mortis can potentially be as useful as it is in terrestrial situations, although limited practical research has been carried out on the temperature effects in aquatic environments. It is also worth noting that preservational processes can also occur in watery environments, including mummification and saponification. Important factors to note with decomposition in water are that the environment can be quite volatile with regard to depth, which can influence flotation behaviour; temperature and chemistry, both of which can markedly affect microbial presence and density; and turbulence i.e. water currents and flow, which can also affect the rate of decomposition. Moreover, while scavenging also occurs in terrestrial circumstances, the types of scavengers can be quite different in aquatic environments (lakes, rivers, oceans etc.). While insect colonisation and succession can occur in aquatic environments (including terrestrial forms where part of the corpse is above the water line), most invertebrate fauna are opportunistic scavengers and will feed on remains when introduced into their environment but there is no real set pattern or timeframe in which this will occur. Felicity and Marc go on to review those few research studies that have explored the estimation of TSD in aquatic environments, including those that have employed analogues of the terrestrial total body score approach. They note the limited value of staged approaches to scoring decomposition and also the need for much more research into the broader range of what are rather variable aquatic environments such as depth, season, location, temperature and water chemistry.

Stewart Fallon and Colin Murray-Wallace review the application of radiocarbon dating and amino acid racemization approaches to estimating TSD, both of which have a long history of use in archaeology. The basic premise behind radiocarbon dating is that living organisms take up carbon 14 (produced in the upper atmosphere) during their lifetimes, with this assimilation ceasing at death. As carbon 14 is an unstable isotope of carbon, it decays over time at a known rate. The concentration of carbon 14 is then able to be measured in a dead organism and the time since death calculated, and with modern methods TSD can be measured in 10s of 1000s of years. Atomic testing in the mid-twentieth century dramatically increased the concentration of atmospheric carbon 14, the concentration of which has been decreasing ever since. The pattern and rate of carbon 14 concentration can therefore be mapped on a 'bomb curve'. Stewart and Colin go on to discuss how this event, and the bomb curve, can be used to our advantage in estimating TSD using C14 dating in more recent remains, including year of birth (given the right conditions). The second half of the chapter deals with amino acid racemization (AAR), which is based on the observation that amino acids in living individuals have a characteristic form termed L, but when an organism dies it's amino acids take on an alternative D form (the process of racemization) at a known rate which can be used to estimate time since death. Advances in analytical techniques and equipment has meant the technique can be used in forensic situations, where TSD is measured on a relatively much shorter scale than the 100s of 1000s of years employed when researching fossil organisms. Indeed, it is also possible to estimate age at death, in contrast to TSD, in some circumstances. In general, a range of factors can negatively affect the use of AAR, particularly temperature, which may be a significant issue when dealing with burned remains. It must be noted, however, that more research is required to assess the value of TSD estimation using AAR techniques within forensically relevant timeframes.

In Chapter 10, Jarvis Hayman and Marc Oxenham explore the history and origins of the use of body scoring systems for the estimation of TSD before discussing more recent approaches using this methodological approach. An important, albeit often overlooked, early study was published by Joseph Bonaventure Orfila and Octave Lesueur in 1831 based on their observation of bodies reclaimed from the Seine, Paris, France. However, it is not until the late 19th century that stages of decomposition were described, in the context of early entomological work by the French army surgeon Jean Paul Mégnin. While other studies of note are explored, it is not until the mid-1960s that the next major advance was made with Jerry Payne's controlled decomposition experiments using animals. With entomologists at the forefront of such research, it was not until the 1980s with work by Alison Galloway and colleagues that decomposition stages were explored outside of the context of insect succession. In the early 1990s a standardised approach to measuring temperature effects (accumulated degree days) was introduced to decomposition staging studies by Arpad Vass. In the 21st century, Mary Megyesi and colleagues introduced more quantitative rigour into staged approaches to decomposition. In 2016 we introduced a new approach to total body score approaches with a retrospective study of human decomposition in Australian indoor conditions. It is concluded that quantitative approaches to body soring systems should be a standard requirement but much more research into human decomposition in as many environments, and conditions as is practically possible, is required before body scoring systems can be considered for practical application. Notwithstanding, such approaches have enormous potential for estimating TSD in a range of time frames.

This volume concludes with Chapter 11 by Giovanna Vidoli, Melanie Beasley, Lee Meadows Jantz, Joanne Bennett and Dawnie Wolfe Steadman. This is an appropriate final chapter because it looks at the future of taphonomic research into TSD as well as reviewing and summarising many of the topics dealt with in this book, but in the context of work at the original human decomposition facility in Knoxville, Tennessee. Interesting new research at the facility includes work on stable isotopes (generally until now used primarily for reconstructing diet and/or mobility patterns in deceased individuals), in one case looking at differential ratios of nitrogen isotopes during the process of decomposition. Other work at the facility has investigated differential rates, and modes, of decomposition among a range of species, including humans. The finding that specific species have their own characteristic decomposition rates and patterns is important when considering the use of non-human analogues in such research. The Tennessee facility was the first in the world to use human body donors for taphonomic research. It continues to lead and to work at the cutting edge of research into a range of procedures and methods used in the forensic sciences, not least being research into more precise estimates of TSD.

In the nearly 15 years since the publication of the study by Megyesi and others, the number of studies into the estimation of the TSD have greatly increased but without necessarily any further advancement in its precision. In order to bring together the various fields of research in this specialised field, the editors are very grateful for all the researchers who have contributed to this book. One of our chief purposes in putting together this volume is to spur current and future researchers to greater efforts in finding new and more accurate approaches to estimating the TSD in all postmortem periods. Some forensic anthropologists and indeed forensic pathologists have questioned the need to exercise so much time and effort on research into the time since death, however, if it results in the refutation of a false alibi in a criminal case or the confirmation of the truth of a statement which provides the release of an innocent person, such an effort will have served its purpose. In addition, if it renders comfort in revealing the truth behind the discovery of a decomposed body to the deceased's relatives, again, efforts to more precisely determine the time since death will have rendered a useful service.

References

[1] McKnight BE. The washing away of wrongs: forensic medicine in thirteenth century China. Ann Arbor: University of Michigan; 1981.

[2] Davy J. Observations on the temperature of the human body after death. In: Researches physiological and anatomical, vol. I. London: Smith, Elder and Co.; 1839. p. 228–48.

[3] Taylor AS, Wilks D. On the cooling of the human body after death. Guy's Hosp Rep 1863;180:211.

[4] Rainy H. On the cooling of dead bodies as indicating the length of time that has elapsed since death. Glasgow. Med. J. 1868;1:323–30.

[5] Mégnin P. La Faune des Cadavres. Application d'Entomologie à la Médecine Légale. Paris: Gauthier et fils; 1894.

[6] Motter MG. A contribution to the study of the fauna of the grave. J N Y Entomol Soc 1898;6(4):201–31. Dec 1898.

[7] Marshall TK. Estimating the time of death: the use of the cooling formula in the study of post-mortem body cooling. J Forensic Sci 1962a;7(2):189–210.

[8] Marshall TK. Estimating the time of death: the use of body temperature in estimating the time of death. J Forensic Sci 1962b;7(2):211–21.

[9] Marshall TK. The use of body temperature in estimating the time of death and its limitations. Med Sci Law 1969;9:178–82.

[10] Marshall TK, Hoare FE. Estimating the time of death: the rectal cooling after death and its mathematical expression. J Forensic Sci 1962;7(1):56–81.

[11] Megyesi MS, Nawrocki SP, Haskell NH. Using accumulated degree days to estimate the post-mortem interval from decomposed human remains. J Forensic Sci 2005;50(3):1–9.

[12] Vass AA. The elusive post-mortem interval. Forensic Sci Int 2011;204:34–40.

[13] Cockle DL, Bell LS. Human decomposition and the reliability of a "Universal" model for post mortem interval. Forensic Sci Int 2015;253:136e1–9.

Chapter 2

Estimation of the time since death in the early postmortem period (24–48 hours)

Roger W. Byard
School of Medicine, The University of Adelaide, and Forensic Science South Australia (FSSA), Adelaide

> *Each part, deprived of supple government, Shall, stiff and stark and cold appear like death.*
>
> William Shakespeare (1564–1616), Romeo and Juliet, Act 4, Scene 1.

> *At the instant of death the organism commences to return to an equilibrium with the outer world.*
>
> Professor Johan Ludwig Caspar (1796–1864), Berlin, Prussia [1].

Introduction

Although a series of characteristic and sequential changes occurs in bodies after death there is considerable variability among individuals in the timing of such processes. The speed of development of both physical and biochemical changes is influenced by a variety of internal and external factors, sometimes acting synergistically [2]. Factors which speed up postmortem changes are summarized in Table 2.1 [3]. As a result of this extreme variability, finding an accurate way to determine time of death has become a type of philosopher's stone for pathologists. More pragmatically the timing of postmortem changes has been referred to as the Achilles heel of forensic pathology [4]. One result of assuming that all bodies behave in a similar manner is that unusual postmortem changes may be incorrectly interpreted at a death scene or an autopsy resulting in investigative authorities receiving inaccurate advice. The following chapter will deal with external and internal pathological findings that may be used as a guide to the time of death in the early postmortem period, as well as investigative methods that have been proposed as measures of postmortem interval.

Estimation of the Time since Death. https://doi.org/10.1016/B978-0-12-815731-2.00002-9

TABLE 2.1 Factors speeding up the onset and extent of postmortem changes [3].
Hot and moist environment
Prolonged time before cool storage
Insulation by warm clothing or bed coverings
Obesity
Diabetes mellitus
Infections or sepsis
Intoxication with illicit drugs such as amphetamines

Algor mortis

Algor mortis is the name used to describe the normal cooling of a body after death as it equilibrates with the ambient temperature. Normal human internal temperatures range from 34.2° to 37.6° with a mean of 36.9° [5], however there is considerable variability which may compromise methods that rely upon 37° as a starting point for time of death estimation. Factors affecting core temperature are summarized in Table 2.2.

Equilibration of the body with environmental temperatures occurs by conduction, convection, radiation, and evaporation, with the major processes

TABLE 2.2 Factors that may alter body temperature [6,7].
Elevated rectal temperature
Physical exertion
Infections/fever
Emotional stress
Organic conditions e.g. malignant hyperthermia, hyperthyroidism
Decreased fluid intake
Neuroleptic medications
Illicit drugs e.g. amphetamines, cocaine
Reduced rectal temperature
Hypothermia
Hypothyroidism
Frailty syndrome

controlling heat exchange being conduction and convection. The rate of cooling of a body after death depends on a number of factors. The Body Mass Index (BMI) is important, as obese bodies retain heat and so cool more slowly than cachexic bodies [6,8]. This is also influenced by sex as females have more subcutaneous fat than males and so lose temperature more slowly. The rate of heat loss is also dependent on the difference between the core temperature and the environmental temperature, as a body exposed to colder temperatures will cool more quickly. Wind and moisture will enhance heat loss, with a naked body in rain cooling faster, particularly if the body is stretched out and not curled into a ball. Clothing acts as an insulator retaining heat, as do bed covers [7].

Immediately after death, or the cessation of cardiorespiratory function, the temperature of the body remains unchanged for some time; this is called the "postmortem temperature plateau" [5]. It has been estimated that this plateau will persist for between one to 3 h in cool to moderate temperatures followed by a linear decrease in temperature of between 0.5 and 1.5 °C per hour for the next 10–16 h [7]. This rate slows the closer the temperature of the body gets to the environmental temperature.

A number of systems have been used in attempts to estimate postmortem interval based on the assumed predictable decline in body core temperature (measured in the rectum, brain and tympanic membrane) [9], but all suffer from problems, as the initial body temperature is not known, the length of the temperature plateau for each individual is uncertain, and they become less and less accurate the closer the body temperature is to the environmental temperature [5]. The most widely used method involves the Hensgge nomogram which requires measuring and plotting the ambient and core temperatures at the death scene, allowing for weight and introducing a corrective factor for clothing, as the calculations are based on a naked body lying extended in still air (Fig. 2.1). There are two charts for temperatures above and below 23° [10,11].

The most accurate estimations occur indoors soon after death rather than in outdoor locations where temperatures may change dramatically over the hours with wind and rain being confounding factors. It has also been noted that reproductions of the nomogram in standard texts [12] may not be accurate representations of the original material [13]. The nomogram is also of no use in infants and children under 10 kg weight.

Livor mortis

Livor mortis or hypostasis refers to the red-blue-purple discolouration that develops in the skin of dependent parts of the body after death. Although the cause is believed to involve gravitational settling of blood within dermal capillaries, usually within 30 min to 3 h after death, the mechanism is obviously more complex as the pattern in a body that has not been moved is not that of a simple line with lividity below and pallor above, but is instead usually quite irregular with livid areas that are not infrequently quite high up on the

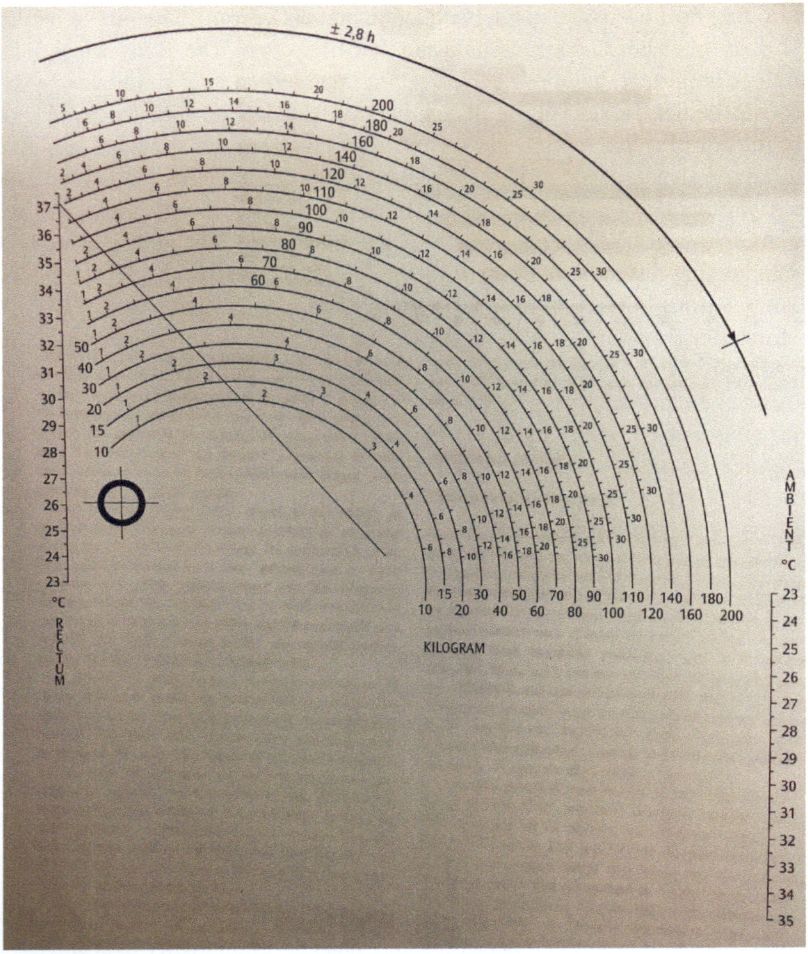

FIG. 2.1 The Hensgge nomogram that is used to estimate time of death based on calculations using rectal and ambient temperatures [10,11].

body. For example, irregular pink patches which may be found on the cheeks have been attributed to the effects of local stasis and have been called *Kirchhofrosen* in German [14].

Early in the development of livor the colour is pink-red due to oxygenation of red blood cells (Fig. 2.2). This becomes darker over time as oxygen levels decline resulting in a more blue-purple hue [2]. The colour may, however, be influenced by a variety of factors such as carbon monoxide or cyanide poisoning, hypothermia, and in bodies stored at cold temperatures where the colour is light red-pink. Classically carbon monoxide toxicity is associated with a "cherry pink/red" discolouration because of the formation of carboxyhemoglobin [5]. Livor may be brown in colour in nitrate or nitrite poisoning

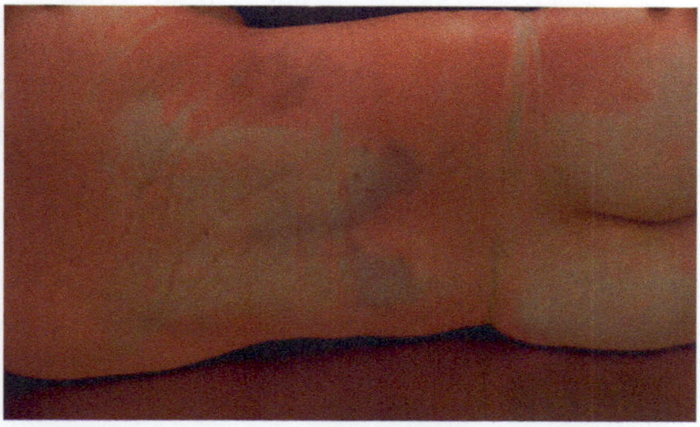

FIG. 2.2 Pink dependent lividity over the back of a recently deceased individual with prominent pressure blanching over the buttocks and centre of the back. Linear blanching can also be seen around the waist from clothing.

due to the formation of methemoglobin and green with putrefactive changes due to the accumulation of sulfhemoglobin [2]. Livor may be markedly reduced or absent if there has been excessive blood loss prior to death or if the decedent was anaemic. It may also be very difficult to discern in individuals who are deeply sun-tanned or dark-skinned.

Livor becomes patterned when the body has had pressure applied to dependent areas which prevents dermal capillaries filling with blood. In Caucasians the compressed skin is pale and white which often contrasts dramatically with the surrounding red-purple congested skin, as can be seen on the back of the decedent in Fig. 2.2. If an object is pressed into the skin, it may leave a distinct outline as was observed on the outer thigh in Fig. 2.3 where the fingers have been resting.

One of the major uses of livor is in identifying the position that the decedent was left in after death, as livor would be expected over the back in someone who has died in the supine position, and over the front in someone who has died and remained in the prone position. Although the finding of

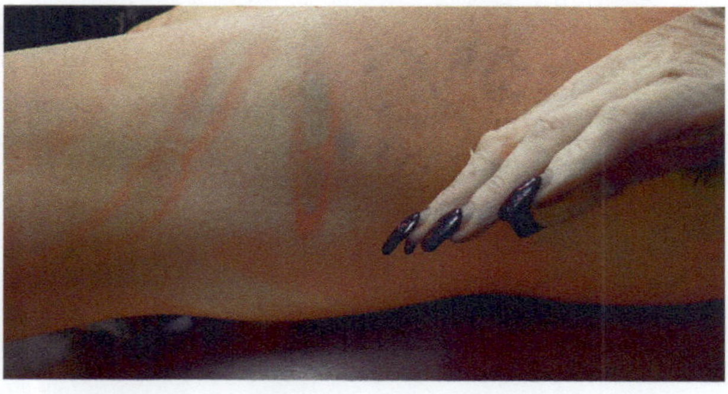

FIG. 2.3 The original position of the fingers over the left side of the body can be seen due to pressure blanching.

anterior lividity with pressure blanching in a body found on its back indicates that the body has been moved after death, it is not uncommon to find posterior lividity in cases at autopsy who also have anterior lividity corresponding to a face down position after death. The reason for this is that most bodies develop posterior livor during the time that they are stored lying on their backs [15].

A related phenomenon which may be encountered in areas of lividity involves postmortem ecchymoses which are small areas of interstitial haemorrhage caused by rupture of subcutaneous capillaries and smaller vessels (predominantly veins) after death due to increased intravascular pressures from blood pooling [16].

While stages in the development of lividity have been used in the past to estimate the time since death the variability among individuals makes this a very inaccurate process [4]. An approximate guide to the chronology of these changes is of livor appearing between 30 min to 3 h as a patchy red discoloration which then becomes confluent, fully developing by four to 8 h, with the maximum intensity reached at approximately 10 h. The timing is summarized in Table 2.3 [7].

Fixation is a term used to describe a failure of livor to blanch when pressure is applied to it because the position of the livor has become permanent. In the first 12–18 h after death livor is not fixed and so applied pressure will force blood out of engorged congested capillaries, rendering the area pale in light skinned individuals. This phenomenon is also seen when a body is moved, as the areas of livor will shift to the newly positioned dependent parts. It has been suggested that this occurs because the red blood cells in congested vessels are still intact and therefore are capable of shifting within the vascular system. After this time livor becomes fixed and so will not blanch under pressure or change if the body is moved. Fixation is thought to be due to haemoconcentration and then lysis of red blood cells producing an indelible stain in surrounding tissues, much as the lining of blood vessel becomes stained from putrefactive haemolysis [17]. The process is markedly affected by environmental temperatures with fixation occurring much earlier in warmer climates or situations.

Differentiating livor from bruising is important as the latter indicates that blunt force trauma has occurred. As noted above, in the early postmortem

TABLE 2.3 Very approximate times for the appearance of livor mortis after death in cool to moderately warm environments [7].

	Earliest	Most common	Latest
Patchy	0.5 h	2 h	3 h
Confluent	4 h	6 h	8 h
Maximum	6 h	10 h	16 h

period livor will blanch with pressure, while bruises will not. A simple incision will clearly demonstrate normal appearing yellow subcutaneous fat in livor, contrasting with red interstitial haemorrhage in bruising [18].

Rigor mortis

Although skeletal muscles relax in the period after death rigor mortis soon develops which refers to the sequential stiffening of various muscle groups [2]. While rigor mortis develops in all muscles it is first noticed in the eyelids and jaw, sometimes as early as 20 min after death. This is followed by stiffening of elbow and knee joints approximately two to 6 h after death. The progression of rigor from the head to the arms and then the legs is known as "Nysten's rule" and is due to the increase in muscle bulk distally, although rigor may develop first in the legs if a decedent had experienced marked physical activity of the legs prior to death (as in forceful running) which may have used up available adenosine triphosphate (ATP) [7]. Rigor mortis may occasionally be useful in helping to assess whether a body has been moved after death if the limbs have stiffened into an unusual position.

Rigor mortis develops as ATP is used up within skeletal muscle myofibrils which results in actin and myosin microfilaments adhering and causing muscles to stiffen. Affected muscles lose their elasticity and shorten, a process which continues until the myofibrils disintegrate due to autolysis and putrefaction.

As in most findings after death the timing of rigor mortis is very variable and is influenced by environmental temperatures; for example, high temperatures are associated with a more rapid onset, sometimes within one to 2 h. This contrasts with cooler temperatures where it may not develop for six to 8 h [3,19]. It also develops more rapidly in infants, but may be undetectable in cachexic individuals with debilitating diseases or in individuals with myopathic or neurological disease such as muscular dystrophy or multiple sclerosis. While the occurrence of instantaneous rigor mortis, known as cadaveric spasm, has been debated [2,20] cases occasionally present to autopsy with objects firmly grasped in their hands (Fig. 2.4) [21]. Factors that may alter the timing of rigor mortis are summarized in Table 2.4.

Loosening of rigor mortis is also temperature dependent and although it begins in cool and temperate climates approximately 24−36 h after death rigor may still be detected many days later at autopsy when bodies have been stored in cold morgue refrigerated rooms. It usually disappears in the order in which it appeared. While rigor mortis is absent in putrefied bodies, gases derived from decomposition may stretch the soft tissues resulting in the artefact of so-called putrefactive 'rigor mortis' [22].

Autolysis and putrefaction

While autolysis and putrefaction are usually thought to occur as late post-mortem changes there are a number of factors and situations where they may

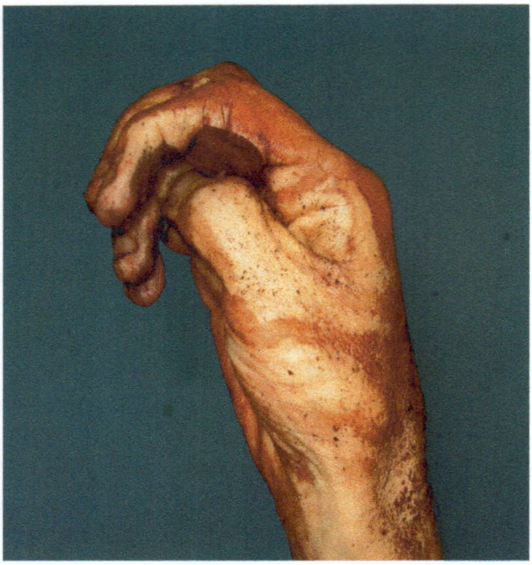

FIG. 2.4 A shard of glass firmly gripped in the hand of a 37-year-old man who died quite rapidly from an incised wound to the throat in keeping with so-called "cadaveric spasm".

TABLE 2.4 Factors effecting the development of rigor mortis [7].

Accelerated rigor mortis
Exertion before death
Fever
Fitting
High environmental temperatures
Delayed rigor mortis
Cachexia/frailty syndrome
Debilitating organic diseases
Low environmental temperatures

be accelerated resulting in these changes occurring relatively soon after death [3]. Autolysis refers to the sterile breakdown of tissues and organs due to disruption of cell membrane integrity after death causing the release of lysosomal enzymes with "autodigestion". This endogenous enzyme activity results in extensive loss of tissue structure [7].

A process which usually accompanies autolysis is putrefaction where there is bacterial growth within the body contributing to organ and soft tissue

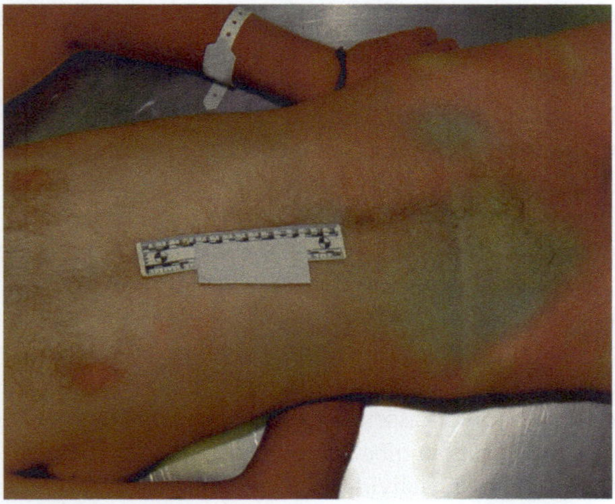

FIG. 2.5 Green putrefactive discoloration of the right lower abdomen within 24 h of death due to accelerated putrefactive changes from high summer environmental temperatures.

disintegration. After death anerobic bacteria (usually *Clostridium* and *Proteus* species) proliferate within the gut and then migrate into adjacent tissues and through the vasculature to the rest of the body [23]. The two processes may act synergistically as autolytic disintegration of the integrity of the gut mucosa assists bacterial migration. One of the earliest signs of putrefaction may be green discoloration of the right iliac fossa which overlies the bacterial filled cecum (Fig. 2.5). The green colour derives from bacteria generated hydrogen sulfide combining with haemoglobin from autolytic red blood cells forming sulfhaemoglobin. Early venous marbling arises from red blood cell autolysis and the intravascular growth of intestinal bacteria that have migrated along blood vessels [5] (Fig. 2.6).

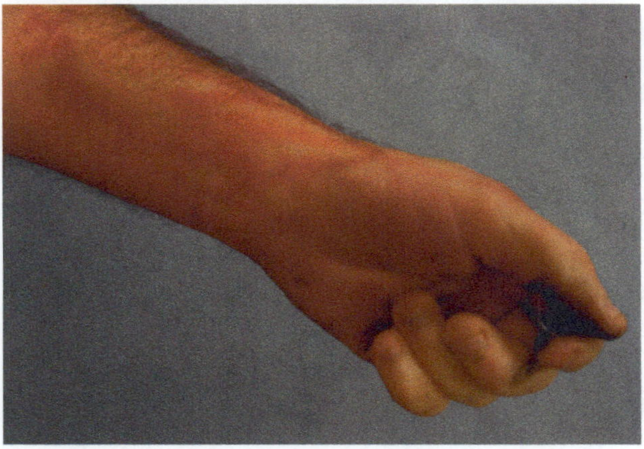

FIG. 2.6 Early venous marbling of the forearm showing the characteristic serpiginous linear discoloration due to bacterial-associated venous haemolysis.

As summarised in Table 2.1 there are a number of exogenous and endogenous factors which may cause accelerated putrefaction and thus confuse a death scene when estimation of the time of death is undertaken. Any conditions that mimic laboratory conditions for growing bacteria may cause this. Thus, putrefaction may begin within hours of death in hot moist ambient environments compared to cold conditions [24,25].

Putrefaction is also accelerated in individuals who have had hyperglycaemia from uncontrolled diabetes mellitus or a systemic infection. High blood sugar levels feed bacteria and in cases of disseminated sepsis bacteria have already spread to multiple organs, and the body temperature is often raised. As obese individuals also maintain a higher body temperature for longer, those with high BMIs are also more likely to putrefy. Thus, time of death estimates based on an assessment of decompositional changes must be modified for the increasing number of large individuals now presenting to our morgues [26,27]. Injured individuals with open and dirty wounds from stabbings or a firearm also present a portal for bacteria to enter the body that may increase the rate of putrefaction [28]. The degree of putrefaction may also vary from one part of the body to another depending on exposure to elements such as the sun or water [29].

Green discoloration of the abdomen will become more generalized over time with the development of skin slippage, putrefactive fluid-filled skin blisters, and purging of putrefactive fluids from the mouth and nose. The case of a prisoner who had died of natural causes but who demonstrated these changes when checked one morning raised the possibility that he had been dead for a number of days. It was not until the heating system beside his cell was found to be faulty that the reason for the accelerated decomposition was established.

It has been suggested that putrefactive changes are more reliable in estimating time of death in bodies that have been immersed in water as the temperature of water tends to be more stable with less fluctuations. Evaluations take into account a large number of putrefactive signs such as peeling of the skin and loss of nails [30,31]. The effect of salt or freshwater immersion on this is unclear as it has been shown that bodies immersed in salt water putrefy more slowly than in fresh water [32] (see Chapter 8, this volume for a detailed discussion of this topic).

Other postmortem changes

The following are briefly listed for completeness merely to mention further postmortem changes that occur, however, they are all generally found some time after death.

Adipocere

Adipocere is also known as grave or corpse wax or the "fat of graveyards", and is produced when adipose tissue decomposes, usually in cold wet conditions, by the hydrolysis of triglycerides into glycerine and free fatty acids [33]. It is gray-white in colour and the early waxy consistency changes to a more solid and crumbling material as the fatty acids crystallize. It occurs more often in females, the well-nourished and the obese, rather than in underweight or cachectic individuals with lower adipose tissue content [34]. Generally, adipocere takes months or years to develop, but it has on occasion been found within days of death [35,36].

Mummification

Mummification refers to the process of the desiccation of soft tissues which usually happens in hot dry environments, although it may also occur in cold regions if conditions are sufficiently arid [2,37]. It may be found in elderly cachexic recluses whose bodies have remained undiscovered for some time [38]. While it usually takes some time to develop, again this may be variable with mummification of the limbs sometimes occurring after only several days exposure to hot and dry weather conditions. As the tissues and organs dehydrate, they shrink, causing considerable loss of body weight (up to 60%–70%) with the skin becoming hard and leathery. The limbs tend to flex [7].

Skeletonization

Reduction of a body to bones occurs once there has been total or partial loss of soft tissues and organs. It usually occurs after prolonged periods of decomposition but may be quite rapid in hot environments if there is also insect colonization of the body and scavenger activity [39,40].

Other parameters

Evaluation of gastric contents

Although it was once considered that the stomach emptied in a uniform and predictable manner and so the time between consumption of the last meal and death could be quite accurately predicted, this is no longer believed. There are numerous variables that affect the rate of gastric emptying including age, underlying disease states such as diabetes mellitus, stress, body mass index (BMI), pain, nausea, surgery, drug ingestion and the nature of the ingested food [41–43]. If the stomach contains food at autopsy, then the most reliable observation to make is that death has occurred sometime after a meal has been eaten. Despite this, there have been notable cases where convictions were influenced by very precise estimates of emptying times. However, even as early as 1985 Horowitz and Pounder considered that the opinions given on the stomach contents and time of death in the Truscott case in Canada and the Van Beelen case in Australia were "scientifically unsound" [41].

Assessment of muscle excitability

As death is a process and not a simple end point, cell and organ metabolism continue long after cardiorespiratory function has ceased. For this reason it has been proposed that skeletal muscle reactivity can be used to estimate time since death [44,45]. While not a standard technique in English speaking jurisdictions, it is used in parts of Europe where the biceps muscle of the upper arm is forcefully struck to elicit one of three reactions. In the first one to two and a half hours after death the whole muscle will contract ("propagated excitation"). Following this, a reversible contraction (the so called "idiomuscular pad") will occur up to four to 5 h postmortem. Then a weaker contraction will occur up to 24 h after death [14].

An alternative to mechanical excitation of muscles is the use of electrical stimulation [46,47]. This technique requires the insertion of two small electrodes into the medial part of the upper eyelid for passage of a current from a 30 mA generator. The muscular response is graded into 6° with the strongest response occurring soon after death (VI) which consists of contraction of the entire ipsilateral muscles of the face. The response of degree V involves only the upper and lower eyelids and ipsilateral forehead muscles, with the degree of contractility decreasing with increasing postmortem interval until it only affects muscle at the site of the electrodes [14].

Assessment of iris reactivity

In a similar manner the reactivity of the iris has been assessed using injections of stimulant drugs into the anterior chamber of the eyeball. These will affect the smooth muscle of the iris within five to 30 min. Tropicamide, norepinephrine and atropine will increase iris diameter compared to acetylcholine which will decrease the diameter. Atropine will have an effect for up to three to 10 h after death compared to acetylcholine and norepinephrine which may have an effect from up to 14–46 h post mortem [14].

Evaluation of cerebral changes

While it was suggested that H magnetic resonance spectroscopy could be used to identify changing metabolite concentrations in decomposing brains and that this could be used to predict post mortem intervals [48], it has been noted this data relies on isolated animal heads which may not be comparable to practical forensic situations [14]. A far simpler animal study has shown a linear increase in brain fluid content with increasing postmortem interval [49].

Measurement of vitreous humor analyte concentrations

The vitreous humor is more resistant to the effects of autolysis than the blood and so provides a ready source for postmortem electrolyte sampling. Electrolytes change in predictable manner after death with a number of studies looking at estimating postmortem interval from increasing potassium levels [50–52]. Unfortunately, as with other parameters, this has not proved to be completely reliable, although it does become more accurate if a multiple linear regression formula is used in conjunction with other analytes such as urea, glucose and sodium [14]. Although it was proposed that the linear increase in vitreous humor hypoxanthine over 120 h postmortem might also be useful [53], it has been shown that potassium levels had a stronger correlation [54,55].

Miscellaneous

The value of immunohistochemical staining of tissues for a variety of substances including thyroglobulin, calcitonin and insulin [56,57] has yet to be proven, as do the results of more recent studies looking at RNA degradation [58,59].

Artefacts

Preservation by freezing

Freezing of a body most often occurs following a homicide to either conceal the body or to allow it to be disposed of at a later time. Freezing halts postmortem changes and so completely confounds time of death estimations. If a body is later dumped outside in a warm to hot environment the degree of putrefactive change is usually greater on the exterior as the internal organs will remain frozen for longer [7].

Animal predation

Colonisation by arthropods may occur immediately after death with considerable damage being done to a body in a relatively short period of time if the conditions are favourable. Flies (Diptera) and beetles (Coleoptera) are attracted to bodies after death and flies may lay eggs around the nostrils and mouth very early in the postmortem period, particularly in hot environments [60]. "Faunal succession" refers to colonization of bodies by specific arthropod species for only a limited period of time [61] (see Chapter 4, this volume, for a detailed discussion of this topic). Postmortem lesions caused by ants consist of very characteristic superficial serpiginous injuries [62].

The significance of arthropod colonisation is twofold – particular species may be found in only one specific area or microenvironment and so their presence out of this range may suggest that a body has been moved. In addition, entomological assessment of the developmental stages of particular species can be used to try to determine the time that a corpse has been inhabited, the so-called "colonisation interval" [7].

Larger animals such as rodents, dogs, foxes and cats can also cause considerable damage to bodies when feeding [37,63,64]. The major issues with animal predation are not around time of death estimations but in trying to determine whether injuries occurred before or after death, and whether significant underlying organic diseases were present. The latter is particularly difficult, if not impossible, if major organs have been consumed by the roving animals [39].

Conclusions

Caspar's comment over 150 years ago that once death occurs an organism "commences to return to an equilibrium with the outer world" [1] remains succinct and accurate. The rate at which these changes occur, however, remains the subject of debate, investigation and some confusion. Idiosyncratic responses of biological systems remain a reality and cannot be underestimated. However, while recognizing that timing of processes in forensic pathology is our Achilles heel [4], new techniques and revisiting older methods may still help to clarify some of these issues over time.

References

[1] Caspar JJL. A handbook of the practice of forensic medicine based upon personal experience, vol. 1. Thanatological division. London: New Sydenham Society; 1861. p. 17.

[2] Prahlow J, Byard RW. Postmortem changes and time of death. Ch 8. In: An atlas of forensic pathology. New York: Springer Publishers; 2012. p. 145–98.

[3] Zhou C, Byard RW. Factors and processes causing accelerated decomposition in human cadavers. An overview. J Forensic Leg Med 2011;18:6–9.

[4] Byard RW. Timing – the Achilles heel of forensic pathology. Forensic Sci Med Pathol 2017;13:113–4.

[5] Knight B, Nokes L. Temperature-based methods I. In: Knight B, editor. The estimation of the time since death in the early postmortem period. 2nd ed. London: Arnold; 2002. p. 3–42.

[6] Byard RW. Frailty syndrome – medicolegal considerations. J Forensic Leg Med 2015;30C:34–8.

[7] Tsokos M, Byard RW. Post mortem changes - overview. In: Payne-James J, Byard RW, editors. Encyclopedia of forensic and legal medicine. 2nd ed., vol. 4. Oxford: Academic Press; 2016. p. 10–31.

[8] Byard RW. The complex spectrum of forensic issues arising from obesity. Forensic Sci Med Pathol 2012;8:402–13.

[9] Baccino E, de Saint Martin L, Schuliar Y, et al. Outer ear temperature and time of death. Forensic Sci Int 1996;83:133–46.

[10] Henssge C. Death time estimation in case work—I. The rectal temperature time of death nomogram. Forensic Sci Int 1988;38:209–36.

[11] Henssge C, Madea B. Estimation of the time since death. Forensic Sci Int 2007;165:182–4.

[12] Saukko P, Knight B. Forensic pathology. 3rd ed. London: Edward Arnold; 2004. p. 84–6.

[13] Burger E, Dempers J, Steiner S, Shepherd R. Henssge nomogram typesetting error. Forensic Sci Med Pathol 2013;9:615–7.

[14] Madea B. Methods for determining time of death. Forensic Sci Med Pathol 2016;12:451–85.

[15] Byard RW, Jensen L. How reliable is reported sleeping position in cases of unexpected infant death? J Forensic Sci 2008;53:1169–71.

[16] Hammer U, Büttner A. Distinction between forensic evidence and post-mortem changes of the skin. Forensic Sci Med Pathol 2012;8:330–3.

[17] Byard RW, Cains G, Tsokos M. Haemolytic staining of the intima of the aortic root – a useful pathological marker of fresh water drowning? J Clin Forensic Med 2006;12:125–8.

[18] Byard RW. Sudden death in the young. 3rd ed. Cambridge, UK: Cambridge University Press; 2010.

[19] Nokes L, Madea B, Knight B. Changes after death. In: Knight B, editor. The estimation of the time since death in the early postmortem period. 2nd ed. London: Arnold; 2002. p. 209–43.

[20] Bedford PJ, Tsokos M. The occurrence of cadaveric spasm is a myth. Forensic Sci Med Pathol 2013;9:244–8.

[21] Byard RW. The 'break, enter and die' syndrome may involve significant injury to major neck vessels. J Forensic Sci 2011;56(Suppl. 1):S252–4.

[22] Tsokos M, Byard RW. Putrefactive "rigor mortis". Forensic Sci Med Pathol 2012;8:200–1.

[23] Byard RW, Tsokos M. The challenges presented by decomposition. Forensic Sci Med Pathol 2013;9:135–72.

[24] Green H, Gilbert J, James R, Byard RW. An analysis of factors contributing to a series of deaths due to exposure to high environmental temperatures. Am J Forensic Med Pathol 2001;22:196–9.

[25] Byard RW, Gilbert JD, Kostakis C, Heath K. Circumstances of death and diagnostic difficulties in brushfire fatalities. J Forensic Sci 2012;57:969–72.

[26] Byard RW, Bellis M. Significant increases in body mass index (BMI) in an adult forensic autopsy population from 1986 to 2006 – implications for modern forensic practice. J Forensic Legal Med 2008;15:356–8.

[27] Eitzen DA, Byard RW. The handling of bariatric bodies. J Forensic Leg Med 2013;20:57–9.

[28] Gill-King H. Chemical and ultrastructural aspects of decomposition. In: Haglund D, Sorg MH, editors. Forensic taphonomy. The postmortem fate of human remains. Boca Raton, FL: CRC Press; 1997. p. 93–108.

[29] Fernando T, Winskog C, Byard RW. An unusual pattern of decomposition associated with suicidal electrocution in the bath. J Forensic Sci 2013;58:1085–7.

[30] Doberentz E, Madea B. Estimating the time of immersion of bodies found in water – an evaluation of a common method to estimate the minimum time interval of immersion. Rev Española Med Leg 2010;36:51–61.

[31] Doberentz E, Madea B. Estimating of duration of immersion. In: Madea B, editor. Estimation of the time since death. 3rd ed. Boca Raton: CRC Press; 2015. p. 189–202.

[32] Byard RW. Putrefaction – an additional complicating factor in the assessment of freshwater drownings in rivers. J Forensic Sci 2018;63:899–901.

[33] Byard RW. Adipocere – the fat of graveyards. Am J Forensic Med Pathol 2016;37:208–10.

[34] Fiedler S, Graw M. Decomposition of buried corpses, with special reference to the formation of adipocere. Naturwissenschaften 2003;90:291–300.

[35] Thali MJ, Lux B, Lösch S, Rösing FW, Hürliman J, Feer P, et al. "Brienzi" – the blue vivianite man from Switzerland: time since death estimation of an adipocere body. Forensic Sci Int 2011;211:34–40.

[36] Mohan Kumar TS, Monteiro FN, Bhagavath P, Bakkannavar SM. Early adipocere formation: a case report and review of literature. J Forensic Leg Med 2009;16:475–7.

[37] Haglund WD, Sorg MH, editors. Forensic taphonomy. The post mortem fate of human remains. Boca Raton: CRC Press; 1997.

[38] Byard RW, Tsokos M. Forensic issues in cases of Diogenes syndrome. Am J Forensic Med Pathol 2007;28:177–81.

[39] Byard RW, James RA, Gilbert JD. Diagnostic problems associated with cadaveric trauma from animal activity. Am J Forensic Med Pathol 2002;23:238–44.

[40] Byard RW. Animals, autopsies and artefacts. Forensic Sci Med Pathol 2011;7:309–10.

[41] Horowitz M, Pounder DJ. Gastric emptying – forensic implications of current concepts. Med Sci Law 1985;25:201–14.

[42] Soenen S, Rayner CK, Horowitz M, Jones KL. Gastric emptying in the elderly. Clin Geriatr Med 2015;31:339–53.

[43] Samsom M, Bharucha A, Gerich JE, et al. Diabetes mellitus and gastric emptying: questions and issues in clinical practice. Diabetes Metab Res Rev 2009;25:502–14.

[44] Madea B, Krompecher T, Knight B. Muscle and tissue changes after death. In: Hnesgge C, Knight B, Krompecher T, Madea B, Nokes L, editors. The estimation of the time since death in the early postmortem period. 2nd ed. London: Edward Arnold; 2002. p. 134–208.

[45] Madea B. Supravitality in tissues. In: Madea B, editor. Estimation of the time since death. 3rd ed. Boca Raton: CRC Press; 2015. p. 17–40.

[46] Madea B. Estimating time of death from measurements of electrical excitability of skeletal muscles. J Forensic Sci Soc 1992;32:117–29.

[47] Madea B, Rödig A. Precision of estimating the time since death using different criteria of excitability. Forensic Sci Med Pathol 2006;2:127–33.

[48] Madea B. Is there recent progress in the estimation of the postmortem interval by means of thanatochemistry? Forensic Sci Int 2005;151:139–49.

[49] Leonard A, Vink R, Byard RW. Brain fluid content related to body position and post mortem interval – an animal model. J Forensic Sci 2016;61:671–3.

[50] Zhou B, Zhang L, Zhang G, Zhang X, Jiang X. The determination of potassium concentration in vitreous humor by low pressure ion chromatography and its application in the estimation of postmortem interval. J Chromatogr B Analyt Technol Biomed Life Sci 2007;852:278–81.

[51] Siddamsetty AK, Verma SK, Kohli A, Puri D, Singh A. Estimation of time since death from electrolyte, glucose and calcium analysis of postmortem vitreous humor in semi-arid climate. Med Sci Law 2014;54:158–66.

[52] Zilg B, Bernard S, Alkass K, Berg S, Druid H. A new model for the estimation of time of death from vitreous potassium levels corrected for age and temperature. Forensic Sci Int 2015;254:158–66.

[53] Rognum TO, Hauge S, Oyasaeter S, Saugsted OD. A new biochemical method for estimation of postmortem time. Forensci Sci Int 1991;51:139–46.

[54] Munoz Barus JL, Suarez-Penaranda J, Otero XL, et al. Improved estimation of postmortem interval based on differential behavior of vitreous potassium and hypoxanthine in death by hanging. Forensci Sci Int 2002;125:67–74.

[55] Madea B, Hensgge C. Eye changes after death. In: Madea B, editor. Estimation of the time since death. 3rd ed. Boca Raton: CRC Press; 2015. p. 161–85.

[56] Wehner F, Wehner H-D, Subke J. Delimitation of the time of death by immunohistochemical detection of calcitonin. Forensic Sci Int 2001;122:89–94.

[57] Wehner F, Wehner H-D, Subke J. Delimitation of the time of death by immunohistochemical detection of glucagon on pancreatic β-cells. Forensic Sci Int 2002;124:241–8.

[58] Ondrizola A, Riancho JA, de la Vega R, et al. miRNA analysis in vitreous humor to determine the time of death: a proof-of-concept pilot study. Int J Leg Med 2013;127:573–8.

[59] Sampaio-Silva F, Magalhaes T, Carvalho F, Dinis-Oliveira RJ, Silvestre R. Profiling fRNA degradation for estimation of post mortem interval. PLoS One 2013;8:e56507.

[60] Byrd JH, Castner JL, editors. Forensic entomology. The utility of arthropods in legal investigations. Boca Raton: CRC Press; 2001.

[61] Benecke M. Forensic entomology: arthropods on corpses. In: Tsokos M, editor. Forensic pathology reviews, vol. 2. Totowa, NJ: Humana Press; 2004. p. 207–40.

[62] Byard RW. Autopsy problems associated with postmortem ant activity. Forensic Sci Med Pathol 2005;1:37–40.

[63] Buschmann C, Solarino B, Püschel K, Czubaiko F, Heinze S, Tsokos M. Postmortem decapitation by domestic dogs: three case reports and review of the literature. Forensic Sci Med Pathol 2011;7:344–9.

[64] Gapert R, Tsokos M. Anthropological analysis of extensive rodent gnaw marks on a human skull using post-mortem multislice computed tomography (pmMSCT). Forensic Sci Med Pathol 2013;9:441–5.

Chapter 3

Biochemical methods of estimating time since death

Lena M. Dubois[1], Katelynn A. Perrault[2]
[1]*Organic and Biological Analytical Chemistry Laboratory, MolSys, University of Liège, Liège, Belgium;* [2]*Laboratory of Forensic and Bioanalytical Chemistry, Forensic Sciences Unit, Division of Natural Sciences and Mathematics, Chaminade University of Honolulu, Honolulu, HI, United States*

Introduction

After death, a number of biochemical changes take place in the human body. In the previous chapter (see Chapter 4, this volume), a focus was placed on the early post-mortem interval (PMI), which typically comprises the period between death and the start of soft tissue decomposition. Beyond the early post-mortem period, the estimation of post-mortem interval using biochemical markers becomes more challenging. If reliable patterns in the biochemical profile of biological fluids or tissue are identified, measurements of this profile in such matrices at the time of discovery of a body can yield valuable information about the PMI. However, the relationship between PMI and biochemical markers is often complex due to the numerous endogenous and environmental variables that play a role in post-mortem chemical reactions [1]. Developments in instrumental sensitivity and specificity in recent years has, however, provided a number of high throughput methodologies for estimating post-mortem interval using biochemical markers [2]. This is beneficial because chemical measurements are often viewed as being more objective than observational methods in court, and error rates can be calculated to encompass their associated scientific uncertainty.

Many studies are aimed at developing models that relate measurements from the body, whether biochemical or physical, to PMI. It must be noted that the scientific method is a crucial component of developing PMI models that can eventually be used as a routine method in post-mortem examination. Recent publications have called forward issues in anecdotal claims for post-mortem interval, as well as the lack of corroborating data for claims of patterns in post-mortem interval that have been perpetuated over time in the literature [3]. As such, it is essential to critically evaluate and understand the state of

Estimation of the Time since Death. https://doi.org/10.1016/B978-0-12-815731-2.00003-0

technology readiness of PMI estimation methods that measure biochemical markers when they are presented in the literature. A large number of preliminary studies claim the possibility for implementation as a PMI estimation method, yet currently lack follow up studies that fully validate their use in casework scenarios [3,4].

An ideal biochemical marker for PMI would meet several criteria. First, the biochemical marker should be present in a matrix that can be collected and analysed within an extended timeframe if it is to be used beyond the early post-mortem period. Biomarkers measured in tissues that decompose quickly in their entirety have less practical potential, as they can only be used if the body is recovered prior to significant post-mortem alteration. In order for biochemical markers to be useful in cases with longer post-mortem periods (i.e. weeks or months) the samples must still be present for collection. Secondly, a predictable relationship should exist between the concentration of the marker and the PMI. In situations where this relationship does not necessarily appear to be predictable, it may still be possible to establish a predictable relationship if other intrinsic and extrinsic factors are accounted for (e.g. temperature, moisture, pH, presence of oxygen). An example of such an approach is to relate biomarker concentration to a scaled time factor, such as accumulated degree days (ADD), rather than number of days. ADD accounts for temperature as a variable influencing concentration, and thereby limits the variance in biomarker concentration which results from individuals decomposing in environments with different temperatures [5,6]. The most successful demonstrations of biochemical markers have exhibited a *linear* relationship between concentration and time. It is possible that this relationship could be a negative linear relationship (i.e. the compound is present in higher concentration and decreases steadily after death) or a positive linear relationship (i.e. the compound is present in lower concentration or entirely absent and steadily increases after death). While a linear relationship is not necessarily required, it does have significant benefits for simplicity of a concentration-time model. In linear relationships, each y-value is only possible at a single x-value, meaning that a particular concentration measurement can only lead to a single possibility for time. Many current studies on biochemical markers characterise temporal trends of compounds that have multi-peak trends or discontinuous presence. It is important for future work developing methods from these preliminary trends to address how measurements in a case scenario would be assessed if the biomarker could represent multiple time points. It is possible that multi-peak biomarker trends could provide accurate PMI estimation if other information (e.g. visual observation) can contribute to an accurate final estimation of PMI.

Electrolytes and elemental analysis

The use of ions to estimate PMI is historically one of the most reliable and widely used methods. Several researchers in the early 1960s [7,8] established a relationship between increasing potassium concentration in vitreous humour and the length of PMI. These studies established a predictable equation to predict PMI up to 100 h with very low error rates that did not vary over time (±4.7 h). After decades of work, that both confirmed and refuted these initial findings, it was determined in the 1990s that PMI estimation using post-mortem vitreous potassium concentration was accurate within 24 h and could be further estimated up to 48–72 h under some circumstances [9]. This biochemical marker has one of the most extensive research backgrounds of all those that have been investigated [4]. Recent research has focused on the use of analytical instrumentation and statistical methods to reduce error rates [10,11], correlating vitreous potassium concentration to physical post-mortem changes (i.e. rigour mortis, algor mortis, and corneal turbidity) [12], as well as correcting for factors such as age and temperature [13]. Zilg et al. highlighted the wide variability in best fit lines from other studies (Fig. 3.1) [13], and ultimately determined that age contributes to 16% of post-mortem vitreous potassium variation while temperature accounted for 5% of variation. It is also proposed that an online tool could facilitate improved PMI estimation using vitreous potassium for practitioners [13]. Although other ions (e.g. sodium, chloride) in vitreous humour have not been correlated to PMI, hypoxanthine has had comparable trends to potassium (see Section Nucleic acids and related compounds). Vitreous potassium still remains the biochemical marker with the most complete literature investigation for its relationship to PMI [4].

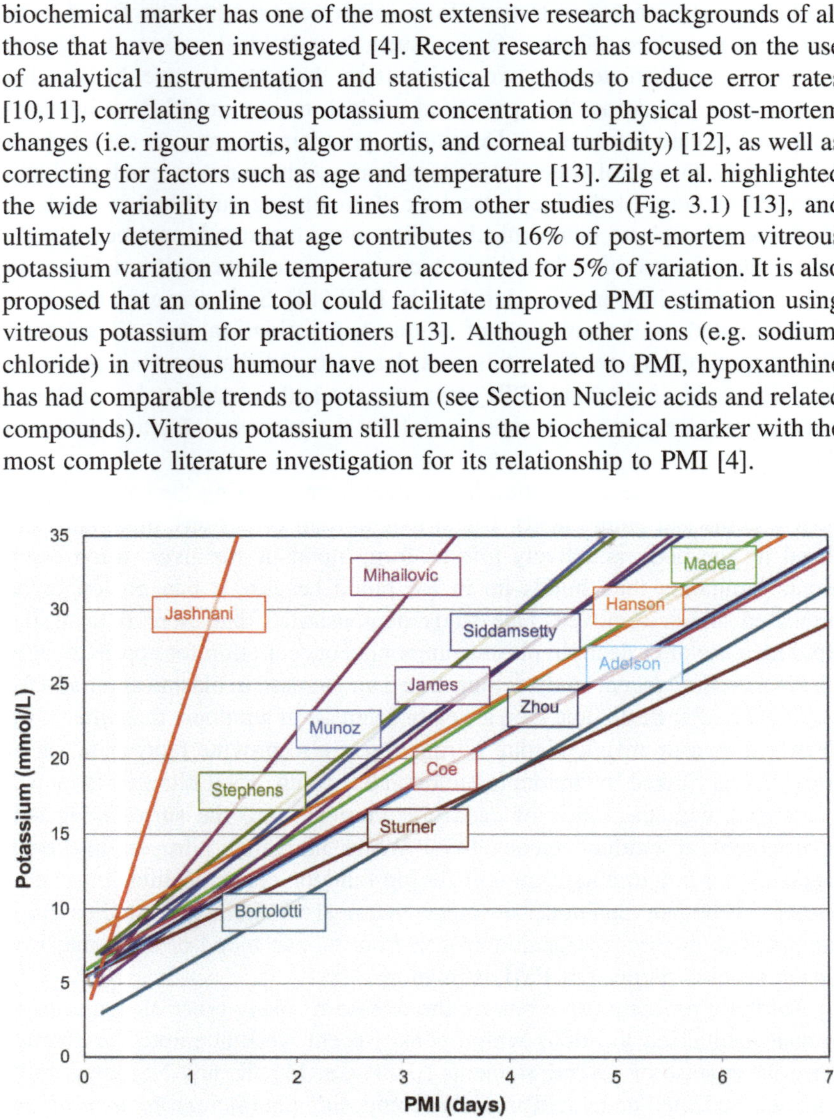

FIG. 3.1 *Regression lines* for the calculations of PMI using vitreous potassium performed in different studies [13].

While a large body of research exists into the use of vitreous humour as a matrix for PMI estimation, more research has emerged on the analysis of ions from other matrices. In 1992, Vass et al. [5] collected data on anions and cations released from decomposing human remains into the surrounding soil in outdoor environments. These ions included chloride, sulphate, sodium, ammonium, potassium, calcium, and magnesium. After accounting for temperature (i.e. through the use of accumulated degree days, ADD), moisture, and body mass, ion concentrations from soil-water extracts were found to be consistent regardless of other factors such as individual or season [5]. Ion concentrations fluctuated in a two-peak pattern; these trends were then applied to two case scenarios that generated logical maximum PMI estimations compared to case information. Despite the promising regression models built in this study, the use of water extractions from soil have not been adopted into forensic practices, likely due to the lack of continuing published research on this topic. Though no biochemical markers were measured, one recent study investigated the use of soilwater conductivity to determine postburial interval (PBI), which by inference is related to the PMI [14]. Soilwater conductivity is indeed related to the presence of anions and cations in the soil solution. Though preliminary work on this area demonstrated that the soilwater conductivity could give reliable PBI estimates, the authors ultimately concluded that the measurements were most useful for the purposes of grave detection [14].

Ammonia is a decomposition by-product formed during the catabolism of nucleic acids and amino acids. Under antemortem conditions, ammonia produced by the body is actively filtered from blood by the liver; when death occurs, ammonia then builds up in the blood because it can no longer be circulated and/or removed. One study demonstrated that there is an initial rapid increase after death in plasma ammonia concentration for approximately 8 h [15]. A more recent study demonstrated an increase in plasma ammonia for the first 9 h after death, and then a steady decrease of ammonia thereafter [16]. Chemical measurements of total nitrogen may also provide representation of nitrogen contributed by ammonia buildup after death. Total nitrogen is known to increase with the influx of cadaveric nutrients into the surrounding soil environment at outdoor scenes [17]. While inorganic nitrogen has been characterised longitudinally in soil during outdoor decomposition in several studies of human analogue or other mammals [17,18], no studies have attempted to monitor inorganic nitrogen from human blood or other matrices for the specific purpose of PMI estimation.

Autolytic processes also initiate the release of many other elements from compartmentalised locations within cells. Recent work attempted to characterise the release of several elements (i.e. P, Ca, Mg, K, and Na) temporally from soil collected under and around decomposing pig (*Sus scrofa domesticus*) remains [19]. Potassium, calcium, and magnesium did not exhibit any significant trends in the study; however, phosphorus and sodium were seen to increase under and in close vicinity to the decomposing remains [19]. Another study investigated a large number of elements in human and porcine adipose tissue (i.e. Na, Mg, Al, Si, K, Ca, Mn, Fe, Zn, Sr, and Pb) over a 30-day period using inductively coupled plasma – mass spectrometry (ICP-MS) [20]. This study demonstrated that the influx of sodium and potassium into the surrounding environment from decomposing remains is due to the loss of sodium and potassium from adipose tissue. These research studies were not conducted for the purposes of estimating PMI, but the longitudinal aspect of their study designs demonstrates potential utility of significant elements for future work in PMI estimation. The investigation of elements such as sodium, potassium, magnesium, and calcium may also provide insight into the use of conductivity measurements from soil-water solution [14], decomposition fluid [21], or tissue to estimate PMI in future work.

Lipids and related compounds

It is speculated that lipids and/or their by-products derived from adipose tissue can potentially be used as biomarkers of decomposition, as lipids and fatty acids have been shown to be persistent in decomposition environments [22]. Human adipose tissue is composed of 5%–30% water, 2%–3% proteins and 60%–85% fat (by weight) [23]. Such fat or lipids are mainly comprised of triglycerides containing numerous fatty acids attached to a glycerol molecule. The most abundant fatty acid commonly associated with adipose tissue is mono-unsaturated oleic acid (C18:1). This is followed by polyunsaturated linoleic acid (C18:2), monounsaturated palmitoleic acid (C16:1), and the corresponding saturated palmitic acid (C16:0) [24]. Immediately after death, neutral fats are hydrolysed by intrinsic lipases resulting in the formation of free fatty acids and glycerin [20,23,24]. In a secondary phase, lipolytic enzymes originating from microorganisms (bacteria and fungi) strongly contribute to the transformation process [20,23]. Fatty acids can undergo oxidation or hydrogenation depending on oxygen availability [23]. Bacterial enzymes lead to the transformation of unsaturated fatty acids into saturated fatty acids, which may further undergo β-oxidation [20,25]. In anaerobic conditions, neutral lipids can be completely converted to adipocere (adipo = fat, cree = wax). Adipocere is known to contain a mixture of saturated fatty acids, which is known to be relatively stable and persistent in soil [22,26].

Previous research focused on the determination of lipids and their by-products in soil below or around where a decaying carcass was placed. Larizza et al. investigated the fatty acid profile in soil containing decomposition fluids of pigs in order to determine the lateral extent of fatty acid release in the cadaver decomposition island (CDI) [27]. Breton et al. aimed to determine the effect of environmental variables on the decomposition process and subsequent changes in gravesoil microbial fatty acids [28]. The authors used fatty acid methyl ester (FAME) profiling to study the community level changes in soil throughout the decomposition process. Changes in FAME profiles coincided with the onset of active decay and persisted through to the dry remains stage. The study emphasises the microbial sensitivity to significant changes in soil moisture levels; hence, FAME profiles can differ greatly between season and year. While these studies did not perform modelling of fatty acids in correlation to PMI, they demonstrate the longitudinal trends of fatty acids resulting from pig decomposition.

Only a few studies have investigated the use of fatty acids for PMI estimation. Vass et al. was one of the first studies that aimed at developing a method for using volatile fatty acids (VFAs) to estimate the post-mortem interval (PMI) [5]. In addition to the anions and cations mentioned above (see Section Electrolytes and elemental analysis), microbial VFAs were analysed from underneath seven decomposing human cadavers [5]. It was found that each body produced the same ratios between propionic, butyric and valeric acid prior to skeletonisation; hence, a range of PMI estimation could be calculated using VFAs (1285 $\pm$ 110 ADD) [5]. Furthermore, it was shown that trends between specific VFAs could be correlated to decomposition stages, which was hypothesised to be a result of VFAs correlating with insect activity, anaerobic fermentation of soft tissues, and/or protolithic activity of microbes [5]. Longer chain fatty acids were interpreted as indicators for decomposition in cold environment [5]. The authors emphasised that soil moisture and body weight prior to decomposition were the two most important variables influencing the concentration of VFA in soil solutions [5].

Swann et al. conducted a study to detect short chain VFAs and long chain fatty acids in decomposition fluid collected from pork belly, piglets, and adult pig carcasses, in the absence of a soil matrix [29]. An increase in short chain VFAs was detected in pork belly until experimental day 15. This was followed by decreasing concentration until the end of the study. This is significant because trends indicate that fatty acid degradation may follow a predictable pattern. Ideally, a useful biochemical marker would exhibit a linear relationship between concentration and time, which was not apparent for the investigated short chain VFAs. This appears to be consistent between the limited longitudinal VFA studies that have been conducted. It is possible that long chain fatty acids exhibit cyclic trends related to the fly life cycle [29]. In addition, ratios between individual fatty acids were investigated; however, no trends were found that would allow their use as effective indicators of PMI [29]. Finally, temporal trends of VFAs require further validation in human studies to prove valuable for forensic casework.

Recent research that characterises fatty acids from decomposing tissue characterises preliminary temporal trends but does not appear to extend these trends to PMI estimations. Additionally, the majority of recent studies were performed on human analogues; therefore, further validation is required on human remains and on applications to forensic case studies. However, the persistence of fatty acid by-products in tissue and the surrounding environment, together in combination with methods developed for their detection in these previous studies, may provide valuable research avenues in the future for identifying biochemical markers.

Proteins and related compounds

Historically, a total protein content measurement from blood was suggested for the estimation of PMI [30–32]. However, reports of high variability [32] and ranges being within ante mortem levels [30,31] ultimately resulted in diminished value of this measurement in post-mortem examination procedures. More recently, Pittner et al. analysed human post-mortem skeletal muscle samples of 40 forensic cases by Western blotting and casein zymography up to 40 ADD [33]. It was stated that particular proteins and the degradation products could be used as markers for specific post-mortem periods, which can be useful tools for time since death estimation. Furthermore, other possible influencing factors, such as temperature, age, sex, body weight, and cause of death, were investigated. The most important external element influencing the suggested proteins was temperature [33], which is consistent with our current knowledge of human tissue decomposition in forensic taphonomy. In addition, these data provide evidence that age and body mass are also important factors that influence post-mortem muscle protein degradation. The authors suggested that a correction for these factors could be used in developing a model for post-mortem interval estimation. Even under the heterogeneous conditions encountered when using non-standardised human subjects, it was demonstrated that protein degradation processes in human muscle can be associated with temperature and the PMI which may be beneficial in renewing a total protein approach to PMI estimation.

Other biochemical markers of proteins, including enzymes and by-products of protein metabolism, have been gaining more attention. Recent work has focused on the detection of specific proteins that are indicative of cellular responses to death. Zapico et al. measured the mRNA expression of the Fas ligand (FasL) and the phosphatase and tensin homologue deletion on chromosome 10 (PTEN) using quantitative-PCR [34]. These are key proteins in the cell death processes associated with autolysis [34]. Significant strong correlations were found between time since death and cell death proteins within 8 h after death ($r = 0.98$ for PTEN and $r = 0.94$ for FasL) [34]. However, the decrease in cell death proteins after 8 h limits their utility for PMI estimation beyond the fresh stage of decomposition [34]. Another recent and unique approach of whole proteins included a study of adenosine triphosphatase (ATPase) activity in human liver tissue with increasing PMI [35]. The linearity between the decrease in ATPase activity and time in hours was found to be $r^2 = 0.9455$ for up to 24 h post-mortem, demonstrating good correlation for such a method [35]. However, the negative linear correlation between activity and time is limited by the eventual inactivity at short post-mortem intervals (24 h). Whole protein or enzyme investigation may be accurate but it is possibly limited to the early post-mortem period due to the extensive degradation that occurs after this time.

A validated method for vitreous humour protein was developed for the estimation of PMI using a simplified equation [36]. In this method, the protein in the vitreous humour forms a complex with a biuret reagent, providing low limits of detection and quantification for bovine serum albumin (i.e. 8 and 10 μg/mL, respectively). The results of this study demonstrated a predictable, negative linear relationship between vitreous humour protein and PMI with a utility up to 60 h. As with other vitreous humour-based methods, the isolation of the vitreous humour from putrefaction, bacteria, and residual enzymatic activity provides increased stability for measurement of biochemical markers [37]. The predictable negative linear relationship that was established is also very useful for PMI estimation, yet has not been shown to be useful beyond the initial 60 h period. Previous approaches measuring total protein from blood may have been more highly variable than in vitreous humour due the near immediate shift in blood pH after death, triggering the initiation of autolytic processes.

Ansari et al. also recently developed a measurement of free tryptophan in vitreous humour [38]. While other studies have measured free amino acids in vitreous humour [39,40], Ansari et al. were the first to demonstrate a strong correlation between PMI and vitreous humour tryptophan [38]. Contrary to the negative trend between vitreous protein and PMI demonstrated up to 60 h, tryptophan concentrations were seen to steadily increase in a predictable manner up to 90 h post-mortem [38]. This predictable positive linear relationship is promising given this extended timeframe. A positive linear relationship is also known to exist between PMI (up to 72 h) and free tryptophan concentration in brain tissues as measured as an indicator of brain tissue quality in brain bank studies [41]. This increase in free tryptophan concentration is hypothesised to be a result of protein degradation, though direct primary studies to investigate this mechanism have not yet been conducted [41]. Girela et al. investigated free amino acid concentrations in vitreous humour and cerebrospinal fluid [40]. Their results supported the increase in free amino acids within vitreous humour as PMI increased. It is hypothesised that increasing amino acid concentrations could be due to the breakdown of the blood-vitreous barrier in addition to proteolysis [40]. Significant correlations have been identified between the concentration of taurine, glutamate, and aspartate with PMI; however, no significant correlation was been observed for tryptophan or other amino acids [40]. Additional research is required to determine whether free amino acids in the vitreous humour could be useful for PMI estimation, especially due to the conflicting results presented across the studies that have been conducted.

The investigation of free amino acids as a biochemical marker for protein degradation has also been investigated to estimate PMI using other matrices.

Vass et al. introduced this concept in 2002 in a research study that investigated the concentration of amino acids and neurotransmitters as chemical biomarkers for longer post-mortem periods (i.e. greater than 300 cumulative degree hours, CDH) and from various organs (i.e. liver, kidney, heart, brain and muscle) [39]. Empirical models were designed in the form of decision trees, which took into account the combination of marker concentrations [39]. PMI estimations could be made up to 608 CDH (~25 days) using this combination biochemical marker approach [39]. This concept is unique in that the empirical model is used to determine a range of CDH, and then linear regression is used within that CDH range to determine a PMI estimation [39]. This assumes a linear relationship between biomarker concentration and CDH exists within that particular CDH range, which was used as an estimation but was not demonstrated empirically. However, this approach claims to narrow the CDH range to within 5 h. This highlights one potential option for dealing with non-linear relationships or discontinuous biomarker concentration over longer post-mortem intervals. This type of approach should, however, be used with caution if further work does not define the linearity of these discrete intervals that are used for quantification. The linear range was inferred within these regions and therefore should be measured in future work.

Donaldson and Lamont identified an increasing concentration of 18 amino acids post-mortem in blood plasma samples from rat models [42]. Their proposed metabolomics approach on blood samples is useful because it is one of few non-targeted approaches that attempts comprehensive characterisation of metabolites simultaneously in a post-mortem matrix. Blood is also an interesting matrix to choose for metabolomics studies because ante mortem samples are possible to obtain for comparison, contrary to a matrix such as liver or vitreous humour. Fig. 3.2 demonstrates the temporal trends for 18 amino acids between antemortem samples and from 0 to 96 h post-mortem [42]. The metabolomics approach employed by Donaldson and Lamont [42] can provide improved information about how different macromolecule breakdown pathways may be correlated and/or linked, as concentrations for various markers are available from the same sample simultaneously. While a non-targeted approach to biochemical markers is not ideal for a final method implemented in routine casework, it has significant research implications and may provide crucial information to determining the mechanisms behind biochemical marker production in future work.

As in the case of ionic and elemental analyses above, research has also targeted the correlation of biochemical markers from external matrices such as soil with PMI for protein by-products. Van Belle et al. studied the concentration of ninhydrin reactive nitrogen (NRN) in grave soil collected from decomposing pig carcasses both aboveground and belowground [43]. NRN is a measure of nitrogen contributed from the combination of proteins, peptides, amino acids, amines and ammonium. While no modelling was performed between NRN and post-mortem time, temporal trends were established for

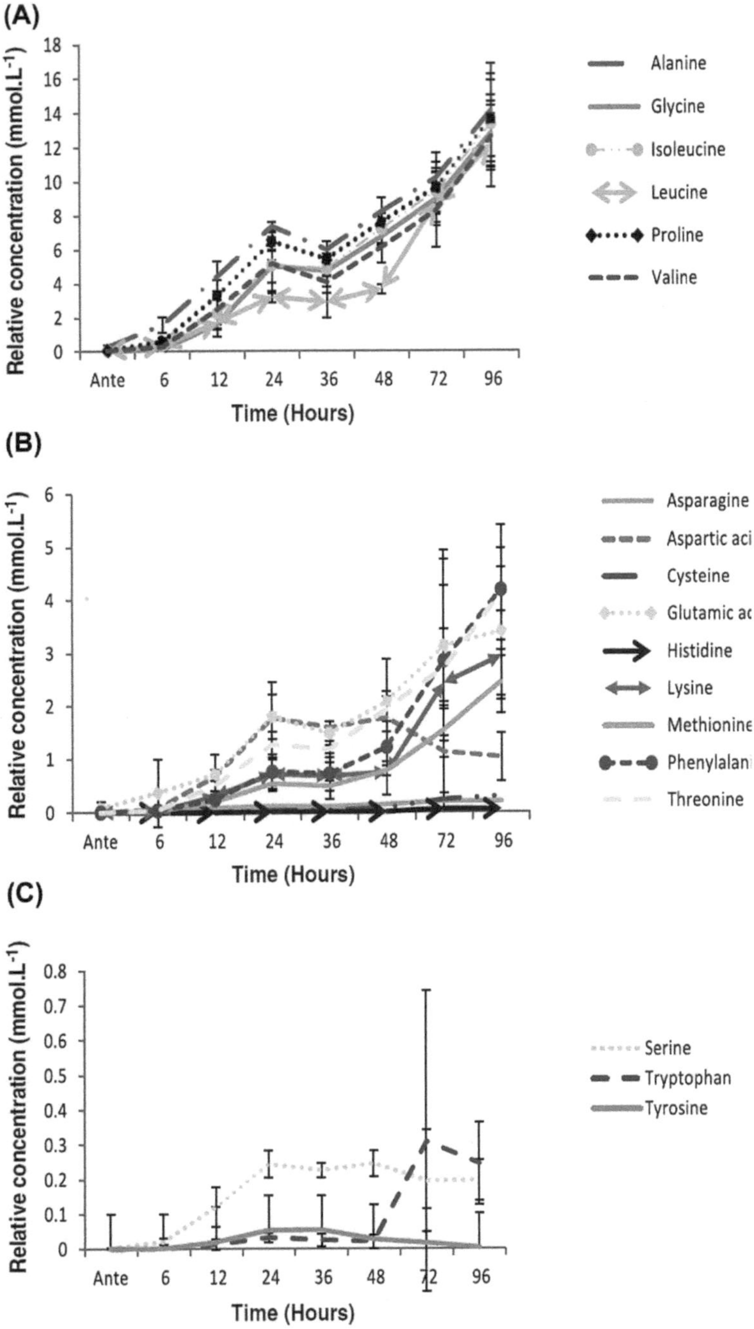

FIG. 3.2 Changes in the concentrations of amino acids postmortem. (A) Six amino acids that have relative concentration changes of 50–500 fold postmortem. (B) Six amino acids that have relative concentration changes of 46–128 fold postmortem. (C) Three amino acids that have little concentration change post-mortem. All values are the average from four rats with the standard deviations shown [42].

three months post-mortem [43]. Further work modelling these relationships on human models may yield tools for outdoor death scenes when remains have decomposed for lengthy periods. Additional comparison between different soil types is also needed to advance the utility of NRN measurements in soil for PMI estimation.

Nucleic acids and related compounds

Concentrations of hypoxanthine, which is a purine derived from the degradation of adenosine nucleotide metabolism, have also been investigated for PMI estimation. Hypoxanthine is formed by several enzymatic reactions and may become elevated due to ante mortem hypoxia resulting in diffusion along the concentration gradient from the retina into the centre of the vitreous [44]. However, it also increases after cessation of the life processes and elevated hypoxanthine concentrations have been identified in plasma, cerebrospinal fluid, and urine [45,46]. Several authors have investigated the correlation between PMI and hypoxanthine concentration in vitreous humour. In 1991, Rognum et al. used high-performance liquid chromatography (HPLC) to detect hypoxanthine levels in vitreous humour in 87 cases, and a strong correlation to PMI was found [44]. In addition, the use of the formulae for hypoxanthine concentration initially appeared to be more precise than that of potassium, particularly in the first 24 h [44]. In another study by the same research group, investigating the impact of hypoxaemia on the hypoxanthine concentration, evidence was found that its concentration increases for the first 24 h after death using a porcine model [46]. Since then, a relationship between vitreous humour hypoxanthine concentration and PMI has since been confirmed by several authors and various formulae have been reported for describing this relationship [46–51]. Donaldson et al. investigated the concentration of hypoxanthine over 96 h in post-mortem blood taken from rats and pigs, and blood from rats and humans stored *in vitro* [52]. An increase in hypoxanthine concentration was observed over time, but the extent and rate of change varied for the different species [52]. Even though there is an increasing amount of literature, there is still some debate as to whether a stronger linear PMI correlation exists for concentrations of hypoxanthine compared with potassium concentrations in relation to PMI [12,16,44,47,49,50]. The results obtained in the different studies may be influenced by several factors such as different statistical approaches and analytical techniques used, as well as the cause of death [47,53,54]. In addition, there is also a positive linear relationship between the hypoxanthine concentration and body temperature [44]. Though hypoxanthine has been used as a linear model, a more recent approach was also developed that took into account potassium and urea levels, and built a flexible model using R code-based software [49]. This allowed for variations in time to be accounted for in the model. However, no clear description about the dynamics of the change in potassium and hypoxanthine concentration over a longer period was provided. These methods remain useful during short post-mortem intervals (i.e. 0–2 days maximum).

Despite studies by numerous research groups, to date, there is no consensus regarding the mathematical equation that best describes the correlation between hypoxanthine concentration in vitreous humour and PMI. Therefore, none of the proposed methods has been implemented routinely in forensic casework [4]. However, with advances in technology and improved statistical approaches using analytical data taken from the vitreous humour, it could in the future prove possible to develop a reliable means to estimate the PMI.

Several studies investigating the changes in deoxyribonucleic acid (DNA) or ribonucleic acid (RNA) degradation as a means of estimating the PMI have also been published. The premise for this research maintains that if the degree of DNA and/or RNA degradation in post-mortem samples could be measured quantitatively, a mathematical model could be established serving as a tool for accurate PMI estimation. In the past, some studies claimed no correlation existed between DNA or RNA degradation and post-mortem interval [55,56]. However, others studies claimed a distinct correlation between degradation and time up to a PMI of 4–5 days [57]. Most studies have focused on the degradation of either deoxyribonucleic acid (DNA) or ribonucleic acid (RNA) by assessing the expression level of target genes or the degradation level of nucleic acids.

Both, DNA and RNA haven been observed to show time-dependent decrease in integrity, but RNA is more susceptible to degradation than DNA [58]. One eventual result was that the first studies utilising molecular forensic techniques mainly focused on DNA integrity determination. However, with the advances in technology, researchers started to examine the effect of PMI on RNA stability as well. Several studies have shown a high variation of degradation for different tissue types, as well as significant impact on trends due to environmental factors [59–61]. In this respect, it is worth mentioning that the use of RNA protein degradation processes in soft tissues have already been described in the context of food science for meat decomposition (e.g. in order to develop tenderness in stored meat or spoilage) [62,63]. Some of the degradation products detected in animal tissues are similar to those found in human tissues, and therefore it is possible to hypothesise that further studies of these degradation products in human tissues could yield possible post-mortem interval correlations.

Sampaio-Silva et al. worked on a murine model and determined RNA integrity in eight different tissues under controlled conditions [60]. This study also demonstrated that the loss of RNA integrity was tissue-specific; however, only a PMI of less than 12 h was considered. Four genes in the femoral quadriceps were determined to be the most reliable dependent variables that correlated with the PMI. Hence, to estimate the PMI, a mathematical model considering the gene transcripts' decay of the four selected genes was developed [60]. The predictive value was tested using specimens from mice stored at room temperature with a PMI of 1, 4 and 10 h and an error mean of 51.4 min was reported. Such preliminary studies are promising but must be further validated using human samples.

More recently, Ferreira et al. investigated the impact of death and post-mortem cold ischaemia on gene expression across multiple human tissues [61]. Data, comprised of 7105 samples, corresponding to 540 donors, were obtained from the Genotype-Tissue Expression (GTEx) project. The GTEx project aims to be a resource database and associated tissue bank for the scientific community to study the relationship between genetic variation and gene expression, and as such, is a good source of samples for research of this nature. In the study, it was demonstrated that the death of an organism has an immediate impact on a tissue's transcriptome [61]. Many genes for different tissue types also displayed expression profiles that were more complex than simple monotonic changes with PMI. The authors suggested a model to determine the PMI based on the tissue-specific response of the transcriptome for the most informative tissues (e.g. particularly skin and subcutaneous adipose). Although such a method may contribute to the understanding of decomposition and post-mortem chemistry, it is currently limited in practical value for the estimation of PMI. Furthermore, the study infers that the analysis of the transcriptome could be related to the cause of death; however, this could not be proven due to small sample sizes used.

Walker et al. noted great differences between the correlation of RNA integrity number (RIN) and total RNA yield with PMI [64]. A whole-body autopsy program was used to take 389 samples from 18 different tissues. The authors concluded that the RNA stability and yield did not depend solely on PMI, but also on other undetermined factors that were not measured. However, the authors excluded age due to the homogenous age distribution of the donors [64]. Thus, further research is required to investigate which factors need to be taken into account for this model to be successful in the future.

Genotyping, gene expression profiling, whole genome sequencing, and RNA sequencing have also been investigated as a collective approach to investigating post-mortem changes. Zhu et al. used these techniques in combination on 2016 samples from the GTEx database [65]. The samples were contributed from 316 donors and ranged from 1 to 27 h after death. In this comprehensive study, 266 differentially variable genes were identified whose expression was significantly dispersed between short PMI and long PMI samples. Two major genes they highlighted for potential were DEFB4B and IFNG. The authors concluded that PMI-related messenger RNA degradation was tissue-specific, gene specific, and even genotype-dependent. These factors mean there may be large variation in the way that RNA degrades, and further work is required to improve the understanding of these different factors.

RNA degradation has also been used as a PMI indicator in combination with colourimetric assays. Young et al. conducted a study using colourimetric assays on tooth pulp samples from pig carcasses [66]. The colourimetric assay was used to quantify the progressive colour changes by means of the analysis of digital photographs. While the colour measurement was not sufficient to produce an accurate estimate of PMI, the combination of RNA degradation rates with colourimetric assay provided an accurate estimate of PMI until day 84 [66]. This PMI is much longer than many PMI estimation studies take into account, which may provide assistance in cases where traditional techniques can no longer be performed due to the state of decomposition of the body. Although the study has not been verified on human samples, future work could be applied to extended PMI scenarios.

Measurement of transcript profiles for particular genes has also been targeted for PMI estimation. Hunter at el. used a high throughput approach to determine the change in gene transcript profiles with PMI in zebrafish and mice [67]. It was demonstrated that transcript abundance of a set of genes yield better post-mortem time predictions than individual gene transcripts. In addition, RNA transcripts from the liver were considered to be better as PMI biochemical markers than gene RNA transcripts from the brain [67]. The next phase of this work would be to assess whether these trends are similar for human analogues such as pig carcasses and then, if so, to extend this work to human remains.

Ma et al. investigated the degradation rate of some RNA markers at 4, 15, 25, and 35 °C in rat brain specimens in order to determine the most suitable RNA markers with the best correlation with prolonged PMI [68]. The authors assumed that a linear regression model would not be sufficient to predict PMI accurately for these markers. Hence, they developed a mathematical model using R software taking into consideration the effect of ambient temperature [68]. In the following study, different RNA markers in both rat and human tissues (i.e. myocardium, liver and brain) were collected to screen valid biomarkers [58]. Similar to the previous study, β-actin was found to exhibit the best correlation coefficient with PMI and the corresponding mathematical model was established [58]. For validation, PMIs for 36 rats and 13 human cases were estimated from the mathematical model. According to the human model, using β-actin in the three types of tissue, the estimated PMI was calculated with a mean estimated error of 5.06 h [58]. As the predictive model showed increased stability for human specimens with a longer PMI, the authors acknowledge that biomarkers that are more sensitive are necessary for PMI estimation, especially with short PMIs.

It is evident that degradation of DNA and RNA is a complex process. Many of these processes are not yet fully understood in the context of forensic taphonomy. However, most research has demonstrated that the degradation of DNA and RNA appears to be tissue-specific. There are currently no PMI estimation formulae developed that use DNA or RNA degradation to predict PMI from measurements from single tissues. However, continuing work in this area may aim to produce these in the future. Moreover, external factors such as temperature appear to have a great impact on the rate of degradation.

Even though promising results were presented in recent years, these proposed approaches still need to be fully validated and tested with independent material. In addition, influencing factors would need to be taking into account quantitatively to be included in a mathematical model permitting accurate PMI estimation.

Volatile organic compounds

For more than ten years, there has been a high interest in decomposition odour due to its implication in many post-mortem phenomena. Research typically aims to develop a better understanding of the interaction between the volatile organic compounds (VOCs) emitted during decomposition and necrophagous insects, since the field of forensic entomology clearly demonstrates predictable attraction patterns to remains based on chemical cues. In the field of search and rescue operations, there is a need for enhanced insight into the compounds that trigger the olfactory system of cadaver-detection canines. This can assist in improving their training procedures and training aids. A large portion of the research in this area has focused on longitudinal profiling over the length of the decomposition process, as the emitted VOCs have been shown to be time-dependent. In the last decade, there has been a significant increase in scientific interest in the comprehensive characterisation of the decomposition VOC profile throughout the entire process of decomposition. Most of the studies rely on gas chromatographic techniques using mass spectrometry as a detection method. More recently, research has been advanced by technical progress in gas chromatographic instrumentation, which allows a more comprehensive characterisation of such samples [69]. Comprehensive two-dimensional gas chromatography coupled to mass spectrometry (GC $\times$ GC-MS) is now being used regularly in research studies to allow improved identification and quantification of components in the decomposition VOC profile [69–72].

Studies from the past five-year period have emphasised the use of longitudinal profiling. Longitudinal profiling is performed when measurements are taken repeatedly throughout the course of the decomposition process, rather than a single measurement at one time point. This data is very useful prior to the extension of a trend in forensic case studies. Several studies have emphasised that the decomposition VOC profile changes over time [69,71,73,74]. Only two studies to date have aimed to specifically correlate VOCs from porcine remains directly with the PMI [75,76]. One of these studies performed four different decomposition trials during 2008 and 2011, each utilising one pig carcass [75]. VOCs were collected using sorbent tubes, then introduced onto gas chromatographic instrumentation using thermal desorption (TD) [75]. Gas Chromatography (GC) is an analytical technique that is commonly used in forensic laboratories because it allows for the detection and identification of a wide range of chemicals. Paczkowski et al. placed sorbent tubes above certain regions of the pig carcasses at different decomposition stages [75]. Three criteria were defined in this study to allow a set of "core volatiles" to be extracted. The goal of the study was to use these core volatiles for PMI estimation [75]. First, VOCs were chosen that were reliably emitted during vertebrate decay. Second, VOCs were included if they were emitted at high concentrations. Third, VOCs were required to demonstrate a reproducible quantitative dynamic during the decay process. Among the 17 VOCs identified and quantified by gas chromatography coupled to mass spectrometry (GC-MS), 14 were determined to be electrophysiologically active on antennae of female *Calliphora vicina*. Since it is known that insects are attracted to decomposing remains in predictable succession patterns (see Chapter 4, this volume for a detailed discussion of this topic), understanding which compounds are active for carrion insects also provides information about potential PMI biochemical markers. Heptanal, nonanal, dimethyl disulfide and dimethyl trisulfide were the core volatiles found to differentiate the fresh stage from the bloat stage of decomposition [75]; however, these stages are visually differentiated and the compounds were not incorporated into a mathematical model that would assist in pinpointing a specific PMI during those stages. Butan-1-ol could differentiate between the bloat and active decay stages. While it is true that the stages of decomposition can usually be visually differentiated, taphonomic processes occur as a continuum. Investigating the change in VOC concentration across the interface between two stages may be particularly helpful in PMI estimation when remains are seen to be transitioning from one stage to another.

Although Paczkowski et al. attempted to correlate PMI with a suite of decomposition VOCs, there are some advocates for approaching the link between VOCs and PMI in a more singular manner. It is not currently known whether one particular VOC from the decomposition VOC profile could be used as a PMI estimation tool, though it is possible that, through the investigation of pre-established longitudinal data or future studies, a biochemical marker for PMI could emerge. One particular chemical compound that has recently been investigated for PMI estimation is trimethylamine [76]. This study is based on the premise from Xia et al. [77] that the content of the total volatile base nitrogen (TVB-N), which is an important parameter to predict meat freshness, increases with PMI. Recently, Li et al. proposed a PMI estimation method based on the measurement of trimethylamine, which is considered to a component of TVB-N [76]. The trimethylamine concentration in post-mortem rat tissues (i.e. liver, myocardial and skeletal muscle tissues) was measured and was found to increase in all three tissues from the time of first detection up to 192 h, and then gradually decreased after 384 h [76]. On this basis, the authors suggested three mathematical equations (Fig. 3.3) to describe the correlation between trimethylamine concentration and PMI (0–720 h). In addition, five cases of human liver samples with a PMI ranging from 14.5 h to 35 h were analysed. Although good agreement was found between human liver samples and the equations generated from rat tissues,

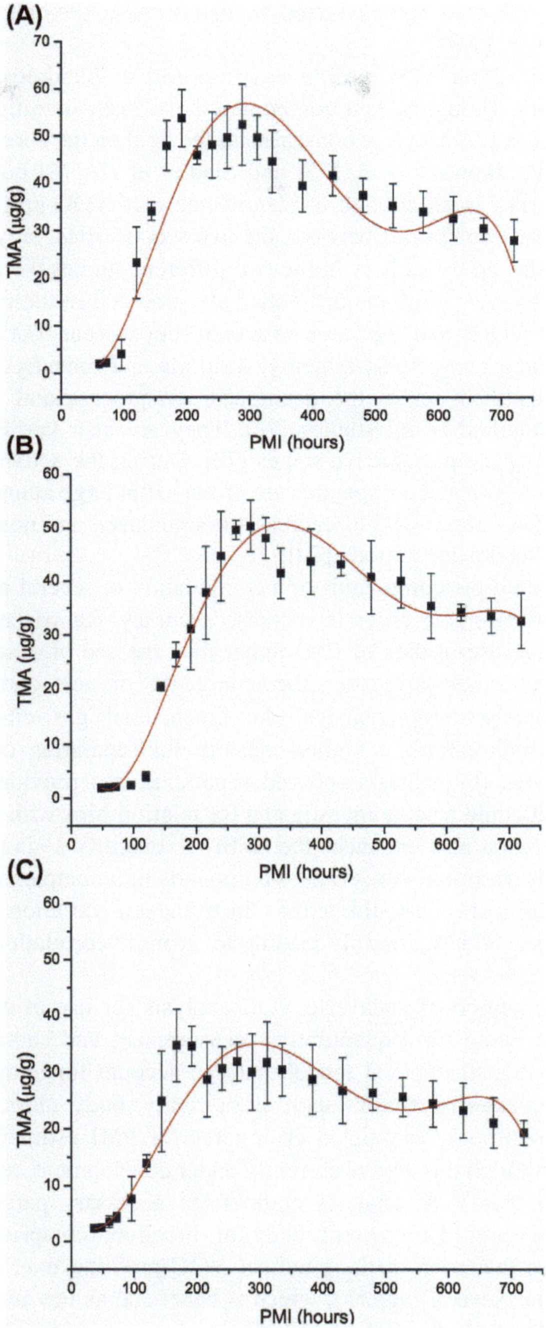

FIG. 3.3 (A) The content of TMA in myocardial muscle increases with PMI (after 60 h), $y = -2.59E^{-11}x^5 + 4.97E^{-8}x^4 - 3.35E^{-5}x^3 + 0.009x^2 - 0.68x + 16.75$ (adj. $R^2 = 0.9535$). (B) The content of TMA in skeletal muscle increases with PMI (after 48 h), $y = -1.39E^{-11}x^5 + 2.90E^{-8}x^4 - 2.15E^{-5}x^3 + 0.006x^2 - 0.55x + 15.92$ (adj. $R^2 = 0.9394$). (C) The content of TMA in liver increases with PMI (after 36 h), $y = -1.22E^{-11}x^5 + 2.30E^{-8}x^4 - 1.51E^{-5}x^3 + 0.004x^2 - 0.22x + 5.68$ (adj. $R^2 = 0.9697$) [76].

further studies need to be conducted to demonstrate the reliability of the method for longer PMIs.

The decomposition VOC profile is comprised of hundreds of chemical compounds [72]. Though a few compounds have been investigated as PMI indicators, there is still a lack of consensus in the field on the core VOC profile. For example, Paczkowski et al. [75] and Stadler et al. [78] both performed multiple field trials in an attempt to identify the core VOC profile. However, under the different conditions between the two sets of trials, only a few of the core volatiles chosen by authors in the two different studies were found to be in common. However, some major trends have emerged in the past decade as to the types of VOCs and the stage in which they appear. For example, the sulphur-containing compounds dimethyl disulfide and dimethyl trisulfide are consistently identified across the decomposition process and appear to be consistently identified in all studies [72]. They are also known to peak in abundance during the putrefactive stages [72]. During the active decay stage, aromatics and oxygenated compounds are produced in large abundance. In late stage decay, VOCs are known to decrease in abundance and non-polar VOCs tend to persist for longer periods [79].

The use of multiple compounds or a combination of several markers could be used for modelling in order to increase accuracy. Ratios between VOCs may also provide useful data of PMI rather than the use of absolute concentrations. Recent trends have seen the emergence of new chromatographic techniques, namely comprehensive two-dimensional gas chromatography (GC × GC), which affords a higher capacity for separating compounds in complex mixtures [69]. This improved separation has provided new VOC targets [69] that could also be investigated for relationships with the PMI. The improved separation also enhances the ability to quantify a single compound accurately apart from numerous other compounds in a complex mixture [69]. Improved quantification should reduce instrumental variation in the measurement of these VOCs, possibly leading to stronger correlation values with PMI.

A standard method of cadaveric VOC analysis for use in estimating the PMI should be based on a quantitative measurement and should be further developed into a mathematical model that can account for temporal fluctuations and other external factors such as humidity, body mass, rainfall etc. Under these conditions, associated error rates for PMI estimation could be determined. Although this area is currently under development, recent research shows promise that VOC analysis could fulfil necessary parameters to be useful for casework. The current body of literature comprises numerous research studies that perform longitudinal VOC profiling over extended periods of time (i.e. several months), which is beneficial as few methods can be extended into this longer duration of PMI.

Completeness of data for biochemical markers

Sections Electrolytes and elemental analysis, Lipids and related compounds, Proteins and related compounds, Nucleic acids and related compounds, and Volatile organic compounds demonstrate the vast research currently being performed in the area of post-mortem biochemical markers. Though numerous studies have been conducted, few biomarkers reach a standard that can currently be used in forensic casework. The rationale for using biochemical markers to estimate PMI is compelling; biochemical markers can allow estimation of the post-mortem interval where conventional visual methods are not objective, or where entomological evidence cannot be used. In addition, a routine method using a biochemical marker has the potential to have high sensitivity and yield high sample throughput with available analytical techniques. However, despite the advantages presented, there is minimal adoption of these techniques by practitioners.

Recent research aimed at categorising biochemical markers of PMI in the literature by using a point scale from 0 to 17 [4]. Practical focus was placed on whether biochemical markers of PMI could reach the Daubert & Frye standards, as well as their significance of change in concentration over the investigated PMI. The point system presented in Meurs et al. [4] defines a specific point system based on several factors, including: significant change in concentration over the post-mortem alteration period, investigation of intrinsic and extrinsic factors, presentation of coefficient of determination (R^2 value), presentation of concentrations with mean and standard deviation, as well as reporting of error values. The point system was then divided into five categories, including: well investigated and practically applicable, well investigated and not practical, poorly investigated and practical, poorly investigated and not practical, or unknown. Note that the unknown category was designated when not enough information was available in the literature to assign the biochemical marker to any of the first four groups. The difference between well investigated and poorly investigated was defined based on whether the biochemical marker had higher or lower than nine points on the scale, respectively. While the assessment of the level of investigation was arbitrarily set at nine points, this provides a valuable starting point for discussion on the level of investigation for biochemical markers. This meta-analysis was the most comprehensive study of post-mortem biochemical markers in literature to date.

Based on this evaluation, only seven biochemical markers have been well investigated according to the point scale [4]. These markers include: potassium, sodium, urea, chloride, magnesium, hypoxanthine, and cardiac troponin T [4]. Of the biochemical markers that were proposed for PMI estimation in the literature up to the year 2016, 364 markers were found to be classified as unknown, 18 were classified as poorly investigated but not practical, and six were found to be well investigated but not practical. None of the biochemical markers investigated to date were classified as being well investigated and practically applicable, which provides some insight into the level of adoption of these techniques in routine work. In addition, 24 biochemical markers under investigation were quoted in their original research articles as being not feasible for PMI estimation [4]. Indeed, the reporting of negative results for PMI estimation is just as important as positive results, in order to prevent reiterations of work on such chemicals.

This classification demonstrates the lack of continuing research currently being done in the area of post-mortem biochemistry. Numerous articles demonstrate proof-of-concept or significant change in concentration at different points in time, but do not provide metrics on analytical data or details of the markers' practical usage. In addition, many studies quote a significant change at different visual stages (e.g. fresh, bloat, active decay); however, since these stages are visually differentiated, the difference in chemical measurements over time must go much more in depth than these statements. While a number of markers have been shown to be promising in the literature, this remains a significant hurdle in the development of a routine laboratory method that can be used for PMI estimation. The large number of biochemical markers categorised as unknown demonstrates the wealth of data that currently exists, which upon further in-depth investigation may yield very valuable tools in the future.

Conclusion

The amount of ongoing research in the area of post-mortem biochemical markers is abundant. Nearly 400 biochemical markers have been proposed to date. The use of biochemical marker concentrations can be powerful in providing quantitative and objective measurements of the time since death, as well as the associated error rate of the technique. While the literature is significantly positive for some biomarkers (e.g. vitreous potassium, vitreous hypoxanthine), many other markers may have only one or two published studies suggesting they may be significant.. The development of ways to assess the level of investigation and practical application of a biochemical marker for PMI will be helpful to assess which of these trends warrant further investigation in future work. It may also provide a practical and quantitative means of assisting judges to determine which biochemical markers reach Daubert and Frye standards for use in trials. In order to reach these standards, true analytical validation will be required for nearly all suggested biomarkers in the current literature. The extent of research that performs full method validation for a specific biochemical marker, specifically demonstrating figures of merit and associated error rates, remains sparse. However, a substantial amount of data exists in the literature and therefore there is promise that some of these markers could be further validated in the future.

Aside from analytical validation, there remains a strong need for studies that use animal models to continue validation of this work on human remains. A number of studies mentioned above discuss biochemical marker trends for models on fish, mice, and pigs. The most predominant animal model used for collecting biochemical marker data throughout decomposition is the pig, which is a valuable analogue for human remains in forensic taphonomy due to similarities in skin, gut flora, and fat distribution [80]. Human remains inherently exhibit a large amount of variation, due to differences in gender, body mass, age, lifestyles factors, and other variables. In addition, many practical limitations exist with obtaining human remains, as well as the fact that it is challenging to have a large number of bodies at the same time for any given study. Studies that use a large number of forensic cases increase the number of bodies available for analysis; however, this means that longitudinal sampling cannot be performed since the remains are typically not recovered immediately after death. The use of pig carcasses for the initial development of trends is valuable because it allows replicate carcasses to be used with lower intrinsic variation between individuals. However, ideally biochemical trends should progress from animal longitudinal profiling to human longitudinal profiling and be finally validated on case studies. Recently, there has been an increase in the number of taphonomic research facilities in the United States, and more facilities are also emerging worldwide. The use of decomposition facilities with body donation programs can provide additional meaningful opportunities to perform longitudinal profiling on human remains prior to advancing to validation on case studies. Progression of work in this manner, rather than starting directly with trying to develop biochemical marker trends on case samples, may be a better approach for these types of studies. When progressing from animal models to human remains in a series of steps, it is possible to improve the characterisation of the effect of intrinsic and extrinsic variables on the disruption of established trends from a previous proof-of-concept.

Finally, care should be taken in the wording used for publishing data on biochemical markers. Many studies claim the establishment of a trend in a particular biochemical marker for PMI estimation, yet provide no mathematical model that relates the biochemical marker concentration to the PMI. While the characterisation of changing concentrations in decomposition by-products based on the stages of decomposition is valuable in understanding taphonomic processes, a true PMI estimation model should have a mathematical model that is continuous along the dependent variable of time (or other scaled time factor such as ADD or CDH). Studies that find an increase or decrease in a particular marker within a stage of decomposition should avoid the use of characterising that method as being useful for PMI estimation, as they will require substantial further investigation to reach a level of practical usage. The use of time-series modelling may also be one consideration to increase the power of biochemical markers' concentration relationship with the PMI in future work.

List of acronyms and abbreviations

ADD Accumulated Degree Days
ATPase Adenosine Triphosphatase
CDH Cumulative Degree Hours
DNA Deoxyribonucleic Acid
FAME Fatty Acid Methyl Ester
FasL Fas Ligand
GC Gas Chromatography
GC-MS Gas Chromatography-Mass Spectrometry
GC×GC-MS Comprehensive Two-dimensional Gas Chromatography-Mass Spectrometry
GTEx Genotype-Tissue Expression
NRN Ninhydrin Reactive Nitrogen
PBI Postburial interval
PMI Post-mortem interval
PTEN Phosphatase and tensin homologue deleted on chromosome 10
RIN RNA integrity number
RNA Ribonucleic acid
VFA Volatile Fatty Acid

References

[1] Forbes SL, Perrault KA, Comstock JL. Microscopic post-mortem changes: the chemistry of decomposition. In: Schostsmas EMJ, Marquez-Grant N, Forbes SL, editors. Taphonomy of human remains: forensic analysis of the dead and the depositional environment. Chichester: John Wiley & Sons; 2017. p. 26–38.

[2] Donaldson AE, Lamont IL. Estimation of post-mortem interval using biochemical markers. Aust J Forensic Sci 2014;46:8–26. https://doi.org/10.1080/00450618.2013.784356.

[3] Simmons T. Post-Mortem interval estimation: an overview of techniques. In: Schotsmans EMJ, Marquez-Grant N, Forbes SL, editors. Taphonomy of human remains: forensic analysis of the dead and the depositional environment; 2017. p. 134–41.

[4] Meurs J, Krap T, Duijst W. Evaluation of postmortem biochemical markers: completeness of data and assessment of implication in the field. Sci Justice 2019;59:177–80.

[5] Vass AA, Bass WM, Wolt JD, Foss JE, Ammons JT. Time since death determinations of human cadavers using soil solution. J Forensic Sci 1992;37:1236–53.

[6] Megyesi MS, Nawrocki SP, Haskell NH. Using accumulated degree-days to estimate the postmortem interval from decomposed human remains. J Forensic Sci 2005;50:618–26.

[7] Adelson L, Sunshine I, Rushforth NB, Mankoff M. Vitreous potassium concentration as an indicator of the PMI. J Forensic Sci 1963;8:503–14.

[8] Sturner WQ, Gantner GE. The postmortem interval. Am J Clin Pathol 1964;42:137–44. https://doi.org/10.1093/ajcp/42.2.137.

[9] Lange N, Swearer S, Sturner WQ. Human postmortem interval estimation from vitreous potassium: an analysis of original data from six different studies. Forensic Sci Int 1994;66:159–74. https://doi.org/10.1016/0379-0738(94)90341-7.

[10] Bocaz-Beneventi G, Tagliaro F, Bortolotti F, Manetto G, Havel J. Capillary zone electrophoresis and artificial neural networks for estimation of the post-mortem interval (PMI) using electrolytes measurements in human vitreous humour. Int J Leg Med 2002;116:5–11. https://doi.org/10.1007/s004140100239.

[11] Tagliaro F, Bortolotti F, Manetto G, Cittadini F, Pascali VL, Marigo M. Potassium concentration differences in the vitreous humour from the two eyes revisited by microanalysis with capillary electrophoresis. J Chromatogr A 2001;924:493–8. https://doi.org/10.1016/S0021-9673(01)00713-0.

[12] Salam HA, Shaat EA, Aziz MHA, MoneimSheta AA, Hussein HASM. Estimation of postmortem interval using thanatochemistry and postmortem changes. Alexandria J Med 2012;48:335–44. https://doi.org/10.1016/j.ajme.2012.05.004.

[13] Zilg B, Bernard S, Alkass K, Berg S, Druid H. A new model for the estimation of time of death from vitreous potassium levels corrected for age and temperature. Forensic Sci Int 2016;254:158–66. https://doi.org/10.1016/j.forsciint.2015.07.020.

[14] Pringle JK, Cassella JP, Jervis JR, Williams A, Cross P, Cassidy NJ. Soilwater conductivity analysis to date and locate clandestine graves of homicide victims. J Forensic Sci 2015;60:1052–60. https://doi.org/10.1111/1556-4029.12802.

[15] Schleyer F. Determination of the time of death in the early post-mortem interval. In: Lundquist F, editor. Methods forensic sci, vol. II. London: John Wiley & Sons; 1963. p. 253–91.

[16] Madea B. Is there recent progress in the estimation of the postmortem interval by means of thanatochemistry? Forensic Sci Int 2005;151:139–49. https://doi.org/10.1016/j.forsciint.2005.01.013.

[17] Benninger LA, Carter DO, Forbes SL. The biochemical alteration of soil beneath a decomposing carcass. Forensic Sci Int 2008;180:70–5. https://doi.org/10.1016/j.forsciint.2008.07.001.

[18] Towne EG. Prairie vegetation and soil nutrient responses to ungulate carcasses. Oecologia 2000;122:232–9. https://doi.org/10.1007/PL00008851.

[19] Perrault KA, Forbes SL. Elemental analysis of soil and vegetation surrounding decomposing human analogues. Can Soc Forensic Sci J 2016;49:138–51. https://doi.org/10.1080/00085030.2016.1184840.

[20] Notter SJ, Stuart BH, Rowe R, Langlois N. The initial changes of fat deposits during the decomposition of human and pig remains. J Forensic Sci 2009;54:195–201. https://doi.org/10.1111/j.1556-4029.2008.00911.x.

[21] Comstock JL, Leblanc HN, Forbes SL. Analysis of decomposition fluid collected from carcasses decomposing in the presence and absence of insects. In: Kars H, van den Eijkel L, editors. Soil in criminal and environmental forensics: proceedings of the soil forensics special, 6th european academy of forensic science conference. The Hague: Springer; 2016. p. 275–96. https://doi.org/10.1007/978-3-319-33115-7.

[22] Ubelaker DH, Zarenko KM. Adipocere : what is known after over two centuries of research. Forensic Sci Int 2011;208:167–72. https://doi.org/10.1016/j.forsciint.2010.11.024.

[23] Dent BB, Forbes SL, Stuart BH. Review of human decomposition processes in soil. Environ Geol 2004;45:576–85. https://doi.org/10.1007/s00254-003-0913-z.

[24] Forbes SL. Decomposition chemistry in a burial environment. In: Tibbet M, Carter DO, editors. Soil anal. forensic taphon. chem. biol. eff. buried remain., Boca Raton; 2008.

[25] Fiedler S, Graw M. Decomposition of buried corpses, with special reference to the formation of adipocere. Naturwissenschaften 2003;90:291–300. https://doi.org/10.1007/s00114-003-0437-0.

[26] Forbes SL, Stuart BH, Dent BB. The identification of adipocere in grave soils. Forensic Sci Int 2002;127:225–30. https://doi.org/10.1016/S0379-0738(02)00127-5.

[27] Larizza M, Forbes SL. Detection of fatty acids in the lateral extent of the cadaver decomposition island. Geol Soc Lond Spec Publ 2013;384:209–19. https://doi.org/10.1144/SP384.11.

[28] Breton H, Kirkwood AE, Carter DO, Forbes SL. The impact of carrion decomposition on the fatty acid methyl ester (FAME) profiles of soil microbial communities in southern Canada. Can Soc Forensic Sci J 2015;5030:1–18. https://doi.org/10.1080/00085030.2015.1108036.

[29] Swann L, Forbes S, Lewis SW. Observations of the temporal variation in chemical content of decomposition fluid: a preliminary study using pigs as a model system. Aust J Forensic Sci 2010;42:199–210. https://doi.org/10.1080/00450610903258102.

[30] Coe J. Postmortem chemistries on blood with particular reference to urea nitrogen, electrolytes, and bilirubin. J Forensic Sci 1974;19:33–42. https://doi.org/10.1520/JFS10067J.

[31] Uemura K, Shintani-Ishida K, Saka K, Nakajima M, Ikegaya H, Kikuchi Y, et al. Biochemical blood markers and sampling sites in forensic autopsy. J Forensic Leg Med 2008;15:312–7. https://doi.org/10.1016/j.jflm.2007.12.003.

[32] Fekete JF, Brunsdon DFV. The use of routine laboratory tests in postmortem examinations. Can Soc Forensic Sci J 1974;7:238–45. https://doi.org/10.1080/00085030.1974.10757216.

[33] Pittner S, Ehrenfellner B, Monticelli FC, Zissler A, Sänger AM, Stoiber W, et al. Postmortem muscle protein degradation in humans as a tool for PMI delimitation. Int J Leg Med 2016;130:1547–55. https://doi.org/10.1007/s00414-016-1349-9.

[34] Zapico SC, Menéndez ST, Núñez P. Cell death proteins as markers of early postmortem interval. Cell Mol Life Sci 2014;71:2957–62. https://doi.org/10.1007/s00018-013-1531-x.

[35] Lodha A, Ansari N, Prajapati T, Rao MV, Menon SK. Novel approach to determine postmortem interval from ATPase activity. Aust J Forensic Sci 2017;49:22–30. https://doi.org/10.1080/00450618.2015.1115128.

[36] Ansari N, Lodha A, Mehta M, Menon SK. A real-time smartphone-enabled time since death estimation from vitreous humour protein. Aust J Forensic Sci 2017;0618:1–17. https://doi.org/10.1080/00450618.2017.1324581.

[37] Thierauf A, Musshoff F, Madea B. Post-mortem biochemical investigations of vitreous humor. Forensic Sci Int 2009;192:78–82. https://doi.org/10.1016/j.forsciint.2009.08.001.

[38] Ansari N, Menon SK. Determination of time since death using vitreous humor tryptophan. J Forensic Sci 2017;62:1351–6. https://doi.org/10.1111/1556-4029.13430.

[39] Vass AA, Barshick S-A, Sega G, Caton J, Skeen JT, Love JC, et al. Decomposition chemistry of human remains: a new methodology for determining the postmortem interval. J Forensic Sci 2002;47:542–53.

[40] Girela E, Villanueva E, Irigoyen P, Girela V, Hernández-Cueto C, Peinado JM. Free amino acid concentrations in vitreous humor and cerebrospinal fluid in relation to the cause of death and postmortem interval. J Forensic Sci 2008;53:730–3. https://doi.org/10.1111/j.1556-4029.2008.00726.x.

[41] Grünblatt E, Proft F, Apfelbacher M, Deckert J, Roggendorf W, Riederer P, et al. Brain tryptophan rather than pH-value is altered as consequence of artificial postmortem interval and storage conditions. Neurochem Int 2010;57:819–22. https://doi.org/10.1016/j.neuint.2010.08.020.

[42] Donaldson AE, Lamont IL. Metabolomics of post-mortem blood: identifying potential markers of post-mortem interval. Metabolomics 2014. https://doi.org/10.1007/s11306-014-0691-5.

[43] Van Belle LE, Carter DO, Forbes SL. Measurement of ninhydrin reactive nitrogen influx into gravesoil during aboveground and belowground carcass (*Sus domesticus*) decomposition. Forensic Sci Int 2009;193:37–41. https://doi.org/10.1016/j.forsciint.2009.08.016.

[44] Rognum TO, Holmen S, Musse MA, Dahlberg PS, Stray-Pedersen A, Saugstad OD, et al. Estimation of time since death by vitreous humor hypoxanthine, potassium, and ambient temperature. Forensic Sci Int 2016;262:160–5. https://doi.org/10.1016/j.forsciint.2016.03.001.

[45] Saugstad OD. Hypoxanthine as a measurement of hypoxia. Pediatr Res 1975;9:158–61. https://doi.org/10.1203/00006450-197504000-00002.

[46] Poulsen JP, Rognum TO, Oyaseter S, Saugstad OD. Changes in oxypurine concentrations in vitreous humor of pigs during hypoxemia and post-mortem. Pediatr Res 1990;28:482–4. https://doi.org/10.1203/00006450-199011000-00013.

[47] Madea B, Rödig A. Time of death dependent criteria in vitreous humor - accuracy of estimating the time since death. Forensic Sci Int 2006;164:87–92. https://doi.org/10.1016/j.forsciint.2005.12.002.

[48] Muñoz JI, Costas E, Rodríguez-Calvo MS, Suárez-Peñaranda JM, López-Rivadulla M, Concheiro L. A high-performance liquid chromatography method for hypoxanthine determination in vitreous humour: application to estimation of post mortem interval. Hum Exp Toxicol 2006;25:279–81. https://doi.org/10.1191/0960327106ht615oa.

[49] Muñoz-Barús JI, Rodríguez-Calvo MS, Suárez-Peñaranda JM, Vieira DN, Cadarso-Suárez C, Febrero-Bande M. PMICALC: an R code-based software for estimating post-mortem interval (PMI) compatible with Windows, Mac and Linux operating systems. Forensic Sci Int 2010;194:49–52. https://doi.org/10.1016/j.forsciint.2009.10.006.

[50] Madea B, Käferstein H, Hermann N, Sticht G. Hypoxanthine in vitreous humor and cerebrospinal fluid - a marker of postmortem interval and prolonged (vital) hypoxia? Remarks also on hypoxanthine in SIDS. Forensic Sci Int 1994;65:19–31. https://doi.org/10.1016/0379-0738(94)90296-8.

[51] James RA, Hoadley PA, Sampson BG. Determination of postmortem interval by sampling vitreous humor. Am J Forensic Med Pathol 1997;18:158–62.

[52] Donaldson AE, Lamont IL. Biochemistry changes that occur after death: potential markers for determining post-mortem interval. PLoS One 2013;8:e82011. https://doi.org/10.1371/journal.pone.0082011.

[53] Muñoz Barús JI, Suárez-Peñaranda JM, Otero XL, Rodríguez-Calvo MS, Costas E, Miguéns X, et al. Improved estimation of postmortem interval based on differential behaviour of vitreous potassium and hypoxantine in death by hanging. Forensic Sci Int 2002;125:67–74. https://doi.org/10.1016/S0379-0738(01)00616-8.

[54] Camba A, Lendoiro E, Cordeiro C, Martínez-Silva I, Rodríguez-Calvo MS, Vieira DN, et al. High variation in hypoxanthine determination after analytical treatment of vitreous humor samples. Forensic Sci Med Pathol 2014;10:627–33. https://doi.org/10.1007/s12024-014-9590-3.

[55] Preece P, Cairns NJ. Quantifying mRNA in postmortem human brain: influence of gender, age at death, postmortem interval, brain pH, agonal state and inter-lobe mRNA variance. Mol Brain Res 2003;118:60–71. https://doi.org/10.1016/S0169-328X(03)00337-1.

[56] Heinrich M, Matt K, Lutz-Bonengel S, Schmidt U. Successful RNA extraction from various human postmortem tissues. Int J Leg Med 2007;121:136–42. https://doi.org/10.1007/s00414-006-0131-9.

[57] Bauer M, Gramlich I, Polzin S, Patzelt D. Quantification of mRNA degradation as possible indicator of postmortem interval - a pilot study. Leg Med 2003;5:220–7. https://doi.org/10.1016/j.legalmed.2003.08.001.

[58] Lv YH, Ma JL, Pan H, Zhang H, Li WC, Xue AM, et al. RNA degradation as described by a mathematical model for postmortem interval determination. J Forensic Leg Med 2016;44:43–52. https://doi.org/10.1016/j.jflm.2016.08.015.

[59] Itani M, Yamamoto Y, Doi Y, Miyaishi S. Quantitative analysis of DNA degradation in the dead body. Acta Med Okayama 2011;65:299–306. https://doi.org/10.18926/AMO/47011.

[60] Sampaio-Silva F, Magalhães T, Carvalho F, Dinis-Oliveira RJ, Silvestre R. Profiling of RNA degradation for estimation of post morterm interval. PLoS One 2013;8. https://doi.org/10.1371/journal.pone.0056507.

[61] Ferreira PG, Muñoz-Aguirre M, Reverter F, Sá Godinho CP, Sousa A, Amadoz A, et al. The effects of death and post-mortem cold ischemia on human tissue transcriptomes. Nat Commun 2018;9. https://doi.org/10.1038/s41467-017-02772-x.

[62] Piõrkowska K, Zukowski K, Nowak J, Połtowicz K, Ropka-Molik K, Gurgul A. Genome-wide RNA-Seq analysis of breast muscles of two broiler chicken groups differing in shear force. Anim Genet 2016;47:68–80. https://doi.org/10.1111/age.12388.

[63] Fonseca LFS, Gimenez DFJ, dos Santos Silva DB, Barthelson R, Baldi F, Ferro JA, et al. Differences in global gene expression in muscle tissue of Nellore cattle with divergent meat tenderness. BMC Genomics 2017;18:1–12. https://doi.org/10.1186/s12864-017-4323-0.

[64] Walker DG, Whetzel AM, Serrano G, Sue LI, Lue LF, Beach TG. Characterization of RNA isolated from eighteen different human tissues: results from a rapid human autopsy program. Cell Tissue Bank 2016;17:361–75. https://doi.org/10.1007/s10561-016-9555-8.

[65] Zhu Y, Wang L, Yin Y, Yang E. Systematic analysis of gene expression patterns associated with postmortem interval in human tissues. Sci Rep 2017;7:1–12. https://doi.org/10.1038/s41598-017-05882-0.

[66] Young S, Wells J, Hobbs G, Bishop C. Estimating postmortem interval using RNA degradation and morphological changes in tooth pulp. Forensic Sci Int 2013;229.

[67] Hunter MC, Pozhitkov AE, Noble PA. Accurate predictions of postmortem interval using linear regression analyses of gene meter expression data. Forensic Sci Int 2017;275:90–101. https://doi.org/10.1016/j.forsciint.2017.02.027.

[68] Ma J, Pan H, Zeng Y, Lv Y, Zhang H, Xue A, et al. Exploration of the R code-based mathematical model for PMI estimation using profiling of RNA degradation in rat brain tissue at different temperatures. Forensic Sci Med Pathol 2015;11:530–7. https://doi.org/10.1007/s12024-015-9703-7.

[69] Perrault KA, Nizio KD, Forbes SL. A comparison of one-dimensional and comprehensive two-dimensional gas chromatography for decomposition odour profiling using inter-year replicate field trials. Chromatographia 2015;78:1057–70. https://doi.org/10.1007/s10337-015-2916-9.

[70] Stefanuto P-H, Perrault KA, Lloyd RM, Stuart BH, Rai T, Forbes SL, et al. Exploring new dimensions in cadaveric decomposition odour analysis. Anal Methods 2015;7:2287–94. https://doi.org/10.1039/C5AY00371G.

[71] Perrault KA, Stefanuto P-H, Stuart BH, Rai T, Focant J-F, Forbes SL. Reducing variation in decomposition odour profiling using comprehensive two-dimensional gas chromatography. J Sep Sci 2015;38:73–80. https://doi.org/10.1002/jssc.201400935.

[72] Verheggen F, Perrault KA, Caparros Megido R, Dubois LM, Francis F, Haubruge E, et al. The odour of death: an overview of current knowledge on characterization and applications. Bioscience 2017;67:600–13. https://doi.org/10.1093/biosci/bix046.

[73] Kasper J, Mumm R, Ruther J. The composition of carcass volatile profiles in relation to storage time and climate conditions. Forensic Sci Int 2012;223:64–71. https://doi.org/10.1016/j.forsciint.2012.08.001.

[74] Rosier E, Loix S, Develter W, Van de Voorde W, Tytgat J, Cuypers E. The search for a volatile human specific marker in the decomposition process. PLoS One 2015;10:e0137341. https://doi.org/10.1371/journal.pone.0137341.

[75] Paczkowski S, Nicke S, Ziegenhagen H, Schütz S. Volatile emission of decomposing pig carcasses (*Sus scrofa domesticus* L.) as an indicator for the postmortem interval. J Forensic Sci 2015;60:s130–7. https://doi.org/10.1111/1556-4029.12638.

[76] Li W, Chang Y, Han L, Liu X, Cai J, Zha L, et al. Trimethylamine in postmortem tissues as a predictor of postmortem interval estimation using the GC method. Leg Med 2018;35:80–5. https://doi.org/10.1016/j.legalmed.2018.09.011.

[77] Xia Z, Zhai X, Liu B, Mo Y. Conductometric titration to determine total volatile basic nitrogen (TVB-N) for post-mortem interval (PMI). J Forensic Leg Med 2016;44:133–7. https://doi.org/10.1016/j.jflm.2016.10.008.

[78] Stadler S, Desaulniers J-P, Forbes SL. Inter-year repeatability study of volatile organic compounds from surface decomposition of human analogues. Int J Leg Med 2015;129:641–50. https://doi.org/10.1007/s00414-014-1024-y.

[79] Perrault KA, Stefanuto P-H, Stuart BH, Rai T, Focant J-F, Forbes SL. Detection of decomposition volatile organic compounds in soil following removal of remains from a surface deposition site. Forensic Sci Med Pathol 2015;11:376–87. https://doi.org/10.1007/s12024-015-9693-5.

[80] Schoenly KG, Haskell NH, Mills DK, Bieme-Ndi C. Recreating death's acre in the school yard: using pig carcasses as model corpses to teach concepts of forensic entomology & ecological succession. Am Biol Teach 2006;68:402–10.

Chapter 4

The application of insects to the estimation of the time since death

James F. Wallman[a,b], Melanie S. Archer[c]
[a]*School of Life Sciences, University of Technology Sydney, Sydney, Australia;* [b]*Centre for Sustainable Ecosystem Solutions, School of Earth, Atmospheric and Life Sciences, University of Wollongong, Wollongong, Australia;* [c]*Victorian Institute of Forensic Medicine and Monash University, VIC, Australia*

Introduction

The use of entomology (the study of insects) for the estimation of the time since death has involved a long history of scientific endeavour, and is integrally associated with awareness of the role of these creatures in the decomposition of animal remains [1]. The available methods for estimating when someone died are inevitably associated with some degree of error given the retrospection required, but the main justification for using the entomological approach is that it may have more accuracy and precision than other techniques, and is not restricted to the first few hours after death [2,3]. The fundamental method in forensic entomology casework is to try to estimate the time that the body or remains became infested by insects, and to use this to infer that the individual had been dead at least this long (the minimum postmortem interval or minPMI). There is also a period between death and the time of first insect infestation, but it is usually not possible to determine the duration of this earlier phase because of various environmental and other factors influencing insect activity and their access to the body [4]. There are two major sources of variability that pose major challenges to the forensic entomologist: the natural variation in behaviour exhibited by all animals, including insects, and the weather. The weather is important because insects, being ectotherms, are heavily influenced physiologically by their ambient conditions.

This chapter provides a concise summary of the main approaches used in the application of insects in forensic investigations and an array of associated

Estimation of the Time since Death. https://doi.org/10.1016/B978-0-12-815731-2.00004-2

complicating factors. An emphasis is placed on the Australian context, but many of the issues in this country apply elsewhere.

Which insects and other invertebrates are used forensically?

A human corpse, like the carcass of any other animal, decomposes over time. This is a complex phenomenon affected by a wide range of factors [5]. Insects and other invertebrates are critical to the decomposition process in natural environments [6]. They follow a process of succession, a classical concept in ecology, in which the activity of each group of species, in combination with abiotic variables (e.g. wind, rain, heat), renders the carrion unsuitable for the species' continued occupation. Instead, the body becomes more suitable for the next set of species that was unable to use the carrion in its previous form [7].

Certain species of flies (the insect order Diptera) are the group of insects that have evolved the most profound association with the remains of dead animals through the reliance on this food source by their larvae, known as maggots. Indeed, maggots in carrion are the major agents of decomposition, although bacterial activity is also very important; there would be catastrophic impairment of the flow of nutrients in natural systems were it not for the role of maggots. The maggots' feeding and mechanical activity has the potential to liquefy the body tissues [8] and remove biomass [9].

Fly species of the family Calliphoridae (blowflies), distributed globally in most habitats, are usually the first to arrive at carrion, although there is often a sequence of species arrival [7,10]. Another family featuring early colonisers are the Sarcophagidae (flesh flies), although they are found more typically in tropical and warm temperate regions [11]. Fly taxa arriving somewhat later in the decomposition process, several days after death, are especially the Muscidae (house flies and allies) and Faniidae (latrine and lesser house flies), which favour decaying organic matter more broadly, but also contain carrion specialists [12,13]. Besides these, there are a number of other families, some of whose members also breed in carrion, and which are also more associated with later stages of decay. These include the Piophilidae (cheese skippers), Sepsidae (ant flies) and Phoridae (scuttle flies), but the maggots of these species will usually be found on corpses in far smaller numbers. The phorids are notable for being able to reach buried remains [14].

Beetles (order Coleoptera) are also a prominent component of the carrion fauna, either as predatory consumers of other insects such as maggots, or as consumers of the carrion. Beetles usually arrive within a few days after death but can persist for months afterwards [15]. The dominant families are the Silphidae (carrion and burying beetles), Histeridae (clown beetles), Staphylinidae (rove beetles), and Dermestidae (hide beetles). The first three groups are predatory, with the hide beetles feeding on skin and dried flesh [14]. In the same way as for the flies, there is a host of additional beetle families that occur on carrion less commonly or in fewer numbers.

In addition to flies and beetles, other terrestrial invertebrates, such as mites (Acari), have potential for the estimation of the time since death because there might be a predictable period of their association with carrion [16]. Certain commensal and parasitic mites (e.g. follicle and mange mites) and parasitic lice (order Phthiraptera) (e.g. head lice) can also be found on humans while alive, but will only persist for a limited time after death [17,18]. Other workers have contended that parasitoids (parasites that kill their host) of insects might be helpful in estimating the minPMI, and this has been applied especially to the species of wasp (order Hymenoptera) that parasitise maggots [19]. There is even scope for invertebrates found in freshwater and marine environments, such as crustaceans, to be indicators of the time elapsed since death based on their colonisation of submerged remains [20]. Terrestrial insects may also infest corpses in water if parts of the body are protruding above the surface. Additionally, it has been proposed that it may be possible to estimate the period of submersion of a corpse that had previously been on land, based on the time taken for the infesting insects to drown [21] (see Chapter 8, this volume).

The timing of insect arrival at a dead body

The estimation of a minPMI is necessary because the gap between death and insect colonisation is so hard to predict. This is largely due to the stochastic factors involved in invertebrate colonisation, but also partially attributable to an incomplete understanding of how colonisation occurs. Flies and beetles seek out and sense carrion using the organic volatiles produced by rotting carcasses. These molecules are detected and recognised with the antennae, although the specifics of how this system operates are still quite poorly known [22]. Some flies can arrive at and colonise a body within an hour after death [23] in the right conditions (usually daylight and warmth), but odour cues are seemingly modified in various ways by factors such as burning of remains [24]. It is also clear that a number of biotic and abiotic variables affect the timing of insect arrival on a body [25], and odour cues are therefore not the full basis for the process of attraction and colonisation (see also Chapter 3, this volume).

A better understanding of the process of insect attraction has the potential to improve the precision of death time estimates, since they would then not depend exclusively on the time of colonisation by the immature stages, but rather on when the remains were first available to insects. To this end, ongoing research has been directed at understanding the electrophysiological and chemical basis of insect attraction to carrion in the laboratory, e.g. Refs. [22,26]. There is also a set of field-based research focussing on prediction of the arrival time of adult carrion beetles [27,28], as well as the factors that influence colonisation by flies [25,29,30]. Recent interest has also been sparked in the interactions between insects and corpse microbes, which include their role in colonisation [31].

Estimating the time since death using insects

Insect development

When a person has been dead for a relatively short period of hours to days, the entomological approach to estimating death time will typically focus on the infesting blowflies and flesh flies, since these are generally the first attendants [14]. In this case the task facing the forensic entomologist will be to estimate the period elapsed from the commencement of development of the immature flies in the corpse until their collection, which will provide the minPMI. This necessitates calculating the period of development required for the specimens to reach the stage and size at which they were collected, which can be derived from reference data on the growth rates of species at different temperatures, e.g. Refs. [32,33]. Temperature is the major determinant of the speed of maggot growth; a curvilinear relationship exists between the time of development and temperature, with the assumption that no development occurs below the minimum threshold temperature and death or abnormal development above the maximum threshold temperature, both thresholds varying between species [34].

Experimental temperatures are usually constant, but those at the scene will almost always be variable, especially outdoors. Also, the growth of maggots will vary among individuals of a given species even at a constant temperature, so the application of growth data must inevitably entail some type of modelling that encompasses this variability and associated error. Such models, at their simplest, derive growth curves for measures of larval mass, length or width versus age at a given temperature [35–37]. A second general approach, called thermal summation, involves models of development that assume a constant increase in development rate with increasing temperature; these are also known as day-degree models, because development equates to the temperature above the minimal developmental threshold multiplied by time spent above the threshold [34]. Other more sophisticated mathematical approaches, such as generalised additive models, have also appeared in the literature [38]. Appropriate margins of error must accompany any approach given the range of assumptions that they incorporate; the most fundamental assumption is that the experimental conditions producing the reference data adequately mimic the situation in the field [39]. The minPMI is, in any case, a conservative estimate, since it does not seek to explicitly account for the earlier period between the death and the infestation time, and there is always the possibility that the oldest specimens were not collected, meaning that the minPMI may not equate with the earliest colonisation time.

The fly life cycle, on which the developmental minPMI is based, involves an initial egg stage laid by the female (often by the hundreds), or 'live-laid' larvae in smaller numbers [40]. Thus, it will depend on the species concerned whether infestation of the corpse by maggots can occur immediately, or whether there will be delay, typically of at least 12 h, before the larvae hatch from the eggs. As they feed, the larvae pass through three instars, or stages, of development. The third larval stage undergoes a process called pupariation, in which the cuticle, or skin, hardens to form a case-like puparium. Within the puparium the third-instar larva becomes a pupa, which then finally metamorphoses into an adult fly. Upon completing their development, the adult flies emerge from their puparia and disperse to continue the life cycle. Beyond the use of modelling, the milestones such as larval instar, pupariation and emergence can also be useful in estimating specimen age [41]. For further information on the biology of blowflies, see Erzinçlioğlu [42].

Although the minPMI is the term most commonly employed in forensic entomology analyses, another term sometimes used is 'maxPMI'. By contrast with the minPMI, this is estimated from the time that the deceased was last seen alive, rather than when the body became insect infested [39]. Some workers also prefer to replace minPMI with terms like 'postcolonisation interval' or 'time of colonisation'; or to use 'precolonisation interval' for the time between death and infestation [43]; or even 'period of insect activity' for the period between the initial detection of the corpse by insects and the collection time [44]. In practical terms, it should not matter what terminology is used by the practitioner as long as it is adequately defined in the case report and its main assumptions made clear [45].

Insect succession

When a person's remains have been exposed to invertebrates for a longer period of weeks to months, there will usually be a greater species richness of invertebrates present at the time of discovery. In addition to blowflies and flesh flies, a host of other fly families will have arrived as part of the process of faunal succession as decomposition has progressed, along with beetles and other invertebrates, such as ants (Formicidae) and mites [46].

A yet more complicated approach awaits the entomologist under these circumstances, as a minimum death time can only be arrived at by reference to further experimental data on species succession on decomposing remains. Succession patterns vary between localities and seasons, so these data should be for the same time of year and general locality and habitat. As alluded to already, many factors, such as temperature and rainfall, can influence the attraction of insects to carrion, even within the same season [47,48]. Here too some type of modelling exercise is required [49,50], although there is currently no consensus on how this should be done [15]. Methodological flaws have been exposed in some research approaches to measuring succession rate [51], and validation of succession data (or any other experimentally derived data in forensic entomology) therefore undoubtedly benefits from field testing before its application to casework [15].

Insect succession reference data have almost always been derived from experiments on various non-human animal species; especially domestic pigs, given assumed similarities to humans in aspects such as physiology and relative hairlessness, e.g. Ref. [52]. While the assumption that pigs or other species are a valid proxy for humans is widely held, it has been little tested [53]. A major responsibility to explore this assumption lies with 'body farms' – human decomposition research facilities – that exist in the USA and Australia and that are planned for other regions [54].

In the case of skeletonised remains, too little evidence might remain to provide a postmortem interval, not to mention too little precision based on the available reference data (see Chapter 7, this volume). However, because fly puparia can resist breakdown in the soil for many years [55], and because the activity of some species is seasonal, such evidence can nonetheless provide information about season of death [56,57].

Factors limiting the minPMI estimate

Insect identification

Since insects are the most diverse group of organisms on Earth, the composition of the entomological communities attracted to carrion can vary greatly from place to place. It is important in forensic casework to be able to rely on baseline data to support the presence of a certain set of species at the site where a body is found. This can be accomplished through knowledge of the geographic distributions of each species, but also through reliable methods for their identification.

Identification is traditionally achieved on the basis of the taxonomic features of the specimens. This can include obvious features such as colour and size, but also many more subtle ones such as the arrangement of bristles on certain part of the body and even the structure of the genitalia. Because of their frequent dominance, it is necessary to be able to identify the immature stages of the insects of forensic importance, as well as the adults. Immatures, especially fly maggots, have fewer diagnostic features than adults so are usually more difficult – or impossible – to identify. Morphological identification has in the past been facilitated by the use of dichotomous keys that mostly require specialist knowledge to use (e.g. Refs. [58,59]), but now online tools also based on morphology are available for some regions that make identification accessible to non-specialists, e.g. Ref. [60].

In recent years data derived from the genetic material of species (mainly DNA) have become a reliable supplement to morphological approaches. Again, the available data vary according to locality, but some countries have developed comprehensive datasets incorporating all species likely to be encountered, especially from the families Calliphoridae and Sarcophagidae, e.g. Refs. [61,62]. Molecular analysis has special value when there are no live immatures able to be reared to the adult stage or when specimens are degraded. Several techniques exist, but the most common involves sequencing the DNA from the so-called DNA 'barcode', which is represented by a portion of the mitochondrial gene, cytochrome oxidase 1 [63]. Some very closely related species cannot be reliably separated using this and other regions of DNA, but in most such instances it remains to be proven if such close relatives differ sufficiently in their growth rates for this to be of practical concern.

Geographic region and seasonality

Like all animals, insect species vary in their geographic distributions according to their habitat and temperature requirements. Knowledge of the species found in a given locality can help refine the associated conclusions, if, for example, the involvement of a foreign species implies that a body has been relocated from one place to another [64]. There is also the possibility of geographic variation in the genetics of a given species, such that the rate of development might vary within its distribution [65]. For both of these reasons, it is important to know the locality from which specimens came. Also, when corpses are relocated, insect evidence may be left behind at the scene and later potentially linked to the body by DNA profiling of its gut contents to demonstrate that it has been feeding on human remains [66]. DNA technology may also be applied to potentially even identifying the deceased [67]. Some species are only active at certain times of year, so their presence in a given case may not always be expected, thus potentially leading to their misidentification [68].

Weather and retrospective temperature analysis

Because temperature is such an important determinant of the development of immature flies, it is vital in forensic entomology cases to attempt to retrospectively estimate the temperature of the ambient air at the death scene. This can then serve as a baseline indicator of the temperature conditions affecting the maggots' growth. Previously, entomologists would commonly obtain weather records from the Bureau of Meteorology for the weather station nearest the death scene, encompassing a period prior to the recovery of the body, and assume that these data were representative of the scene itself. The problem with this approach is that the nearest weather station may be a long distance from the scene or in some other way climatically unrepresentative of it. To help overcome this concern, there is now a validated technique that creates a correlation between the nearest weather station and the scene for a period after the body is discovered, using data recorded at the scene, which in turn can be applied to the earlier weather station data for the approximate period that the body was *in situ* [69,70] (Fig. 4.1). The advantage of this method is that it provides a statistical test of whether the temperatures at the scene are indeed accurately reflected by those at the nearest weather station. The most recent studies on this topic have shown that the accuracy of the

Weather station temperature data collection period														
Body *in situ* period					Correlation period (*in situ* temperature data)									
1	2	3	4	5	6	7	8	9	10	11	12	13	14	15

FIG. 4.1 Example of the method used to retropectively estimate death scene ambient temperature (after Fig. 2 in Ref. [70]). Body *in situ* period (days 1—5) temperatures are estimated by statistically comparing *in situ* temperatures with weather station temperatures for days 6—15 and applying the resulting regression equation to weather station temperatures for days 1—5.

correction of the weather station data in providing a retrospective estimate of the scene data does not appear to be significantly affected by season, the length of the correlation period, or by distances up to 15 km between the site of the body discovery and the weather station. However, corrected weather data can be made less representative of actual scene temperatures if the correlation is done when there is a difference of >5 °C between the average weather station data collected *in situ* (prior to the body recovery) and the correlation period (after the body recovery) [70]. To offset this complication, it is recommended that the correlation period be at least 10 days in duration. However, as long as the correlation data have a high periodicity (of every 3 h or less), correlation periods can also be as short as two days if this is all that can be accommodated. For example, in some circumstances it may be difficult for the police to have access to a death scene in a domestic residence for longer than a week after discovery of the remains.

Nocturnal oviposition

The flies that breed in carrion are usually active only in daylight, leading to the frequent assumption that the period represented by the minPMI cannot commence at night. Such an assumption could affect estimates of minPMI by up to 12—14 h, depending on latitude and season. Studies have shown that the probability of the nocturnal deposition by female flies of their eggs (oviposition) or larvae (larviposition) in the laboratory may be quite high, depending on species, and can be enhanced by artificial lighting [71,72]. Workers have also demonstrated nocturnal oviposition occurring outdoors, again under both lit and unlit scenarios, but it is much less common than in a controlled environment [73,74]. The possibility of nocturnal ovi/larviposition therefore cannot be discounted, but it appears that cues other than just lighting, such as temperature and humidity, are involved.

Thermogenesis

Another factor requiring consideration where maggot development in concerned is the substantial increase in temperature above ambient that can occur in larval aggregations or maggot 'masses' [75–77]. Fly larvae group together in this way to enhance the feeding process, and, since higher temperatures boost their activity rates, minPMI calculations should accommodate such larval thermogenesis, or heating [78]. Data also point to a role in corpse heating from bacterial activity – bacteria are another key driver in the decomposition process [79] – and heat from the sun can be yet another contributing factor [80].

Larval thermogenesis has been a major area of experimental investigation in recent years, because without an indication of the temperature increase above ambient available to the developing larvae, it is difficult to produce an accurate assessment of their growth rate in a given case. Two techniques have been developed that have potential for assisting with the assessment of larval mass heating. Computed tomography (CT) scanning has been optimised and validated for casework in order to visualise maggot masses in dead bodies to provide information about mass size and location, including in inaccessible body regions [81,82] (Fig. 4.2); the estimation of mass volume has the potential to imply the associated heat production [75]. A second approach, thermal imaging, can be used to measure the actual temperatures generated within masses [83].

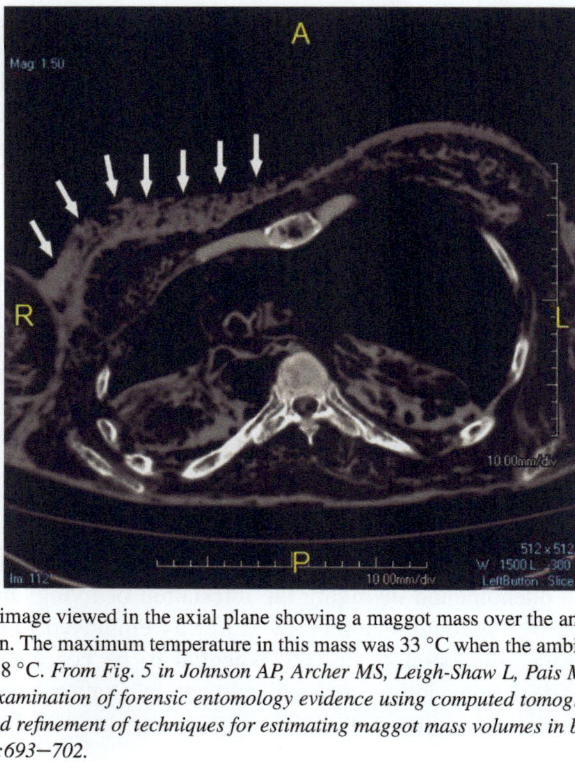

FIG. 4.2 CT image viewed in the axial plane showing a maggot mass over the anterior chest of a deceased person. The maximum temperature in this mass was 33 °C when the ambient temperature was only 17–18 °C. *From Fig. 5 in Johnson AP, Archer MS, Leigh-Shaw L, Pais M, O'Donnell C, Wallman JF. Examination of forensic entomology evidence using computed tomography scanning: case studies and refinement of techniques for estimating maggot mass volumes in bodies. Int J Leg Med 2012;126:693–702.*

Drugs

Corpses may commonly contain pharmaceutical and illicit drugs, ingested or injected prior to death for therapeutic or recreational purposes. Whether or not the drugs themselves have been the cause of death, they will persist in the decomposing remains for a period thereafter. Colonising insects will in turn ingest these drugs, and the compounds can be identified by analysis of the insects' tissues even when those of the corpse no longer remain or are unsuitable for analysis [84]. Fly larvae will mostly be analysed for drugs, but these compounds have also been extracted from fly puparia and beetle exuviae (skins) [85]. It has further been found that commonly used drugs, such as cocaine and methamphetamine, can affect maggot development, thus biasing minPMI estimates [86,87]. This sub-discipline of forensic entomology has been termed *entomotoxicology* [88]. Another complicating issue is that, in the same way that the primary drug compound will be metabolised in the living human body, drugs can change form in the developing insect [89]; this must be considered by studies investigating the effect of drugs on insect development.

Developmental substrate

It is well known that diet affects growth and development in all animals, so it would therefore be surprising if maggot development did not vary in different parts of corpses, subject to the different nutritional qualities and state of decomposition of the body tissues on which the maggots have fed. A number of studies have found significant developmental effects on fly larvae among fresh and decayed tissue types in pigs, sheep and other non-human animals [90–93].

Some differences might be expected to translate to human tissues. However, in the same way that PMI estimates based on succession data from animal models are frequently employed in casework, growth rate data for various fly species are almost always derived from laboratory experiments. These data are assumed to apply to the equivalent growth in human bodies, but this has hardly been examined. Comparisons of growth in the same species in tissues from different animals have shown differences [94], but interestingly no difference was found when maggot development on pork muscle and liver was compared with human muscle [95].

Maggot infestation prior to death

Myiasis is the phenomenon involving the infestation of living animal tissues by fly larvae [96]. Although entomology is mostly employed to estimate the time since death, this estimate has the potential to be confounded by rare scenarios in which the victim sustained maggot infestation *prior* to death. This could occur under circumstances involving attraction of flies to blood resulting from injuries with associated incapacitation, decubitus ulcers or faeces arising from incontinence in the elderly, infirm or very young [97,98]. Myiasis itself may lead to death due to invasion of major organs, sepsis or alkalosis [99−101], or death may be the result of some other cause. Even if myiasis is not fatal, it may nonetheless imply criminal neglect, with the time since the onset of such neglect useful in legal proceedings. Maggot infestation of living domestic animals may also lead to criminal charges, and insects also have potential to provide a minPMI when animals die through neglect or are killed illegally [102].

Manner of death

While the presence of drugs in a body, dealt with above, may provide important information concerning the cause of death, other entomological factors are also relevant to how someone died. The location and pattern of larval infestation in a corpse may imply that death occurred in a certain way [103]. For example, because maggot infestation normally begins in the facial orifices, infestation in some other part of the body, such as the hands, would therefore not normally be present early in decomposition, and may indicate wounds sustained prior to death, to which female flies may preferentially be attracted for ovi/larviposition [104]. It should however always be remembered that fly colonisation is variable, and that postmortem animal scavenging (rather than ante-mortem wounding) may have been responsible for creating defects that alter expected colonisation patterns [105].

In a related way, the marks left by insects feeding on corpses may challenge pathologists in their interpretation of the autopsy findings. Holes in skin caused by maggots can be misinterpreted for gunshot injuries, and erosions on skin produced by ants and cockroaches may be confused with abraded or chemical injury incurred prior to death, e.g. Ref. [106]. Additionally, insects can obscure trauma when maggots have been feeding in an antemortem injury, such as a stab wound or laceration. An appreciation of the often irregular, soft and ragged edges produced by maggot feeding can help the pathologist differentiate maggot feeding from features of wounds, such as crushing or abrasion of wound margins, bruising and patterning. Radiological imaging and autopsy investigation can also assist with ensuring that maggot feeding is not obscuring an ante-mortem injury by identifying underlying fractures, or embedded foreign objects, such as a projectile or broken knife blade.

Collecting methods

Unless rigorous approaches are used to collect entomological evidence, there is always the risk that samples have been missed that might have given a more accurate result. There are a number of published guidelines on how entomological evidence from death scenes should be collected. A comprehensive set of such information is provided by Amendt et al. [107].

Specimen selection

Because a body may contain specimens arising from separate episodes of colonisation, it is important that samples represent all parts of the corpse (head, torso and limbs), as well as beneath it and on and in the adjacent environment. Fly larvae may be found in different parts of the body because they are competing with each other, either among or within species. The larvae of certain species, such as the 'hairy' maggots of *Chrysomya rufifacies* (Calliphoridae), are predatory, leading to the 'smooth' maggots of the prey species separating from them to avoid attack [108].

It is sometimes recommended that only the largest specimens be collected, but some species can deposit an egg in a clutch that is much more developed than the others, leading to the presence of a larva that seems older than when it was actually deposited [109,110]. Also, smaller maggots are not necessarily younger, and may simply belong to a species that is constitutionally small.

Specimen preservation

Since it is often difficult for logistical reasons for an entomologist to attend a death scene in person, it is frequently the police or mortuary personnel who collect the insect evidence in their place. In these circumstances the entomologist should be consulted promptly about the circumstances to ensure that the collecting process is optimised.

How the evidence is processed by the police or other collectors acting on behalf of the entomologist may have ramifications for the accuracy of its interpretation. In particular, measuring the size of maggots collected from a body can be important in determining their age. In order to provide a record of the size reached at collection, a sample should always be killed and preserved. It has, however, been shown experimentally that the size of specimens can be influenced by the type of preservative. Some substances will cause larvae to shrink while others will make them expand, thus giving the false indication that they are younger or older, respectively, than their real age [111–113].

After specimens have been collected from the body at a scene, the corpse will usually be conveyed directly to the mortuary where it will be refrigerated prior the autopsy. Supplementary specimens should also be collected at the autopsy, but it is important to understand the capacity for maggots to continue to develop even when chilled. Maggot masses can still produce heat in mortuary fridges, thus permitting growth to continue [114]. And, since it has also been shown that maggot development can continue in live *unfed* samples, it is unwise to delay their preservation after collection [115].

Contamination

Depending on the location of a body, there is the possibility that the specimens collected from or around it could have originated in the remains of a nearby non-human animal [116]. Such carcasses are widespread in the landscape and corpses deposited outdoors could easily be placed alongside or even atop other carrion. Additional problems may arise with elevated numbers of deceased animals on rural properties due to hunting, farm animal attrition or home slaughter practices. Multiple deceased people [117] or their dead domestic pets [118] may also occasionally be encountered at scenes. Pre-existing remains will contain older specimens that may skew minPMI estimates. Police personnel must therefore note any secondary carcasses or other sources of misleading specimens, such as human refuse, when collecting entomological evidence from a death scene, but there is also the potential for contamination occurring in the mortuary [119].

Collecting rigour

Shortcomings in crime scene police personnel and pathologists acting as proxies for forensic entomologists can be mitigated by them undertaking the appropriate training. Opportunities for entomologists to talk to law enforcement agencies can occur quite regularly, and these agencies are usually very keen for regional practitioners to help them update their internal standard operating procedures for entomology collection, and even help them develop standardised collecting kits to be used at scenes. Australian entomologists have now developed online training, including video footage, which anyone with the appropriate credentials can access [120].

Even with the benefit of such training, there is a potential limitation through collecting being done inadequately. There are two areas that are commonly overlooked. The first involves the need to search carefully for fly pupae and puparia, which represent the later stages of a fly's lifecycle. These may often be found some distance away from the corpse, especially in indoor scenes, since fly larvae have the capacity to crawl considerable distances away from remains [121]. Omission of pupal and puparial specimens can reduce the estimated minPMI. The second area of concern relates to the treatment of insect specimens once recovered. The importance of the method of preservation of maggot specimens being killed has already been mentioned, but it is also critical that specimens being kept alive be handled appropriately; it is common for police agencies to delay sending the evidence, during which time fly larvae will die if denied food, moisture and oxygen.

Summary of collecting steps

The general approach to be adopted involves the following general steps:

1. Contact the forensic entomologist for initial advice.
2. Record the crime scene, especially the nature and extent of the insect infestation of the corpse (include photos).
3. Record the temperatures of the corpse, maggot masses and the surrounding air and soil.
4. Collect all kinds and sizes of immature and adult insects associated with the corpse. Kill a large maggot sample in very hot water (just under boiling is ideal), then preserve the specimens in 70-80% ethanol. Keep a further sample of fly eggs, larvae and pupae alive; keep the maggots moist, fed and aerated. 'Hairy' maggots should be separated from 'smooth' ones to avoid the latter being killed and eaten (see 'Specimen selection', this chapter).
5. Look for fly pupae and pupal cases around and beneath the corpse. Collect soil and leaf litter samples to ensure that no specimens are missed.
6. Check for adjacent animal remains that could be a source of contamination.
7. Collect additional insects and temperature measurements at the autopsy.
8. Deliver insect specimens promptly to the forensic entomologist.
9. Obtain weather data for the death scene from the start of the approximate body *in situ* period until at least 10 days after collection of the insect evidence.

General standards among forensic entomology practitioners

Personal experience is an important determinant of the approaches applicable to a given case and the conclusions able to be drawn from it. Indeed, it is only through such experience that a practitioner will be able to determine if an entomological opinion is even appropriate. As in any forensic discipline, benefit will be derived from practitioners communicating with one another and coordinating their efforts with regard to appropriate guidelines, protocols and standards. For example, there is much merit in experts applying some form of peer review to their reports, especially if they are being tendered as evidence in court. Many workers have also developed collecting protocols of the sort mentioned earlier in this chapter, including working with police agencies to ensure that the same methodologies are used repeatedly, even across different jurisdictions. In some countries, such as Australia, there are also official standards endorsed by a federal-level forensic agency within which entomology activities fit, especially connected with matters such as recovery and storage, examination and interpretation, and reporting [120].

All sub-disciplines of forensic science are subject to what have been referred to as context effects, in which the thinking and decision-making of analysts may be influenced by information unnecessary for them to do their job [122–124]. This might not be a concern were it not for the fact that it can lead to workers being negatively biased by factors that they did not know or expect would influence them. While of course some context can be useful, it is accepted that steps should be taken to minimise anything deemed unhelpful. Ultimately, entomology evidence in court can be more readily challenged if attempts are not made to remove bias. In entomological analyses, bias can arise through, for example, assumptions regarding the identity of specimens due to the locality from which they were collected; and assuming a certain minPMI because of information provided by the police about the last time the victim was seen alive. Such risks of bias can be managed in practice through a process called sequential unmasking, in which only the information absolutely necessary is available at each stage of the analytical process (Fig. 4.3). Ideally therefore, the entomologist would have no initial information about the origin of a given set of specimens, nor the case with which they were associated [125].

In any judicial matter there may also be occasions when the opinions of those called upon to provide an expert opinion do not agree. Forensic entomology is not immune here, and there have been some very public cases reported in the USA in particular. These have often centred on key issues such as the minPMI, the taxonomic identity of specimens, the effect of drugs on maggot development, retrospective estimation of scene temperature and the appropriateness of providing an opinion from photographs only, e.g. Refs. [126,127]. One such court room controversy culminated with the Western Australian Coroner providing a concise assessment of the risks inherent in practitioners failing to (1) collect all relevant information, (2) reveal their information sources, (3) give the basis of their opinions and (4) clarify the limits of their testimony [128].

Case studies

The forensic entomology literature already contains an abundance of case reports that can help the reader understand the practical application of insects to forensic science, e.g. Refs. [14,104,129]. However, to provide final context to this chapter, summaries of three anonymised Australian cases are also given here.

Case 1

The double murder of a husband and wife took place in their home in rural New South Wales. The body of the husband was found on the kitchen floor, while that of the wife was found in her bed. Maggots from both bodies were analysed and a minPMI estimated, based on growth data for the fly species concerned at an appropriate temperature. Since it appeared that the crimes had occurred at the same time, there was initially some confusion about the fact

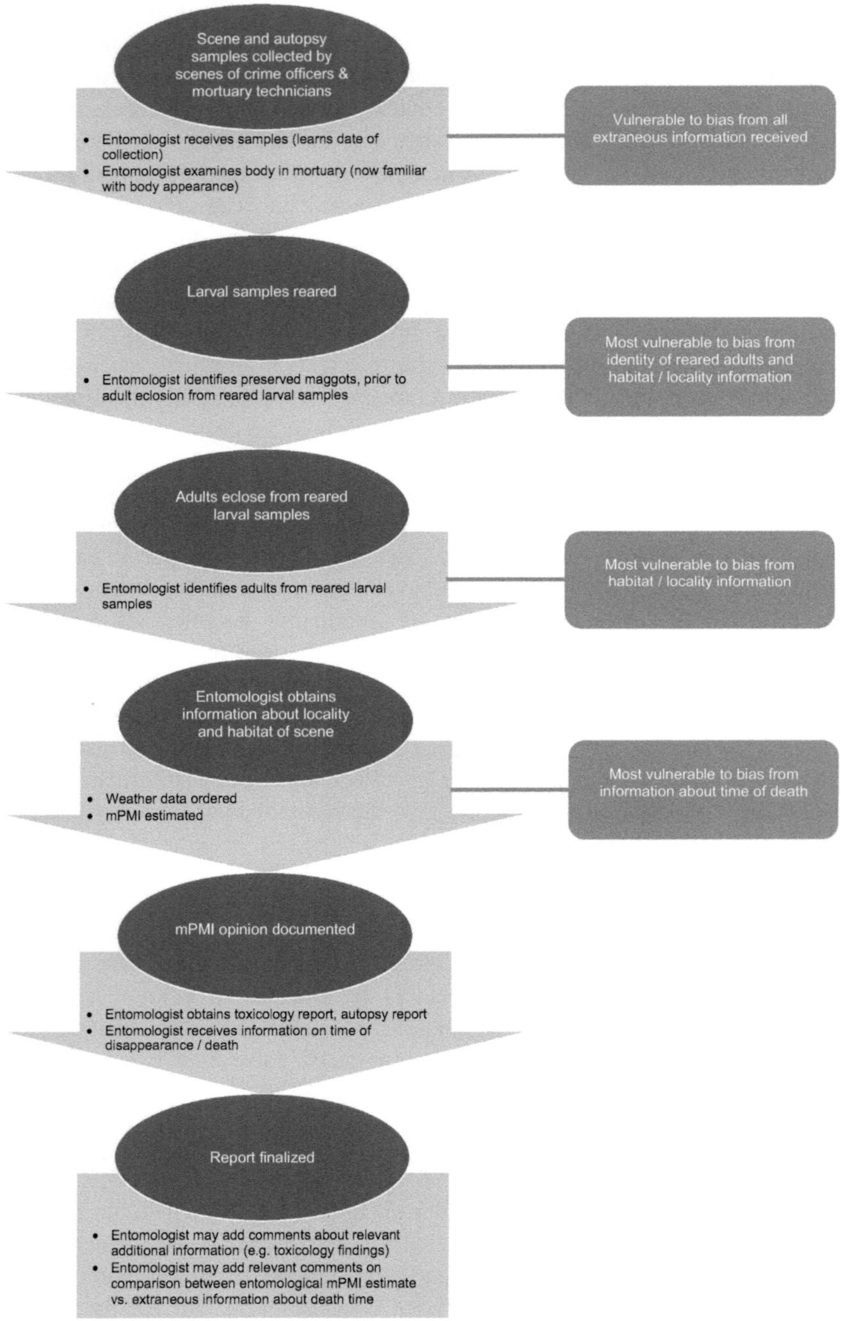

FIG. 4.3 An example of the order in which tasks might be carried out to enable a sequential unmasking approach to context-free casework in forensic entomology. *From Fig. 1 in Archer MS, Wallman JF. Context effects in forensic entomology and use of sequential unmasking in casework. J Forensic Sci 2016;61:1270–1277.*

that the maggots from the woman's body were better developed than those from the man's, and thus appeared older. It was then revealed that the woman's body was lying on an electric blanket that was switched on; the extra heat had accelerated the maggots' development. The entomologist's estimate of the minPMI suggested a different death time than that provided by other police evidence, such as when the last phone call was made from the house and when the female victim was last seen alive. This resulted in the original evidence being re-checked by the police, and found to be flawed. The revised timeframe enabled the police to refocus their investigation, leading to the trial and conviction of a suspect lacking an alibi for the time in question [117].

Case 2

A young woman was found dead in the ground-floor storeroom of a block of apartments in suburban Sydney. Her body had been placed in a sports bag. Insect evidence, comprising the adults and immature stages of at least eight fly and two beetle species, were collected at the scene as well as at the subsequent autopsy. Using data from a nearby weather station and readings taken at the scene, the estimated temperature in the storeroom during the tenure of the remains was estimated using the methodology of Archer [69]. The presence of fly puparia from which flies had already emerged, combined with maggots of species that occur later during decomposition, suggested a minPMI of at least four weeks based on previous studies of these taxa. The trial of the main suspect in the case found consistency between the insect evidence and when the victim was last seen alive, contributing to his subsequent conviction for the murder.

Case 3

The body of a woman was found in forest near Melbourne, Victoria. The corpse was fully clothed, with a plastic bag containing the partially severed head and a carpet wrapped around the torso. The woman had been killed with a combination of gunshot, sharp force, and blunt force trauma. Maggot masses in the body were generating significant heat. The estimated mean ambient temperature at the scene was calculated for the entire time the body might have been present (between two and four weeks). The immature stages of six species of carrion-breeding flies and immatures and adults of three species of beetles were collected from the remains. Data from succession experiments on dead pigs (arrival and departure times of different species), undertaken nearby at the same time of year, were applied to the case, despite the pigs being unclothed and not dismembered. All potential experimental shortcomings were given in the report tendered to the police. Court proceedings revealed that the estimated mPMI range encompassed the day of death and body disposal, which was established by eyewitnesses as 21 days before the body was discovered; the suspects were found guilty [15].

Conclusions

Forensic entomology can be a powerful tool for answering various questions surrounding the time since death, especially when encountering cases involving medium to longer term postmortem intervals. However, the application of entomological techniques can be complex and requires careful evidence collection and interpretation. Research into various aspects of the association of insects with decaying bodies is gradually helping to ameliorate traditional problems in the analysis of forensic entomology evidence, and increasing collaboration between practitioners has led to a vibrant and progressive research culture. Nonetheless, the discipline remains small and faces considerable challenges in the future related to ongoing problems such as modelling of larval growth and insect succession, and taxonomic identification.

References

[1] Greenberg B, Kunich JC, editors. Entomology and the law: flies as forensic indicators. Cambridge: Cambridge University Press; 2002.

[2] Wallman JF. The practice of crime scene investigation. Boca Raton: CRC Press; 2004.

[3] Turner BD. Blowfly maggots: the good, the bad and the ugly. Comp Clin Pathol 2005;14:81–5.

[4] Tomberlin JK, Wallace JR, Byrd JH. Forensic entomology: myths busted! Forensic Mag 2006. p. 10–4.

[5] Schotsmans EMJ, Márquez-Grant N, Forbes SL, editors. Taphonomy of human remains. Chichester: John Wiley & Sons Ltd; 2017.

[6] Putman RJ. Carrion and dung: the decomposition of animal wastes. London: Edward Arnold; 1983.

[7] Fuller ME. The insect inhabitants of carrion: a study in animal ecology. Council Sci Ind Res, Australia, Bull 1934;82:1–63.

[8] Hobson RP. Studies on the nutrition of blow-fly larvae. III. The liquefaction of muscle. J Exp Biol 1932;9:359–65.

[9] Putman RJ. Dynamics of the blowfly, *Calliphora erythrocephala*, within carrion. J Anim Ecol 1977;46:853–66.

[10] Norris KR. The bionomics of blowflies. Annu Rev Entomol 1965;10:47–68.

[11] Pape T. In: Gupta VK, editor. Catalogue of the Sarcophagidae of the world. Gainesville: Associated Publishers; 1996.

[12] Pont A. Studies on Australian Muscidae (Diptera). IV. A revision of the subfamilies Muscinae and Stomoxyinae. Aust J Zool Suppl Ser 1973;51:129–296.

[13] Pont A. A revision of the Australian Fanniidae (Diptera: Calyptrata). Aust J Zool Suppl Ser 1977;51:1–60.

[14] Smith KGV. A manual of forensic entomology. London: Trustees of The British Museum (Nat. Hist.) and Cornell University Press; 1986.

[15] Archer M. Comparative analysis of insect succession data from Victoria (Australia) using summary statistics versus preceding mean ambient temperature models. J Forensic Sci 2014;59:404–12.

[16] Goff ML. Gamasid mites as potential indicators of postmortem interval. In: Channabasavanna GP, Viraktamath CA, editors. Progress in acarology, vol. 1. New Delhi: Oxord and IBH Publishing; 1989. p. 443–50.

[17] Perotti MA, Goff ML, Baker AS, Turner BD, Braig HR. Forensic acarology: an introduction. Exp Appl Acarol 2009;49:3–13.

[18] Gonzales TA, Vance M, Helpern M, Umberger CJ. Legal medicine: pathology and toxicology. 2nd ed. New York: Appleton-Century-Crofts; 1954.

[19] Voss SC, Spafford H, Dadour IR. Hymenopteran parasitoids of forensic importance: host associations, seasonality, and prevalence of parasitoids of carrion flies in Western Australia. J Med Entomol 2009;46:1210–9.

[20] Merritt RW, Wallace JR. The role of aquatic insects in forensic investigations. In: Byrd JH, Castner JL, editors. Forensic entomology: the utility of arthropods in legal investigations. 2nd ed. Boca Raton: CRC Press; 2010. p. 271–319.

[21] Singh D, Greenberg B. Survival after submergence in the pupae of five species of blow flies (Diptera: Calliphoridae). J Med Entomol 1994;31:757–9.

[22] Frederickx M, Dekeirsschieter J, Verheggen FJ, Haubruge E. Responses of *Lucilia sericata* (Diptera: Calliphoridae) to cadaveric volatile compounds. J Forensic Sci 2012;57:386–90.

[23] Hall RD, Doisy KE. Length of time after death: effect on attraction and oviposition or larviposition of midsummer blow flies (Diptera: Calliphoridae) and flesh flies (Diptera: Calliphoridae) of medicolegal importance in Missouri. Ann Entomol Soc Am 1993;86:589–93.

[24] Catts EP, Goff ML. Forensic entomology in criminal investigations. Annu Rev Entomol 1992;37:253–72.

[25] George KA, Archer MS, Toop T. Abiotic environmental factors influencing blowfly colonisation patterns in the field. Forensic Sci Int 2013;229:100–7.

[26] Dekeirsschieter J, Frederickx M, Lognay G, Brostaux Y, Verheggen FJ, Haubruge E. Electrophysiological and behavioral responses of *Thanatophilus sinuatus* Fabricius (Coleoptera: Silphidae) to selected cadaveric volatile organic compounds. J Forensic Sci 2013;58:917–23.

[27] Matuszewski S. Estimating the preappearance interval from temperature in *Creophilus maxillosus* L. (Coleoptera: Staphylinidae). J Forensic Sci 2012;57:136–45.

[28] Matuszewski S. Estimating the pre-appearance interval from temperature in *Necrodes littoralis* L. (Coleoptera: Silphidae). Forensic Sci Int 2011;212:180–8.

[29] George KA, Archer MS, Toop T. Effects of bait age, larval chemical cues and nutrient depletion on colonization by forensically important calliphorid and sarcophagid flies, Med Vet Entomol 2012;26:188–93.

[30] Reibe S, Madea B. How promptly do blowflies colonise fresh carcasses? A study comparing indoor with outdoor locations. Forensic Sci Int 2010;195:52–7.

[31] Jordan HR, Tomberlin JK. Abiotic and biotic factors regulating inter-kingdom engagement between insects and microbe activity on vertebrate remains. Insects 2017;8:54.

[32] Byrd JH, Butler JF. Effects of temperature on *Chrysomya rufifacies* (Diptera: Calliphoridae) development. J Med Entomol 1997;34:353–8.

[33] Anderson GS. Factors that influence insect succession on carrion. In: Byrd J, Castner E, editors. Forensic entomology: the utility of arthropods in legal investigations. 2nd ed. Boca Raton: CRC Press; 2010. p. 201–50.

[34] Higley LG, Haskell NH. Insect development and forensic entomology. In: Byrd JH, Castner JL, editors. Forensic entomology: the utility of arthropods in legal investigations. 2nd ed. Boca Raton: CRC Press; 2010. p. 389–405.

[35] Wells JD, Kurahashi H. *Chrysomya megacephala* (Fabricus) (Diptera: Calliphoridae) development: rate, variation and the implications for forensic entomology. Jpn J Sanit Zool 1994;45:303–9.

[36] Donovan SE, Hall MJR, Turner BD, Moncreiff CB. Larval growth rates of the blowfly, *Calliphora vicina*, over a range of temperatures. Med Vet Entomol 2006;20:106–14.

[37] Day DM, Wallman JF. Width as an alternative measurement to length for post-mortem interval estimations using *Calliphora augur* (Diptera: Calliphoridae) larvae. Forensic Sci Int 2006;159:158–67.

[38] Tarone AM, Foran DR. Generalized additive models and *Lucilia sericata* growth: assessing confidence intervals and error rates in forensic entomology. J Forensic Sci 2008;53:942–8.

[39] Villet MH, Richards CS, Midgely JM. Contemporary precision, bias and accuracy of minimum post-mortem intervals estimated using development of carrion-feeding insects. In: Amendt J, editor. Current concepts in forensic entomology. Dordrecht: Springer; 2008. p. 109–37.

[40] Mackerras MJ. Observations on the life-histories, nutritional requirements and fecundity of blowflies. Bull Entomol Res 1933;24:353–62.

[41] Greenberg B. Flies as forensic indicators. J Med Entomol 1991;28:565–77.

[42] Erzinçlioğlu YZ. Blowflies. Slough. Richman Publishing Co Ltd; 1996.

[43] Tomberlin JK, Mohr R, Benbow ME, Tarone AM, VanLaerhoven S. A roadmap for bridging basic and applied research in forensic entomology. Annu Rev Entomol 2011;56:401–21.

[44] Gallagher MB, Sandhu S, Kimsey R. Variation in developmental time for geographically distinct populations of the common green bottle fly, *Lucilia sericata* (Meigen). J Forensic Sci 2010;55:438–42.

[45] Tarone AM, Sanford MR. Is PMI the hypothesis or the null hypothesis? J Med Entomol 2017;54:1109–15.

[46] Merritt RW, De Jong GD. Arthropod communities in terrestrial environments. In: Benbow EM, Tomberlin JK, Tarone AM, editors. Carrion ecology, evolution, and their applications. Boca Raton: CRC Press; 2016.

[47] Archer MS. Annual variation in arrival and departure times of carrion insects at carcasses: implications for succession studies in forensic entomology. Aust J Zool 2003;51:569–76.

[48] Archer MS. Rainfall and temperature effects on the decomposition rate of exposed neonatal remains. Sci Justice 2004;44:35–41.

[49] Wells JD, LaMotte L. The role of a PMI-prediction model in evaluating forensic entomology experimental design, the importance of covariates, and the utility of response variables for estimating time since death. Insects 2017;8:47.

[50] Michaud JP, Moreau G. A statistical approach based on accumulated degree-days to predict dcomposition-related pocesses in forensic studies. J Forensic Sci 2011;56:229–32.

[51] Michaud JP, Schoenly KG, Moreau G. Sampling flies or sampling flaws? Experimental design and inference strength in forensic entomology. J Med Entomol 2012;49:1–10.

[52] Anderson GS, VanLaerhoven SL. Initial studies on insect succession on carrion in southwestern British Columbia. J Forensic Sci 1996;41:617–25.

[53] Schoenly KG, Haskell NH, Hall RD, Gbur JR. Comparative performance and complementarity of four sampling methods and arthropod preference tests from human and porcine remains at the Forensic Anthropology Center in Knoxville, Tennessee. J Med Entomol 2007;44:881–94.

[54] Wallman JF. Body farms. Forensic Sci Med Pathol 2017;13:487–9.

[55] Gautier A, Schumann H. Puparia of the subarctic black blowfly *Protophormia terraenovae* (Robineau-Desvoidy, 1830) in a skull of a late Eemian(?) bison at Zemst, Brabant (Belgium). Palaeogeogr Palaeoclimatol Palaeoecol 1973;14:119–25.

[56] Nuorteva P. Empty puparia of *Phormia terraenovae* R.-D. (Diptera, Calliphoridae) as forensic indicators. Ann Entomol Fennici 1987;53:53–6.

[57] Archer MS, Elgar MA. Yearly activity patterns in southern Victoria (Australia) of seasonally active carrion insects. Forensic Sci Int 2003;132:173–6.

[58] Wallman JF. A key to the adults of species of blowflies in southern Australia known or suspected to breed in carrion [corrigendum in Med Vet Entomol 16:223]. Med Vet Entomol 2001;15:433–7.

[59] Meiklejohn KA, Dowton M, Pape T, Wallman JF. A key to the Australian Sarcophagidae (Diptera) with special emphasis on *Sarcophaga (sensu lato)*. Zootaxa 2013;3680:148–89.

[60] Kavazos CRJ, Meiklejohn KA, Archer MS, Wallman JF. A LUCID key for the online identification of the Australian flies known or suspected to breed in carrion. Wollongong: University of Wollongong; 2012.

[61] Wallman JF, Leys R, Hogendoorn K. Molecular systematics of Australian carrion-breeding blowflies (Diptera: Calliphoridae) based on mitochondrial DNA. Invertebr Syst 2005;19:1–15.

[62] Meiklejohn KA, Wallman JF, Cameron SL, Dowton M. Comprehensive evaluation of DNA barcoding for the molecular species identification of forensically important Australian Sarcophagidae (Diptera). Invertebr Syst 2012;26:515–25.

[63] Nelson LA, Wallman JF, Dowton M. Using COI barcodes to identify forensically and medically important blowflies. Med Vet Entomol 2007;21:44–52.

[64] Erzinçlioğlu YZ. Entomology and the forensic scientist: how insects solve crimes. J Biol Educ 1989;23:300–2.

[65] Nelson LA, Dowton M, Wallman JF. Thermal attributes of *Chrysomya* species. Entomol Exp Appl 2009;133:260–75.

[66] Wells JD, Stevens JR. Application of DNA-based methods in forensic entomology. Annu Rev Entomol 2008;53:103–20.

[67] Wells JD, Introna F, Di Vella G, Campobasso CP, Hayes J, Sperling FAH. Human and insect mitochondrial DNA analysis from maggots. J Forensic Sci 2001;46:685–7.

[68] Kavazos CRJ, Wallman JF. Community composition of carrion-breeding blowflies (Diptera: Calliphoridae) along an urban gradient in south-eastern Australia. Landsc Urban Plan 2012;106:183–90.

[69] Archer MS. The effect of time after body discovery on the accuracy of retrospective weather station ambient temperature corrections in forensic entomology. J Forensic Sci 2004;49:1–7.

[70] Johnson AP, Wallman JF, Archer MS. Experimental and casework validation of ambient temperature corrections in forensic entomology. J Forensic Sci 2012;57:215–21.

[71] Williams KA, Wallman JF, Lessard BD, Kavazos CRJ, Mazungula DN, Villet MH. Nocturnal oviposition behavior of blowflies (Diptera: Calliphoridae) in the southern hemisphere (South Africa and Australia) and its forensic implications. Forensic Sci Med Pathol 2017;13:123–4.

[72] George KA, Archer MS, Toop T. Nocturnal colonization behavior of blowflies (Diptera: Calliphoridae) in southeastern Australia. J Forensic Sci 2013;58:S112–6.

[73] Greenberg B. Nocturnal oviposition behaviour of blow flies (Diptera: Calliphoridae). J Med Entomol 1990;27:807–10.

[74] Singh D, Bharti M. Further observations on the nocturnal oviposition behaviour of blow flies (Diptera: Calliphoridae). Forensic Sci Int 2001;120:124–6.

[75] Slone DH, Gruner SV. Thermoregulation in larval aggregations of carrion-feeding blow flies (Diptera: Calliphoridae). J Med Entomol 2007;44:516–23.

[76] Charabidze D, Bourel B, Gosset D. Larval-mass effect: characterisation of heat emission by necrophagous blowflies (Diptera: Calliphoridae) larval aggregates. Forensic Sci Int 2011;211:61–6.

[77] Cianci TJ, Sheldon JK. Endothermic generation by blow fly larvae *Phormia regina* developing in pig carcasses. Bull Soc Vector Ecol 1990;15:33–40.

[78] Turner B, Howard T. Metabolic heat generation in dipteran larval aggregations: a consideration for forensic entomology. Med Vet Entomol 1992;6:179–81.

[79] Johnson AP, Mikac K, Wallman JF. Thermogenesis in decomposing carcasses. Forensic Sci Int 2013;231:271–7.

[80] Shean BS, Messinger L, Papworth M. Observations of differential decomposition on sun v. shaded pig carrion in coastal Washington State. J Forensic Sci 1993;38:938–49.

[81] Johnson AP, Archer MS, Leigh-Shaw L, Pais M, O'Donnell C, Wallman JF. Examination of forensic entomology evidence using computed tomography scanning: case studies and refinement of techniques for estimating maggot mass volumes in bodies. Int J Leg Med 2012;126:693–702.

[82] Johnson AP, Archer MS, Leigh-Shaw L, Brown M, O'Donnell C, Wallman JF. Non-invasive visualisation and volume estimation of maggot masses using computed tomography scanning. Int J Leg Med 2013;127:185–94.

[83] Johnson AP, Wallman JF. Infrared imaging as a non-invasive tool for documenting maggot mass temperatures. Aust J Forensic Sci 2013;46:73–9.

[84] Gagliano-Candela R, Aventaggiato L. The detection of toxic substances in entomological specimens. Int J Leg Med 2001;114:197–203.

[85] Miller ML, Lord WD, Goff ML, Donnelly B, McDonough ET, Alexis JC. Isolation of amitriptyline and nortriptyline from fly puparia (Phoridae) and beetle exuviae (Dermestidae) associated with mummified human remains. J Forensic Sci 1994;39:1305–13.

[86] Mullany C, Keller PA, Nugraha AS, Wallman JF. Effects of methamphetamine and its primary human metabolite, p-hydroxymethamphetamine, on the development of the Australian blowfly, *Calliphora stygia*. Forensic Sci Int 2014;241:102–11.

[87] Goff ML, Omori AI, Goodbrod JR. Effect of cocaine in tissues on the development rate of *Boettcherisca peregrina* (Diptera: Sarcophagidae). J Med Entomol 1989;26:91–3.

[88] Goff ML, Lord WD. Entomotoxicology. A new area for forensic investigation. Am J Forensic Med Pathol 1994;15:51–7.

[89] Parry S, Linton SM, Francis PS, O'Donnell MJ, Toop T. Accumulation and excretion of morphine by *Calliphora stygia*, an Australian blow fly species of forensic importance. J Insect Physiol 2011;57:62–73.

[90] Day DM, Wallman JF. Influence of substrate tissue type on larval growth in *Calliphora augur* and *Lucilia cuprina* (Diptera: Calliphoridae) [erratum in J Forensic Sci 51:1221]. J Forensic Sci 2006;51:657–63.

[91] Thyssen PJ, de Souza CM, Shimamoyo PM, Salewski T, Moretti TC. Rates of development of immatures of three species of *Chrysomya* (Diptera: Calliphoridae) reared in different types of animal tissues: implications for estimating the postmortem interval. Parasitol Res 2014;113:3373–80.

[92] Kaneshrajah G, Turner B. *Calliphora vicina* larvae grow at different rates on different body tissues. Int J Leg Med 2004;118:242–4.

[93] Richards CS, Rowlinson CC, Cuttiford L, Grimsley R, Hall MJR. Decomposed liver has a significantly adverse affect on the development rate of the blowfly *Calliphora vicina*. Int J Leg Med 2013;127:259–62.

[94] Clark K, Evans L, Wall R. Growth rates of the blowfly, *Lucilia sericata*, on different body tissues. Forensic Sci Intl 2006;156:145–9.

[95] Bernhardt V, Schomerus C, Verhoff MA, Amendt J. Of pigs and men - comparing the development of *Calliphora vicina* (Diptera: Calliphoridae) on human and porcine tissue. Int J Leg Med 2017;131:847–53.

[96] Hall MJR, Wall R. Myiasis of humans and domestic animals. Adv Parasitol 1995;35:257–334.

[97] Benecke M, Lessig R. Child neglect and forensic entomology. Forensic Sci Int 2001;120:155–9.

[98] Goff ML, Charconneau BA, Sullivan W. Presence of fecal material in diapers as a potential source of error in estimations of postmortem interval using arthropod development rates. J Forensic Sci 1991;36:1603–6.

[99] Groves BA, Bates PG. Preliminary investigations of plasma ammonia levels in sheep infested with *Lucilia sericata* and their potential in the ageing of blowfly lesions in cases of neglect, Med Vet Entomol 1998;12:208–10.

[100] Lysaght TB, Wooster ME, Jenkins PC, Koniaris LG. Myiasis-induced sepsis: a rare case report of *Wohlfahrtiimonas chitiniclastica* and *Ignatzschineria indica* bacteremia in the continental United States. Medicine 2018;97:52.

[101] James MT. The flies that cause myiasis in man. US Dept Agr Misc Publ 1947;631:1–175.

[102] Anderson GS, Huitson NR. Myiasis in pet animals in British Columbia: the potential of forensic entomology for determining duration of possible neglect. Can Vet J 2004;45:993–8.

[103] Erzinçlioğlu YZ. Proceedings of the BAFM meeting held in Tunbridge Wells on 6 July 1991. 1. Forensic entomology. Med Sci Law 1992;32:43–4.

[104] Lord WD. Case histories and the use of insects in investigations. In: Catts EP, Haskell NH, editors. Entomology and death: a procedural guide. Clemson: Joyce's Print Shop; 1990. p. 9–37.

[105] Byard RW, James RA, Gilbert JD. Diagnostic problems associated with cadaveric trauma from animal activity. Am J Forensic Med Pathol 2002;23:238–44.

[106] Byard RW. Autopsy problems associated with postmortem ant activity. Forensic Sci Med Pathol 2005;1:37–40.

[107] Amendt J, Campobasso CP, Gaudry E, Reiter C, LeBlanc H, Hall M. Best practice in forensic entomology - standards and guidelines. Int J Leg Med 2007;121:90–104.

[108] Wells JD, Kurahashi H. *Chrysomya megacephala* (Fabr.) is more resistant to attack by *Ch. rufifacies* (Macquart) in a laboratory arena than is *Cochliomyia macellaria* (Fabr.) (Diptera: Calliphoridae). Pan-Pacific Entomol 1997;73:16–20.

[109] Erzinçlioğlu YZ. On the interpretation of maggot evidence in forensic cases. Med Sci Law 1990;30:65–6.

[110] Wells JD, King J. Incidence of precocious egg development in flies of forensic importance (Calliphoridae). Pan-Pacific Entomol 2001;77:235–9.

[111] Day DM, Wallman JF. Effect of preservative solutions on preservation of *Calliphora augur* and *Lucilia cuprina* larvae (Diptera: Calliphoridae) with implications for post-mortem interval estimates. Forensic Sci Int 2008;179:1–10.

[112] Tantawi TI, Greenberg B. The effect of killing and preservative solutions on estimates of maggot age in forensic cases. J Forensic Sci 1993;38:702–7.

[113] Adams ZJO, Hall MJR. Methods used for the killing and preservation of blowfly larvae, and their effect on post-mortem interval length. Forensic Sci Int 2003;138:50–61.

[114] Huntington TE, Higley LG, Baxendale FP. Maggot development during morgue storage and its effect on estimating the post mortem interval. J Forensic Sci 2007;52:453–8.

[115] Archer MS, Jones SD, Wallman JF. Delayed reception of live blowfly (*Calliphora vicina* and *Chrysomya rufifacies*) larval samples: implications for minimum postmortem interval estimates. Forensic Sci Res 2018;3:27–39.

[116] Archer M, Elgar MA, Briggs CA, Ranson DL. Fly pupae and puparia as potential contaminants of forensic entomology samples from sites of body discovery. Int J Leg Med 2006;120:364–8.

[117] Miller H. Final payment. In: Indelible evidence: an international collection of true crimes which have been solved by forensic science. London: BBC Books; 1991. p. 58–68.

[118] Sanford MR. Forensic entomology of decomposing humans and their decomposing pets. Forensic Sci Int 2015;247:e11–7.

[119] Archer MS, Ranson DL. Potential contamination of forensic entomology smaples collected in the mortuary: a case report. Med Sci Law 2005;45:89–91.

[120] Archer MS, Wallman JF. The development of forensic entomology in Australia and New Zealand: an overview of casework practice, quality control and standards. Aust J Forensic Sci 2016;49:125–33.

[121] Greenberg B. Behaviour of postfeeding larvae of some Calliphoridae and a muscid (Diptera). Ann Entomol Soc Am 1990;83:1210–4.

[122] Found B, Ganas J. The management of domain irrelevant context information in forensic handwriting examination casework. Sci Justice 2013;53:154–8.

[123] Miller LS. Bias among forensic document examiners: a need for procedural changes. J Police Sci Adm 1984;12:407–11.

[124] Dror IE, Charlton D, Péron A. Contextual information renders experts vulnerable to making erroneous identifications. Forensic Sci Int 2006;156:74–8.

[125] Archer MS, Wallman JF. Context effects in forensic entomology and use of sequential unmasking in casework. J Forensic Sci 2016;61:1270–7.

[126] Porter G. Zak coronial inquest and the interpretation of photographic evidence. Curr Issues Crim Justice 2012;24:39–49.

[127] Wells JD. A forensic entomological analysis can yield an estimate of postmortem interval, and not just a minimum postmortem interval: an explanation and illustration using a case. J Forensic Sci 2019;64:634–7.

[128] Hope A. Coronial inquest findings. Perth: Western Australian Coroners' Court; 2007.

[129] Byrd JH, Castner JL. Forensic entomology: the utility of arthropods in legal investigations. 2nd ed. Boca Raton: CRC Press; 2010.

Chapter 5

TSD estimation in the advanced stages of decomposition

Eline M.J. Schotsmans[a,b], Wim Van de Voorde[c,d], Shari L. Forbes[e,f]
[a]*Centre for Archaeological Science, University of Wollongong, Wollongong, NSW, Australia;* [b]*PACEA De la Préhistoire à l'Actuel: Culture, Environnement et Anthropologie, UMR 5199, CNRS-Université de Bordeaux, Bordeaux, France;* [c]*Department of Imaging and Pathology, Forensic Biomedical Sciences, KU Leuven - University of Leuven, Leuven, Belgium;* [d]*Department of Forensic Medicine, University Hospitals Leuven, Leuven, Belgium;* [e]*Département de Chimie, Biochimie et Physique, Université du Québec à Trois-Rivières, Trois-Rivières, QC, Canada;* [f]*Australian Facility for Taphonomic Experimental Research, University of Technology Sydney, Sydney, NSW, Australia*

Introduction

The study of human remains in the advanced stages of decomposition is challenging. Not only is it difficult to estimate time since death (TSD) due to the decrease in accuracy with increasing time affected by a multitude of variables, human remains in the advanced stages of decay also fall between two disciplines. Forensic pathologists are more used to estimating TSD in the early post-mortem stages (see Chapter 2, this volume), while biological anthropologists prefer to analyse skeletal material (see Chapter 7, this volume). Another problem is that the remains are not always analysed *in situ* by the appointed scientist or investigator. Human remains in the advanced stages of decay should be analysed in their broader depositional context in order to give the scientist an idea of the whole picture. As an anecdotal example, during the writing of this chapter, the authors heard a forensic anthropologist saying that she did not have any interest in the soft tissue stages of decomposition. Similarly, another biological anthropologist stated that she did not like to go to the field and preferred to analyse the bones in the laboratory.

Without having seen the remains *in situ*, and without considering soft tissue decay when analysing bones, it is likely that certain aspects will be missed. The investigation of 'forensic' human remains goes further than a single analysis of the remains but also aims to understand the taphonomic variables

Estimation of the Time since Death. https://doi.org/10.1016/B978-0-12-815731-2.00005-4

and the actions of the perpetrator (in case of homicide). Therefore, taphonomic profiling of the depositional context is important as it can assist with TSD estimation. Moreover, the presence of a forensic pathologist and/or anthropologist (best practice is together) at the scene is obligatory to determine cause, manner of death and other behaviours of the deceased and of the perpetrator.

This chapter will review the many variables that influence a decaying body and focus on the status of research into TSD estimation of remains in the advanced stages of decay. A case study will demonstrate that TSD estimation can be challenging.

Factors influencing cadaver decomposition

Decomposition is a complex process whereby the soft tissues break down and eventually disintegrate, resulting in skeletonisation, or beyond, because bones can also disintegrate depending on the depositional factors. Every deposition is unique due to a combination of intrinsic and extrinsic factors, a division that was originally described by Henderson [1]. Intrinsic factors depend on the nature of the body itself, while extrinsic, or 'external' factors consist of environmental variables, aspects from the depositional context as well as aspects related to human behaviour. It is evident that all the variables are in interaction with each other and that it is impossible to study them one by one. For example, the choice of the perpetrator regarding belowground or aboveground disposal, has an important influence on temperature and insect access and thus on the rate of decay and on PMI estimation. The description below forms a theoretical base meant to describe the individual variables. It is by no means a complete list and should not be viewed as independent factors as many of these variables interact with each other.

Environmental variables

Temperature is one of the most important variables that affects decomposition. An increase in temperature is associated with an accelerated rate of cadaver decomposition (e.g. Refs. [2,3]), while cool or freezing temperatures slow the decomposition considerably [4,5]. This is mostly due to high temperatures providing optimal conditions for the reproduction of bacteria, the increase of invertebrate activity such as insects [2,3,6] and the increase of the speed of enzymatic and catalytic decomposition [7]. Until around 2010 it was common for papers to report that it took 'xx days' for a body to reach certain decomposition stages [8]. Nowadays almost every investigator recognises the important effect of temperature on decomposition and accumulated degree days (see below) are now more commonly used to express chronological days (see also Chapter 10, this volume for a detailed discussion of ADD).

Another important factor that is associated with the rate of decomposition is humidity. Again, this factor is correlated with increased insect activity [2] as well as the introduction of moisture to the internal enzymatic decomposition process [7,9]. Directly linked with humidity is the factor rainfall. Smith [10] suggested that rehydration of dried remains by rain sometimes allows recolonisation of carcasses by flies and their larvae. Archer [11] suggested that the effect of rainfall might speed decomposition by mechanically breaking-up flesh, by leaching body contents and by keeping the surroundings of the carcass moist. Moist soil prevents carcasses from drying and therefore encourages maggot and bacterial action.

Oxygen plays a role in decomposition too, as anaerobic microorganisms are less efficient than aerobe decomposers. Reduced oxygen conditions might slow the decomposition down as observed in, for example, airtight containers or deep burials (see below) [7,12,13].

The depositional environment

The soil

The four major components of soil are minerals, organic matter, water and air, with soil particle size distribution having a direct effect on factors such as drainage, temperature and soil oxygen content. As described above, temperature, humidity and oxygen are important variables during decomposition.

Buried bodies are influenced by the soil that surrounds them. Researchers used to think that the impact of soil type on decomposition was of minor importance within the first two years of burial [2], or at the onset of advanced decay [14]. However, Wilson et al. [15] concluded that soil has an important effect on decay because the general soil conditions such as temperature, moisture, pH and nutrient availability control microbial communities and hence microbial activity. As such, soil analysis is recognised to be important for understanding biodegradation and decomposition. Specific soil types are known to have specific decomposition dynamics and periods. Fine textured soil, such as clay, has been associated with an inhibition of cadaver decomposition (e.g. Refs. [13,16]) caused by the low rate of gas and moisture diffusion. The low rate at which oxygen is exchanged with CO_2 might not be sufficient to meet aerobic microbial decay [14]. In contrast, coarse-texture soils, such as sand, are associated with a high rate of gas diffusion and movement of moisture [17], creating good decomposition conditions. However, the situation is more complex with the presence of groundwater and the water table playing an important role. Where drainage is impeded or where there is a high water table, waterlogged soils have voids filled with water. The small amount of oxygen will rapidly be depleted by microbial activity and only slowly be replaced by circulation [18]. Soil pH is directly related to site hydrology and the location of the water table. pH is determined by the activity of hydrogen ions (H^+). Very acid ($pH < 4$) or very alkaline ($pH > 10$) depositional environments will slow the decomposition down as bacteria will not flourish [19] and intracellular chemical reactions and the catalytic ability of enzymes will be affected [7].

In turn, cadaver decomposition has an effect on soil pH and other localised changes to the depositional soil. It is generally accepted that a decomposing body initially results in an alkaline environment, followed by an acidic environment and eventually normalises [14]. Providing localised changes in moisture, carbon and nutrients, the decaying body produces a concentrated island of fertility surrounding the corpse, called a cadaver decomposition island (CDI). The CDI's biophysicochemical characteristics change over time. It can initially have a negative effect on surrounding vegetation, and then turn into a positive effect and eventually normalise [14].

Faunal agents

If the remains are accessible to scavengers, decay will typically be accelerated due to soft tissue destruction and literally the consuming of flesh and bone [2]. All scavengers do not share the same scavenging behaviour or scatter patterns. Likewise, species-typical scavenging behaviours and scatter patterns will be affected by different crime scene scenarios. They are influenced by factors pertaining to the deposition site (e.g. region, environment, weather, season), human remains (e.g. carcass size, condition) and/or scavenger species (e.g. Refs. [20–25]).

Apart from vertebrate scavenging, it is widely acknowledged that invertebrate activity plays an essential role in the degradation of remains. Therefore, forensic entomology and insect knowledge can be used for minimum PMI (mPMI) estimation (see Chapter 4, this volume). Here too, there are many factors affecting the composition of the fauna feeding on a cadaver including temperature, rain, season, clothes and injuries [11,26]. For example, maggots are responsible for a large majority of mass loss during decomposition. During the active stages of decomposition, large maggot masses create a microenvironment by generating their own heat. This might influence larval development rates and should be considered in during TSD estimation [6,27,28]. The opposite is also true, if a body is not exposed to insects, for example due to being sealed, decomposition is likely to go slower [2,26,29].

Human behaviour

People managing the dead decide how, where and when the deceased is deposited or buried, whether it is the perpetrator or whether they are relatives. Treatment of the body, such as artificial mummification, embalming or the application of chemicals, has an influence on decay (e.g. Refs. [30–32]). Clothing and other coverings such as coffins or tarps can partially negate the effect of the depositional environment and may delay the process of decay (e.g. Refs. [33,34]). Airtight containers reduce the amount of oxygen, and slow the cadaver decomposition down because anaerobic microorganisms are less efficient than their aerobe counterparts. However, coffins do not present a constant burial environment since they also breakdown gradually. This means that the initial prevention from direct contact with burial sediments and its biota such as bacteria, fungi, plants and other organisms does not remain [35]. Metallic artefacts deposited around the decaying body can lead to localised conditions of toxicity which can decrease microbial activity, but even when a body is buried with extensive metal grave goods, there is usually insufficient metal to result in large-scale soft tissue preservation [18].

Burial or surface deposition has an important influence. The deeper a body is buried, the longer the decomposition takes as a result of lower temperatures, less oxygen and decreased access by insects and scavengers. When a body is deposited on the surface or buried in a shallow grave, it is more accessible by insects and scavengers and influenced by seasonal fluctuations (e.g. Refs. [18,36]). Furthermore, the decay of tissues will be profoundly influenced by the period between death and burial [37,38]. Several researchers have stated that a body with trauma(s) decomposes faster than a body that did not encounter trauma, mainly caused by the attraction of insects to the open wounds (e.g. Refs. [2,14]). This was contested by Cross & Simmons [39] who showed in a controlled experiment with a large sample size ($n = 34$) that decomposition rates in bodies with penetrating trauma did not differ from those without trauma.

When buried in a mass grave, the location in the grave has an influence on the decomposition rates due to a combination of effects described in the above variables [40].

The subject

Personal characteristics of the deceased such as age, sex, body size and physique are of importance regarding decomposition rates. Not only will there be internal biochemical differences, personal characteristics will also have an influence on the external factors. As with the other variables the literature contains contradictions. Based on observations by Mant [41], Janaway [18] states that thin bodies skeletonise more rapidly than larger ones. On the contrary, Mann et al. [2] observed that obese bodies lose body mass more quickly. Of course, observations need to be scientifically tested in experimental standardised studies. Simmons et al. [36] showed that body size is a significant factor when carcasses are accessed by insects with small carcasses decomposing faster than large carcasses. However, when insects are excluded, the decomposition progress happens at the same rate regardless of body size. Several other investigations about the effect of body size on rate of decomposition were carried out on animal remains without clear consensus in the results (e.g. Refs. [42,43]) probably due to the other variables at play which are not taken into account.

In addition, antemortem and perimortem medical conditions might accelerate decay caused by a high body temperature such as fever [44]. In contrast, other medical conditions, such as cancer treatment, can slow the decomposition down due to chemicals in the body which are less attractive for insects, and which slow microbial growth down [32]. This has been also been observed with surface depositions at the Australian Facility for Taphonomic Experimental Research (AFTER) by the authors.

Delayed decay rates and soft tissue preservation

Over shorter timescales, bodies may be actively decaying without having reached the skeletonised stage when they are discovered. However, the presence of soft tissue does not always indicate a recent death. Forensic cases have been reported of individuals being found with preserved soft tissue weeks or years after death (e.g. Refs. [45–49]). For example, on first sight, the individual in Fig. 5.1 seems to be recently deceased (Fig. 5.1). However, closer inspection showed that the deceased was desiccated. Based on unopened mail in his letterbox and the period he was last seen by the neighbours, the TSD interval was about four months. Clearly, under appropriate conditions decomposition processes can be slowed down and the body preserved. In addition, minor differences in the local micro-environment might lead to major variation in preservation within the same body. All these conditions should be just right, also called the 'Goldilocks Principle' [50]. Attempts to produce soft tissue preservation, might therefore not always succeed. Brooks Garcia et al. [51] tried to understand pre-Inca mummification by conducting an experiment with dead pigs in two imitated pre-Inca tombs. However, overall mummification did not occur.

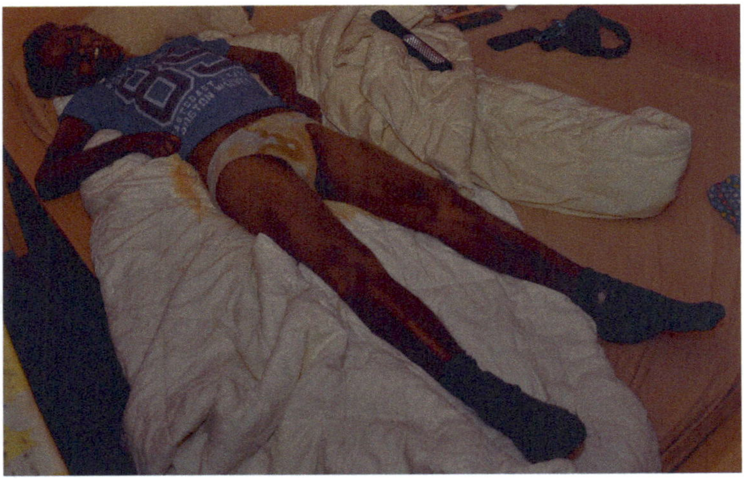

FIG. 5.1 The individual seems to be recently deceased, but on closer inspection he appeared to be desiccated with a TSD of four months.

Important in this context is that arrested decay can change if the depositional environment changes. Therefore, preserved soft tissue is never a final stage. According to Piombino-Mascali et al. [52] there are two main categories of taphonomic impact that need to be considered when analysing preserved human remains: the environment (e.g. temperature, humidity, wind, sun, freeze-thaw cycles, water, gravity etc.) and local fauna. Any disruptions to the preserved remains increase the rate of taphonomic change. The impact of these variables must always be considered during the process of TSD estimation. One has to bear in mind that most preserved human remains, no matter how effective the natural forces were in the process of preservation, are all on their taphonomic journey back to the elements [53].

The following section will discuss mostly natural preservation processes. While the origins of the word mummy originally referred to artificial anthropogenic preservation of soft tissue, the word mummification is widely applied to all preserved bodies, including those caused by natural factors. The authors, however, prefer to use the word preservation or desiccation when it comes to natural mummification.

Dry environments

Desiccation results from rapid drying and dehydration of soft tissues with the skin eventually becoming dark, dry and leathery. Usually it affects body parts which are generally exposed to either airflow or dry aerated burial conditions as they allow drying of soft tissue and limit putrefaction by destructive microorganisms. As such, desiccation requires a dry environment, an absence of humidity and an air current [54,55]. According to Janaway et al. [18,56] desiccation would normally not occur in bodies that have been buried directly into the soil due to the need for good air flow. However, Aturaliya and Lukasewycz [33] suggested that desiccation is equally as effective by soil interment as by air exposure. Of course, the soil type plays a role. Desiccation is promoted in porous soils such as sand based on the assumption that moisture is drawn away from the body's surface due to the capillary action and better drainage in these soils [14].

However, in natural body preservation (mummification) it is often seen that the outer layers of the body are preserved, and the interior contains only bones [57]. Under normal conditions human remains deteriorate from the inside outwards. Soft tissue is mainly subject to bacterially driven putrefaction processes. As such, it is often observed that the decay continues from the inside of the subject, driven by micro-organisms derived mainly from the body itself. Janaway et al. [55] examined natural mummification by burying three pigs in the coastal desert of Peru. After two years of burial the remains had been subject to considerable desiccation of the outer tissues, while the core of the carcasses remained moist. The same observations were made by Schotsmans et al. [58] on limed pig experiments.

Cold environments

Cold temperatures can slow down or (temporarily) arrest the process of decomposition [3,4,59]. The effect of freezing and thawing on the process and rate of decomposition is not often studied. Research undertaken by Micozzi [60] investigated the differences in decomposition of frozen-thawed and freshly killed rats. The results showed that previously frozen rats showed more aerobic decomposition, exhibiting an outside-in process of decay compared to the fresh rats which showed an inside-out manner of decomposition due to decreased enteric bacteria caused by the freezing process. Two other studies found no significant difference between previously frozen remains and fresh remains on percentage of tissue mass loss or insect activity [61,62]. Finally, Roberts and Dabbs [63] conducted research on pig remains and concluded that previously frozen subjects decompose at a slower overall rate. The decreased number of viable bacteria in the respiratory and digestive tracts will result in slower internal decay. This means that PMI in cases where remains have experienced freezing temperatures may be underestimated. When conducting taphonomic experiments with human remains, it is not recommended to use previously frozen subjects, as it will not reflect the typical decomposition rates.

Soft tissues can be preserved in cold environments by two different processes; freeze-drying and freezing. Freeze-drying, also known as cryodesiccation, is a dehydration process which involves sublimation of frozen water under low pressure in freezing temperatures. This means that a freeze-dried individual no longer contains water. In contrast, a frozen body still contains water. When a frozen body returns to temperatures above the freezing point, the internal ice will melt and the body will more likely continue the decomposition process as opposed to a frozen-dried individual [52]. The preservative effects of frozen environments upon soft tissue have been studied through examples such as Iceman 'Ötzi' who dates back to the end of the Neolithic era [64,65] or the three frozen Llullaillaco children who were discovered in Andean Argentina [66].

Adipocere formation

Adipocere formation occurs by alteration of subcutaneous fat of a corpse into a grey-white lipid mixture (see also Chapter 8, this volume). With time, it becomes a hard, brittle shell, which retards decomposition [67,68]. The chemical processes of adipocere formation are largely understood, with the basic process resulting from the hydrolysis and hydrogenation of adipose fat. Extensive studies regarding its chemical composition demonstrate that adipocere consists predominantly of saturated fatty acids, namely myristic, palmitic and stearic acids, with lesser amounts of hydroxyl and oxo-fatty acids [68–70]. The formation of adipocere is considered to result from bacterial action and occurs largely under anaerobic conditions wherein sufficient moisture is also present in the tissue [50,70–74]. Adipocere can also yield important information about the environmental context in which a body was deposited [75]. It can persist for years as long as the environment is stable. However, it is not necessarily a stable product, with certain conditions inducing further decomposition [68,70,76,77].

Desiccation and adipocere are usually presented as contrasting conditions. However, slight adipocere formation is common in desiccation. The two are related in that the utilisation of the internal body water can be sufficient to hydrolyse the fat and in turn help to dehydrate the tissues. Dehydration and desiccation will accompany adipocere formation in bodies where little or no exogenous water is available [67,70,78]. This is called the atypical condition for adipocere because most reported instances of adipocere are associated with conditions such as water immersion, wet graves or damp vaults [78]. Because adipocere is influenced by many differing factors, it has been questioned if adipocere could be used to predict PMI [50].

Bog environments

The decomposition might be altered in wet environments. There are two types of peat environments. Minerotrophic environments, known as fens, have a water supply from streams or springs. This makes them generally alkaline (pH 5.5–7.5) so that human remains found in these minerotrophic wetlands are usually completely skeletonised [79].

The second type of wetlands are ombotrophic sites, also known as peat bogs. Peat bogs are generally cold, acidic (pH 3–5), anaerobic and characterised by the presence of sphagnum moss which grows on the surface. Sphagnum moss decomposes into sphagnan which possesses chelating properties, allowing the depletion of metal ions. As a result, metal ions such as iron, copper or zinc are no longer available to bacteria, depriving them from an important source of nourishment and bacterial activity is slowed down. In addition, calcium chelation causes the calcium to be leached out of the skeletal material so that only collagen remains [52]. Bog bodies are preserved human corpses found in acidic peat bogs. However, not all tissue types are equally well preserved. In general, those tissues with high levels of collagen and keratin, such as skin, hair and nails tend to be well preserved in acidic bog environments. In contrast, skeletal material is demineralised and often absent. As a result of the weight of the overlying peat putting pressure on the remains, bog bodies often have a flattened appearance [80].

Differential decomposition

One of the main difficulties for PMI estimation during the later stages of decomposition is differential decay. The above described preservation conditions are often reported independent of each other, while they commonly co-exist. For example, desiccation and adipocere are not contrasting conditions. Slight adipocere formation is common in desiccation. The two are related in that the utilisation of the internal body water can be sufficient to hydrolyse the fat and in turn help to dehydrate the tissues. Dehydration and desiccation will accompany adipocere formation in bodies where little or no exogenous water is available [54,55,67,78]. Cotte et al. [81] studied desiccated skin of an Egyptian mummy and identified adipocere as one of the main degradation products of the skin. In temperate climates, differential decomposition due to the combination of decay, desiccation and adipocere is often observed but not often published (e.g. Refs. [82,83]).

Another example, commonly encountered in warmer climates such as on the South-East coast of Australia, is superficial desiccation on the side of the body exposed to solar radiation. However, when the remains are turned over, they are completely skeletonised. The human remains consist of only bones with a protective desiccated skin layer on top (Fig. 5.2). This superficial desiccation is caused by the temperatures, the air flow and sun light. The insects, however, do not like to be exposed to sun, so they typically hide and feed below the body in the dark, moist areas. These observations have been

FIG. 5.2 Superficial desiccation observed at the Australian Facility for Taphonomic Experimental Research (AFTER). The remains consist of only bones with a protective desiccated skin layer on top.

made on many surface depositions at the Australian Facility for Taphonomic Experimental Research (AFTER) by the authors.

Postmortem interval estimations are generally based on the degree of soft tissue decomposition and identifiable stages of tissue alteration that occur in a predictable, sequential and semi-continuous pattern at a rate that is dependent on several variables, amongst which temperature and insect access as very important factors. Total body scores, the assignment of a numerical value to the decomposition stage of different body parts (see below) becomes very difficult when bodies are showing differential decay. Minor differences in the local micro-environment might lead to major variation in preservation within the same body. Figs. 5.3 and 5.4 show the head, upper body and back of an individual in the advanced stages of decay, discovered in a garage in Belgium. At the anterior side of the body, the head was partially skeletonised but also revealed desiccation and fungal growth. The neck area displayed wet decomposition. The trunk, upper and lower limbs were desiccated with wet decomposition around the groin(Fig. 5.3). In contrast, the posterior side of the body showed wet, greasy decomposition with adipocere, and skeletonisation at the posterior part of the right upper leg(Fig. 5.4). The individual was identified

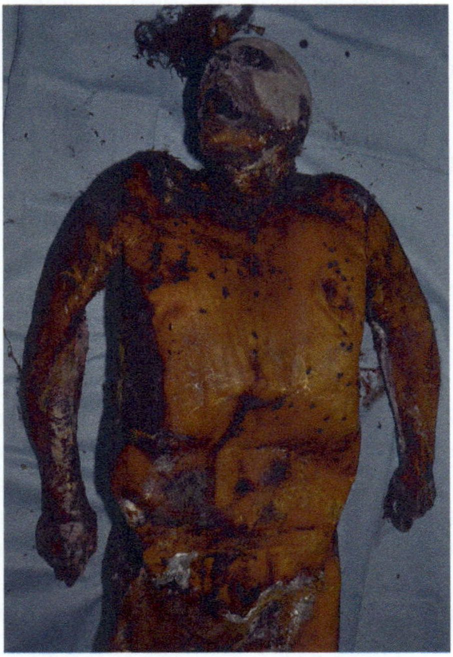

FIG. 5.3 Individual showing differential decomposition. At the anterior side, the head was partially skeletonised in combination with desiccation and fungal growth. The neck area showed wet decomposition. The trunk, upper and lower limbs were desiccated with wet decomposition around the groin.

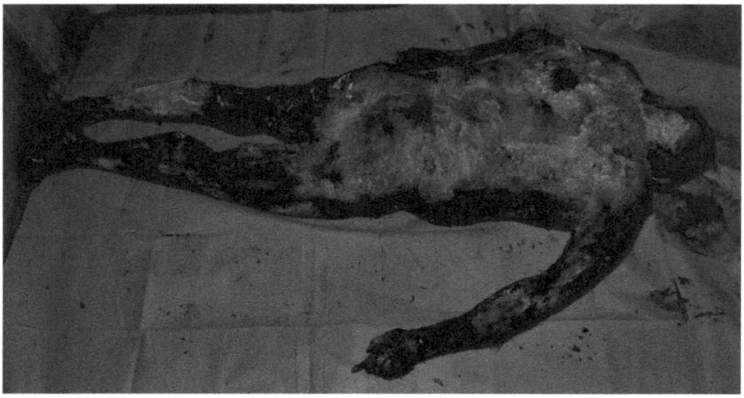

FIG. 5.4 The posterior side of the deceased displayed wet, greasy decomposition with adipocere formation and skeletonisation at the posterior part of right upper leg.

based on DNA. The TSD could not be established based on the visual analysis of the stage of decomposition, but was estimated about nine months based on 'person last seen' data.

Differential decay is not only noticeable within a single body, it is also noticed when multiple individuals are deposited together. It has, for example, been observed in mass graves with the same postmortem and post-burial interval, as documented in forensic archaeological [40,41,84] or experimental contexts [85]. Bodies at the edges of a mass grave tend to exhibit accelerated decomposition in comparison with bodies in the centre of the burial. This phenomenon is called the feather edge effect 'feather edge effect' [40,41].

PMI estimation

With the above-described factors that influence cadaver decomposition and the combination of variables that could cause soft tissue preservation, it becomes evident that accurately estimating PMI in the advanced stages of decay is a daunting task and in some (most?) cases even impossible over an increasing timescale. A number of studies have been conducted to understand the rate and variability of decomposition within specific regions (e.g. Refs. [86–91]) and experimental studies have shown important differences in decay rates between sites within one specific region [15]. Environmental factors are not static during decomposition and seasonal changes have an important influence on decay rates.

Some researchers suggested that it might be possible to attempt to provide a continent-wide template of human decomposition by taking different regional models [87]. Similarly, other researchers proposed to establish a standardised visual reference guide for estimation of soft tissue loss by increasing case reports and experiments [92]. However, theory and practice do not always match. Taking the variables from the depositional environment into account, it is widely acknowledged that decomposition varies within geographic regions. There is currently no scientifically recognised PMI estimation method for a specific geographic region and this will probably never be possible due to the multitude of variables described above.

Postmortem interval estimation

Techniques used by the pathologist to estimate TSD in the early postmortem period (see Chapter 2, this volume), are no longer useful in cases where the body is going through the advanced stages of decay. Despite the variables and the difficulties, some researchers have made an attempt for a universally applicable PMI method in cases where the body is no longer fresh. Vass et al. in 1992 [93] first introduced the concept of accumulated degree days (ADD), using the concentration of volatile fatty acids in the soil below cadavers to estimate time since death (see also Chapter 10, this volume). Inter-regional comparisons appeared to be very difficult when using 'days' because of the important effect of temperature on decay. By using accumulated average daily temperature over time to describe the progression of decomposition, comparisons of multiple geographic regions could be made possible. According to Vass 1285 ADD is the empirically determined value at which volatile fatty acid liberation from soft tissue ceases [7,93], also applicable to desiccated human remains [7]. 1285 ADD does not stand for the standard amount of time a body will take to decompose, as wrongly stated in certain articles (e.g. Refs. [86,92]).

In 2011 Vass published two formulae for PMI estimation for surface-deposited (Formula I) and buried (Formula II) remains, developed with human decay data collected over 20 years of experiments at the University of Tennessee's Anthropology Research Facility in Knoxville, in the United States [7] (Table 5.1). The two formulae are based on temperature, moisture/humidity, the aforementioned 1285 ADD and decomposition scoring. However, there seems to be a degree of flexibility in the use of these formulae. For example, temperature and humidity can reflect the average value at the site on the day of discovery or 'over a period of time by taking an average of days, weeks or months of temperature data'. This period should be calculated with the 1285 value. Furthermore, the researcher must make a visual assessment of the degree of decomposition of the entire body by scoring the degree of soft tissue decomposition as a percentage between 1 (little decay) and 100 (fully skeletonised), a score that could differ between two researchers.

Taking into account ADD, Megyesi et al. [3] quantified decomposition by assigning a numerical value to descriptive decomposition stages of different body parts, called total body score (TBS), based on the original classification of Galloway et al. [88]. Based on 68 forensic human remain cases, Megyesi et al. [3] derived a predictive formula for estimating time since death, although confusion was created by mixing up temperature data between Fahrenheit and Celsius (Table 5.1). Their paper became well known and the formula is currently widely used in time since death estimations.

TABLE 5.1 An overview of the most commonly used PMI estimation formulae for remains in the later stages of decay.

	Megyesi et al. [3]	Moffatt et al. [94]	Vass [7] - Formula I	Vass [7] - Formula II
PMI formula	$ADD = 10^{((0.002 \times TBS \times TBS)+1.81)} \pm 388.16$	$TBS_{surf}^{1.6} = 125 \times \log_{10} ADD - 212$	$PMI_{Aerobic} = \frac{1285 \times (decomposition/100)}{0.0103 \times temp. \times humidity}$	$PMI_{Anaerobic} = \frac{1285 \times (decomposition/100) \times 4.6 \times adipocere}{0.0103 \times soil\ temp. \times (soil\ moisture)}$
Additional materials needed		Accompanying table 1 provides prediction interval from observed TBS	Formula explanation and requirements detailed in Vass [7]	Formula explanation, multiplier values for adipocere and other requirements detailed in Vass [7]
Information	The result is in ADD	Table 1 in Moffatt et al. [94] gives the results in ADD (C°)	The result is in days	The result is in days

However, Moffatt et al. [94] raised shortcomings concerning the statistical treatment of the data in Megyesi et al.'s formula. They presented a more appropriate regression model to predict accumulated degree days from total body scores (Table 5.1). In addition, Dabbs et al. [95] examined the reliability of the TBS method by testing interobserver error rates. They concluded that there is a high reliability for the overall TBS score, as well as for each of the three component categorical scores that are used to calculate TBS.

Important to mention regarding ADD is Dabbs' research on the use of data from national weather stations [96]. Practitioners are advised to examine the temperature fluctuations at the crime scene over a period of several days and then choose which local weather station parallels its temperatures most closely. Contrary to Vass' [7] suggestion, no correction of weather station data should be attempted as these methods create more significant differences than using data from the weather station with the closest approximation to the site [96,97].

Over the years, only a few researchers have tested the above methods on human remains with mixed results. Cockle and Bell [98] attempted to validate Vass' [7] Formula I for aboveground PMI using 42 Canadian case studies with known PMI. The results indicated that the PMI was consistently over-estimated for decomposing bodies in warmer conditions or under-estimated for bodies exposed to colder temperatures. A study by Maile et al. [92] evaluated the Vass' [7] equation for aboveground PMI at 9 indoor death scenes with known PMI in Nebraska and 10 indoor death scenes in Hawaii. The results indicate that the Vass' equation was accurate in 79% of the scenes [92]. Marhoff-Beard et al. [86] conducted a similar evaluation by comparing the Megyesi et al. [3] method to the Vass [7] equation on human remains and pigs in the Greater Western Sydney region in Australia. The Vass [7] method was shown to under-estimate the PMI of the remains, while the Megyesi et al. [3] method over-estimated the PMI of the remains. When the remains were in fresh or early stages of decay, both methods seemed to estimate the PMI within 1–2 weeks, which could help to narrow the PMI. The later the stage of decay, the more inaccurate both formulae seemed to be [86].

Postburial interval estimation

Postburial interval (PBI) refers to the period between burial and recovery. This period might differ from PMI which aims to estimate the entire period since death. When a victim is not buried immediately after death, the PBI can be used as an estimate of the lower limit of the PMI. As mentioned above, the exclusion of insects in burials might have an influence on the rate of decomposition [36].

When an individual is buried, any plant material around the human remains, as well as any material buried with the remains can be valuable to a forensic investigation [99]. Botanical evidence such as roots, branches, leaves, pollen or fungi might help to determine the time of deposition. Digging a grave disturbs and damages plants in the area. Additional damage could be caused by the spoil heap and refill of the burial. Botanical analysis may provide seasonal indications and information about when the plant was damaged, thus providing a PBI [100]. This was demonstrated in several case studies [100–104]. In addition, botanical evidence from stomach contents could aid with PMI estimation using the rate of digestion of ingested food [103]. Pollen, fungi and algae can be also used for the determination of geographic locations and DNA of plant material for linking botanical evidence to a suspect or scene of crime [100]. Finally, Pringle et al. [105] suggested that analysing groundwater conductivity might be a way to provide a PBI estimate.

Advanced expertise in PMI estimation

More specialised methods for PMI estimation in the later stages of decomposition involve studying the post-mortem microbial succession [106–109], ribonucleic acid degradation [110–113], gene expression [114,115] or using neutron radiography [116]. The problem is that these methods require advanced expertise and specific instrumentation. Furthermore, they become less reliable with increasing PMI time. None of these methods have yet been proven to be the key to accurate TSD estimation and some of them have only been tested on animal models.

Experiments and retrospective studies

The above described factors that influence decay and the below described PMI estimation is mainly based on retrospective case studies and experimental research with human donors as well as animal models. Controlled experimental research with human remains are dependent on the donations and cannot be planned. As a result, the sample sizes are often small and statistical analysis cannot be performed. On the contrary, experimental research conducted on animal models can be planned and can consist of larger sample sizes. However, because of their lateral decay, different body proportions and differential decay, researchers have to be careful to apply the results directly to humans. For example, Dautartas et al. [117] showed that neither rabbits, nor pigs captured the pattern, rate and variability of human decomposition. Even more caution is necessary when translating results from experiments with animal tissues to whole bodies. For example, Schotsmans et al. [58] showed that it was much easier to desiccate a small cube of tissue than a whole carcass with complete viscera due to the different surface area to volume ratio.

A taphonomic experiment should start with a well-planned experimental design. Researchers should carry out a literature review before the start of the project and become familiar with the decomposition patters of the region. The experiment itself should consist of a reasonable sample size (ideally large enough to assess statistical significance) with control subjects.

Furthermore, a single variable should be studied and other variables should ideally be controlled. A good experiment also consists of replicates carried out under the same conditions. Protocols for data collections and intervals should be decided upon before the start of the experiments [8].

Case study

A case report from Belgium on a 65-year-old male who was partially buried for about seven months was published by Schotsmans et al. [82] in order to better understand the taphonomic variables resulting in differential decomposition with desiccation and adipocere formation. At that time, TSD estimation methods were not yet commonly used, certainly not with bodies in the later stages of decay. For this publication, the authors wanted to re-visit the case and evaluate the three scoring methods by Vass [7], Megyesi et al. [3] and Moffatt et al. [94] in order to verify their accuracy based on a known PMI in a temperate climate such as Belgium.

The remains of an adult male were found in private coniferous woodland in Belgium during spring. There had been no disturbance to the remains prior to police involvement. The deceased had been buried naked, lying on his left side in a semi flexed position and partly covered with brush. The grave was small and shallow, with dimensions of 110 by 136 cm and a depth of 30–42 cm. The soil had not been compacted and the victim's right lower limb protruded out of the ground. The right arm and a part of the temporal bone were also visible. The woodland consisted of conifers, spread within a distance of three to four meters. There was no specific undergrowth, only dead wood, needles and brush.

Extensive soft tissue remained, with only a small exposed part of the temporal bone being skeletonised (Fig. 5.5). The victim's head, neck, right shoulder, upper part of the torso and left lower limb were covered with adipocere. The right lower limb was desiccated and exhibited reddish brown, hard and dry tissue. The rest of the torso and the arms looked relatively fresh (Fig. 5.5). Localised blue staining derived from body exudates was visible in the surrounding soil. There was no noticeable strong odour.

Rodent gnawing was confined to a small part of the temporal bone and the distal ends of the left metacarpals. The phalanges of this hand were absent, probably taken by scavengers. Despite part of the body lying exposed at the surface, there were no other signs of carnivore activity. Equally, there was little entomological evidence. A few larvae and pupae were collected by a forensic entomologist.

The suspect confessed to having smothered the victim and although he could not remember the exact date of killing, his wife confirmed that it had happened around the timeframe when the victim had been reported missing, seven months earlier. Based on police investigation and confessions of the perpetrator's wife, the victim was estimated as being killed during a 25-day time frame in September and October. The partially buried body had been buried through autumn, winter and the first weeks of spring.

FIG. 5.5 The remains of an adult male exhibited marked differential decomposition with both natural tissue desiccation (right lower limb) and adipocere formation (head, neck, right shoulder, upper torso and left lower limb).

The minimal postmortem interval calculated by the entomologist was about 3 months. This was not an exact estimation because so few larvae and pupae of only one species were found. With a minimal postmortem interval of three or more months, a large assemblage of different insects on the body would normally be expected. It is assumed that the differential preservation of the body influenced the insect activity.

Based on Megyesi et al. [3] the best match for the decomposition scoring of the head and neck was category C, stage 2: 'Moist decomposition with bone exposure less than one-half that of the area being scored' which equals 8 points. This judgement was reached based on the photographs taken during the start of the autopsy, when the adipocere was removed from the head, neck and shoulder region. For the torso region, category B, stage 4 was assigned 5 points 'postbloating following release of the abdominal gases, with discoloration changing from green to black'. This judgement was based on the images taken during the start of the autopsy showing greenish-black patches and on the statement of the medical examiner that the body had reached the primary bloat stage. The scoring of the limbs appeared to be more difficult as the right lower limb was desiccated while the left lower limb and the upper limbs appeared to be fresh but not dry. After reflection, it was decided to assign 4 points from category B, stage 3 'discolouration and/or brownish shades particularly at edges drying of fingers, toes and other projecting extremities'. The sum of the regions yielded at TBS of 17. The predicted ADD using the Megyesi et al. [3] method is 244 ADD ($\pm$ 388.16) (Table 5.2). The Moffatt et al. [94] method provided a point estimate of 274 ADD with a 95% prediction interval range of 126–611 ADD, or a 75% prediction interval range of 178–425 ADD (Table 5.2).

TABLE 5.2 Summary of the predicted and actual PMI by applying the Megyesi et al. (2005), Moffatt et al. [94] and Vass (2011) methods to a case study in Belgium (ADD = Accumulated Degree Days; mPMI = minimum PostMortem Interval).

	Megyesi et al. [3]	Moffatt et al. [94]	Vass [7] - Formula I	Vass [7] - Formula II	Entomology	Actual result
Calculated PMI for case study	ADD = 244	ADD = 274	5 days	382 days	> 3 months	**7 months**
Predicted interval	ADD = 244 ± 388.16	ADD (95%) = 126-611				**ADD = 967-1296**
Converted PMI in days based on real temp.	32 days (interval: 0–152 days)	41 days (95% interval: 15–147 days)	5 days	382 days	> 90 days	**178-202 days**
Result	Under-estimation	Under-estimation	Under-estimation	Over-estimation		

For the Vass [7] method, formula I ($PMI_{Aerobic}$) for above ground decomposition was first used based on the fact that the corpse was not entirely buried at a depth between 0.46 and 1.07 m. The decomposition score of the remains, which refers to the extent of total body soft tissue decomposition [7], was based on the original estimation of the Soft Tissue Index after Aufderheide [57]. With an assigned Soft Tissue Index of 96% [82], the extent of total body soft tissue decomposition was calculated at 4%. Taking the average temperature and humidity on the day of discovery (respectively 10 °C and 94.1), the PMI was estimated at 5 days with the Vass [7] formula (Table 5.2).

Because of the presence of adipocere on the corpse and the deposition in a shallow burial (but not buried between 0.46 and 1.07 m), it was decided to also test Vass' [7] second formula. $PMI_{Anaerobic}$ was estimated with a 4% decomposition score, with 9 °C soil temperature and 20% soil moisture. The multiplicative value of adipocere was 3, based on 35 % of adipocere estimated to be associated with the corpse (See table 2 in [7]). Putting all the values into the equation the estimated $PMI_{Anaerobic}$ was 382.6 days (Table 5.2).

In summary (Table 5.2), when calculating the ADD results into days based on the real average temperatures that were measured at the closest weather station from where the human remains were found, the Megyesi et al. [3] method predicted a PMI of 32 days, the Moffatt et al. [94] method calculated a 95% prediction interval range of 15−147 days. The Vass [7] $PMI_{Aerobic}$ formula calculated 5 days and the $PMI_{Anaerobic}$ estimation was 382 days. In addition, the entomologist estimated a PMI of 3 months or more (about 90 days). The actual timeframe since death, as detailed in the article [82], was between 178 and 202 days or ADD = 967−1296.

The Megyesi et al. [3] and the Moffatt et al. [94] methods were not able to produce an accurate PMI estimate, with the upper-level of their intervals about one month less than the actual result. To find out if this error is related to the presence of adipocere and desiccation, more Belgian case studies should be tested.

The Vass method [7] failed to estimate the PMI of the remains from this case study with a serious under-estimation, or an over-estimation of almost six months, depending which formula was used. One of the difficulties was the uncertainty about which of the two formulae to apply because the individual showed a mix of anaerobic an aerobic decay. It has to be mentioned that the Vass method was developed based on cases in the mid to eastern section of the United States. However, Vass [7] also mentions that 'the surface decomposition formula is applied to many cases worldwide with remarkable success'. He states that a common source of error is that the period has exceeded 1285 ADDs [7], but in this case study the upper level of the actual ADD interval reaches 1296, which is 11 °C more and thus not even a day more.

In conclusion, the mPMI of three months estimated by the entomologist gave the best estimation. This appeared to be a better prediction than the mPMI of 0, 15 and 5 days as calculated by the formulae by Megyesi et al. [3],

Moffatt et al. [94] and Vass [7] respectively. Or than the visual observations of the remains which gave a 'fresh' impression.

While this case is 'special' in the sense that the individual showed differential decomposition with adipocere and desiccation, this example of retrospective PMI calculation indicates that more research should be carried out on PMI estimations in Belgium (Flanders). It also indicates that there is a need for PMI determination methods for human remains in the later stages of decay, and for desiccated remains that have passed the active stages of decay.

Conclusions

Forensic scientists are regularly asked to estimate the postmortem interval or time since death. Unfortunately, the more advanced the decomposition, the more difficult TSD estimation becomes. Substantial research has been conducted in an attempt to identify an accurate method for estimating PMI or PBI with mixed success. It is generally agreed that so many different variables come into play during decomposition that they are not sufficiently uniform or accurate to provide a precise PMI in the later stages of decay. While it might not be possible to create a 'universal' method, regional studies on human decomposition might give a better understanding of the impact and rate of decay within a specific geographic region.

This chapter shows that a large knowledge base is appropriate in this interdisciplinary field of forensic taphonomy. It highlights that human remains should be analysed by an interdisciplinary team in their broader depositional context. The combination of several disciplines might have the potential to narrow the PMI estimate, but the formula for an accurate PMI estimation will probably remain an illusion.

Acknowledgements

The authors wish to thank Dr Luc Debontridder from the Royal Meteorological Institute (RMI) of Belgium for providing detailed meteorological data. The photographs used in this paper are taken by the authors. Specific dates and locations regarding the case examples could not be provided due to the anonymity of the cases.

References

[1] Henderson J. Factors determining the state of preservation of human remains. In: Boddington A, Garland AN, Janaway RC, editors. Death, decay and reconstruction. Manchester: Manchester University Press; 1987.

[2] Mann RW, Bass WM, Meadows L. Time since death and decomposition of the human body: variables and observations in case and experimental field studies. J Forensic Sci 1990;35:103–11.

[3] Megyesi MS, Nawrocki SP, Haskell NH. Using accumulated degree-days to estimate the postmortem interval from decomposed human remains. J Forensic Sci 2005;50:618–26.

[4] Meyer J, Anderson B, Carter DO. Seasonal variation of carcass decomposition and grave soil chemistry in a cold climate. J Forensic Sci 2013;58:1175–82.

[5] Cockle DL, Bell LS. The environmental variables that affect human decomposition in terrestrially exposed contexts within Canada. Sci Justice 2017;57:107–17.

[6] Campobasso CP, DI Vella G, Introna F. Factors affecting decomposition and Diptera colonization. Forensic Sci Int 2001;12:18–27.

[7] Vass AA. The elusive universal post-mortem interval formula. Forensic Sci Int 2011;204:34–40.

[8] Simmons T. Post-mortem interval estimation: an overview of techniques. In: Schotsmans EMJ, Marquez-Grant N, Forbes SL, editors. Taphonomy of human remains: forensic analysis of the dead and the depositional environment. Chichester: Wiley; 2017.

[9] Aufderheide AC. Soft tissue taphonomy: a paleopathology perspective. Intl J Paleopathol 2011;1:75–80.

[10] Smith KGV. A manual of forensic entomology. London: Trustees of the British Museum; 1986.

[11] Archer MS. Rainfall and temperature effects on the decomposition rate of exposed neonatal remains. Sci Justice 2004;44:35–41.

[12] Dent BB, Forbes SL, Stuart BH. Review of human decomposition processes in soil. Environ Geol 2004;45:576–85.

[13] Fiedler S, Schneckenberger K, Graw M. Characterization of soils containing adipocere. Arch Environ Contam Toxicol 2004;47:561–8.

[14] Carter DO, Tibbett M. Cadaver decomposition and soil: processes. In: Tibbett M, Carter DO, editors. Soil analysis in forensic taphonomy. Boca Raton: CRC Press; 2008.

[15] Wilson AS, Janaway RC, Holland AD, Dodson HI, Baran E, Pollard AM, Tobin DJ. Modelling the buried human body environment in upland climes using three contrasting field sites. Forensic Sci Int 2007;169:6–18.

[16] Turner BD, Wiltshire PEJ. Experimental validation of forensic evidence: a study of the decomposition of buried pigs in a heavy clay soil. Forensic Sci Int 1999;101:113–22.

[17] Moldrup P, Olesen T, Rolston DE, Yamaguchi T. Modeling diffusion and reaction in soils: predicting gas and ion diffusivity in undisturbed and sieved soils. Soil Sci Soc Am J 1997;162:632–40.

[18] Janaway RC. The decay of buried human remains and their associated materials. In: Hunter J, Roberts C, Martin A, editors. Studies in crime. An introduction to forensic archaeology. London: Routledge; 1996.

[19] Schotsmans EMJ, Fletcher JN, Denton J, Janaway RC, Wilson AS. Long-term effects of hydrated lime and quicklime on the decay of human remains using pig cadavers as human body analogues: field experiments. Forensic Sci Int 2014b;238:141.e1–141.e13.

[20] Young A. The effects of terrestrial mammalian scavenging and avian scavenging on the body. In: Schotsmans EMJ, Marquez-Grant N, Forbes SL, editors. Taphonomy of human remains. Forensic analysis of the dead and the depositional environment. Chichester: Wiley; 2017.

[21] O'brien RC, Forbes SL, Meyer J, Dadour IR. Forensically significant scavenging guilds in the southwest of Western Australia. Forensic Sci Int 2010;198:85–91.

[22] O'brien RC, Appleton AJ, Forbes SL. Comparison of taphonomic effects due to the necrophagic activity of geographically disparate scavenging guilds. Can Soc Forensic Sci J 2017;50:42–53.

[23] Steadman DW, Dautartas A, Kenyhercz MW, Jantz LM, Mundorff A, Vidoli GM. Differential scavenging among pig, rabbit, and human subjects. J Forensic Sci 2018;63:1684–91.

[24] Jeong Y, Jantz LM, Smith J. Investigation into seasonal scavenging patterns of raccoons on human decomposition. J Forensic Sci 2016;61:467–71.

[25] Dabbs GR, Martin DC. Geographic variation in the taphonomic effect of vulture scavenging: the case for Southern Illinois. J Forensic Sci 2013;58:S20–25.

[26] Vanin S, Huchet J-B. Forensic entomology and funerary archaeoentomology. In: Schotsmans EMJ, Marquez-Grant N, Forbes SL, editors. Taphonomy of human remains: forensic analysis of the dead and the depositional environment. Chichester: Wiley; 2017.

[27] Heaton V, Moffatt C, Simmons T. Quantifying the temperature of maggot masses and its relationship to decomposition. J Forensic Sci 2014;59:676–82.

[28] Johnson AP, Wallman JF. Effect of massing on larval growth rate. Forensic Sci Int 2014;241:141–9.

[29] Payne JA, King EW, Beinhart G. Arthropod succession and decomposition of buried pigs. Nature 1968;219:1180–1.

[30] Micozzi MS. Postmortem change in human and animal remains. Springfield: Charles Thomas; 1991.

[31] Sledzik PS, Micozzi MS. Autopsied, embalmed and preserved human remains: distinguishing features in forensic and historic contexts. In: Haglund WD, Sorg MS, editors. Forensic taphonomy. The postmortem fate of human remains. Boca Raton: CRC Press; 1997.

[32] Schotsmans EMJ, Van de Voorde W. Concealing the crime: the effects of chemicals on human tissues. In: Schotsmans EMJ, Marquez-Grant N, Forbes SL, editors. Taphonomy of human remains: forensic analysis of the dead and the depositional environment. Chichester: Wiley; 2017.

[33] Aturaliya SMD, Lukasewycs A. Experimental forensic bioanthropological aspects of soft tissue taphonomy: 1. Factors influencing postmortem tissue desiccation rate. J Forensic Sci 1999;44:893–6.

[34] Card A, Cross P, Moffatt C, Simmons T. The effect of clothing on the rate of decomposition and Diptera colonization on Sus Scrofa carcasses. J Forensic Sci 2015;60:979–82.

[35] Pokines JT, Baker JE. Effects of burial environment on osseous remains. In: Pokines J, Symes SA, editors. Manual of forensic taphonomy. Boca Raton: CRC Press; 2013.

[36] Simmons T, Adlam RE, Moffatt C. Debugging decomposition data - comparative taphonomic studies and the influence of insects and carcass size on decomposition rate. J Forensic Sci 2010;55:8–13.

[37] Boddington A, Garland AN, Janaway RC. Death, decay and reconstruction. Manchester: Manchester University Press; 1987.

[38] Dadour IR, Harvey ML. The role of invertebrates in terrestrial decomposition: forensic applications. In: Tibbett M, Carter DO, editors. Soil analysis in forensic taphonomy. Boca Raton: CRC Press; 2008.

[39] Cross P, Simmons T. The influence of penetrative trauma on the rate of decomposition. J Forensic Sci 2010;55:295–301.

[40] Barker C, Alicehajic E, Naranjo Stantana J. Post-mortem differential preservation and its utility in interpreting forensic and archaeological mass burials. In: Schotsmans EMJ, Marquez-Grant N, Forbes SL, editors. Taphonomy of human remains: forensic analysis of the dead and the depositional environment. Chichester: Wiley; 2017.

[41] Mant AK. Knowledge acquired from post-war excavations. In: Boddington A, Garland AN, Janaway RC, editors. Death, decay and reconstruction. Manchester: Manchester University Press; 1987.

[42] Spicka A, Johnson R, Bushing J, Higley LG, Carter DO. Carcass mass can influence rate of decompositionand release of ninhydrin-reactive nitrogen into gravesoil. Forensic Sci Int 2011;209:80–5.

[43] Sutherland A, Myburgh J, Steyn M, Becker P. The effect of body size on the rate of decomposition in a temperate region of South Africa. Forensic Sci Int 2013;231:257–62.

[44] Zhou C, Byard RW. Factors and processes causing accelerated decomposition in human cadavers. An overview. J Forensic Legal Med 2011;38:111–5.

[45] Campobasso CP, Falamingo R, Grattagliano I, Vinci F. The mummified corpse in a forensic setting. Am J Forensic Med Pathol 2009;30:307–10.

[46] Jit I, Sehgal S, Sahni D. An Indian mummy: a case report. Forensic Sci Int 2001;117:57–63.

[47] Ventura F, Portunato F, Pizzorno E, Mazzone S, Verde A, Rocca G. The need for an interdisciplinary approach in forensic sciences: perspectives from a peculiar case of mummification. J Forensic Sci 2013;58:831–6.

[48] Introna F, De Donno A, Santoro, Corrado S, Romano V, Porcelli F, Campobasso CP. The bodies of two missing children in an enclosed underground environment. Forensic Sci Int 2011;207:e40–7.

[49] Catanese G, Bloom T. Recovery of amummified pregnant woman from a 55-gallon drum more than 30 years after her death. Am J Forensic Med Pathol 2002;23:245–7.

[50] O'brien TG, Kuehner AC. Waxing grave about adipocere: soft tissue change in an aquatic context. J Forensic Sci 2007;52:294–301.

[51] Brooks Garcia AM, Beckett RG, Watson JT. Internal environmental characteristics of a Chiribaya style tomb holding swine remains and their taphonomic impact on decomposition delay, a requisit for mummification. Pap Anthropol 2014;23:45–62.

[52] Piombino-Mascali D, Gill-Frerking H, Beckett RG. The taphonomy of natural mummies. In: Schotsmans EMJ, Marquez-Grant N, Forbes SL, editors. Taphonomy of human remains: forensic analysis of the dead and the depositional environment. Chichester: Wiley; 2017.

[53] Piñar G, Piombino-Mascali D, Maixner F, Zink A, Sterflinger K. Microbial survey of the mummies from the Capuchin Catacombs of Palermo, Italy: biodeterioration risk and contamination of the indoor air. FEMS (Fed Eur Microbiol Soc) Microbiol Ecol 2013;86:341–56.

[54] Knight B. Forensic pathology. New York: Arnold; 1996.

[55] Janaway RC, Wilson AS, Caprio Diaz G, Guillen S. Taphonomic changes to the buried body in arid environments: an experimental case study in Peru. In: Ritz K, Dawson L, Miller D, editors. Criminal and environmental soil forensics. London: Springer; 2009b.

[56] Janaway RC, Percival SL, Wilson AS. Decomposition of human remains. In: Percival SL, editor. Microbiology and aging. London: Springer; 2009a.

[57] Aufderheide AC. The scientific study of mummies. Cambridge: Cambridge University Press; 2003.

[58] Schotsmans EMJ, Denton J, Fletcher JN, Janaway RC, Wilson AS. Short-term effects of hydrated lime and quicklime on the decay of human remains using pig cadavers as human body analogues: laboratory experiments. Forensic Sci Int 2014a;238:142.e1–142.e10.

[59] Pilloud MA, Megyesi MS, Truffer M, Congram D. The taphonomy of human remains in a glacial environment. Forensic Sci Int 2016;261:161e1–8.

[60] Micozzi MS. Experimental study of post mortem change under field conditions: effects of freezing, thawing and mechanical injury. J Forensic Sci 1986;31:953–61.

[61] Stokes KL, Forbes SL, Tibbett M. Freezing skeletal muscle tissue does not affect its decomposition in soil: evidence from temporal changes in tissue mass, microbial activity and soil chemistry based on excised samples. Forensic Sci Int 2009;183:6–13.

[62] Bugajski KN, Seddon CC, Williams RE. A comparison of blow fly (Diptera: calliphoridae) and beetle (Coleoptera) activity on refrigerated only versus frozen-thawed pig carcasses in Indiana. J Med Entomol 2011;48:1231–5.

[63] Roberts LG, Dabbs GR. A taphonomic study exploring the differences in decomposition rate and manner between frozen and never frozen domestic pigs (*Sus Scrofa*). J Forensic Sci 2015;60:588–94.

[64] Ruff CB, Holt M, Sladek V, Berner M, Murphy WA, Zur Nedden D, Seidler H, Recheis W. Body size, body proportions and mobility in the Tyrolean Iceman. J Hum Evol 2006;51:91–101.

[65] Janko M, Zink A, Gigler AM, Heckl WM, Stark RW. Nanostructure and mechanics of mummified type I collegan from the 5,300-year-ol Tyrolean Iceman. Proc Royal Soc B 2010;227:2301–9.

[66] Wilson AS, Brown EL, Villa C, Lynnerup N, Healey A, Ceruti MC, Reinhard J, Previgliano CH, Araoz FA, Diez JG, Taylor T. Archaeological, radiological, and biological evidence offer insight into Inca child sacrifice. Proc Natl Acad Sci 2013;110:13322–7.

[67] Clark MA, Worrell MB, Pless JE. Postmortem changes in soft tissues. In: Haglund WD, Sorg MS, editors. Forensic taphonomy. The postmortem fate of human remains. Boca Raton: CRC Press; 1996.

[68] Fiedler S, Graw M. Decomposition of buried corpses, with special reference to the formation of adipocere. Naturewissenschaften 2003;90:291–300.

[69] Fiedler S, Buegger F, Klaubert B, Zipp K, Dohrmann R, Witteyer M, Zarei M, Graw M. Adipocere withstands 1600 years of fluctuating groundwater levels in soil. J Archaeol Sci 2009;36:1328–33.

[70] Forbes SL. Decomposition chemistry in a burial. In: Tibbett M, Carter DO, editors. Soil analysis in forensic taphonomy. Boca Raton: CRC Press; 2008.

[71] Stuart BH, Forbes SL, Dent BB, Hodgson. Studies of adipocere using diffuse reflectance infrared spectroscopy. Vib Spectrosc 2000;24:233–42.

[72] Takatori T. The mechanism of human adipocere formation. Leg Med 2001;3:193–204.

[73] Yan F, Mcnally R, Kontanis EJ, Sadik OA. Preliminary quantitative investigation of postmortem adipocere formation. J Forensic Sci 2001;46:609–14.

[74] Schoenen D, Schoenen H. Adipocere formation - the result of insufficient microbial degradation. Forensic Sci Int 2013;226:301.e1–6.

[75] Notter SJ, Stuart BH, Rowe R, Langlois N. The initial changes of fat deposits during the decomposition of human and pig remains. J Forensic Sci 2009;51:195–201.

[76] Forbes SL, Dent BB, Stuart BH. The effect of soil type on adipocere formation. Forensic Sci Int 2005;154:35–43.

[77] Fiedler S, Berns A, Schwark L, Woelk AT, Graw M. The chemistry of death. Adipocere degradation in modern graveyards. Forensic Sci Int 2015;257:320–8.

[78] Nushida H, Adachi J, Takeuchi A, Asano M, Ueono Y. Adipocere formation via hydrogenation of linoleic acid in a victim kept under dry concealment. Forensic Sci Int 2008;175:160–5.

[79] Healy F, Housley RA. Nancy was not alone: human skeletons of the Early Bronze Age from the Norfolk peat fen. Antiquity 1992;66:948–55.

[80] Brothwell DR, Gill-Robinson H. Taphonomic and forensic aspects of bog bodies. In: Haglund WD, Sorg MH, editors. Advances in forensic taphonomy. Boca Raton: CRC Press; 2002.

[81] Cotte M, Walter P, Tsoucaris G, Dumas P. Studying skin of an Egyptian mummy by infrared microscopy. Vib Spectrosc 2005;38:159–67.

[82] Schotsmans EMJ, Van De Voorde W, De Winne J, Wilson AS. The impact of shallow burial on differential decomposition to the body: a temperate case study. Forensic Sci Int 2011;206:e43–8.

[83] Beaumont G. Body on the beach. A case of foot and mouth? Journal of Forensic and Legal Medicine 2007;14:54–7.

[84] Loe L, Barker C, Brady K, Cox M, Webb H. 'Remember me to all': the archaeological recovery and identification of soliders who fought and died in the Battle of Fromelles 1916. Oxford: Oxford Archaeology; 2014.

[85] Troutman, Moffatt C, Simmons T. A preliminary examination of differential decomposition patterns in mass graves. J Forensic Sci 2014;59:621–6.

[86] MarhofF-Beard SJ, Forbes SL, Green H. The validation of 'universal' PMI methods for the estimation of time since death in temperate Australian climates. Forensic Sci Int 2018;291:158–66.

[87] Rhine S, Dawson J. Estimation of time since death in the Southwestern United States. In: Reichs KJ, editor. Forensic osteology: advances in the identification of human remains. Springfield, Illinois: Charles C Thomas; 1998.

[88] Galloway A, Birkby WH, Jones AM, Henry TE, Parks BO. Decay rates of human remains in an arid environment. J Forensic Sci 1989;34:607–16.

[89] Komar DA. Decay rates in a cold climate region: a review of cases involving advanced decomposition from the medical examiners office in Edmonton, Alberta. J Forensic Sci 1998;43:57–61.

[90] Prieto J, Magana C, Ubelaker DH. Interpretation of post mortem change in cadavers in Spain. J Forensic Sci 2004;49:1–6.

[91] Sorg MH, Dave E, Rebmann A. Cadaver dogs, taphonomy, and postmortem interval in the Northeast. In: Reichs KJ, editor. Forensic osteology. Advances in the identification of human remains. Illinois: Charles C Thomas; 1998.

[92] Maile AE, Inoue CG, Barksdale LE, Carter DO. Toward a universal equation to etimate postmortem interval. Forensic Sci Int 2017;272:150–3.

[93] Vass AA, Wolt JD, Foss JE, Ammons JT, Bass WM. Time since death determinations of human cadavers using soil solution. J Forensic Sci 1992;37:1236–53.

[94] Moffatt C, Simmons T, Lynch-Aird J. An improved equation for TBS and ADD: establishing a reliable postmortem interval framework for casework and experimental studies. J Forensic Sci 2016;61:S201–7.

[95] Dabbs GR, Connor M, Bytheway JA. Interobserver reliability of the Total Body Score system for quantifying human decomposition. J Forensic Sci 2016;61:445–51.

[96] Dabbs GR. How should forensic anthropologists correct National Weather Service temperature data for use in estimating the postmortem interval? J Forensic Sci 2015;60:582–7.

[97] Dabbs GR. Caution! All data are not created equal: the hazards of using National Weather Serice data for calculating accumulated degree days. Forensic Sci Int 2010;202:e49–52.

[98] Cockle DL, Bell LS. Human decomposition and the reliability of a 'Universal' model for post mortem interval estimations. Forensic Sci Int 2015;253:136.e1–9.

[99] Hall DW. Forensic botany. In: Haglund WD, Sorg MS, editors. Forensic taphonomy. The postmortem fate of human remains. Boca Raton: CRC Press; 1997.

[100] Courtin GM, Fairgrieve SI. Estimation of postmortem interval as revealed through the analysis of annual growth in woody tissue. J Forensic Sci 2004;49:781–3.
[101] Vanezis P, Sims BG, Grant JH. Medical and scientific investigations of an exhumation in unhallowed ground. Med Sci Law 1978;18:209–21.
[102] Denne MP. Dating of events from tree growth and wood structure. J Forensic Sci Soc 1977;17:257–64.
[103] Miller J. Forensic botany and stomack contents analysis: established practice and innovation. In: Schotsmans EMJ, Marquez-Grant N, Forbes SL, editors. Taphonomy of human remains: forensic analysis of the dead and the depositional environment. Chichester: Wiley; 2017.
[104] Szibor R, Schubert C, Schoning R, Krause D, Wendt U. Pollen analysis reveals murder season. Nature 1998;395:450–1.
[105] Pringle JK, Cassella JP, Jervis JR, Williams AC, Cross P, Cassidy NJ. Soilwater conductivity analysis to date and locate clandestine graves of homicide victims. J Forensic Sci 2015;60:1052–60.
[106] Damann FE, Williams DE, A.C., L. Potential use of bacterial community succession in decaying human bone for estimating postmortem interval. J Forensic Sci 2015;60:844–50.
[107] Metcalf JL. Estimating the postmortem interval using microbes: knowledge gaps and a path to technology adoption. Forensic Sci Int: Genetics 2019;38:211–8.
[108] Metcalf JL, Xu ZZ, Weiss S, Lax S, W., V. T., Hyde ER, Song S, Amir A, Larsen P, Sangwan N, Haarmann D, Humphrey GC, Ackermann G, Thompson LR, Lauber C, Bibat A, Nicholas C, Gebert MJ, Petrosino JF, Reed SC, Gilbert JA, Lynne AM, Bucheli SR, Carter DO, Knight R. Microbial community assembly and metabolic function during mammalian corpse decomposition. Science 2016;351:158–62.
[109] Hyde ER, Haarmann DP, Petrosino JF, Lynne AM. Initial insights intobacterial succession during human decomposition. Int J Leg Med 2015;129:661–71.
[110] Lv Y, Ma J, Pan H, Zhang H, Li W, Xue A, Wang H, Ma K, Chen L. RNA degradation as described by a mathematical model for postmortem interval determination. J Foren Legal Med 2016;44:43–52.
[111] Young ST, Wells JD, Hobbs GR, Bishop CB. Estimating postmortem interval using RNA degradation and morphological changes in tooth pulp. Forensic Sci Int 2013;229:163.e1–6.
[112] Sampaio-Silva E, Magalhaes T, Carvalho F, Dinis-Oliveira R, R., S. Profiling of RNA degradation for estimation of post-mortem interval. PlLoS One 2013;8:e56507.
[113] Poor VS, Lukacs D, Nagy T, Racz E, Sipos K. The rate of RNA degradation in human dental pulp reveals post-mortem interval. Int J Leg Med 2016;130:615–9.
[114] Kimura A, Ishida Y, Hayashi T, Nosaka M, Kondo T. Estimating time of death based on the biological clock. Int J Leg Med 2011;125:385–91.
[115] Javan GT, Can I, Finley SJ, Soni S. The apoptotic thanatotranscriptome associated with the liver of cadavers. Forensic Sci Med Pathol 2015;11:509–16.
[116] Bilheux HZ, Cekanova M, Vass AA, Nichols TL, Bilheux JCRI,D, Finochiarro V. A novel approach to determine postmortem interval using neutron radiography. Forensic Sci Int 2015;251:11–21.
[117] Dautartas A, Kenyhercz MW, Vidoli GM, Jantz LM, Mundorff A, Steadman DW. Differential decomposition among pig, rabbit and human remains. J Forensic Sci 2018;63:1673–82.

Chapter 6

The importance of microbial communities in the estimation of the time since death

David O. Carter
Laboratory of Forensic Taphonomy, Forensic Sciences Unit, Division of Natural Sciences and Mathematics, Chaminade University of Honolulu, Honolulu, HI, United States

Introduction

Estimating Time since Death (TSD) is one of the most difficult components of medicolegal death investigation. The difficulty is because the relationships between decomposition, decomposer communities, decomposing remains, and environment are largely misunderstood. This is the result of two primary factors. First, corpse decomposition is subject to an immense number of variables such as cause of death, temperature, and decomposer access. Many of these variables have received little detailed research while others have never been investigated in a systematic manner. These variables will likely be addressed over time as more research is conducted, however, all of these data must eventually be analysed in a cohesive manner, so that the multitude of variables can be interpreted across scenes, climates, and seasons.

The second primary factor for the difficulty in estimating TSD is that it is not always necessary to close a death investigation; it is quite common to close a death investigation and complete a death certificate without establishing a reliable TSD. Based on professional experience, this factor has resulted in little research into TSD being conducted by investigative personnel. Quite frankly, most investigative agencies in the USA do not have the resources to investigate and analyse nonessential data. Rather, estimates of PMI are typically only pursued in cases of extreme interest, such as a Homicide where the TSD plays a significant role in verifying an alibi.

Although TSD is not the focus of most death investigations, forensic taphonomy has benefited from many multidisciplinary investigations. One area of significant potential is forensic microbiology and microbial ecology. Microorganisms are relevant to death investigation because they are ubiquitous and participate in every stage of decomposition. In fact, decomposition is one

Estimation of the Time since Death. https://doi.org/10.1016/B978-0-12-815731-2.00006-6

of the primary contributions that microbial communities make to the function of our planet, along with maintaining our atmosphere, filtering our water, and contributing to the growth and function of other organisms. It is difficult to overstate the importance of microbial communities to the function of Earth.

The ubiquity of microbial communities means that they will always be found at death scenes. Furthermore, microbial communities make several direct contributions throughout the decomposition process from translocation and putrefaction to bone diagenesis. Recent research has shown that these contributions are predictable and can be used as a basis to estimate TSD. This predictability can result in the generation of a minimum or maximum TSD as well as a range of TSD, depending on the analytical approach. Microbial communities are also important to the estimation of TSD because they make several indirect contributions to decomposition by cycling decomposition fluids and releasing chemicals into the atmosphere, which can attract and repel insects and decomposers (Fig. 6.1). Microorganisms even contribute to the development of insects and scavengers. Microbial communities are important to the estimation of TSD because they contribute to nearly every process associated with decomposing remains.

The purpose of this chapter is to review our understanding of the structure and function of microbial communities during decomposition. This foundation will then be used to discuss the current approaches for using microbial

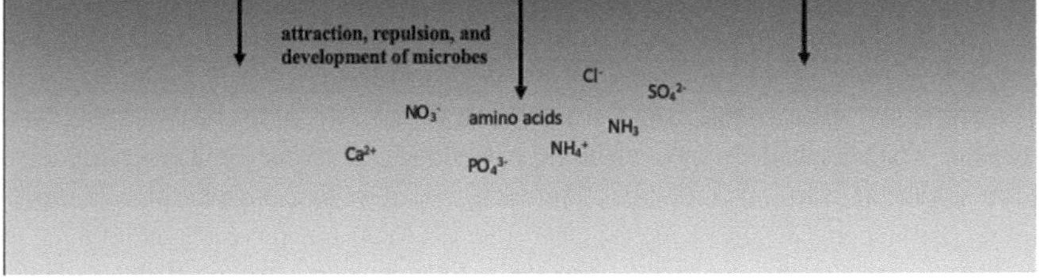

FIG. 6.1 Microorganisms participate in several decomposition processes including putrefaction, the cycling of decomposition fluids, and the release of volatile organic compounds (VOCs). These contributions result in the release of several chemicals throughout the Cadaver Decomposition Island including amino acids, ammonia (NH_3), ammonium (NH_4^+), atmospheric nitrogen (N_2), calcium (Ca_2^+), carbon dioxide (CO_2), chloride (Cl^-), hydrogen sulfide (H_2S), methane (CH_4), nitrate (NO_3^-), phosphate (PO_4^{3-}), and sulfate (SO_4^{2-}). These microbial activities provide several ecosystem services including the attraction, repulsion, and development of insects, scavengers, and other microorganisms. In doing so, postmortem microbial activity also facilitates access to cadaveric moisture and nutrients that are otherwise unavailable.

communities to estimate TSD. Finally, this chapter will review the strengths and weaknesses of using microbial communities to estimate TSD.

What is a microbial community?

The term microorganism can be used to refer to any microscopic organism, regardless of species. A bacterial cell will likely have a diameter of 1−5 μm. Some multicellular microorganisms can be several millimetres in length, although microscopy is necessary to view them in any detail. Oftentimes the term microbe is used as a synonym for microorganism, as it will in the current text. Microorganisms can be found in all three domains of life: Archaea, Bacteria, and Eukarya [1]. Some microbes are single celled organisms (prokaryotes: Archaea, Bacteria) while others are multicellular organisms (eukaryotes: Eukarya). Microbes are widely distributed throughout the planet and inhabit virtually every habitat on Earth; they are certainly found everywhere humans are found because humans serve as hosts for countless microbes.

A single microbe if often called a cell or, when referring to eukaryotes, an individual. A group of cells/individuals is a population. In other words, a population is a group of microbes that are all the same species, such as an isolated colony in a Petri dish. A microbial community, in contrast, is a group of microbes that includes at least two species. The study of microbial communities is the study of multiple species simultaneously, which introduces great complexity. One swab from a carcass, for example, can contain thousands of microbial species [2]. Species can differ in many ways including their morphology, function, and environmental requirements [3]. These species interact with their environment, including other species, and can respond rapidly to changes in their environment. As a result, microbial communities change over time. This is particularly true for microbial communities associated with decomposing remains. Decomposing remains are one of the most nutritious resources on our planet and, depending on their size, can support abundant, diverse, and rapidly changing microbial communities for finite periods.

This text will use terminology from microbiology and microbial ecology, and a concise review of this terminology is provided where necessary. See Metcalf et al. [4] and Carter et al. [3] for more detailed terminology and concepts related to forensic microbiology. See Madigan et al. [5], Brown [6], Dyer [7], and Swanson et al. [8] for terminology and concepts related to general microbiology and microbial ecology.

Microbial community structure and function

Microbial communities can be defined in two fundamental ways: structure and function. Microbial community structure refers to the microbial taxa that comprise the community. Microbial community structure is usually presented as a taxonomic level. Forensic microbiology tends to present structure as a phylum, family, genus, and/or species (see Table 6.1). Understanding microbial community structure is important because certain microorganisms are associated with different stages of decomposition; microbial community structure shifts over time. For example, the visible presence of fungi associated with decomposing remains occurs after maggots have migrated [9] or when remains are stored in a cool, damp environment that retards insect and scavenger activity [10]. In fact, the proliferation of fungi is a constant concern for body donation programs that maintain embalmed bodies for teaching and research (C. Carter, personal communication).

Understanding microbial communities is also important because certain microorganisms carry out certain functions. Acquiring insight into these functions is important to death investigation because it leads to a comprehensive understanding of the decomposition processes at a given death scene. For example, *Proteus mirabilis* (Proteobacteria: Enterobacteriaceae), a bacterial species regularly associated with decomposing remains (e.g. Ref. [8]), is known to release chemicals to attract insects that can be used to estimate TSD [11]. Microbial community function provides a foundation for reconstructing the death scene because microbes play a role in many decomposition processes, particularly translocation and putrefaction [12]. Like microbial community structure, function shifts over time in response to the change in the availability and composition of the remains [2]. These functional shifts are often associated with structural shifts, as different species may carry out different functions. The change in microbial communities over time is called microbial succession and it is a crucial process for using microbial communities to estimate TSD.

Succession is an ecological concept that is used to describe the process where one microbial community replaces another microbial community over time (see [6]). Succession can result from a change in the availability or type of food and moisture as the remains decompose. For example, decomposing remains in an outdoor location during the early postmortem period often support communities dominated by bacteria and flies with relatively few fungi and beetles. Over time, as moisture and soft tissue are depleted, these organisms become less abundant as fungi and beetles proliferate. Postmortem insect succession in particular has long been an area of interest for this reason – certain insects tend to be associated with certain postmortem intervals [13] (see Chapter 4, this volume). A growing body of research has also shown that microbial communities shift over time and it is this succession on which estimates of TSD are based [2,14–18].

Lastly, it is necessary to discuss the term microbiome. The current text will use microbiome interchangeably with microbial community, although microbiome has been used to refer to the genes contained within a microbial community [4]. The postmortem microbiome can be referred to as the necrobiome, the community of all organisms (prokaryote and eukaryote)

TABLE 6.1 Microorganisms from all three domains of life (Archaea, Bacteria, and Eukarya) are associated with decomposing remains, a very small proportion of which are listed here.

Domain	Phylum	Family	Genus	Species	Citations
Archaea	Euryarchaeota	Methanobacteriaceae	*Methanobacterium*	sp.	Kwon et al. [77]
		Methanosarcinaceae	*Methanosarcina*	sp.	Kwon et al. [77]
Bacteria	Actinobacteria	Bifidobacteriaceae	*Bifidobacterium*	sp.	Tuomisto et al. [32]
	Bacteroidetes	Bacteroidaceae	*Bacteroides*	sp.	Hyde et al. [23]
	Firmicutes	Clostridiaceae	*Clostridium*	spp.	Javan et al. [34]
		Lactobacillaceae	*Lactobacillus*	sp.	Hauther et al. [26]
		Staphylococcaceae	*Staphylococcus*	sp.	Pechal et al. [22]
	Proteobacteria	Enterobacteriaceae	*Proteus*	*mirabilis*	Iancu et al. [30]
		Xanthomonadaceae*	*Ignatzschineria*	*indica*	Chun et al. [53]
Eukarya	Annelida	Enchytriadeae	*Enchytronia*	*parva*	Schlaghamerský and Krawczynski [80]
	Arthropoda	Entomobryidae	*Sinella*	*tenebricosa*	Merritt et al. [79]
		Hypogastruridae	*Hypogastrura*	*vernalis*	Klonowski et al. [78]
	Ascomycota	Eurotiomycetidae	*Penicillium*	*expansum*	Di Piazza et al. [10]
		Trichocomaceae	*Aspergillus*	spp.	Ridgway et al. [58]
	Basidiomycota	Trichosporonaceae	*Trichosporon*	sp.	Szelecz et al. [39]
	Cercozoa	Euglyphidae	*Euglypha*	*rotunda*	Seppey et al. [42]
	Nematoda	Rhabditidae	*Oscheius*	*tipulae*	Metcalf et al. [14]

The microbes listed here are meant to serve as examples of microbial taxa that are frequently associated with decomposing remains. The designations sp. and spp. indicate one unidentified species and multiple unidentified species, respectively. *Indicates that Xanthomonadaceae is a taxon name that does not conform with the International Code of Nomenclature of Bacteria.

associated with decomposing remains [19]. It is also common for the postmortem microbiome to be subdivided into two components, the thanatomicrobiome and the epinecrotic microbiome [17]. Thanatomicrobiome is defined as the microbiome associated with internal organs, e.g. liver, spleen, heart. The epinecrotic microbiome is defined as the microbial communities on the surfaces of decomposing remains, e.g. skin, mouth.

Antemortem microbial communities differ from postmortem microbial communities

To date, several studies have investigated microbial communities during decomposition and samples have been collected from several body sites including the skin [2,14,15,20–24], gastrointestinal/rectal locations [2,14,18,20–23,25–30], oral sites [15,20,23,27,29,30], eyes [21,22], nose and/or ear [16,21,22,31], internal organs [17,28,32–34], bone [35,36], grave soils [2,14,37–52], and insect larval masses [53,54]. These studies have helped us to understand that there exist a number of fundamental concepts that must be understood when using microbial communities to estimate TSD. First, it is important to recognize the distinction between antemortem microbial communities (those that are associated with living organisms) and postmortem microbial communities (those that are associated with decomposing remains) because microbial communities change after death. In addition, postmortem microbial communities continue to change throughout the course of decomposition; microbial succession. Third, postmortem microbial succession is predictable, which provides the basis for estimating TSD.

Understanding antemortem microbial communities is essential to estimate TSD because antemortem microbial communities represent the starting point of the decomposition process. Much of what is known about antemortem microbiomes is the result of the Human Microbiome Project [55]. One of the most forensically relevant observations resulting from this project is that each person hosts a microbial community that is unique and stable over time [56]. Skin microbiomes are sufficiently unique to serve as a means of identification, like a fingerprint [24], and they have great potential as trace evidence because humans constantly transfer their microbiomes to objects and surfaces with which they interact. This transfer appears to have implications for estimating TSD because the microbiomes dissipate from objects and surfaces when they are not replenished by repeated interaction; they exist for only a finite time. The time required for the microbiome to fade is unknown, but recent research shows that significant loss of microbial material can occur after 24 h [57].

The unique nature of antemortem microbiomes is very important to the estimation of TSD because it means that each corpse begins decomposing with a microbiome that is unique. At some point in the early postmortem period, apparently approximately 48 h postmortem [22,24], antemortem microbes are succeeded by postmortem microbes. This shift is probably the result of many processes including the cessation of the host immune system, translocation, putrefaction, insect activity, scavenger activity, and desiccation. The shift to a postmortem microbiome indicates that the host has ceased to function as a living organism and, instead, serves as a habitat suitable for the activity of decomposers – microbes, insects, and scavengers [9]. A corpse is a highly attractive habitat because it comprises nutrient rich resources (protein, lipid) and significant moisture. A habitat of these characteristics will select for microorganisms that can acquire energy through the decomposition of organic and inorganic compounds, compete in a moisture rich environment, and tolerate the availability of little to no oxygen. In general, a habitat of this type tends to favour bacteria.

Historically, microbes were of great interest because they can cause death (e.g. Ref. [55]). Early forensic microbiology was focused on the identification of microbes that cause death, which is an approach that exists today particularly with infant and elderly deaths where the host is susceptible to infection [58]. This application helped to establish the understanding that microbial communities change after death because the ability to collect pathogenic microbes can become compromised over time, a process currently referred to as translocation [12]. Translocation is a form of microbial succession where postmortem microbes succeed the pathogenic microbes and, in doing so, compromise the ability to establish cause of death because all of the pathogens have been killed by the decomposers [12,32,58,59].

More recent microbiome research, which has focused on domain Bacteria, has repeatedly observed four bacterial phyla associated with decomposing remains: Actinobacteria, Bacteroidetes, Firmicutes, and Proteobacteria (e.g. Refs. [2,27]). A few other phyla, such as Fusobacteria, Tenericutes, and Verrucomicrobia, have also been observed in multiple studies (e.g. Refs. [16,34,51,60]). For example, Pechal et al. [15] observed a microbiome comprising Proteobacteria (70% of the microbial community), Firmicutes (~20%), Actinobacteria (~5%), and Bacteroidetes (~5%) associated with decomposing swine carcasses on the day of death. These bacteria were associated with greater than 20 families including Aerococcaceae, Alcaligenaceae, Moraxellaceae, and Pasteurellaceae. Lauber et al. [45] observed similar microbiomes associated with decomposing mouse carcasses. From one perspective, it is not surprising that these taxa are associated with decomposing remains because they are widely distributed throughout nature. In fact, all of these phyla can be found among antemortem microbial communities. This observation represents an important point – many of the changes in postmortem microbial communities occur at the family, genus, and species levels of taxonomy.

Postmortem microbial communities shift repeatedly during decomposition

A postmortem microbial community does not remain stable once it established; it continues to shift as remains decompose. It is difficult to definitively describe these changes because relatively little research has been conducted but some common trends have emerged. The initial shifts associated with decomposing remains tend to be the loss of the antemortem microbial community (environmental, pathogenic microbes), an increase in microbial abundance and activity [2,38,50,61,62], and a decrease in microbial diversity [14,15,18,41,52]. These shifts are most likely due to the nature of the remains. The high concentration of nutrients and moisture is capable of supporting increased microbial activity and a larger microbial community. In fact, significantly greater [61,62] and more diverse [22] microbial activity has been observed within 48 h postmortem. However, decomposing remains are a highly specialised habitat, which probably explains the loss of diversity over time. Decomposing remains select for a microbial community that is able to breakdown protein and lipid in an environment of warm temperature (~40–50 °C) and antimicrobial compounds released by insects [63]. Not every microbe can survive that environment.

One major microbially mediated process is putrefaction. Putrefaction has an interesting history because it was well established as a decomposition process several years before it was associated with microorganisms [64]. Putrefaction is fermentation, a common decomposition process in which a microorganism uses an organic compound as an electron acceptor to generate adenosine triphosphate for energy [3]. Putrefaction results in the bloating, colour changes, and many of the odours commonly associated with decomposition. The bacteria that drive putrefaction originate from the gastrointestinal tract and may represent the largest component of the whole postmortem microbial community. Putrefaction represents a structural and functional shift as these microbes are now able to decompose the gastrointestinal tract and other internal structures. For example, Javan et al. [34] and Debruyn and Hauther [18] observed a significant increase of bacterial genus *Clostridium* in postmortem samples. *Clostridium* is an anaerobic taxon that can proliferate during decomposition because little or no oxygen is present within the decomposing remains; decomposition is so intense at this stage that all available oxygen will be consumed rapidly. Several species of *Clostridium* have been associated with decomposing remains, so this genus is probably a major contributor to several postmortem processes. Other bacterial genera commonly associated with putrefaction include *Bacteroides* [18,23,26–28, 32,34,65], *Bifidobacterium* [26,32], *Escherichia* [27,28,34,53,65,66], *Enterococcus* [28,34], *Ignatzschineria* [30,52,53,67], *Lactobacillus* [26,27,34], *Proteus* [27,30,53], *Pseudomonas* [23,30,34,53,67], *Staphylococcus* [32,53,65, 66,68], and *Wohlfahrtiimonas* [23,30,53].

It is common for the accumulation of putrefactive gases to result in the rupture of the remains, usually in the abdominal region. The rupture of decomposing remains and release of decomposition fluids appear to represent a major event in postmortem microbial succession. Several studies [2,14,45,51,52] have observed significant shifts following rupture, which is usually associated with the Bloat and Active Decay stages of decomposition [9]. Rupture represents an important event in microbial succession because it exposes the internal cavity to air. This can have a significant effect on microbial communities because many postmortem microbes, such as *Clostridium*, are anaerobic. As a result, it is common to see the abundance of anaerobic taxa decrease following rupture. Metcalf et al. [14], for example, observed a decrease in the abundance of phylum Firmicutes in the abdominal activity of mouse carcasses on soil. Conversely, the abundance of some microbes can increase following rupture. Carter et al. [51] and Finley et al. [37] observed an increase in the abundance of the bacterial family Chitinophagaceae in grave soil following the rupture of swine (*Sus scrofa domesticus*) carcasses on the soil surface. This taxon is known to decompose the polysaccharide chitin, which is a major component of insect exoskeletons. It is possible that these bacteria are using dead insects as a food source, which is an excellent example of a postmortem food web.

Postmortem microbial communities are a component of a complex postmortem food web

Although much of the current research in forensic microbiology focuses on bacteria, postmortem bacterial communities do not function in isolation from other microbes. Microbes from domains Bacteria, Archaea, and Eukarya are part of the same community and can interact constantly with each other. In fact, one of the primary stimuli for the proliferation and succession of bacteria is the proliferation of other microorganisms. This type of shift occurs when an increase in the abundance of one group of microbes is followed by an increase in the abundance of the organisms that feed on those microbes. One consistently observed example of this is the proliferation of bacterivorous nematodes following the growth of bacterial communities and rupture [14]. Nematodes are a highly diverse group of roundworms that are ubiquitous in nature and can consume many different types of food including bacteria and other nematodes [41]. They are often used as environmental indicators because they can respond rapidly to changes in their habitat such as temperature, nutrient availability.

Relatively few studies have investigated postmortem nematode communities, yet the results are very promising for forensic application [39]. Szelecz et al. [41] conducted the first experiment focused on the structure of postmortem nematode communities in grave soils and several significant effects were observed. Nematode abundance increased by an order of magnitude during the initial 15 days postmortem, but this was followed by a decrease in abundance to near zero by 22 days postmortem. This decrease in abundance could be due to a saturation of decomposition fluids following rupture and/or a significant increase in temperature during Active Decay [41]. Nematode abundance then steadily increased from 36 days postmortem to 123 days postmortem. These postmortem nematode communities were dominated by families Rhabditidae, Diplogasteroididae, and Neodiplogasteridae and these shifts were partly driven by nutrient availability, including grave soil pH, nitrate, ammonium, phosphorus, and potassium.

Recent microbiome studies observed similar shifts in postmortem nematode communities [2,14,45,51,52]. Metcalf et al. [14] observed a significant increase in the abundance of *Oscheius tipulae* from family Rhabditidae. This shift represents an excellent example of postmortem microbial succession: increase in bacterial food → increase in bacterial abundance → increase in bacterivorous nematode abundance. Similar observations have been observed [2,45,51,52], which is important because it has implications for estimating the TSD during the extended postmortem interval after fly larvae have migrated (see below). Other nematode groups that may be abundant during the extended postmortem interval include families Cephalobidae, Plectidae, and Myolaimidae [39]. All of these families represent bacterivorous nematodes that are probably responding the proliferation of postmortem bacterial communities.

Microbial activity and function also shift during decomposition

The structural changes discussed above are associated with several functional changes, although microbial community function is far less understood than microbial community structure. We currently know that postmortem microbial activity can increase significantly within 24 h of death [20,31,49,50,61,62] and this activity can differ between season [20], temperature [61], and moisture availability [62]. Functional shifts in the postmortem nematode community have also been observed. Szelecz et al. [41] observed a shift from a nematode community dominated by bacterivores and plant feeding nematodes to a community dominated by bacterivores and predacious nematodes.

To date, the research into postmortem microbial community function has focused on the functions associated with the cycling of carbon [20,38,50,61,62,69], nitrogen [2,49,61,62,69,70], and phosphorus [61,62,69,70]. However, several other elements and compounds are subject to microbial activity. All of these studies indicate that microbial activity increases and functions shift in response to nutrient availability and competition for these nutrients. These activities decrease and eventually return to basal levels as the remains decompose and nutrients are depleted. One of the most common ways to measure microbial activity is via carbon dioxide respiration [38,50,61]. Carbon dioxide is regularly used as an index of microbial activity because microbes are constantly seeking out organic compounds as food. Some of the carbon will be assimilated into the microbe for energy and cell maintenance while some of the carbon will be released as carbon dioxide.

Carbon dioxide concentration increases rapidly and significantly during decomposition but this effect can be significantly altered by temperature and moisture [38,50,61,62]. Carbon dioxide concentration can also remain elevated well into the latter stages of decomposition, up to two years postmortem [38,50]. Interestingly, Cobaugh et al. [50] observed a functional shift associated with human remains between 7 and 12 days postmortem. This shift comprised a sustained rate of carbon dioxide respiration with a decrease in microbial biomass conversion, measured as leucine incorporation. This shift in microbial growth efficiency may indicate that the readily available nutrients had been depleted by 7—12 days postmortem forcing the microbial community to invest its energy into activities other than growth, such as enzyme production, to acquire more nutrients. This functional shift coincided with a structural shift where anaerobic bacteria from phylum Firmicutes were more abundant.

The production of enzymes by microorganisms is another commonly used index of microbial activity and is important to understand because microbial community function is often discussed from the perspectives of extracellular function and intracellular function. Extracellular function is often associated with microbial enzyme activity because microbes release enzymes from the cell. These enzymes react with substrates outside of the microbial cell so that the microbes can take up the lower molecular weight product through the cell membrane.

It is important to remember that using enzymes as an index of microbial activity comes with two compromises. First, enzyme assays tend to measure optimal enzyme activity, which may be significantly greater than true enzyme activity. Second, extracellular enzymes can accumulate in a habitat, particularly soils. Accumulated enzymes can function separately of microbial activity, which can also lead to an overestimate of true microbial activity and function. These conditions are very important to consider when interpreting enzyme activity data. As with most microbial activities, the dynamics of enzymes are significantly influenced by environment, particularly temperature, moisture, and environmental chemistry. For example, enzyme activity tends to increase as temperature increases, up to approximately 45 °C when they become denatured. Moisture is also crucial to microbial activity because many of these enzymes are hydrolytic enzymes that require water to react.

Carter et al. [61,62] directly investigated extracellular enzyme activity in grave soils. These studies demonstrated that the decomposition of rat (*Rattus rattus*) remains was repeatedly associated with the activity of enzymes associated with the decomposition of proteins (protease) and nucleic acids (phosphodiesterase). Protease and phosphodiesterase are associated with the cycling of nitrogen and phosphorus, respectively, and the concentration of these enzymes increased significantly within 7 days of death and remained elevated for several weeks [48,61,62]. Howard et al. [48] conducted a similar study to investigate postmortem lipase activity (lipid decomposition) in grave soils associated with swine (*S. scrofa domesticus*) remains. A significant increase in lipase activity was observed within 9 days postmortem, which indicates that microorganisms were probably contributing to the decomposition of lipids by that time. These time periods are similar to those observed by Cobaugh et al. [50], which may indicate that decomposing remains are associated with significant functional shifts by 10 days postmortem when the remains are in a warm, outdoor habitat (see also Chapter 3, this volume).

Our understanding of intracellular function is quite limited. Some of it is related to postmortem enzyme activity and shows that microbes respond rapidly to changes in their environment, which can include increases and decreases in microbial function. Metcalf et al. [2] provided novel insight into postmortem microbiome function during the initial 30 days postmortem by predicting enzyme activity based on microbial gene abundance. Postmortem microbial function was significantly related to key steps in the nitrogen cycle. Increased gene abundance was associated with amino acid (glutamate, glycine, lysine, ornithine) decomposition and ammonia production (Fig. 6.1). In contrast, an increased abundance of genes associated with nitrate reduction was not observed. Similarly, Moreno et al. [49] observed a down regulation of the *nifH* gene, which codes for the enzyme nitrogenase reductase. Nitrogenase reductase is associated with the cycling of nitrogen because it reduces atmospheric nitrogen (N_2) to ammonia (NH_3). This process is crucial to ecosystem function because ammonia is used regularly by microbes and plants. The reason why a decrease in this function was observed is because decomposing mammal remains release sufficient ammonia into their surrounding habitat, probably due to amino acid degradation [2]. In other words, it is unnecessary for microbes to engage in nitrate reduction because sufficient ammonia is already available via amino acid degradation. Both of these studies are important because they demonstrate that a decrease in intracellular function can be associated with decomposing remains for as long as 16 weeks postmortem [49].

Pechal et al. [22] also provides remarkably helpful insight into postmortem microbial function. They observed greater functional redundancy in postmortem microbiomes at TSDs < 49 h; many of the microbes were carrying out similar functions and this functional redundancy was associated with a stable community structure. However, 49+ h microbiomes were associated with shifts in functions associated with cell motility. In particular, Pechal et al. [22] observed an increase in chemotaxis, motility proteins, and flagellar assembly that indicated the shift to a more mobile microbial community that was increasingly represented by bacteria from family Enterobacteriaceae. This coincided with a general increase in the abundance of phylum Proteobacteria over time. This may help to explain postmortem bacterial translocation [12], as a motile microbial community would be able to better facilitate the decomposition of remains.

Postmortem microbial succession continues through the extended postmortem period

To date, the majority of postmortem microbial community analysis has focused on the early postmortem period, defined in the current text as the TSD leading up to the migration of fly larvae. The time required for this to occur varies according to environmental conditions and the ability for decomposers to access the remains; fly larvae tend to migrate 10–14 days postmortem at outdoor terrestrial death scenes in Hawaii (e.g. Ref. [53]). These studies primarily focus on bacteria because they are the dominant microbial group during this initial period of rapid breakdown and elevated nutrient status. However, several other groups of microorganisms continue to proliferate during the extended postmortem period after fly larvae have migrated and decomposing remains comprise dry skin, bone, hair, and nails. Research into postmortem microbial communities during the extended postmortem period tends to focus on the microbial eukaryotes, particularly fungi, nematodes, and amoebae. The extended postmortem period is arguably the TSD during which microbial tools to estimate TSD are most needed. Relatively little is known about microbial communities during Advanced Decay and Skeletonisation, but these are stages during which microbial eukaryotes have received more attention than the prokaryotes.

Postmortem microbial eukaryotes also proliferate in response to the availability of nutrients, such as ammonium and nitrate, and there is growing interest in postmortem microbial eukaryote communities particularly those including fungi, mites, nematodes, and testate amoebae. For example, fungi tend to proliferate during the extended postmortem period [71,72] or in habitats that retard bacterial and scavenger activity [10,73]. Fungi also demonstrate a succession where the earliest colonizers, usually > one-month postmortem, typically comprise fungi from phyla Ascomycota and Basidiomycota with Deuteromycota, which is an artificial grouping of fungi that do not fit elsewhere [10,74]. These phyla can then be succeeded by a community comprising Basidiomycota and Mucoromycota that may persist for several years postmortem [39,45]. It is not yet possible to comprehensively list the fungi that are typically associated with decomposing remains because the body of research is so small. However, some fungi that have been observed in great abundance or in multiple investigations include genera *Aspergillus* [73], *Coprinus* [71], *Hebeloma* [71], *Mortierella* [39], *Penicillium* [10,73], *Rhopalomyces* [39], and *Trichosporon* [39]. Interestingly, *Rhopalomyces* is a parasite of nematode eggs [75], which is another example of the interactions that comprise the postmortem food web. A number of recent studies have identified additional postmortem fungi for the first time including *Talaromyces udagawae* [74] and *Cladosporium cladosporoides* [10].

Szelecz et al. [40] recently investigated the relationships between soil testate amoebae and decomposing remains. Testate amoebae are commonly called shelled amoebae, or testaceans. The shell component is forensically relevant because they can remain *in situ* for several years following amoebae death and therefore serve as an indicator well into the extended PMI. This process is similar to the persistence of fly pupal casings following eclosion. Testate amoebae are widely distributed throughout nature and used as environmental indicators because they can respond rapidly to changes in their habitat, e.g. temperature, nutrient availability. Like the fungi, testate amoebae responded negatively to the decomposition of remains [44]. Szelecz et al. [40] observed a decrease in abundance, richness, and diversity during the first-year postmortem, shifts that are driven by pH, the addition of decomposition fluids, and high levels of nutrients. A similar finding was observed by Wanner et al. [44] when consulting on a death investigation a few years later [39] and in recent microbiome studies [51,52] where rupture of swine (*S. scrofa domesticus*) carcasses was followed by a significant decrease in the abundance of the amoeboid Thecofilosea, which was the most abundant eukaryote prior to rupture. Some of the most commonly observed postmortem testaceans in grave soil include species *Centropyxis aerophila*, *Arcella arenaria*, *Euglypha rotunda*, and superclass Monadofilosa [40,42,44].

Microbial communities and bone

Although postmortem microbiology samples have been collected from several body sites (e.g. skin, mouth, blood), very few have been collected from bone; the microbiology and microbial ecology of bone is poorly understood. The dearth of research in this area is surprising considering that microbes, particularly fungi, are known to modify bone, which can compromise the interpretation of taphonomy [36]. Damann et al. [35] conducted a study to investigate the bacterial communities associated with decomposing human rib bones in an initial attempt to provide insight into microbes that colonise an osseous habitat. The results from this study, in some ways, are similar to those investigating more frequently sampled body sites. Decomposing bone was inhabited by frequently observed bacterial phyla including Proteobacteria, Firmicutes, Bacteroidetes, Actinobacteria, and Acidobacteria. Furthermore, this similarity was observed at the family level as Pseudomonadaceae, Clostridiaceae, and Tissierellaceae were dominant components of the microbial communities [31,34].

Damann et al. [35] observed the abundance of Proteobacteria, Bacteroidetes, Actinobacteria, and Acidobacteria increase over time while the abundance of Firmicutes decreased over time. These findings contrast, in part, with soft tissue microbiology where the abundance of Proteobacteria decreases while the abundance of Firmicutes increases [2,15,23]. Another significant difference between bone microbiology and soft tissue microbiology is that the diversity of bone microbial communities was observed to increase over time [35]. These shifts showed that the bone microbial communities became more similar to soil microbial communities over time. Similarly, Seppey et al. [42] observed the convergence of testate amoebae communities in grave soils with those in control soils after 309 days postmortem. The convergence of these communities is expected because that is one of the major functions of decomposer microbial communities: decompose waste material and return habitats to basal conditions (see Chapter 7, this volume, for a discussion of TSD in skeletonised remains).

Understanding the differences between the microbial communities of bone and soft tissues is important for estimating TSD because they apparently follow different successional patterns. Soft tissues are high quality resources [9] that select for specialised microbial communities with relatively little diversity. In contrast, bones are low quality resources that acquire diversity over time via microbial succession. From a basic ecology perspective, bone may be associated with microbial succession similar to primary succession where a relatively stable, nutrient poor habitat (such as a newly formed lava field) is associated with the gradual development of a complex biological community. Conversely, soft tissue succession may be more similar to secondary succession when a disturbance event (such as a carcass, flood, or fallen tree) provides access to previously unavailable nutrients so that a microbial community can colonise and reproduce rapidly. The implications of these differences on the estimation of TSD have yet to be established, but it is likely that they will play a crucial role in the forensic application of bone microbial communities.

Decomposing remains affect many microorganisms of untapped forensic potential

The diversity of microbes in nature is immense, and a robust understanding of the importance of many postmortem microorganisms has yet to be achieved. Yet occasionally some of these taxa, such as archaea, collembola, and enchytraeids have been observed in association with decomposing remains. The importance of these microbes in the estimation of TSD is slowly becoming clear but much more detailed research is needed.

Archaea are prokaryotes (single celled) typically associated with extreme environments although they are probably found in many habitats associated with humans [76]. Archaea are actually well positioned for more detailed study because, like bacteria, they are analysed using the 16S rRNA gene. In fact, the postmortem microbiome datasets [2,22] probably contain insightful information about postmortem archaeal communities. These datasets need to be analysed and published. Recently Kwon et al. [77] investigated the structure of archaeal communities associated with 3989 decomposing swine carcasses that were buried in response to an outbreak of foot-and-mouth disease. Samples were collected from associated groundwater and compared to archaeal communities collected from groundwater associated with a manure heap. Kwon et al. [77] observed two significantly different archaeal communities.

The archaeal community associated with carcass decomposition was dominated by microbes from phylum Euryarchaeota, particularly genera *Methanobacterium* and *Methanosarcina* (Table 1). The implications of these observations for estimating TSD are not yet known, but postmortem archaea certainly deserve more detailed study.

Collembola are microscopic (0.2 mm−10 mm length) arthropods widely distributed throughout terrestrial ecosystems. These microbial eukaryotes, commonly called springtails, feed on other microbes including fungi and yeast and have been observed in association with decomposing remains on multiple occasions. Klonowski et al. [78] collected 7606 collembolan individuals comprising 13 species from grave soil one year after the death of a badger (*Meles meles*) carcass. This grave soil also contained elevated concentrations of ammonium, nitrate, and phosphate. Nearly 95% of the collembola community was represented by *Hypogastrura vernalis* (Collembola: Hypogastruridae) and the abundance of this species was significantly positively correlated with the concentration of nitrate and phosphate. These organisms may be feeding on the other postmortem microbes and have the potential to serve as estimates of extended TSD [39]. For example, Merritt et al. [79] observed thousands of collembolans in association with the remains of buried, embalmed human remains after 28 years postmortem. This microbial community was comprised exclusively of *Sinella tenebricosa* (Collembola: Entomobryidae). This observation is important because it demonstrates that collembolans can burrow to a depth of 1.8 m and can remain established on remains for up to 28 years. The full forensic potential of these microorganisms requires further research.

Enchytraeids are microscopic (10 mm−20 mm length) worms that are anatomically similar to earthworms. Commonly called potworms, these microorganisms inhabit terrestrial, freshwater, and marine habitats. Their primary food source is probably other microbes, particularly fungi and bacteria, and they appear to be negatively affected by the decomposition of remains. Schlaghamerský and Krawczynski [80] investigated the soil chemistry and enchytraeid communities in grave soil associated with a decomposing red deer (*Cervus elaphus*) carcass. They observed 715 enchytraeid individuals comprising 8 species at 6.5 months postmortem. 78% of this community was represented by *Enchytronia parva* while 11% of the community comprised *Achaeta* spp. This grave soil was characterized by increased pH (~6.2) and electrical conductivity as well as elevated concentrations of ammonium, nitrate, and phosphate. However, the abundance of enchytraeids was negatively correlated to most of these parameters; enchytraeid abundance increased with distance from the carcass. Enchytraeids clearly respond to decomposing remains and this interaction merits more details research.

Estimating time since death – microbial communities are predictable

The observations described above clearly demonstrate that a vast diversity of microorganisms is present during every stage of decomposition. This is a valuable characteristic not shared by many types of physical evidence that are commonly used to estimate TSD, including telephone records, social media activity, and insects. These studies also demonstrate that microorganisms respond rapidly, positively and negatively, to decomposing remains. The subsequent succession of microbes, like insect succession, is another helpful characteristic; postmortem microbial communities that remain stable during decomposition would have little, if any, probative value. In fact, microbial based estimates of TSD become more accurate the more rapidly microbial succession occurs [81]. One of the most intriguing recent observations is the apparent convergence of postmortem microbial communities [2]. Convergence is an ecological process where two separate microbial communities become similar to one another over time, typically following the introduction of nutrients or contaminants. Metcalf et al. [2] observed the convergence of microbial communities from mouse and human remains across seasons and soil types. In fact, the microbiome from one was used to accurately predict the TSD of the other. If consistent across all variables, postmortem convergence has significant implications for forensic microbiology.

The primary impact of postmortem convergence is that it would allow PMI models to be developed using nonhuman models. This would greatly speed the development of PMI models because it would allow for replicated decomposition studies to be conducted anywhere, not strictly in association with human decomposition facilities or medicolegal death investigation agencies. Developing PMI models using human remains is absolutely crucial, but it is a slow process because of the myriad variables associated with humans, e.g. cause of death, age, medications, clothing. Collecting sufficient data to understand the effect of these variables is a long-term project. The benefit of postmortem convergence is that it would allow these human models to be bolstered by data from nonhuman models, as is done in forensic entomology.

Postmortem microbial communities can represent a minimum or maximum TSD

Microbial communities can be used to estimate TSD in two primary ways. One approach is to use microbes as "milestones" so that a particular species, population, or community represents a fixed, approximate TSD. The other approach is to associate the structure of a microbial community, oftentimes using a machine learning algorithm, to a range of time within the continuum of microbial succession. Both of these approaches can generate reliable estimates of TSD and should be used together when possible.

Using microbes and microbial communities as milestones of TSD generates a minimum TSD or a maximum TSD and can result in several lines of probative physical evidence. An excellent example of this approach is provided by Szelecz et al. [39], which reports a medicolegal death investigation that used several species of microorganisms to estimate the TSD of a decedent known to be alive 22 months prior to discovery. Their [39] sampling yielded specimens of nematodes, mites, and amoebozoa that indicated a minimum TSD of 8 months, but more likely > 1 year. A similar approach that complements the observations of Szelecz et al. [69] was employed by Carter and Tibbett [71] to synthesize the observations of several disparate investigations into the appearance of postmortem fungi. The analysis indicates that different groups of fungi form fruiting structures (mushrooms) at different stages of decomposition. Fungi from Zygomycota and Ascomycota tend to fruit at a TSD < 1 year while fungi from Basidiomycota tend to fruit at a TSD > 1 year. Carter et al. [9] state that a TSD of 28 days is they earliest that they have observed a fungal fruiting structure in association with decomposing remains in an outdoor setting. Although anecdotal, their observations serve as an example that fungi are not able to compete with bacterial and insect communities that can dominate earlier stages of decomposition. Thus, postmortem fungi appear to have greatest probative value during the latter (>1 month) stages of decomposition.

The milestone approach employed by Szelecz et al. [39] can also be extended to microbial function, particularly the products of microbial activity in grave soil such as pH and the concentration of chemicals. For example, Szelecz et al. [39,69] and Carter et al. [61,62] recognize increases in grave soil pH and ammonium as markers of a TSD < 1 year. A TSD < 1 year has also been associated with elevated levels of total nitrogen, phosphorus, and potassium [69]. A TSD > 1 year has been associated with ammonium returning to basal levels [69,82] and pH decreasing below basal levels [69,82] while other compounds, such as nitrate [69,82], phosphorus [69], and potassium [69], increase to greater than basal levels. This aspect of microbial community function is an area of forensic taphonomy that deserves much greater research because it aids in the understanding of microbial community structure [2,20,38,50] and can serve as standalone physical evidence [39,69,82].

Postmortem microbial succession can represent a range of TSD

Another approach to estimate TSD is based on the succession of microbial communities acquired via microbiome sequencing. This is a newer approach that is similar to the use of insect succession for estimating TSD [13]. The novelty of this approach means that relatively few studies have been conducted to date even though these have shown great potential – the TSD of decomposing remains has been estimated with an error as little as $\pm$ 2 days [2,15,16,60].

Essentially, microbiome data collected from decomposition studies with a known TSD are used to build a model for estimating TSD so that a known microbial community structure is associated with a particular TSD. Building these TSD models relies on the use of three genetic markers: 16S rRNA (Archaea, Bacteria), 18S rRNA (Eukarya), and Internal Transcribed Spacer Regions (ITS: Fungi). These markers are used to track microbial succession and can be used in combination with one another or individually. Thus far a few different models have been developed and applied. Pechal et al. [15] built a number of regression models (generalised linear model, generalised additive model) using bacterial phyla and families observed during a 5-day decomposition study. This study found that the family level of taxonomy explained greater than 90% of observed variation in bacterial community structure and TSD. Hauther et al. [26] built an exponential decay model using the relative abundance of three bacterial taxa (*Bacteroides*, *Bifidobacterium*, *Lactobacillus*) over a period of 20 days. The abundance of these genera declined during decomposition with *Bacteroides* and *Lactobacillus* following a significant, predictable pattern.

Machine learning algorithms are an effective option for estimating TSD using microbial succession [2,14,16,22,60]. In fact, Belk et al. [60] posit that a machine learning approach results in the greatest precision because it uses the whole microbiome instead of a select group of indicator taxa. A machine learning approach can be used to categorise outcomes, such as whether TSD was greater or less than 48 h [22], or it can incorporate a regression model. Several different regression algorithms can be used to estimate TSD, e.g. linear regression, Support Vector Regression. Johnson et al. [16] found the greatest precision using the K-nearest neighbour regression model while a Random Forest regression model has also shown great promise [2,14,60]. Regardless of regressor, a machine learning algorithm builds and selects a model by dividing data into one of two groups, a training set or a testing set. The training set serves as the "known" where it provides the timeline for microbial community structure, and once the model is constructed it is applied to the testing set, which is used to estimate error. Most models make use of k-fold cross validation, which continually re-divides the data so that all samples are included in both a training set and testing set. The accuracy of the trained model is then assessed using the testing set which provides an error ($\pm$ unit of time) for the TSD estimate. From this perspective the training set functions similarly to any evidence database such as an Automated Fingerprint Identification System. These datasets can be built with data from one study [16] or from several studies [60], which is a great benefit as the reliability of the TSD model improves as more data are added. The precision associated with these approaches is remarkable with an observed error rate of as little as $\pm$ 2 days [16,60].

The reliability of these models is influenced by a number of variables including sample location, sequence marker (16S, 18S, ITS), frequency of sampling, duration of sampling, and informative microbial taxa. Belk et al.

[60] found that microbial samples collected from grave soil was most precise in a series of controlled laboratory decomposition studies [14]. Using datasets from outdoor decomposition studies of human remains [14], Belk et al. [60] observed an interaction between sample location and sequence marker where the most precise 16S dataset was collected from the skin while the most the most precise 18S and ITS datasets were collected from grave soils. The reliability of microbial communities from grave soils and skin may prove to be a significant advantage as these locations can be sampled at the death scene, however, several body sites can be sampled to generate a reliable estimate of TSD [15,16,22]. The machine learning research also provides an opportunity to identify the most informative microbial taxa, i.e. those taxa that have the greatest effect on the TSD model. Although using the entire dataset is probably the most reliable strategy [16] the datasets used by Belk et al. [60] indicated that bacterial phyla Fusobacteria, Actinobacteria, and Firmicutes played a substantial role in the reliability of the TSD estimates. Johnson et al. [16] identified Verrucomicrobia, Actinobacteria, and Armatimonadetes as useful microbes for estimating TSD. In general, Belk et al. [60] found that using the 16S rRNA genetic marker (compared to 18S rRNA and ITS) summarised at the phylum level provided the most overall accurate estimates of PMI.

The use of microbial succession and machine learning to estimate TSD is promising, although due to the small number of datasets and low sample sizes, knowledge gaps remain [81]. It will become clear if current results are able to be generalised as more datasets are published. In fact, the greatest hurdle to developing a method to estimate TSD in this way is the relative lack of access to microbiome datasets from decomposition studies. It is not yet known which regression model is the most effective, however, it is important to recognise that all regression models have strengths and weaknesses that must be explored in great detail. The Random Forest algorithm, for example, tends to overestimate TSD in the early postmortem period and underestimate TSD in the extended postmortem period. The effect of this weakness can be reduced by adding more datasets and more frequent sampling over extended periods of time. This will be an extremely interesting area of research that may have significant implications for estimating TSD.

Microbial communities can affect other methods for estimating TSD

In addition to providing a direct estimate of TSD, microbial communities also have indirect effects on other estimators of TSD. In particular, microorganisms play a significant role in the release and cycling of decomposition fluids and volatile organic compounds (VOCs) that can be used to estimate the TSD while influencing the behaviour of insects and scavengers. These are important interactions to consider when using decomposition fluids, VOCs, insects, and/or scavengers to estimate the TSD.

Decomposition fluids and volatile organic compounds

Decomposition fluids can be a conspicuous component of a death scene. The decomposition of remains can result in the release of significant fluids that will collect on nonporous surfaces (e.g. linoleum, granite) or be taken up by porous surfaces (e.g. clothing, carpet, soil). These fluids can cover several square meters of nonporous surfaces and leach several centimetres into the soil. This is the primary stimulus for the development of the Cadaver Decomposition Island concept [9], i.e. important taphonomy occurs outside, sometimes meters from, the actual remains.

The release of decomposition fluids is the release of several compounds and elements, including carbon, nitrogen, ammonium, nitrate, potassium, and phosphorus [69]. When released into grave soil, decomposition fluids usually stimulate an increase in pH [2,62,82]. This release is a significant factor in microbial succession because all of these materials represent food for some portion of the postmortem microbial community. Microorganisms actively cycle these compounds and nutrients until the death scene returns to basal levels when chemical concentrations return to their original status. This process can take many years [38,69,83] because decomposing remains release vast quantities of chemicals. As discussed above, a detailed understanding of the processes driven by microbial communities has yet to be achieved but it is clear that they play a significant role in the cycling of carbon [61,62] and nitrogen [2]. As an example, multiple studies have shown that the release of decomposition fluids into grave soil results in an elevated concentration of ammonium followed by an increase in nitrate [2,69,82,84], which can be used as an estimator of TSD [39,69]. These chemical shifts represent natural decomposition processes as the cycling of amino acid → ammonium → nitrate represent key steps in the nitrogen cycle. It is a virtual certainty that microbial communities play a significant role in the cycling of every chemical released considering that the cycling of energy and nutrients is a primary function of microbial communities in every ecosystem.

In addition to decomposition fluids, some compounds and elements are released into the atmosphere as VOCs. Volatile organic compounds are a valuable form of physical evidence because they can be used to locate clandestine graves [85] as well as serve as a basis for the estimation of TSD (see Chapter 3, this volume). Microbial communities also play a significant role in the release of VOCs and microbial succession may explain, in part, the change in VOC profiles over time. For instance, Pascual et al. [31] observed that microbial community structure is significantly related to VOC profile. They [31] observed an apparent relationship between the release of acetic acid, indole, and phenol and bacterial families Enterobacteriaceae, Tissierellaceae, and Xanthomonadaceae, respectively. More recently Eckert et al. [86] observed the bacterial species *Bacillus subtilis* release a significant amount of dimethyl disulfide, a key postmortem VOC. The relationships between microbial communities and VOCs are an area that should merit increased research, as they have several implications for the ability to estimate TSD and locate clandestine graves.

Microbe – insect interactions

It is crucial to recognise that microbial communities do not exist in isolation from other organisms. Microorganisms are always involved in the activities of other organisms, particularly their attraction, repulsion, growth, and development [87]. Postmortem bacteria, particularly genera *Proteus*, *Providencia*, and *Ignatzschineria* can release VOCs that attract forensically important flies from genera *Cochlyomyia*, *Hermetia*, and *Lucilia* [11]. Furthermore, these relationships can change over time. The release of VOCs such as phenylacetic acid during early decomposition stages can attract gravid flies and stimulate oviposition [88]. In contrast, the release of dimethyl disulfide during latter stages of decomposition attracts male flies at a time when virgin females are attracted [87].

Microbial communities also contribute to the growth and development of forensically relevant insects [87]. First, putrefaction and rupture provide additional surface area for insect colonisation. Also, flies may secrete bacteria that generate protective antibiotics onto eggs and larvae to increase the likelihood of growth and development. Bacteria can be taken up by larvae where they serve as symbionts beneficial to larval development. Crooks et al. [89] observed that the presence of bacterial species *Escherichia coli* and *Staphylococcus aureus* affected the growth rates of blow fly species *Calliphora vomitoria* and *Calliphora vicina*. A robust understanding of the relationships between microbes and insects is crucial for the estimation of TSD, as many of these estimates are based on the rapid colonisation of remains as well as the growth and development of fly larvae.

Insects can also transport microbes to and from decomposing remains. A number of recent studies have observed postmortem bacteria, such as *Ignatzschineria* and *Wohlfahrtiimonas*, in close association with forensically relevant insects. Indeed, much of what is known about *Ignatzschineria* is due to research into the interactions between this bacterium and flesh flies (Diptera: Sarcophagidae) [90]. This type of relationship (phoresy) is well established between flies and nematodes and may play a critical role in the structure and function of postmortem microbial communities. For example, *Rhabditis stammeri*, an obligate carrion feeder, is transported by insects, particularly the burying beetle *Nicrophorus vespilloides* [91]. This relationship contributes directly to the structure of postmortem microbial communities and biodiversity, as it is critical to the survival of this nematode.

Microbe – scavenger interactions

There is interest in the use of scavenging activity to estimate the TSD of skeletal remains [92], which is greatly needed. One woefully understudied component of scavenging is the interaction between microbes and scavengers. This situation is improving, however, as scavenging is becoming an important area of research in forensic taphonomy and basic ecology [93]. Scavenging activity has taken on increased importance for two reasons. First, it is clear that scavengers play a more prominent role in decomposition than previously thought, as they can consume up to 90% of all remains in an ecosystem [94]. Secondly, scavengers are also receiving more attention because of the increase in the number of anthropological decomposition facilities; scavengers are often conspicuous members of the decomposer community and observed with relative ease.

Many organisms (e.g. vultures, mongooses, deer) will scavenge and a few of them rely exclusively on remains as a food source. Scavenging activity is limited by the ability of scavengers to locate remains. As a result, scavengers have developed excellent visual and olfactory perception. Olfactory cues are probably the result of microbial metabolism releasing VOCs and other chemicals into the atmosphere (Fig. 6.1). Scavengers also need to possess the ability to tolerate the presence of microbes and their metabolic by-products, as they will be consumed along with the remains. Microbial communities will often release chemicals, including toxins, in an attempt to repel scavengers. Burkepile et al. [95] observed that microbially-laden remains were four times less likely to be consumed by scavengers. This reduction in scavenging was related to the presence of multiple fatty acids including hexadecenoic acid, octadecenoic acid, and octadecanoic acid. Furthermore, these remains hosted a microbial community dominated by anaerobic bacteria from phyla Bacteroidetes and Firmicutes. In contrast, the scavenged remains hosted microbial communities dominated by aerobic bacteria from phyla Proteobacteria. These observations support the concept that putrefaction can be viewed as a defence strategy because putrefied remains are unattractive resources and can significantly reduce scavenger activity [93]. This is another intriguing example of competition with the postmortem food web.

Interactions between microbes and scavengers are strongly influenced by weather, climate, and elevation. DeVault et al. [94] observed scavengers feeding on 30% more remains in colder weather (5.8–17.0 °C) compared with warmer weather (22.6–27.8 °C). This difference is probably due to a temperature driven suppression of microbial and insect activity. Low temperature slows the activity of these organisms which increases the time required for them to reproduce and generate chemicals to repel scavengers. These observations indicate that scavenger-based estimates of TSD are significantly influenced by season.

Meng et al. [96] recently demonstrated that, like insects, vultures may be responsible for transporting microbes to/from decomposing remains. They collected microbial samples from vulture rectal swabs and observed microbial communities dominated by bacteria from phyla Firmicutes and Proteobacteria. Two species, *Clostridium perfringens* and *Peptostreptococcus russellii* represented more than 50% of these communities. Other bacteria found in all vulture samples included genera *Enterococcus*, *Peptoniphilus*, *Sphingomonas*, and *Sporacetigenium*. It is unknown how these microbe-scavenger interactions affect the estimation of TSD, but it appears that the activity of scavengers and microbes are strongly linked and represent another component of the complex postmortem food web.

Strengths and weaknesses of using microbial communities to estimate TSD

The greatest attribute of microbial communities in estimating the TSD is that they will always be present at a death scene or a scene of decomposition. Microbes will be present in any location that humans inhabit, and these humans will also bring their own microbial communities with them. This does not mean that microbes will always provide probative information, but at least they are always available for collection. This can't be said for many other types of temporal evidence, such as insects and mobile devices. This availability is a huge advantage because it allows an investigator to arrive at a scene prepared for their collection and storage. This preparation should not be a painstaking process because microbial communities are easy to collect, which is another advantage. The collection of microbial communities requires essentially the same swabbing technique for collecting human genetic material [97]. This is a huge advantage because it should translate to easy incorporation into the investigative workflow. In fact, the use of a double headed swab [24] could potentially save time by allowing an investigator to collect microbial and human DNA simultaneously.

The apparent convergence of postmortem microbial communities, regardless of host species is another huge advantage. Like the development of insect models for estimating TSD this convergence would allow for microbial models of TSD to be built using data from all types of decomposition studies, including actual death scenes, human decomposition research, and human analogue decomposition research. Drawing from these sources will result in larger datasets, which should provide more reliable estimates of TSD. In addition, using human analogue studies may result in the ability to estimate the TSD of nonhuman remains in cases of neglect and poaching that are often under-resourced areas of forensic investigation.

The above advantages refer to postmortem microbial communities collected from the remains themselves or objects immediately associated with decomposing remains, such as grave soil on/in which the remains are located.

However, it is also possible that antemortem microbial communities from commonly used objects and surfaces may also provide an estimate of TSD even if they are not in contact with the remains. This very new area of research would require us to identify the time at which microbial communities fade from these locations, which would then be used as a minimum TSD. Consider a future where research has shown that antemortem microbial communities fade from handheld objects and surfaces within 48 h of last contact [22,24]. The inability to sequence microbial communities from these objects may then indicate that the decedent is associated with a TSD $>$ 48 h. This is an exciting area of forensic microbiology that should expand in the near future.

Microbial communities also have several weaknesses when used to estimate TSD, many of which are practical in nature [81]. First, microbes are difficult to identify for many reasons. Many microbes look similar under microscopy so further testing is usually required to confirm the identity of microorganisms. This differs from the identification of many of the larger eukaryote decomposers like insects and scavengers that can be identified based on physical features observed with the naked eye. Furthermore, microbiome analysis is expensive, complicated, and time consuming. This process is similar to the analysis of human DNA in that it requires multiple personnel with training on advanced analytical equipment that generates sequences that can be used in conjunction with a microbial database [98]. Microbiome analysis can require several months, which may be problematic in some cases.

Another important weakness of microbial communities is that they are practically invisible. This can introduce difficulties when explaining microbial communities to non-microbiologists such as investigators, lawyers, judges, and juries. Microbial communities are not typically something that one would look at, for example, like a community of flies or vultures. The abstract nature of microbial communities can make them difficult for many people to understand. In this sense, microbes are similar to human DNA and blood alcohol evidence in that they are viewed as a data table or graph instead of actual tangible evidence, such as a bloodstain or a friction ridge pattern. This is not a weakness that precludes the successful communication of microbiological analysis, but it is important to consider when preparing to communicate microbiology to an audience of non-scientists.

Conclusions

Microbial communities are critical to the function of all ecosystems because they contribute to the decomposition of waste materials, maintenance of the atmosphere, and processing of fluids for the water cycle. These roles extend to death investigation as microbial communities contribute to the decomposition of remains, release of VOCs, and cycling of decomposition fluids. Thus, microbial communities are important to virtually every process associated with forensic taphonomy. Recent research has shown that microbial communities can be used to estimate TSD in two primary ways. A "milestone" approach provides a minimum or maximum TSD while a machine learning algorithm based on microbial succession can provide a range as narrow as ±2 days postmortem. These findings have poised forensic microbiology as one of the most rapidly developing and exciting areas of forensic science with significant potential for providing improved estimates of TSD. Like the microorganisms it studies, forensic microbiology may well be a ubiquitous component of medicolegal death investigation if these applications continue to develop at their current rate.

Acknowledgements

I kindly thank A. Belk, C. Carter, R. Carter, H. Deel, J. Metcalf, and K. Perrault for helpful discussions during the preparation of this manuscript.

References

[1] Woese CR, Kandler O, Wheelis ML. Towards a natural system of organisms: proposal for the domains Archaea, Bacteria, and Eucarya. Proc Natl Acad Sci USA 1990;87:4576–9.

[2] Metcalf JL, Xu ZZ, Weiss S, Lax S, Van Treuren W, Hyde ER, et al. Microbial community assembly and metabolic function during mammalian corpse decomposition. Science 2016;351:158–62.

[3] Carter DO, Junkins EN, Kodama WA. A primer on microbiology. In: Carter DO, Tomberlin JK, Benbow ME, Metcalf JL, editors. Forensic microbiology. Chichester, UK: John Wiley & Sons, Ltd.; 2017. p. 1–24.

[4] Metcalf JL, Xu ZZ, Bouslimani A, Dorrestein P, Carter DO, Knight R. Microbiome tools for forensic science. Trends Biotechnol 2017;35:814–23.

[5] Madigan M, Martinko J, Stahl D, Clark D. Brock biology of microorganisms. 13th ed. San Francisco (CA): Pearson Education, Inc.; 2012.

[6] Brown JW. Principles of microbial diversity. Washington (DC), USA: ASM Press; 2015.

[7] Dyer BD. A field guide to bacteria. Ithaca (NY), USA: Cornell University Press; 2003.

[8] Swanson M, Reguera G, Schaechter M, Neidhardt FC. Microbe. 2nd ed. Washington (DC), USA: ASM Press; 2016.

[9] Carter DO, Yellowlees D, Tibbett M. Cadaver decomposition in terrestrial ecosystems. Naturwissenschaften 2007;94:12–24.

[10] Di Piazza S, Zotti M, Barranco R, Cecchi G, Greco G, Ventura F. Post-mortem fungal colonization pattern during 6 weeks: two case studies. Forensic Sci Int 2018;289:e18–23.

[11] Ma Q, Fonseca A, Liu W, Fields AT, Pimsler ML, Spindola AF, et al. *Proteus mirabilis* interkingdom swarming signals attract blow flies. ISME J 2012;6:1356–66.

[12] Mesli V, Neut C, Hedouin V. Postmortem bacterial translocation. In: Carter DO, Tomberlin JK, Benbow ME, Metcalf JL, editors. Forensic microbiology. Chichester, UK: John Wiley & Sons, Ltd.; 2017. p. 192–211.

[13] Wells JD. A forensic entomological analysis can yield an estimate of postmortem interval, and not just a minimum postmortem interval: an explanation and illustration using a case. J Forensic Sci 2019;64:634–7.

[14] Metcalf JL, Parfrey LW, Gonzalez A, Lauber CL, Knights D, Ackermann G, et al. A microbial clock provides an accurate estimate of the postmortem interval in a mouse model system. eLife 2013:e01104. https://doi.org/10.7554/eLife/01104.

[15] Pechal JL, Crippen TL, Benbow ME, Tarone AM, Dowd S, Tomberlin JK. The potential use of bacterial community succession in forensics as described by high throughput metagenomic sequencing. Int J Leg Med 2014;128:193–205.

[16] Johnson HR, Trinidad DD, Guzman S, Khan Z, Parziale JV, DeBruyn JM, et al. A machine learning approach for using the postmortem skin microbiome to estimate the postmortem interval. PLoS One 2016;11. https://doi.org/10.1371/journal.pone.0167370.

[17] Javan GT, Finley SJ, Can I, Wilkinson JE, Hanson JD, Tarone AM. Human thanatomicrobiome succession and time since death. Sci Rep 2016;6. https://doi.org/10.1038/srep29598.

[18] DeBruyn JM, Hauther KA. Postmortem succession of gut microbial communities in deceased human subjects. PeerJ 2017;5. https://doi.org/10.7717/peerj.3437.

[19] Benbow ME, Lewis AJ, Tomberlin JK, Pechal JL. Seasonal necrophagous insect community assembly during vertebrate carrion decomposition. J Med Entomol 2013;50:440–50.

[20] Pechal JL, Crippen TL, Tarone AM, Lewis AJ, Tomberlin JK, Benbow ME. Microbial community functional change during vertebrate carrion decomposition. PLoS One 2013;8:1–11.

[21] Pechal JL, Schmidt CJ, Jordan HR, Benbow ME. Frozen: thawing and its effect on the postmortem microbiome in two pediatric cases. J Forensic Sci 2017;62:1399–405.

[22] Pechal JL, Schmidt CJ, Jordan HR, Benbow ME. A large-scale survey of the postmortem human microbiome, and its potential to provide insight into the living health condition. Sci Rep 2018;8:5724. https://doi.org/10.1038/s41598-018-23989-w.

[23] Hyde ER, Haarmann DP, Petrosino JF, Lynne AM, Bucheli SR. Initial insight into bacterial succession during human decomposition. Int J Leg Med 2015;129:661–71.

[24] Kodama WA, Xu ZZ, Metcalf JL, Song SJ, Harrison N, Knight R, et al. Trace evidence potential in postmortem skin microbiomes: from death scene to morgue. J Forensic Sci 2019;64:791–8.

[25] Iancu L, Dean DE, Purcarea C. Temperature influence on prevailing necrophagous Diptera and bacterial taxa with forensic implications for postmortem interval estimation: a review. J Med Entomol 2018. https://doi.org/10.1093/jme/tjy136.

[26] Hauther KA, Cobaugh KL, Jantz LM, Sparer TE, DeBruyn JM. Estimating time since death from postmortem human gut microbial communities. J Forensic Sci 2015;60:1234–40.

[27] Guo J, Fu X, Liao H, Hu Z, Long L, Yan W, et al. Potential use of bacterial community succession for estimating post-mortem interval as revealed by high-throughput sequencing. Sci Rep 2016;6. https://doi.org/10.1038/srep24197.

[28] Heimesaat MM, Boelke S, Fischer A, Haag L-M, Loddenkemper C, Kühl AA, et al. Comprehensive postmortem analyses of intestinal microbiota changes and bacterial translocation in human flora associated mice. PLoS One 2012;7. https://doi.org/10.1371/journal.pone.0040758.

[29] Hyde ER, Haarmann DP, Lynne AM, Bucheli SR, Petrosino JF. The living dead: bacterial community structure of a cadaver at the onset and end of the bloat stage of decomposition. PLoS One 2013;8. https://doi.org/10.1371/journal.pone.0077733.

[30] Iancu L, Carter DO, Junkins EN, Purcarea C. Using bacterial and necrophagous insect dynamics for post-mortem interval estimation during cold season: novel case study in Romania. Forensic Sci Int 2015;254.

[31] Pascual J, von Hoermann C, Rottler-Hoermann A-M, Nevo O, Geppert A, Sikorski J, et al. Function of bacterial community dynamics in the formation of cadaveric semiochemicals during *in situ* carcass decomposition. Environ Microbiol 2017;19:3310–22.

[32] Tuomisto S, Karhunen PJ, Vuento R, Aittoniemi J, Pessi T. Evaluation of postmortem bacterial migration using culturing and real-time quantitative PCR. J Forensic Sci 2013;58:911–6.

[33] Can I, Javan GT, Pozhitkov AE, Noble PA. Distinctive thanatomicrobiome signatures found in the blood and internal organs of humans. J Microbiol Methods 2014;106:1–7.

[34] Javan GT, Finley SJ, Miller J, Wilkinson JE. Cadaver thanatomicrobiome signatures: the ubiquitous nature of *Clostridium* species in human decomposition. Front Microbiol 2017;8. https://doi.org/10.3389/fmicb.2017.02096.

[35] Damann FE, Williams DE, Layton AC. Potential use of bacterial community succession in decaying human bone for estimating postmortem interval. J Forensic Sci 2015;60:844–50.

[36] Damann FE, Jans MME. Microbes, anthropology, and bones. In: Carter DO, Tomberlin JK, Benbow ME, Metcalf JL, editors. Forensic microbiology. Chichester, UK: John Wiley & Sons, Ltd.; 2017. p. 312–27.

[37] Finley SJ, Pechal JL, Benbow ME, Robertson BK, Javan GT. Microbial signatures of cadaver gravesoil during decomposition. Microb Ecol 2016;71:524–9.

[38] Singh B, Minick KJ, Strickland MS, Wickings KG, Crippen TL, Tarone AM, et al. Temporal and spatial impact of human cadaver decomposition on soil bacterial and arthropod community structure and function. Front Microbiol 2018;8:2616. https://doi.org/10.3389/fmicb.2017.02616.

[39] Szelecz I, Lösch S, Seppey CVW, Lara E, Singer D, Sorge F, et al. Comparative analysis of bones, mites, soil chemistry, nematodes and soil micro-eukaryotes from a suspected homicide to estimate the post-mortem interval. Sci Rep 2018;8:25. https://doi.org/10.1038/s41598-017-18179-z.

[40] Szelecz I, Fournier B, Seppey CVW, Amendt J, Mitchell EAD. Can soil testate amoebae be used for estimating the time since death? A field experiment in a deciduous forest. Forensic Sci Int 2014;236:90–8.

[41] Szelecz I, Sorge F, Seppey CVW, Mulot M, Steel H, Neilson R, et al. Effects of decomposing cadavers on soil nematode communities over a one-year period. Soil Biol Biochem 2016;103:405–16.

[42] Seppey CVW, Fournier B, Szelecz I, Singer D, Mitchell EAD, Lara E. Response of forest soil euglyphid testate amoebae (Rhizaria: Cercozoa) to pig cadavers assessed by high-throughput sequencing. Int J Leg Med 2016;130:551–62.

[43] Thomas TB, Finley SJ, Wilkinson JE, Wescott DJ, Gorski A, Javan GT. Postmortem microbial communities in burial soil layers of skeletonized humans. J Forensic Leg Med 2017;49:43–9.

[44] Wanner M, Betker E, Shimano S, Krawczynski R. Are soil testate amoebae and diatoms useful for forensics? Forensic Sci Int 2018;289:223–31.

[45] Lauber CL, Metcalf JL, Keepers K, Ackermann G, Carter DO, Knight R. Vertebrate decomposition is accelerated by soil microbes. Appl Environ Microbiol 2014;80(16).

[46] Olakanye AO, Nelson A, Komang Ralebitso-Senior T. A comparative *in situ* decomposition study using still born piglets and leaf litter from a deciduous forest. Forensic Sci Int 2017;276:85–92.

[47] Olakanye AO, Komang Ralebitso-Senior T. Soil metabarcoding identifies season indicators and differentiators of pig and *Agrostis/Festuca* spp. decomposition. Forensic Sci Int 2018;288:53–8.

[48] Howard GT, Duos B, Watson-Horzelski EJ. Characterization of the soil microbial community associated with the decomposition of a swine carcass. Int Biodeterior Biodegrad 2010;64(4):300–4.

[49] Moreno LI, Mills D, Fetscher J, John-Williams K, Meadows-Jantz L, McCord B. The application of amplicon length heterogeneity PCR (LH-PCR) for monitoring the dynamics of soil microbial communities associated with cadaver decomposition. J Microbiol Methods 2011;84:388–93.

[50] Cobaugh KL, Schaeffer SM, DeBruyn JM. Functional and structural succession of soil microbial communities below decomposing human cadavers. PLoS One 2015;10. https://doi.org/10.1371/journal.pone.0130201.

[51] Carter DO, Metcalf JL, Bibat A, Knight R. Seasonal variation of postmortem microbial communities. Forensic Sci Med Pathol 2015;11:202–7.

[52] Weiss S, Carter DO, Metcalf JL, Knight R. Carcass mass has little influence on the structure of gravesoil microbial communities. Int J Leg Med 2016;130:253–63.

[53] Chun LP, Miguel MJ, Junkins EN, Forbes SL, Carter DO. An initial investigation into the ecology of culturable aerobic postmortem bacteria. Sci Justice 2015;55:394–401.

[54] Weatherbee CR, Pechal JL, Benbow ME. The dynamic maggot mass microbiome. Ann Entomol Soc Am 2017;110(1):45–53.

[55] Gilbert JA, Blaser MJ, Caporaso JG, Jansson JK, Lynch SV, Knight R. Current understanding of the human microbiome. Nat Med 2018;24:392–400.

[56] Costello EK, Lauber CL, Hamady M, Fierer N, Gordon JI, Knight R. Bacterial community variation in human body habitats across space and time. Science 2009;326:1694–7.

[57] Wilkins D, Leung MHY, Lee PKH. Microbiota fingerprints lose individually identifying features over time. Microbiome 2017;5. https://doi.org/10.1186/s40168-016-0209-7.

[58] Ridgway EJ, Subramanian BM, Raza M. Clinical microbiology and virology in the context of the autopsy. In: Carter DO, Tomberlin JK, Benbow ME, Metcalf JL, editors. Forensic microbiology. Chichester, UK: John Wiley & Sons, Ltd.; 2017. p. 146–91.

[59] Palmiere C, Egger C, Prod'Hom G, Greub G. Bacterial translocation and sample contamination in postmortem microbiological analyses. J Forensic Sci 2016;61:367–74.

[60] Belk A, Xu ZZ, Carter DO, Lynne A, Bucheli S, Knight R, et al. Microbiome data accurately predicts the postmortem interval using random forest regression models. Genes 2018;9. https://doi.org/10.3390/genes9020104.

[61] Carter DO, Yellowlees D, Tibbett M. Temperature affects microbial decomposition of cadavers (*Rattus rattus*) in contrasting soils. Appl Soil Ecol 2008;40(1):129–37.

[62] Carter DO, Yellowlees D, Tibbett M. Moisture can be the dominant environmental parameter governing cadaver decomposition in soil. Forensic Sci Int 2010;200(1–3):60–6.

[63] Bexfield A, Nigam Y, Thomas S, Ratcliffe NA. Detection and partial characterisation of two antibacterial factors from the excretions/secretions of the medicinal maggot *Lucilia sericata* and their activity against methicillin-resistant *Staphylococcus aureus* (MRSA). Microb Infect 2004;6:1297–304.

[64] Casper JL. A handbook of the practice of forensic medicine, based upon personal experience. 3rd ed. London, UK: The New Sydenham Society; 1861.

[65] Kellerman GD, Waterman NG, Scharfenberger LF. Demonstration *in vitro* of postmortem bacterial transmigration. Am J Clin Pathol 1976;66:911–5.

[66] Lobmaier IV, Vege Å, Gaustad P, Rognum TO. Bacteriological investigation - significance of time lapse after death. Eur J Clin Microbiol Infect Dis 2009;28:1191–8.

[67] Yang SH, Ahn HK, Kim BS, Chang SS, Chung KY, Lee EM, et al. Comparison of bacterial communities in leachate from decomposing bovine carcasses. Asian Australas J Anim Sci 2017;30:1660–6.

[68] Maujean G, Guinet T, Fanton L, Malicier D. The interest of postmortem bacteriology in putrefied bodies. J Forensic Sci 2013;58:1069–70.

[69] Szelecz I, Koenig I, Seppey CVW, Le Bayon R-C, Mitchell EAD. Soil chemistry changes beneath decomposing cadavers over a one-year period. Forensic Sci Int 2018;286:155–65.

[70] Benninger LA, Carter DO, Forbes SL. The biochemical alteration of soil beneath a decomposing carcass. Forensic Sci Int 2008;180(2–3).

[71] Carter DO, Tibbett M. Taphonomic mycota: fungi with forensic potential. J Forensic Sci 2003;48:168–71.

[72] Chimutsa M, Olakanye AO, Thompson TJU, Komang Ralebitso-Senior T. Soil fungal community shift evaluation as a potential cadaver decomposition indicator. Forensic Sci Int 2015;257:155–9.

[73] Hitosugi M, Ishii K, Yaguchi T, Chigusa Y, Kurosu A, Kido M, et al. Fungi can be a useful forensic tool. Leg Med 2006;8:240–2.

[74] Cecilia TM, Noemi CM. The mycology as forensics tool. Adv Tech Biol Med 2017;5(226). https://doi.org/10.4172/2379-1764.1000226.

[75] Barron GL. Nematophagous fungi: *Rhopalomyces elegans*. Can J Bot 1973;51:2505–7.

[76] Bang C, Schmitz RA. Archaea associated with human surfaces: not to be underestimated. FEMS Microbiol Rev 2015;39:631–48.

[77] Kwon MJ, Yun S-T, Ham B, Lee J-H, Oh J-S, Jheong W-W. Impacts of leachates from livestock carcass burial and manure heap sites on groundwater geochemistry and microbial community structure. PLoS One 2017;12. https://doi.org/10.1371/journal.pone.0182579.

[78] Klonowski B, Rössler A, Gu X, Krawczynski R, Wiegleb G. Influence of a badger carcass on soil chemistry and Collembola. Acta Soc Zool Bohem 2015;79:235–41.

[79] Merritt RW, Snider R, de Jong JL, Benbow ME, Kimbirauskas RK, Kolar RE. Collembola from the grave: a cold case history involving arthropods 28 years after death. J Forensic Sci 2007;52:1359–61.

[80] Schlaghamerský J, Krawczynski R. Does carcass decomposition affect soil-dwelling enchytraeids? Soil Org 2015;87:91–100.

[81] Metcalf JL. Estimating the postmortem interval using microbes: knowledge gaps and hurdles. Forensic Sci Int Genet 2019;38:211–8.

[82] Anderson B, Meyer J, Carter DO. Dynamics of ninhydrin-reactive nitrogen and pH in gravesoil during the extended postmortem interval. J Forensic Sci 2013;58(5).

[83] Meyer J, Anderson B, Carter DO. Seasonal variation of carcass decomposition and gravesoil chemistry in a cold (Dfa) climate. J Forensic Sci 2013;58(5):1175–82.

[84] Vass AA, Bass WM, Wolt JD, Foss JE, Ammons JT. Time since death determinations of human cadavers using soil solution. J Forensic Sci 1992;37(5):1236–53.

[85] Verheggen F, Perrault KA, Megido RC, Dubois LM, Francis F, Haubruge E, et al. The odor of death: an overview of current knowledge on characterization and applications. Bioscience 2017;67:600–13.

[86] Eckert KE, Carter DO, Perrault KA. Sampling dynamics for volatile organic compounds using headspace solid-phase microextraction arrow for microbiological samples. Separations 2018;5(45). https://doi.org/10.3390/separations5030045.

[87] Tomberlin JK, Crippen TL, Tarone AM, Chaudhury MFB, Singh B, Cammack JA, et al. A review of bacterial interactions with blow flies (Diptera: Calliphoridae) of medical, veterinary, and forensic importance. Ann Entomol Soc Am 2017;110:19–36.

[88] Liu W, Longnecker M, Tarone AM, Tomberlin JK. Responses of *Lucilia sericata* (Diptera: Calliphoridae) to compounds from microbial decomposition of larval resources. Anim Behav 2016;115:217–25.

[89] Crooks ER, Bulling MT, Barnes KM. Microbial effects on the development of forensically important blow fly species. Forensic Sci Int 2016;266:185–90.

[90] Gupta AK, Dharne MS, Rangrez AY, Verma P, Ghate HV, Rohde M, et al. *Ignatzschineria indica* sp. nov. and *Ignatzschineria ureiclastica* sp. nov., isolated from adult flesh flies (Diptera: Sarcophagidae). Int J Syst Evol Microbiol 2011;61:1360–9.

[91] Richter S. Phoretic association between dauerjuveniles of *Rhabditis stammeri* (Rhabditidae) and life history stages of the burying beetle *Nicrophorus vespilloides* (Coleoptera: Silphidae). Nematologica 1993;39:346–55.

[92] Klippel WE, Synstelien JA. Rodents as taphonomic agents: bone gnawing by brown rats and gray squirrels. J Forensic Sci 2007;52(4):765–73.

[93] Beasley JC, Olson ZH, DeVault TL. Ecological role of vertebrate scavengers. In: Benbow ME, Tomberlin JK, Tarone AM, editors. Carrion ecology, evolution, and their applications. Boca Raton (FL), USA: CRC Press; 2015. p. 107–28.

[94] DeVault TL, Brisbin IL, Rhodes Jr OE. Factors influencing the acquisition of rodent carrion by vertebrate scavengers and decomposers. Can J Zool 2004;82:502–9.

[95] Burkepile DE, Parker JD, Woodson CB, Mills HJ, Kubanek J, Sobecky PA, et al. Chemically mediated competition between microbes and animals: microbes as consumers in food webs. Ecology 2006;87:2821–31.

[96] Meng X, Lu S, Yang J, Jin D, Wang X, Bai X, et al. Metataxonomics reveal vultures as a reservoir for *Clostridium perfringens*. Emerg Microb Infect 2017;6:e9.

[97] Pechal JL, Benbow ME, Crippen TL. Sampling methods and data generation. In: Carter DO, Tomberlin JK, Benbow ME, Metcalf JL, editors. Forensic microbiology. Chichester, UK: John Wiley & Sons, Ltd.; 2017. p. 72–93.

[98] Zhulin IB. Databases for microbiologists. J Bacteriol 2015;197:2458–67.

Chapter 7

The postmortem interval and skeletal remains

Alyce Cameron, Marc Oxenham
School of Archaeology and Anthropology, Australian National University, Canberra, ACT, Australia

Introduction

Determining the length of time between death and recovery of forensically relevant remains is a key issue for the forensic sciences. It has been well-established in the literature that determining an estimate of the postmortem interval (PMI) from skeletal remains is necessary for medico-legal investigations, though this is often a difficult task to achieve. There are well-established methods of determining the PMI for individuals recovered earlier in the postmortem period, especially prior to advanced decomposition of soft tissues (see Chapter 2, this volume). While still influenced by environmental and taphonomic factors, these methods have been extensively tested. Determining time since death (TSD) becomes more difficult the longer the postmortem period and the more advanced the decomposition of the remains.

This chapter focuses on methods of determining the PMI from skeletal remains which have not been covered in other chapters of this book. Attempts at determining the PMI or TSD from skeletonised remains is both varied and innovative. When assessing skeletal remains with an unknown PMI, one of the first concerns is to determine whether the remains are of 'forensic relevance' [1]. The time range for skeletal remains to be of forensic relevance is different in different countries and may even differ between jurisdictions within the same country. Swift [2] stats that approximately 75 years PMI was the cut-off date in the United Kingdom. This seems to be the general criterion used in published literature, though often criteria are shortened to post 1950 being classified as being 'forensically relevant' (e.g. Refs. [3,4]).

UV fluorescence

The use of ultra-violet (UV) fluorescence in assessing whether skeletal remains are of forensic interest was initially investigated by Knight and Lauder

Estimation of the Time since Death. https://doi.org/10.1016/B978-0-12-815731-2.00007-8

[5] and Facchini and Pettener [6] with subsequent work by Hoke et al. [7] and Swaraldahab and Christensen [8]. UV fluorescence of bone is possible due to the organic protein component of bone, made up mostly of collagen, which is responsible for the fluorescence properties of bone [8]. The principle behind using UV fluorescence to determine the PMI of skeletonised remains is that the proteins which cause the fluorescence will denature over time, and so the fluorescence properties of bone should also decrease over time.

The results of early studies [5,6] on UV fluorescence analysis indicated that fluorescence could be recorded in bone samples up to a period of 50–200 years after death. The results of Hoke et al. [7] into the viability of using UV fluorescence as a means of differentiating between historical and recent skeletal remains determined that solely using UV fluorescence is inappropriate. They found that at least 2% of recent bone (less than 60 years old) was falsely excluded from being of forensic interest based on UV fluorescence [7]. Despite this, there was a correlation between the PMI and fluorescence colour (either blue or yellow), but not with fluorescence intensity.

The results of Swaraldahab and Christensen's [8] study into using UV fluorescence on bone, also demonstrated that there was a correlation between fluorescence and the age of skeletal remains. Using four groups of skeletal remains (recent, semi-recent, historical and ancient), they [8] showed that there was a decrease in fluorescence with time.

Yoshino et al. [9] used UV fluorescence in conjunction with microradiography and electron microscopy to estimate TSD in skeletal remains. Postmortem changes in human compact bone were examined using the three methods. The study used 51 human bone samples which had a range of 0–15 years after death. Of the 51 bone samples, 33 were left in the open air, 14 were placed in soil, and four samples placed in the sea. All samples were taken from humeri near the neck of the bone. The relative intensity of UV fluorescence in the bone samples decreased with TSD, and the correlation coefficient was high ($r = -0.648$ in the open air and $r = -0.823$ in soil), though the error rate was approximately two years. No morphological changes were identified using micro-radiographic examination, except for one bone sample from the oldest sample group (15 years after death). The histological and microradiographic examination revealed no morphological changes in bones left in the open air for extended periods of time, except one from the 15 years since death group. For the bones left in the soil, vacuoles, which contained a honeycomb-like structure formed by smaller vacuoles, were found in the peripheral zone of the substantia compacta approximately five years after death, and in bones of six years or more the change extended to the mid-zone of the bones. For those samples left in the sea for four to five years, vacuoles were observed in the outer peripheral zone of the substantia compacta. The relative intensity of UV fluorescence in bones decreased with TSD, and the correlation coefficient between UV fluorescence and time was considerably high [9].

Sterzik et al. [10] conducted a further study testing the dating of forensically relevant skeletal remains using UV fluorescence and a new method which utilises a forensic portable light source with varying wavelengths and coloured filters (Lumatec Superlite 410). The 30 samples analysed had a PMI range of 1–49 years, with all samples displaying a proportion of blue fluorescent light (using UV light) and/or red fluorescent light (using a 490 nm wavelength with a dark red filter on the forensic light source) on the surface of the bone cross-section. The results of this study agreed with Hoke et al. [7], where there was a correlation between UV fluorescence colour and PMI. Sterzik et al. [10] stated that a combination of both methods provided the best results. The majority of the samples were accurately assessed as being less than 30 years PMI, or greater than 30 years PMI, though the margin of error was rather large (between 20% and 30% of samples were incorrectly dated) due to the smaller sample size.

UV fluorescence is a reasonable means of differentiating generally between skeletal remains which are more recent, and those which are older (i.e. over 100–200 years old). It is unlikely considering the results of earlier [5,6] and more recent research [7,8] that further differentiation of skeletal remains into absolute PMI time frames will be possible with UV fluorescence alone, though the study conducted by Sterzik et al. [10] raises the possibility.

Luminol and chemiluminescence

Luminol chemiluminescence has been trialed for estimating the PMI from skeletal remains [3,4,11–13]. Luminol methods are based on the reaction between luminol and hydrogen peroxide which is catalyzed by iron in hemoglobin found in fluids and tissues from bodies. This reaction results in a chemiluminescence light which can be measured by various means [12,14,15].

An experiment by Introna et al. [4] involved using the luminal test on five groups of 80 femora which had a known TSD: less than three years; 1015 years; 2535 years; 5060 years; and greater than 80 years. Samples consisted of bone powder taken from the inner compact bone at the femoral mid-shaft. The results demonstrated that there was a decrease in the chemiluminscence observed as the PMI of the femora increased. Femora with a PMI of one month to three years had an intense chemiluminescence observed after a few seconds; those with a PMI of 1015 years had a clear chemiluminescence that was visible to the naked eye in 80% of the sample; the femora with a PMI of 2535 years had a weaker chemiluminescence in 33% of the sample; the femora with a PMI of 5060 years had a faint reaction observed only in a single femur; and in none of the femora with a PMI of over 80 years was any chemiluminescence observed. Introna et al. [4] note that there is a possible quantitative relationship between the PMI and luminal chemiluminescence in powdered bone, but further tests need to be conducted on a wider sample of bones with a closer PMI range to establish statistical significance.

The results of Ramsthaler et al.'s [12] study took a different approach to Introna et al.'s [4], by dividing samples between recent (less than 100 years old) and non-recent (over 100 years old). This classification means that Ramsthaler et al.'s results are less useful when considering shorter PMIs. The results of the study do indicate that by using a luminol test and observing the reaction with bone, the remains can be placed in the correct categories of recent or non-recent with 88.7% accuracy. Creamer and Buck [11] also conducted a study similar to Ramsthaler et al. [12] and obtained similar results, with the luminol chemiluminescence intensities differing statistically between recent (less than 100 years old) and historical (greater than 100 years old) samples.

A further study by Ramsthaler et al. [13] tested and compared UV fluorescence and luminol chemiluminescence in estimating the PMI of skeletal remains, with two screening tests (Hexagon-OBTI test and Combur test) which are used to identify blood. The results of this study indicated that when skeletal remains had a negative chemiluminescence to the luminol test and reduced UV fluorescence, the remains could be excluded from being of forensic interest. However, the two screening tests are unsuitable for use with skeletal remains, as even tests on recent remains were negative.

Capella et al. [3] conducted a comparative study using luminol and the Oxford Histology Index (OHI) against radiocarbon dates of twenty skeletal remains of unknown age. The purpose of the study was to test whether luminol and the OHI could potentially be useful as pre-screening techniques to determine the PMI (as being either from before or after 1950) before undertaking radiocarbon analysis of skeletal remains. They found that the combination of luminol and the OHI were useful in identifying suspected modern (after 1950) skeletal remains, though further analysis was needed to test these preliminary results [3].

A recent study by Sarabia et al. [15] measured the degree of chemiluminescence of luminol in relative light units using a luminometer. This method differed from previous studies by using the luminometer to measure the chemiluminescence reaction caused by the luminol, resulting in an accurate and quantitative measurement. The study used 102 human femora with a range of PMI between 15 and 64 years. The results of the study indicated that this method of measuring the chemiluminescence reaction could determine whether bones were less than or greater than 20 years postmortem.

These studies indicate that the use of measuring a chemiluminescence reaction based on a luminol test is broadly useful in assessing the PMI of skeletal remains. Apart from Introna et al.'s [4] results, which indicated the usefulness of determining the PMI, there have been no other studies which have documented similar results. Further research, with larger samples, would be needed to test the technique and increase the accuracy.

Citrate content

At least 90% of citrate within the human body is located within bone. It is essential for important biomechanical properties of bone such as strength, stability and resistance to fracture [16]. Citrate content of bone was first researched in the 1940s and 1950s, however, interest in it decreased over the intervening decades following the mid-1970s [16,17]. Recently, measuring the citrate content within bone has been proposed and tested as a method of estimating the PMI from skeletal remains [17,18]. The use of citrate content as a means of estimating PMI was considered possible because it is not affected by age-at-death or biological sex of individuals, and the fact that it appeared to decrease in skeletal remains after death [17].

The first recent study to test citrate content for a correlation with the PMI was Schwarcz et al. [17]. Their study focused on testing whether the residual citrate content in bone samples could be used as an index of TSD. Four types of samples were used: fresh pig ribs which had been buried and then frozen at one month intervals ($n = 6$); rib samples of recently deceased individuals which had been stored in a laboratory ($n = 23$); samples from forensic cases ($n = 6$); and rib samples from deceased individuals which had been stored for several years ($n = 3$). Their results [17] demonstrated that the concentration of citrate in skeletal remains which had been subjected to different environmental conditions, remained constant for about four weeks, after which it decreased linearly as a function of log (time), although the rate of loss stopped with storage temperatures below 0°C. Moreover, citrate content has a maximum range of 100 years with the precision of its determination decreasing with age [17].

Kanz et al. [18] used Schwarcz et al.'s [17] method of determining the PMI based on quantification of the citrate content in bone. This study involved using temporal bones and femora from 20 individuals who had been buried in wooden coffins or in body bags. The study found there was a significant difference between the citrate content of temporal bones and femora from the same individuals if buried in body bags, but the differences were not significant between those buried in wooden coffins. The PMI was also underestimated when the femora were used to calculate PMI for samples from both treatments (wooden coffins or body bags), however, there was less citrate preserved in the temporal bones when compared to the femora. The authors concluded that using the femora for citrate-based PMI estimations is preferred, as the femora appear to be less affected by variations in environmental conditions. In terms of PMI estimates, Kanz et al. [18] stated that when using Schwarcz et al.'s [17] equation the accuracy of PMI determination was low.

One of the main factors in differences between studies of citrate content in bone, is in the processing and analytical techniques used. Several more recent studies have highlighted this problem and attempted to assess the variation seen in results concerning the amount of citrate able to be extracted from recent/fresh bone samples [14,19]. To date, these studies, while demonstrating potential for better sample processing and analytical techniques, have not managed to correct these problems. Furthermore, neither the original amount of citrate content in living or fresh bone has yet to be determined nor has enough data been compiled with which to determine the PMI. As this method relies on the measurement of citrate content remaining in bone samples after death, it is important to know the original amount in bone at death or any models based on residual citrate content will overestimate or underestimate the PMI [14,19].

DNA degradation

The use of DNA is widespread in forensic investigations, especially concerning identification of individuals (e.g. Ref. [20]). So far, the use of DNA in estimating the PMI of deceased individuals has been limited, especially for skeletal remains [21–25].

Kaiser et al. [24] examined DNA degradation in human bones which had a PMI between one and 7200 years. The bones were sourced from a range of cemeteries in Munich, Germany. For the analysis, cross-section samples from femora were separated into three sections of inner, middle and outer bone cortex, and the quantity of DNA was determined in each of the sections. The results of the study found that with DNA quantity there was a significant correlation between the region of bone and the amount of DNA present, but there was no correlation between the amount of DNA and the PMI. However, there was a correlation between DNA degradation into increasingly smaller fragments and the PMI. Kaiser et al. [24] concluded that this degradation was time-dependent and could potentially be used as a predictor of PMI in human bones from known environmental conditions.

In contrast, Alaeddini et al. [21,22] when exploring environmental effects on DNA preservation within bone over varying PMIs, did not find any correlation between DNA stability or fragmentation and PMI. They did conclude that DNA was affected by the type of environmental context in which the bone was placed, with conditions of ambient air temperature and freezing having little effect on the DNA stability, while shallow burial and high humidity conditions resulted in almost complete DNA degradation [21]. Moreover, postmortem alterations to DNA in bone can occur very soon after death [22].

Mundorff and Davoren [25] compiled a rank order of skeletal elements by likelihood of being able to extract useable DNA at varying PMIs. They concluded that small cancellous bones yielded more DNA than cortical bones, especially for advanced PMIs. Issues concerning sampling DNA from skeletal material were also the focus of Higgins et al.'s [23] study into which tooth components yielded the highest and least degraded DNA. They used 150 human third molars, buried for periods of zero, one, two, four, eight and sixteen months. It was found that even small variations in soil temperature (2 °C) influenced DNA yields from all types of dental tissues. Furthermore, they found that different types of DNA (nuclear and mitochondrial) was not evenly distributed through the teeth, and that each type degraded at different rates in different dental tissues.

Higgins et al.'s [23] study indicates that further research is required before DNA degradation rates become useful in determining the PMI. Further research needs to be undertaken, into the different skeletal elements and the quantity and quality of DNA able to be extracted from remains with varying PMIs. Larger sample sizes and different types of bone from different environmental contexts should also be considered during future research in order to more fully understand this potential method of estimating PMI from skeletal remains.

Vibrational spectroscopy

Vibrational spectroscopy measures the vibrations emitted from a sample when a broad source of radiation is applied. Infra-red (IR) and Raman spectroscopy (RS) both provide information on the molecular vibrations exhibited by a given sample. These technologies cause molecules to undergo changes in their vibrational energy state by subjecting them to excitation radiation. As there are differences between IR and RS in the transfer of energy to a molecule and the instrumentation used, the data acquired also has differing characteristics. IR and RS are complementary, and the molecular vibrational frequencies observed are nearly the same, but some vibrational band intensities differ [26]. Using IR or RS to study the PMI or TSD of skeletal remains is a relatively recent innovation.

IR is a useful tool in characterizing and identifying molecules within a sample and has been used for many different purposes in archaeological, forensic and medical research. IR has been used on archaeological materials, especially bone, for various purposes. The use of IR on archaeological bone samples has been used to identify whether diagenesis alters the characteristics of bone. The type of alterations researched include alterations to the bone mineral and carbonate contents and whether diagenesis affects analyses such as stable isotope reconstructions [27]. IR has also been extensively used in archaeological research when dealing with heated, burnt or cremated bone [28,29].

IR has been often used in medical research in three areas. First, examining the relationship between bone mineral changes with respect to biological age [30]. Second, the potential differences in bone mineral due to genetic differences [31]. Finally, the effect of osteoporosis and osteomalacia on bone mineral compositions [32,33]. There has also been research conducted into deconvoluting IR spectra peaks and identifying key peaks of interest [34,35].

The use of IR in forensic contexts have included using the technique to differentiate forensically relevant skeletal remains from archaeological remains [36,37], while the potential effects of burial on skeletal remains has also been examined [38]. When a sample is saturated with IR radiation, the molecules are excited to a higher vibrational state by directly absorbing the radiation. This higher vibration state is transmitted, and a given wavenumber calculated. The spectrum used to analyze these data is obtained by plotting the transmittance (absorbance) versus the IR wavenumber [26]. IR can provide information concerning the molecular structure of mineralised and non-mineralized connective tissues, such as bone. The wavelengths of IR absorption bands are characteristic of specific types of chemical bonds, and IR is often used to identify compounds [39].

IR spectra of bone can show the presence of major molecular compounds such as phosphate (from the mineral hydroxyapatite); carbonate; and Amide I, II and III [39]. IR is also useful in the study of bone and other biological specimens as it does not produce fluorescence, which can saturate the sample and make obtaining spectra to analyze difficult [40]. There are limited published studies which focus on using IR on bone within a forensic context. Nagy et al. [36], Patonai et al. [37] and Longato et al. [41] focused on using IR to differentiate between forensic and archaeological bone, while Howes et al. [38] used IR to examine any possible changes to the chemistry of bone as a result of burial in soil.

Nagy et al.'s [36] work illustrated the possibility of using IR to differentiate between archaeological and modern bone. They also employed chemical analyses of various non-pathological, tuberculosis and syphilis-infected bone samples from different burial environments using Fourier-transform Infra-Red spectroscopy (FT-IR) [36]. The aim of the research was to propose a new method of dating human skeletal remains using the crystallinity index and mineral carbonate as a means of distinction between recent and archaeological bone samples. The analysis also determined that there were significant differences in the crystallinity index and mineral carbonate of the infected bone samples compared with the healthy samples, even if the samples were from the same age period.

Patonai et al. [37] focused on developing a screening method using FT-IR and the crystallinity index and mineral carbonate to differentiate between paleoanthropological remains and recent forensic or clinical bone samples. Results demonstrated there were significant changes in the crystallinity index and mineral carbonate values between the forensic and archaeological skeletal samples, corroborating Nagy et al.'s [36] preliminary work suggesting it was possible to use IR to differentiate forensic and archaeological bone.

Longato et al. [41] also used IR, as well as micro-computed tomography and energy dispersive X-ray mapping to differentiate between archaeological and forensically relevant remains. Bone from an archaeological site covering a range of dates between 650 and 1260 years ago were compared against forensic remains with PMIs of 3, 25 and 70 years. Using the same crystallinity index and mineral carbonate indices as Patonai et al. [37], Longato et al. [41] determined that the forensic bone samples had more organic bands present in the IR spectra than the archaeological samples, in particular the CH-Aliphatic band around 2900–2700 cm^{-1}. Longato et al.'s [41] results were consistent with the results from Patonai et al.'s [37] study, where samples with a shorter PMI have a higher crystallinity index and mineral carbonate values than samples with longer PMIs.

Howes et al. [38] used IR to conduct an experimental study with pig carcasses to explore bone chemistry changes 3 and 23 months PMI. There was also a controlled laboratory experiment where ribs of cattle, sheep, and pigs with different pre-treatments (defleshed, fleshed, degreased and boiled) were buried in different types of soil (neutral, acidic and basic, loam, clay, silt, and sand) for up to eight months. The IR analyses of the bone used the crystallinity index, mineral carbonation and mineral content (phosphate to Amide I) indices. They found a decrease in the organic (Amide I) and carbonate contents and an increase in the crystallinity index over the period of the experiment. Regarding specific environments, the acidic soil had the most significant effect on the determination of burial time, with bone decomposition accelerating within an acidic soil environment. Howes et al. [38] noted that species type, pre-treatment of bones, soil pH, soil moisture content and temperature did not have any significant effects on the bone chemistry during burial and that their preliminary data indicated IR can potentially be used to estimate time since burial.

There has been some debate as to whether spectroscopic methods, like IR and RS, can distinguish between forensic and archaeological remains. Hochleitner et al. [42] noted that the peaks used to calculate the crystallinity index are actually at least five different peaks, and any correlation between these peaks cannot be simplified by the crystallinity formula. Hochleitner et al. [42] used forensic and archaeological samples to test the theory, demonstrating that even if samples were of a similar post-mortem age, the crystallinity index varied widely. Despite Hochleitner et al.'s [42] assertion, the results of this study are yet to be formally published.

Indeed, while the IR peaks at 605 and 565 cm^{-1} are likely to be caused by several different component bands (identified through utilizing curve fitting techniques), this is more useful in understanding the secondary structure of these peaks. There has been similar component band analysis undertaken on the Amide I peak [43], the various phosphate peaks [35,44], and carbonate peaks [34]. Identifying the secondary structures of these main components within bone does not make the indices based on them irrelevant. Instead, it adds another layer of analysis which makes it possible to identify more subtle changes within the component itself.

Unlike IR, Raman spectroscopy uses a visible-wavelength excitation source. As RS is based on scattering and IR on absorbance, RS facilitates smaller scale study and is not limited to either transparent or powered samples. Moreover, RS is not affected by water, facilitating a more diverse examination of various types of biological specimens [40]. In the past, RS used a green laser as the excitation source, which caused bone proteins to fluorescence and produced a higher background noise than the Raman signal. The development of near-RS using a deep red excitation source has eliminated most of the fluorescence and meant that bone does not need to be de-proteinated before study using RS [40].

RS is used extensively in forensic contexts for analyzing various samples such as hair, paints and inks, fibres, explosive materials, drugs, and identifying ivory and art forgery [45–51]. As with IR, RS is also used extensively in medical research. Some examples of studies include differences in bone related to biological age, the effect of fluoride treatment on bones and the composition of synthetic hydroxyapatites used in reconstruction surgeries as proxies for bone [52–54]. RS has also been used to assess the quality of stored food [55]. Also, like IR, RS on bone has seen many in-depth studies focusing on identifying and deconvulting carbonate and phosphate vibrational bands [56,57].

The employment of RS to estimate the PMI or time since burial has received limited attention [58,59]. Bertoluzza et al. [58] used Fourier-transform Raman Spectroscopy (FT-RS) on five ancient molar teeth and a modern deciduous canine tooth from an infant to explore if there were any differences between the inorganic and organic components over time. They used a ratio of 2941/960 cm^{-1} as being indicative of the organic to the inorganic component, with 960 cm^{-1} being the $\upsilon_1 PO_4^{3-}$ phosphate band and 2941 cm^{-1} being indicative of organic material remaining in the bone. The results suggested that the organic component is released in proportion to the burial period only from the enamel surface of the teeth and not from the dentine.

McLaughlin and Lednev [59] conducted an experiment using RS to study trends in the chemical composition of bones from a burial environment. They used sectioned turkey bone buried for intervals of between 12 and 62 days. These sections were analysed using RS and it was found that there were chemical changes in the bone due to soil bacteria which are time-dependent. McLaughlin and Lednev [59] found that the RS bands assigned to mineral vibrational modes (mainly the bands indicative of phosphate) were nearly identical, with minimal changes occurring over the duration of the burial period. However, there were changes in several of the organic bands, including the CH_2 regions, Amide I, NH and Amide III in the buried sections. A visual comparison of buried bones showed a consistent decrease in organic Raman bands with increasing burial time, the most noticeable being the broadening and diminishing of the Amide I band, also visible in the CH_2 region and NH band.

McLaughlin and Lednev [59] used peak area and discovered that between buried samples there was a high degree of correlation when integrated peak area ratios were plotted against burial duration. They reported that the best fit was on the peak area ratio of the $\upsilon_2 PO_4^{3-}$ (485–400 cm^{-1}) and CH_2

(3040−2810 cm^{-1}) region, which is indicative of the organic to inorganic ratio similar to that used by Bertoluzza et al. [58], but instead utilizing a different phosphate peak. The authors stated that this trend could be caused by enzymatic digestion of collagen via soil bacteria, though further study would be required to confirm this hypothesis.

Delannoy et al. [60] recently used RS as part of a study comparing the environmental effects on bone mass with the PMI. The study used defleshed human ribs placed in different environments including being buried or on the surface at controlled inside and outside locations for a period of 90 days. The moisture and temperature effects on bone mass were recorded over time. Though the spectroscopic data was only a small part of the overall study, the results indicated that within three months the Raman spectra displayed a 'flattening' of peaks associated with organic components within the bone. The study concluded that 30%−40% of bone mass is lost within 10 days, though the decreasing trend does continue in small amounts over the long term.

Creagh and Cameron [61] used IR and RS on a sample of kangaroo and pig remains which had been decomposing for intervals of four, eight, twelve, sixteen, twenty and twenty-four months. The results showed a decrease in the CH-aliphatic ratio as PMI advanced. Overall, the CH-aliphatic ratio reached a minimum value in the skeletal samples by eight months PMI. The study also showed that the PMI as measured by the CH-aliphatic ratio is species dependent, and that studies using human bone of known PMI is necessary if this method of determining the PMI from skeletal remains is to be of use.

Woess et al. [62] also tested the validity of estimating PMI from skeletal samples using spectroscopic methods. Peak ratios such as the mineral content ratio and the CH-aliphatic ratio were calculated from obtained reflection, attenuated total reflection (ATR) and RS. Six samples were used in the study: four forensic samples ranging from a PMI of 1 day, 3 years, 25 years and 85 years; and two archaeological samples from 650 to 870 years and 1030−1260 years. Results were similar to Creagh and Cameron [61], with the mineral content ratio increasing and the CH-aliphatic content (organic to mineral) ratio decreasing with time.

A recent article by Chikhani et al. [63] focused on determining the least destructive and most effective method of preparing bone samples for Raman spectroscopy. They looked at whether chemical bleaching or scraping reduced the fluorescence from bone samples during Raman spectroscopy analysis. The results demonstrated that scraping was more effective at reducing fluorescence than chemical bleaching.

IR and RS have been shown to have promise with regard to further research in the use of spectroscopic methods to estimate the PMI from skeletal remains. However, more research is necessary regarding spectroscopic methods in relation to human bone with known PMIs and taphonomic histories as most studies so far have used animal substitutes.

Microscopic methods

The microscopic analysis of bone involves many different techniques. The most prevalent employ bone thin sections and histological analysis. Histological analysis has been used extensively in assessing the degradation or diagenesis of bone, especially for archaeological specimens [64]. Histology has also been used archaeologically to estimate biological age [65]; and in species identification [66].

The advantage of histological techniques is that an analysis of the preservation of the microstructure is unable to be assessed by the macroscopic appearance alone [67]. During studies of diagenesis in archaeological contexts, there have been four pathways of bone diagenetic alteration identified: accelerated collagen hydrolysis; bioerosion; dissolution; and fossilization [68]. Some research has demonstrated that alteration to the microstructure of bone can begin early during the PMI [9,69,70].

Bell et al. [69] assessed the potential speed of post-mortem alteration to skeletal microstructures by examining 11 human skeletal specimens from different Canadian environmental contexts and time periods. The human material was taken from various environments including terrestrial, intertidal and lacustrine settings, and covered a time range of three months to 83 years from the time of death. The examination used backscattered electron imaging which provided information on microstructure and relative density. The results of Bell et al.'s [69] study has brought forward the time of known onset for post-mortem alteration of three morphological types of microstructural changes, the earliest of which occurred at three months post-mortem. Bell et al. [69] stated that the contribution of the depositing environment is shown to influence the microstructural and morphological type of post-mortem alterations. They hypothesized that microstructural changes to bone could occur within days of death as a result of endogenous bacterial migration to the skeleton. Further studies are needed to establish the earliest moment that such changes can occur before full skeletonisation. Although the results are interesting there are some reservations regarding the human specimens used, especially the comparability between different bones (e.g. the tibia, ribs, and teeth) and structures.

Histology has also been used to quantify the PMI of skeletal remains through the degradation of bone collagen [70]. In one study two limb bone samples from five pigs recovered at 2, 4, 6, 10 and 12-month intervals were embedded, and then stained using Sirius red/fast green, which is designed to stain collagenous proteins pink and non-collagenous proteins green. There was a decrease in the ratio of collagenous to non-collagenous protein concentrations over time.

The majority of microscopy utilized for bone surfaces focuses on identifying differences in surface morphology. This includes differentiating and characterizing trauma such as cut marks [71]; and differentiating fractures due to heating and fire alteration [72]. Studies utilizing microscopy to identify changes to bones surfaces over time are limited [73,74].

Rogers [74] used bone samples from pig femora and tibiae to conduct macroscopic (changes in colour and texture and adhering features such as fungi, plant or insect materials) and scanning electron microscope (SEM) analysis of bone samples. Part of the analysis was to assess the outer cortical bone in the samples. It was determined that there was a colour change in the cortical bone over time, though other macroscopic changes were not consistent. The SEM analysis was also inconclusive, and Rogers stated that post-depositional modifications to the surface of bone were of limited value for determining the PMI.

Raja [73] also examined cortical bone surfaces as a means of estimating the post-burial time of skeletal material. Testing included SEM, thermogravimetric analysis, pyrolysis gas chromatography-mass spectrometry, and x-ray diffraction. Of interest was the use of SEM. An environmental scanning electron microscope (ESEM) was used on rib bone samples buried at intervals of up to 18 months. The purpose of using the ESEM was to compare surface morphology between the samples and observe if there were changes in the porosity of the bone. Raja [73] identified that the surface of the bone changed as the post-burial time increased. The youngest samples of one to four months had smooth surfaces. Samples six months and older varied and were either smooth or rough. Striations were observed on the bone samples older than four months while samples older than eight months had shallow grooves present. All the pores identified in all samples were circular or relatively circular.

Raja [73] also measured the number of visible pores and found that while there was scatter in the data, the number of pores increased over post-burial time, and more than doubled after six months of burial. Raja [73] stated that it was possible to determine whether samples were 'younger' (less than six months post-burial) or 'older' (between 8 and 18 months post-burial) based on the surface conditions of rough or smooth surfaces and the number of pores observed on the bone surface.

The two studies which have used microscopic differences in the bone surface for estimating PMI have conflicting results. Rogers [74] concluded that there were few differences over time which were useful except for colour change, while Raja [73] noted that there were changes in the pores on the surface of bone, which tended to increase over time.

Weathering

There has been extensive research on the weathering of the surface of bone, with the chief focus being surface weathering of bone. Initially, research focused on broadening our knowledge regarding the manner in which fossil accumulations were formed [75,76]. From the 1990s onwards, bone weathering became of interest to forensic anthropologists who used the earlier archaeological and palaeoecological studies to make inferences about skeletal remains from the more recent past [77–80].

There have been many studies which have examined the weathering of bone using either actualistic experiments or long-term observational studies. The archaeological or palaeoecological studies compare results of research conducted in different environmental conditions with Behrensmeyer's [75] original weathering stages [81], while some of the forensic studies adapt Behrensmeyer's [75] stages to fit with their specific data [79]. Weathering has also been examined in order to understand the effect it would have on subsequent analyses involving isotopic analysis [82] and DNA extraction [83].

The physical process of bone weathering involves a loss of moisture and organic content with subsequent bleaching and cracking of the surface layers [75,84]. The characteristics of weathering by cracking and delamination slowly reduces the overall size and integrity of a bone. The cracks produced during the weathering process typically run parallel to the orientation of the osteons and follow the split-line orientation of the bone [85]. Miller [84] and Behrensmeyer [75] first outlined the physical process and sequences of subaerial bone weathering.

Behrensmeyer [75] developed a set of bone weathering stages during research in the Amboseli National Park, Kenya, for the purpose of better understanding fossil and archaeological bone assemblages. Weathering is defined by Behrensmeyer (75: 153) as being 'the process by which the original microscopic organic and inorganic components of a bone are separated from each other and destroyed by physical and chemical agents operating on the bone *in situ*, either on the surface or within the soil zone'. Behrensmeyer [75] states that the bones of recent mammals will exhibit distinctive weathering characteristics which can be related to the TSD and the local conditions of temperature, humidity and soil chemistry.

The changes caused by weathering were categorised by Behrensmeyer [75] into six stages (0–5), which are recognizable based on descriptive criteria of the bone surface. The time necessary to achieve each successive weathering stage was calibrated using known-age carcasses. The results of Behrensmeyer's [75] study indicated that most bone decomposes beyond recognition in 10–15 years and that the bones of animals under 100 kg (and juveniles) will weather more rapidly than adults or larger animals. Behrensmeyer stated that small-scale environmental factors had the greatest influence on the rate of weathering and distinctive characteristics. Behrensmeyer's [75] weathering stages have been tested in different environmental conditions [81,86] and the same weathering processes have been recorded.

Several studies indicate that the sequence of subaerial bone weathering is consistent with Behrensmeyer's [75] weathering stages [81,86]. This is despite the difference in the geographic and environmental contexts between the studies. A variety of environmental factors can contribute to the subaerial weathering on bone, including UV radiation [78,81,82,87,88]; moisture [75,81,84]; heating and cooling [89]; and freezing and thawing [90].

Bone weathering during burial has also been examined by White and Hannus [91], Ross and Cunningham [79] and Dunphy et al. [19]. White and Hannus [91] examined three excavated sites within South Dakota, USA. The aim of the study was to determine the mechanisms of chemical decomposition and preservation of bone in archaeological sites. As a comparison, modern cow bones (with a TSD of two years) were used. The study concluded that chemical weathering of bone at the South Dakota sites was probably initiated by acids created as micro-organisms decompose the collagen in bone. The authors described the bone weathering process as overlapping reactions controlled by water, acid, oxygen and calcium content in bone and soils.

Ross and Cunningham [79] conducted excavations and analysis of burials on the Isla de Coiba in Panama during summer 2003. The aim of the excavations was to identify several individuals believed to be part of the 'disappeared' people murdered by the Torrijos and Noriega military regimes. A specific decomposition and weathering timeline was developed for the Coiba micro-environment based on Behrensmeyer's [75] stages, adapted to the specific climate, and correlated by using two skeletons with known dates of death. The weathering timeline developed by Ross and Cunningham [79] for bones buried within a tropical environment, specifically Coiba, described the gradual deterioration of the buried bone over time. The timeline covered five stages where Stage 0 had a TSD of less than 10 years; Stage 1 a period of 10−15 years TSD; Stage 2 was between 15 and 20 years TSD; Stage 3 was 20−30 years TSD; and Stage 4 covered a TSD greater than 30 years. Ross and Cunningham [79] concluded that comparing weathering with the estimation of the PMI needed further specific geographic studies, but that weathering did not cease in buried remains in a tropical environment.

The study conducted by Dunphy et al. [19] focused on creating simulated environments, specifically soil type and temperature, through bioreactor chambers. The bioreactor chambers were tested using samples cut from fresh-frozen pig rib bones with fourteen different environmental conditions controlled over a 90-day period. The bone samples which had been buried inside the bioreactor chambers, were then assessed using weathering characteristics, such as colour of the bone; presence of bone marrow tissue; and reduced density (weight) and bone grease. Dunphy et al. [19] concluded that greater changes in bone weathering was seen in the samples from the bioreactors with different temperature regimes, and that differences in soil type did not impact the bone weathering over a 90-day period.

Environmental factors such as UV radiation, moisture, freeze-thaw cycles and temperature will affect the outer surface of the bone and the weathering process. Bone can also continue to undergo weathering changes when buried, which is caused by the acids within the burial soil [79,91]. Furthermore, Dunphy et al. [19] have demonstrated that temperature also impacts the weathering of bone when buried.

Research indicates that while the sequence of weathering is relatively consistent across different environments, the rate of weathering changes between environments. Behrensmeyer [75] assigned periods of time to her weathering stages, ranging from Weathering Stage 0 occurring up to one year since death to Weathering Stage 5 occurring 615 years since death. Tappen [81] noted during her study that the rate of weathering in two different Central African sites (a rainforest and a savannah) were both slower than Behrensmeyer's [75] reported ranges. Andrews and Cook [92] demonstrated that in the United Kingdom, there was no weathering occurring after eight years, while Fiorillo [93] noted Weathering Stage 5 being apparent at a site in Nebraska, USA, at eight years. Fernandez-Jalvo et al. [88] reported bones remaining on the ground surface for between 2 and 25 years displayed, at most, characteristics of Behrensmeyer's [75] weathering Stage 1, and that most bones displayed almost no subaerial weathering at all.

Despite the apparent discrepancies between rates of weathering in different environments, weathering is still noted as being of use in determining the PMI [80]. There have been several studies which have attempted to determine weathering rates for specific environments [78]. Janjua and Rogers [78] conducted an experiment observing 25 defleshed pig femora and metatarsals over 291 days (approximately nine months). The experiment's aim was to establish bone weathering patterns to help estimate TSD in Southern Ontario, Canada and to determine whether larger (femora) or smaller (metatarsals) bones would provide a more accurate TSD indicator using weathering stages. The weathering stages were developed based on several criteria: bleaching; the amount of periosteum and soft tissue; greasiness of the bone; and cracking and flaking of the cortical bone. The results of the study found that insects and climate affected the soft tissue decomposition, animal activity (scavengers) affected the bone weathering and the soft tissue decomposition, and microenvironment (such as soil type) caused variation in the bone weathering rates [78]. The authors developed four stages of bone weathering unique to the study environment. They also found that femora were more resilient and showed more weathering changes than the metatarsals. Janjua and Rogers [78] do not discuss it, but it is possible that the size of the femora, the higher bone density and thicker cortical bone of the femora have a bearing on the results.

Jaggers and Rogers [77] also used pig bone in studying the effects of soil environment on estimating the PMI using macroscopic analyses. They assessed 120 femora and tibiae over a period of two and five months for macroscopic changes such as colour, texture, amount of soft tissue, condition, some cracks, the length of the crack, and weight and hydration. The analyses, which focused on the outer surface of the bones, found that the macroscopic characteristics did not change over a period of five months, regardless of the burial soil environment.

Lyman and Fox [76] undertook a critical review of weathering stages and the use of such stages for determining the time between death and burial. The aim of the review was to critically rethink Behrensmeyer's [75] weathering stages in conjunction with bone assemblage formations, as there are too many variables which weathering stages cannot consider. They concluded that while bone weathering data does provide significant taphonomic information, it does not necessarily reflect the duration of bone assemblage formation. Lyman and Fox [76] stated that this is because there are many taphonomic factors which are involved in the formation of an assemblage of weathered bone, which cannot be factored in or controlled in the analyses of bone weathering data. Lyman and Fox [76] also raised the issue of exposure rates, and how the decomposition process from fresh to skeletonised bone influenced the weathering stages. Exposure rates are a very relevant point, and to date, no research or studies have been conducted which exclusively examine the rate of bone exposure.

McGregor [94] aimed to provide a quantifiable method of assessing TSD based on weathering from the surface of bone without damage. There were two components to the study, a field experiment and laboratory experiment. The field experiment took place in southern Western Australia, with pieces of long bones, ribs, short bones and skulls placed outside to weather for varying periods of time. The laboratory experiment consisted of heating the same types of skeletal elements in ovens at different temperatures to test the accumulated heat load of the materials. A descriptive classification system was used to categorize each skeletal element. McGregor [94] concluded that the cracking seen on ribs was the best assessment of TSD and weathering, in particular between six to nine months post-mortem.

While Behrensmeyer's [75] weathering stages are reliable over a range of different environments [81,86], differential environmental conditions affect the rate at which bone weathering occurs.

Other methods

There have been a range of other methods tested for estimating PMI from skeletal remains. Some of these methods include using thermos-gravimetric analysis [95]; residuals (e.g. lipids, triglycerides etc.) remaining in bone [96]; bacterial colonization within bone [97]; and botanical evidence [98].

Raja et al. [95] used thermos-gravimetric analysis (TGA) to examine pig bone specimens of various post-mortem ages. TGA is a method utilizing thermal analysis where changes in materials, both in physical and chemical properties, are measured as a function of increasing temperature or time. The study used pig rib bones ranging from three months to seven years PMI, which were buried 60 cm below the ground surface. Results indicated that there was a decrease in total bone mass with increasing PMI with the bone mass loss due to the decomposition of the organic components within the bone.

Raja et al. [95] stated that the results of the study showed that TGA could be a viable technique for estimating the PMI of forensic bone samples, although further research into this area has yet to occur.

Castellano et al. [96] presented the results of a previous study into estimating the TSD using bone residuals such as total lipids, triglycerides, cholesterol, free fatty acids, total proteins, zinc, manganese and phosphorus. While it was suggested that they could quantify proteins and triglycerides in determining the TSD of skeletal remains, no corroborating work has been carried out to date.

Damann et al. [97] conducted a preliminary study into using bacterial communities to estimate the PMI from skeletal remains. The study used 15 bone samples taken from ribs of deceased individuals. The individuals were classified as being either partially skeletonised, skeletonised or dry remains, with each classification having increasingly longer PMIs. They found that there was a subsequent shift in the bacterial communities within the bone samples depending on the PMI. The partially skeletonised remains had bacterial communities associated with the human gut, but the dry skeletal remains had bacterial communities that were closer to those of the surrounding soil. This study was preliminary, but the results are promising, and more research focused on using bacterial communities is required.

Cardoso et al. [98] used a case study to illustrate that botanical evidence is useful in helping to establish a minimum PMI. The case study involved the skeletal remains of an adult male whose skeleton showed the presence of green algae, bryophytes and shrub roots in and around the remains. The age of the shrub roots and bryophytes were estimated and it was concluded that the minimum TSD was three years, plus/minus several months through to a few years, depending on the state of the soft tissue decomposition of the remains (see Chapter 6, this volume).

Conclusions

Providing a reliable estimate of the PMI is an important part of forensic investigations concerning human remains and there has been a significant amount of research into the topic. This review of previous research has highlighted some of the different methods and techniques used, focusing on techniques for use with skeletonized remains.

There is clearly significant scope for further research in this area, especially in testing several techniques which so far have only been attempted on animal analogues. Many of these techniques, like infra-red and Raman spectroscopy, have shown potential in use on animal remains, and should be tested using human skeletal remains with known PMIs and, if possible, known taphonomic histories. Several techniques, such as luminol and chemiluminescence, show promise for quantitative rather than qualitative assessment; while recent studies into weathering of bone has demonstrated that weathering is closely aligned with environmental variables and any PMI based on weathering would have to be micro-environment specific.

Finally, although there has been extensive research into estimating the PMI of skeletal remains, no single method or technique has proven itself to be completely reliable with many techniques having large error margins. This is particularly the case for skeletal remains with shorter post-mortem periods (i.e. less than 10 years PMI).

References

[1] Schultz JJ. Determining the forensic significance of skeletal remains. In: Dirkmaat D, editor. A companion to forensic anthropology. 1st ed. Blackwell Publishing; 2012. p. 66–84.

[2] Swift B. The timing of death. In: Rutty GN, editor. The essentials of autopsy practice: current methods and modern trends. Springer; 2016. p. 189–214.

[3] Capella A, Gibelli D, Muccino E, Scarpulla V, Cerutti E, Caruso V, Sguazza E, Mazzarelli D, Cattaneo C. The comparative performance of PMI estimation in skeletal remains by three methods (C-14, luminol test and OHI): analysis of 20 cases. Int J Leg Med 2015:1–10.

[4] Introna F, Di Vella G, Campobasso CP. Determination of postmortem interval from old skeletal remains by image analysis of luminol test results. J Forensic Sci 1999;44:535–8.

[5] Knight B, Lauder I. Methods of dating skeletal remains. Hum Biol 1969;41:322–41. 1969.

[6] Facchini F, Pettener D. Chemical and physical methods in dating human skeletal remains. Am J Phys Anthropol 1977;47:65–70.

[7] Hoke N, Grigat A, Grupe G, Harbeck M. Reconsideration of bone postmortem interval estimation by UV-induced autofluorescence. Forensic Sci Int 2013;228. 176-e1.

[8] Swaraldahab MAH, Christensen AM. The effect of time on bone fluorescence: implications for using alternate light sources to search of skeletal remains. J Forensic Sci 2016;51:442–4.

[9] Yoshino M, Kimijima T, Miyasaka S, Sato J, Seta S. Microscopical study on estimation of time since death in skeletal remains. Forensic Sci Int 1991;49:143–58.

[10] Sterzik V, Jung T, Jellinghaus K, Bohnert M. Estimating the postmortem interval of human skeletal remains by analysing their optical behavior. Int J Leg Med 2016;130:1557–66. 2016.

[11] Creamer JI, Buck AM. The assaying of haemoglobin using luminol chemiluminescence and its application to the dating of human skeletal remains. J Biol Chem Lumin 2009;24:311–6.

[12] Ramsthaler F, Kreutz K, Zipp K, Verhoff MA. Dating skeletal remains with luminol-chemiluminescence. Validity, intra- and interobserver error. Forensic Sci Int 2009;187:47–50. 2009.

[13] Ramsthaler F, Ebach SC, Birngruber CG, Verhoff MA. Postmortem interval of skeletal remains through the detection of intraosseal hemin traces. A comparison of UV-fluorescence, luminol, Hexagon-OBTI, and Combur tests. Forensic Sci Int 2011;209:59–63.

[14] Froome C. Citrate content of bone: a potential measure of postmortem interval. In: National conference on undergraduate research; 2014. p. 1100–8.

[15] Sarabia J, Perez-Martinez C, Hernandez del Rincon JP, Luna A. Study of chemiluminescence measured by luminometry and its application in the estimation of postmortem interval of bone remains. Leg Med 2018;33:32–5.

[16] Costello LC, Chellaiah M, Zou J, Franklin RB, Reynolds MA. The status of citrate in the hydroxyapatite/collagen complex of bone; and its role in bone formation. J Regen Med Tissue Eng 2015;3:4.

[17] Schwarcz HP, Agur K, Jantz LM. A new method for determination of postmortem interval: citrate content of bone. J Forensic Sci 2010;55:1516–22.

[18] Kanz F, Reiter C, Risser DU. Citrate content of bone for time since death estimation: results from burials with different physical characteristics and known PMI. J Forensic Sci 2014;59:613–20.

[19] Dunphy MA, Weisensee KE, Mikhailova EA, Harman MK. Design and evaluation of a bioreactor with application to forensic burial environments. Forensic Sci Int 2015;257:242–51.

[20] Brenner CH, Weir BS. Issues and strategies in the DNA identification of World Trade Center victims. Theor Popul Biol 2003;63:173–8.

[21] Alaeddini R, Walsh SJ, Abbas A. Molecular studies of time- and environment- dependent effects on bone DNA survival. Aust J Forensic Sci 2010;42:211–20.

[22] Alaeddini R, Ahmadi M, Walsh SJ, Abbas A. Semi-quantitative PCR analysis of DNA degradation. Aust J Forensic Sci 2011;43:53–64.

[23] Higgins D, Rohrlach AB, Kaidonis J, Townsend G, Austin JJ. Differential Nuclear and Mitochondrial DNA preservation in post-mortem teeth with implications for forensic and ancient DNA studies. PLoS One 2015;10(5):e0126935.

[24] Kaiser C, Bachmeier B, Conrad C, Nerlich A, Bratzke H, Eisenmenger W, Peschel O. Molecular study of time dependent changes in DNA stability in soil buried skeletal residues. Forensic Sci Int 2008;177:32–6.

[25] Mundorff A, Davoren JM. Examination of DNA yield rates for different skeletal elements at increasing post mortem intervals. Forensic Sci Int 2014;8:55–63.

[26] Lin-Vien D, Colthup NB, Fateley WG, Grasselli JG. The handbook of infrared and Raman characteristic frequencies of organic molecules. San Diego: Academic Press; 1991.

[27] Wright LE, Schwarcz HP. Infrared and isotopic evidence for diagenesis of bone apatite at Dos Pilas, Guatemala: palaeodietary implications. J Archaeol Sci 1996;23:933–44.

[28] Squires KE, Thompson TJU, Islam M, Chamberlain A. The application of histomorphometry and Fourier transform infrared spectroscopy to the analysis of early Anglo-Saxon burned bone. J Archaeol Sci 2011;38:2399–409.

[29] Thompson TJU, Islam M, Piduru K, Marcel A. An investigation into the internal and external variables acting on crystallinity index using Fourier Transform Infrared Spectroscopy on unaltered and burned bone. Palaeogeogr Palaeoclimatol Palaeoecol 2011;299:168–74.

[30] Petra M, Anastassopoulou J, Theologis T, Theophanides T. Synchrotron micro-FT-IR spectroscopic evaluation of normal paediatric human bone. J Mol Struct 2005;733:101–10.

[31] Boskey AL, Young MR, Kilts T, Verdelis K. Variation in mineral properties in normal and mutant bones and teeth. Cells Tissue Organs 2005;181:144–53.

[32] Boskey AL. Assessment of bone mineral and matrix using backscatter electron imaging and FTIR imaging. Curr Osteoporos Rep 2006;4:71–5.

[33] Boskey A, Mendelsohn R. Infrared analysis of bone in health and disease. J Biomed Opt 2005;10(3). 031102-1 – 031102-9.

[34] Rey C, Collins B, Goehl T, Dickson IR, Glimcher MJ. The carbonate environment in bone mineral: a resolution-enhanced Fourier transform infrared spectroscopy study. Calcif Tissue Int 1989;45:157–64.

[35] Rey C, Shimizu M, Collins B, Glimcher MJ. Resolution-enhanced Fourier transform infrared spectroscopy study of the environment of phosphate ions in the early deposits of a solid phase of calcium-phosphate in bone and enamel, and their evolution with age. I: investigations in the v_4 PO_4 domain. Calcif Tissue Int 1990;46:384–94.

[36] Nagy G, Lorand T, Patonai Z, Montsko G, Bajnoczky I, Marcsik A, Mark L. Analysis of pathological and non-pathological human skeletal remains by FT-IR spectroscopy. Forensic Sci Int 2008;175:55–60.

[37] Patonai Z, Maasz G, Avar P, Schmidt J, Lorand T, Bajnoczky I, Mark L. Novel dating method to distinguish between forensic and archaeological human skeletal remains by bone mineralization indexes. Int J Leg Med 2013;127:529–33.

[38] Howes JM, Stuart BH, Thomas PA, Raja S, O'Brien C. An investigation of model forensic bone in soil environments studies using Infrared spectroscopy. J Forensic Sci 2012;57:1161–7.

[39] Boskey A, Camacho NP. FT-IR imaging of native and tissue-engineered bone and cartilage. Biomaterials 2007;28:2465–78.

[40] Carden A, Morris MD. Application of vibrational spectroscopy to the study of mineralized tissues (review). J Biomed Opt 2000;5:259–68.

[41] Longato S, Woss C, Hatzer-Grubwieser P, Bauer C, Parson W, Unterberger SH, Kuhn W, Pemberger N, Pallua AK, Recheis W, Lackner R, Stalder R, Pallua JD. Post-mortem interval estimation of human skeletal remains by micro-computed tomography, mid-infrared microscopic imaging and energy dispersive X-ray mapping. Anal Methods 2015;7:2917–27.

[42] Hochleitner R, Hoke N, Kaliwoda M, Fehr KT, Gunther A, Beck A, Reul A, Rott A, Harbeck M. Can spectroscopic methods distinguish forensic and archaeological human skeletal remains?. In: Conference on Raman and luminescence spectroscopy in the earth sciences CORALS-2013; 2013. p. 45–6.

[43] Chadefaux C, Le Ho A, Bellot-Gurlet L, Reiche I. Curve-fitting micro-ATR-FTIR studies of the amide I and II bands of type I collagen in archaeological bone materials. e-Preserv Sci 2009;6:129–37.

[44] Miller LM, Vairavamurthy V, Chance MR, Mendelsohn R, Paschalis EP, Betts F, Boskey AL. In situ analysis of mineral content and crystallinity in bone using infrared micro-spectroscopy of the v_4 PO_4^{3-} vibration. Biochim Biophys Acta 2001;1527:11–9.

[45] Kalasinsky KS. Forensic analysis of hair by Infrared spectroscopy. In: Chalmers JM, Edwards HGM, Hargreaves MD, editors. Infrared and Raman spectroscopy in forensic science. John Wiley & Sons; 2012. p. 111–20.

[46] Claybourn M, Ansell M. Using Raman Spectroscopy to solve crime: inks, questioned documents and fraud. Sci Justice 2000;40:261–71.

[47] Fredericks PM. Forensic analysis of fibres by vibrational spectroscopy. In: Chalmers JM, Edwards HGM, Hargreaves MD, editors. Infrared and Raman spectroscopy in forensic science. John Wiley & Sons; 2012. p. 153–69. 2010.

[48] Otieno-Alego V, Speers N. Counter terrorism and homeland security. In: Chalmers JM, Edwards HGM, Hargreaves MD, editors. Infrared and Raman spectroscopy in forensic science. John Wiley & Sons; 2012. p. 205–32.

[49] Izake EL. Forensic and homland security applications of modern portable Raman spectroscopy. Forensic Sci Int 2010;202:1–8.

[50] Hargreaves MD, Edwards HGM. Identification of ivory by concentional backscatter Raman and SORS. In: Chalmers JM, Edwards HGM, Hargreaves MD, editors. Infrared and Raman spectroscopy in forensic science. John Wiley & Sons; 2012. p. 447−54.

[51] Deneckere A, Vandenabeele P, Moens L. Vibrational spectroscopy as a tool for tracing art forgeries. In: Chalmers JM, Edwards HGM, Hargreaves MD, editors. Infrared and Raman spectroscopy in forensic science. John Wiley & Sons; 2012. p. 369−81.

[52] Ager JW, Nalla RK, Breeden KL, Ritchie RO. Deep-ultraviolet Raman spectroscopy study of the effect of aging on human cortical bone. J Biomed Opt 2005;10. 034012-1 − 034012-8.

[53] Freeman JJ, Wopenka B, Silva MJ, Pasteris JD. Raman spectroscopic detection of changes in bioapatite in mouse femora as a function of age and in vitro fluoride treatment. Calcif Tissue Int 2001;68:156−62.

[54] Smith R, Rehman I. Fourier transform Raman spectroscopic studies of human bone. J Mater Sci Mater Med 1995;5:775−8.

[55] Herrero AM. Raman spectroscopy a promising technique for quality assessment of meat and fish: a review. Food Chem 2008;107:1642−51.

[56] Awonusi A, Morris MD, Tecklenburg MMJ. Carbonate assignment and calibration in the Raman spectrum of apatite. Calcif Tissue Int 2007;81:46−52.

[57] Penel G, Delfosse C, Descamps M, Leroy G. Composition of bone and apatitic biomaterials as revealed by intravital Raman microspectroscopy. Bone 2005;36:893−901.

[58] Bertoluzza A, Brasili P, Castri L, Facchini F, Fagnano C, Tinti A. Preliminary results in dating human skeletal remains by Raman spectroscopy. J Raman Spectrosc 1997;28:185−8.

[59] McLaughlin G, Lednev IK. Potential application of Raman spectroscopy for determining burial duration of skeletal remains. Anal Bioanal Chem 2011;201:2511−8.

[60] Delannoy Y, Colard T, Le Garff E, Mesli V, Aubernon C, Penel G, Hedouin V, Gosset D. Effects of the environment on bone mass: a human taphonomic study. Leg Med 2016;20:61−7.

[61] Creagh D, Cameron A. Estimating the Post-Mortem Interval of skeletonized remains: the use of infrared spectroscopy and Raman spectro-microscopy. Radiat Phys Chem 2016;137:225−9. 2017.

[62] Woess C, Unterberger SH, Rolder C, Ritsch-Marte M, Pemberger N, Cemper-Klesslich J, Hatzer-Grubweiser P, Parson W, Paulla JD. Assessing various Infrared (IR) microscopic imaging techniques for post-mortem interval evaluation of human skeletal remains. PLoS One 2017;12:e0174552.

[63] Chikhani M, Wuhrer R, Green H. Optimization of sample preparation processes of bone material for Raman spectroscopy. J Forensic Sci 2018;63:1809−12.

[64] Turner-Walker G, Jans M. Reconstructing taphonomic histories using histological analysis. Palaeogeogr Palaeoclimatol Palaeoecol 2008;266:227−35.

[65] Harsányi L. Differential diagnosis of human and animal bone. In: Grupe G, Garland AN, editors. Histology of ancient human bone: methods and diagnosis. Berlin: Springer; 1993. p. 79−94.

[66] Hillier ML, Bell LS. Differentiating human bone from animal bone: a review of histological methods. J Forensic Sci 2007;52:249−63.

[67] Jans MME, Kars H, Nielsen-Marsh CM, Smith CI, Nord AG, Arthur P, Earl N. In Situ Preservation of archaeological bone: a histological study within a multidisciplinary approach. Archaeometry 2002;44:343−52.

[68] Nielsen-Marsh CM, Smith CI, Jans MME, Nord A, Kars H, Collins MJ. Bone diagenesis in the European Holocene II: taphonomic and environmental considerations. J Archaeol Sci 2007;34:1523−31.

[69] Bell LS, Skinner MF, Jones SJ. The speed of post mortem changes to the human skeleton and its taphonomic significance. Forensic Sci Int 1996;82:129–40.

[70] Boaks A, Siwek D, Mortazavi F. The temporal degradation of bone collagen: a histochemical approach. Forensic Sci Int 2014;240:104–10.

[71] Kooi RJ, Fairgrieve SI. SEM and stereomicroscopic analysis of cut marks in fresh and burned bone. J Forensic Sci 2013;58:452–8.

[72] Herrmann NP, Bennett JL. The differentiation of traumatic and head-related fractures in burned bone. J Forensic Sci 1999;44:461–9.

[73] Raja S. A study of bone chemistry in forensic applications [Ph.D. thesis]. Sydney: University of Technology; 2013.

[74] Rogers CJ. Dating death: forensic taphonomy and the postmortem interval [Ph.D. thesis]. University of Wolverhampton; 2010.

[75] Behrensmeyer AK. Taphonomic and ecological information form bone weathering. Paleobiology 1978;4:150–62.

[76] Lyman RL, Fox GL. A critical evaluation of bone weathering as an indication of bone assemblage formation. In: Haglund WD, Sorg MH, editors. Forensic taphonomy: the postmortem fate of human remains. CRC Press; 1997. p. 223–47.

[77] Jaggers KA, Rogers TL. The effects of soil environment on postmortem interval: a macroscopic analysis. J Forensic Sci 2009;54:1217–22.

[78] Janjua MA, Rogers TL. Bone weathering patterns of metatarsal vs. femur and the postmortem interval in Southern Ontario. Forensic Sci Int 2008;178:16–23.

[79] Ross AH, Cunningham SL. Time-since-death and bone weathering in a tropical environment. Forensic Sci Int 2011;204:126–33.

[80] Ubelaker DH. Taphonomic applications in forensic anthropology. In: Haglund WD, Sorg MH, editors. Forensic taphonomy: the postmortem fate of human remains. CRC Press; 1997. p. 77–90.

[81] Tappen M. Bone weathering in the tropical rain forest. J Archaeol Sci 1994;21:667–73.

[82] Koch PL, Behrensmeyer AK, Stott AW, Tuross N, Evershed RP, Fogel MI. The effects of weathering on the stable isotope composition of bones. Anc Biomol 2001;3:117–34.

[83] Misner LM, Halvorson AC, Dreier JL, Ubelaker DH, Foran DR. The correlation between skeletal weathering and DNA quality and quantity. J Forensic Sci 2009;54:822–8.

[84] Miller GJ. A Study of cuts, grooves, and other marks on recent and fossil bone: II Weathering cracks, fractures, splinters, and other similar natural phenomena. In: Swanson EW, editor. Lithic technology: making and using stone tools. Walter de Gruyter; 1975. p. 129–36.

[85] Tappen NC, Peske GR. Weathering cracks and split-line patterns in archaeological bone. Am Antiq 1970;35:383–6.

[86] Madgwick R, Mulville J. Investigating variation in the prevalence of weathering in faunal assemblages in the UK: a multivariate statistical approach. Int J Osteoarchaeol 2012;22:509–22.

[87] Andrews P, Whybrow P. Taphonomic observations on a camel skeleton in a desert environment in Abu Dhabi. Palaeontol Electron 2005;8:1–17.

[88] Fernandez-Jalvo Y, Andrews P, Pesquero D, Smith C, Marin-Monfort D, Sanchez B, Geigl E, Alonso A. Early bone diagenesis in temperate environments Part I: surface features and histology. Palaeogeogr Palaeoclimatol Palaeoecol 2010;288:62–81.

[89] Dupras TL, Schultz JJ. Taphonomic bone staining and color changes in forensic contexts. In: Pokines JT, Symes SA, editors. Manual of forensic taphonomy. CRC Press; 2014. p. 315–40.

[90] Pilloud MA, Megyesi MS, Truffer M, Congram D. The taphonomy of human remains in a glacial environment. Forensic Sci Int 2016;261. 161-e1.

[91] White EM, Hannus LA. Chemical weathering of bone in archaeological soils. Am Antiq 1983;48:316–22.

[92] Andrews P, Cook J. Natural Modifications to bones in a temperate setting. Man 1985;20:675–91.

[93] Fiorillo AR. An experimental study of trampling: implications for the fossil record. In: Bonnichsen R, Sorg MH, editors. Bone modification. Center for the Study of the First Americans; 1989. p. 61–71.

[94] McGregor M. The influence of heating and weathering on the surface appearance of bone [Masters thesis]. The University of Western Australia; 2011.

[95] Raja S, Thomas PS, Stuart BH, Guerbois JP, O'Brien C. The estimation of pig bone for forensic application using thermogravimetric analysis. J Therm Anal Calorim 2009;98:173–6.

[96] Castellano MA, Villanueva EC, von Frenckel R. Estimating the date of bone remains: a multivariate study. J Forensic Sci 1984;29:527–34. 1984.

[97] Damann FE, Williams DE, Layton AC. Potential use of bacterial community succession in decaying human bone for estimating postmortem interval. J Forensic Sci 2015;60:844–50.

[98] Cardoso HFV, Santos A, Dias R, Garcia C, Pinto M, Sergio C, Magalhaes T. Establishing a minimum postmortem interval of human remains in an advanced state of skeletonization using the growth rate of bryophytes and plant roots. Int J Leg Med 2010;124:451–6.

Chapter 8

Estimation of the TSD in an aquatic environment

Felicity Gilbert, Marc Oxenham
School of Archaeology and Anthropology, Australian National University, Canberra, ACT, Australia

Introduction

According to the World Health Organisation, there are an estimated 372 000 annual drowning deaths worldwide [1]. This figure does not include those deaths found to be the result of homicide, suicide, and natural causes in water environments, hypothermia, misadventure (non-drowning), or animal attack.

Aquatic environments are many and varied, and in terms of their biological, chemical, and physical properties, all are unique. Human remains found in any given water system will have been subject to the distinct, and often changing, conditions these properties produce. The decomposition process, and the movement of remains, will be specific to the particular aquatic environment a body is recovered from.

Significant to any medicolegal investigation is the determination of Time Since Death (TSD) or Postmortem Interval (PMI). As TSD has the potential to contribute to identification of a body, and to establishing the circumstances of death, it is an essential (indeed, sometimes pivotal) factor in any investigation. Extensive research has been conducted into TSD in terrestrial environments (see especially Chapters 2–5, this volume). This research has led to the development of various methods (such as the succession of corpse-colonising insects and their specific life stages) that are recognised as accurate indicators of TSD [2]. Currently, the methods used to assess TSD in aquatic environments lack the same level of precision.

Until recently, the dominant school of thought was that the decomposition sequence in aquatic environments closely resembled that of terrestrial environments, only at a slower rate. As Haglund explained, "In temperate climates, a general rule of thumb is that decomposition for one week in air is equivalent to decomposition for two weeks in water" [3: 29]. While this 'rule of thumb' has some value as a vague guide, in estimates of TSD it is far from exact. Consequently, research into aquatic decomposition has frequently applied

Estimation of the Time since Death. https://doi.org/10.1016/B978-0-12-815731-2.00008-X

terrestrially derived methods, expecting to receive the same positive results but often unable to replicate the same level of precision.

With the increase in research conducted over the past few decades, it has become clear that remains found in aqueous environments decompose in a different manner to those found in terrestrial environments as they are exposed to very different agents of destruction, particularly those that are submerged for long periods of time [4–6]. Despite this, the process of decomposition in aquatic environments is still poorly understood and very few longitudinal experiments have been attempted.

The ability to reconstruct the sequence of decomposition requires an intimate knowledge of the environment of deposition. In aquatic contexts the number of variables that may affect this sequence are extensive. The decomposition process in aquatic environments will be affected by water temperature as well as ambient temperatures in the given environment. It is also affected by several other variables that are not considerations in a terrestrial environment, such as salinity, water acidity, and time and extent of submergence.

This chapter provides an overview of the processes involved in the decomposition of remains in aquatic environments. It will discuss the basic process and explore variables that are unique to an aquatic environment. It will then give an overview of research that has been conducted on estimating the Time Since Death (TSD) of remains found in aquatic environments.

The process of decomposition in aquatic environments

Autolysis

Within a few minutes from the moment of death, the decomposition process begins. This consists of two initially parallel processes known as Autolysis and Putrefaction. Cells are deprived of oxygen and begin to die off and rupture releasing fluids in the process known as Autolysis [7]. Autolysis enables several gross morphological processes that present in a body soon after death in the early period of decomposition including; Algor Mortis, Livor Mortis and Rigor Mortis. The onset and rate of all these are affected by extrinsic and intrinsic factors.

Algor Mortis refers to the cooling of a body after death to surrounding temperatures. Immediately after death the body maintains a constant temperature or 'temperature plateau' for a period of time as a steady temperature state develops between the core and the surface of the body. This will generally last a few hours but is variable and dependant on the temperature of the environment and the initial body temperature. After this initial phase the body will cool at a relatively linear rate until it reaches ambient temperature [8].

This rate of cooling is determined by the temperature of the body and its surrounding environment and the difference between the two. Factors such as the presence or absence of clothing, body size and pathology and the type of environment all affect the cooling rate and contribute to variability between remains. Measurement of the Algor Mortis process is generally the most accurate PMI indicator for the first 24 h after death prior to the body reaching ambient temperature (see Chapter 2, this volume) but variability does exist and a large amount of research has and continues to be conducted to increase the accuracy of quantifying body cooling rates after death. For examples see Refs. [9–12].

While research has been limited, the cooling rate of a body immersed in an aquatic environment has often been found to occur more rapidly than in terrestrial environments but follows a similar curve largely due to the high thermal conductivity of water [12]. The normal temperature of a human body (37°C) is generally higher than that of a body of water. The body will cool rapidly to the surrounding temperature but then slow considerably once it meets equilibrium. Several confounding variables such as water flow, the presence or absence of clothing and floating behaviour may dramatically affect the cooling rates and PMI estimations using standard techniques compared with those in terrestrial environments [12].

Karhunen et al. [13] tested the reliability of five commonly used temperature-based PMI methods on two bodies (suspected homicides) found in similar cold water environments with known post mortem intervals. The techniques applied included Henssge's temperature–time of death nomogram, Triple-exponential formula (TEF) method by Al Alousi et al. and James and Knight's method (which takes into account environmental correction factors). The authors found that overall, Henssge's nomogram method with correction factors provided the most accurate results. However, the authors cautioned the use of temperature-based methods on bodies found in water without detailed knowledge of the environment and recommended that further research was needed using experimental studies and the close examination of case studies. The application of temperature-based methods in real case scenarios in water environments is not often reported [13] and their validity remains unclear, particularly for cases with a PMI more than 24 h.

Once the heart ceases to beat and blood no longer circulates, blood will pool in the lower parts of the body in a process known as Livor Mortis or Postmortem Hypostasis. This is caused by the gravitational settling of the red blood cells and presents as a pink-blue discoloration at the lower points of the body and becomes fixed until putrefaction begins. The appearance of Livor Mortis will differ from body to body as the distinct patterning will depend on the surface the body is in contact with and the body's physical position. Some surfaces will prevent pooling as a result of surface compression, which can also be caused by the presence of tight clothing [8].

Livor Mortis has been thought to be useful as a PMI indicator in the early stages of decomposition, with a large percentage of research focusing on quantifying colour and luminance changes [14,15]. However, several factors need to be taken into account such as temperature, environment and condition of the body and a considerable variability exists in the appearance and fixation rate as a PMI indicator [16]. Once putrefactive colour changes begin, Livor mortis becomes difficult to identify, is generally fixed by this stage and will not progress to enable establishment of later PMI.

In remains found in water, Livor Mortis may not present at all. Factors such as water temperature, body movement and water pressure may prevent or delay the characteristic discoloration [8]. When Livor Mortis does present on a body found in water, its location on the body depends on the position and movement of the body in its environment. As a human body generally floats in a face and limb down position, discoloration is more likely to be found on the face and limbs and the upper parts of the chest [17].

Rigor Mortis, in simple terms, is the contraction (proceeded by a relaxation) of the muscles of the body after death through chemical changes in the muscles. The initial onset and time of Rigor Mortis is highly variable and is dependent on environmental temperature, individual muscle mass, body temperature and activity prior to death [8]. In warm environments the putrefaction process may progress extensively enough early on and displace the Rigor process completely, whereas in cool environments the onset may be delayed.

Rigor Mortis will occur in remains in aquatic environments but will also be subject to the same variability of the above mentioned intrinsic and extrinsic factors. On the one hand, the generally lower temperatures in aquatic environments may impede the development of rigor. On the other, the potential muscle spasms or physical exertion that may occur if the victim drowned could accelerate the onset and lengthen its duration when compared to terrestrial environments [17]. Despite many investigations, inconsistency in the Rigor Mortis process makes it fairly unreliable as a PMI indicator, particularly in aquatic environments.

Putrefaction

Putrefaction is the destruction of soft tissues by bacterial action. Anaerobic Bacteria are released as a result of autolysis and multiply rapidly, spreading throughout the entire body [8]. These microorganisms are responsible for the destruction of soft tissue, breaking it down into putrefactive gases, liquids and acids [7]. The early process of putrefaction is characterised by gross visible changes such as green discoloration of the abdomen and putrid odour formation contributed to through the production of gases such as methane and hydrogen sulphide. As these gases accumulate in the body tissues, the body will increasingly bloat as putrefaction progresses. Unless the conditions favour preservation putrefaction will continue, resulting in the liquefaction and eventual destruction of all soft tissue with subsequent skeletonisation.

Several extrinsic variables such as temperature, environment and insect activity as well as intrinsic factors such as body size and pathology all affect the rate and sequence of the putrefactive process. A body decomposing in an aquatic environment goes through the same basic biological process as in terrestrial environments but is exposed to its own unique extrinsic variables that differ significantly to those found on land.

One early putrefactive change that is specific to water environments, occurring usually after only a few hours, is the wrinkling and whitening of skin on hands and feet due to water exposure and absorption commonly known as 'washerwoman's skin'. As time in the water increases, the skin on the hands and feet starts to separate. With prolonged immersion, the upper epidermal layer of skin will progressively loosen and eventually slip off the underlying dermal layer. This is often referred to as gloving due to its glove or stocking like appearance. The speed at which this process occurs is highly dependent on water temperature and has been found to present earlier in warmer water [18,19] but large variation exists in the time sequence between individuals in an aquatic environment [17].

The internal and external changes brought on by autolysis occur quickly and while variable, are in many cases easily recognised on a body in the early post-mortem period. Once the process of putrefaction begins to change the physical appearance of a body, estimates of PMI becomes increasingly challenging as the process does not necessarily follow a set progression and is radically affected by extrinsic variables.

Skeletonisation/disarticulation

Soft tissue loss, in the absence of preservation, will result in skeletonisation and subsequent disarticulation. Over time the structure of the bone will break down further through the process of diagenesis, which refers to the physical, chemical and microbiological changes that take place (see Chapter 7, this volume). The physical appearance of bone in water environments may be altered and its integrity compromised by multiple taphonomic agents, such as those caused by aquatic organisms in the form of encrustation (growth of organisms on the bone) and bioerosion (corrosion through boring or grazing by organisms). Or through physical or chemical interactions with the surrounding environment in the form of abrasion through movement or chemical changes/differences in the water causing dissolution [20]. These agents have the potential to change the morphological appearance of the bone and could be misinterpreted as being in the aquatic environment for longer periods of time than is accurate. A clear knowledge of the potential taphonomic agents in the specific aquatic environment is then essential to avoid misinterpretation.

Haglund [21] described a general disarticulation sequence in aquatic environments as occurring first with the bones of the hands and wrists, feet and ankles, and the mandible and cranium. Then followed the lower legs and upper arms, while sections of the trunk as well as the pelvic girdle were the last to disarticulate. However, this sequence may be altered by the different taphonomic agents described above as well as differences in currents, tidal fluctuations and wave action in the given environment and even body coverings that could preserve soft tissues and prevent disarticulation.

Preservation

Depending on the particular aqueous post-mortem environment and certain conditions, a body's soft tissues may be preserved in the form of either Mummification or Adipocere formation, slowing or halting the decomposition process. Mummification usually occurs in an environment with dry heat and low humidity. The remaining tissue and organs shrivel through dehydration causing skin to become leathery and cling to the skeleton. Mummification is not common in aquatic environments but may still occur on the parts of the body that are continually on the surface and exposed to air, desiccating the skin, giving it a mummified appearance. Haglund [21] reported a body displaying mummification of the anterior thorax that had been floating above the water line and exposed to sun and wind for enough time (PMI unknown) to cause this type of preservation. However, the remainder of the body that was below the water line did not present with signs of mummification. If a body sinks at any stage the tissue will re-hydrate but still display discoloration indicative of desiccation, which may indicate to investigators that the body has spent time floating on the surface. To our knowledge no documented research specifically on mummification in aquatic environments or as a PMI indicator has been conducted.

Adipocere, is a decomposition product which forms through the hydrolysis and hydrogenation of the body's neutral fats converting into fatty acids [22]. It can vary in its appearance and consistency, from white to more grey in colour and appears as a soft, greasy wax like substance to a crumbly, flaky or even hard consistency. Adipocere is common in damp, anaerobic environments but can form in a variety of environments both terrestrial and aquatic. It can inhibit bacterial growth and the process of decomposition resulting in varying levels of preservation.

Adipocere in aquatic environments can start to form early in the decomposition process but has also been found to be highly variable. Using pig cadavers as analogues Yan et al. [23] reported initial formation only a few hours after death. In a cool freshwater environment Forbes et al. [24] described early formation at around one month. In bodies recovered from a shipwreck at approximate depths of 65–85 m in a cold marine environment Kahana et al. [6] found focal adipocere formation after 38 days and Dumser and Turkay [25] report formation after approximately 3 months on a body also found in a shipwreck but at a much greater depth (540–580 m). Once adipocere has formed on a body it can remain for extensive periods of time if the environmental conditions do not foster eventual breakdown. Makristathis et al. [26] analysed the fatty acid composition of tissue specimens in the remains of the Tyrolean Iceman which is estimated to be approximately 5000 years old and found signs of adipocere formation and mummification.

Numerous attempts have been made to quantify the process of Adipocere formation as a PMI indicator [5,6,27,28] but this is a very environment specific process and large variability exists. For example, O'Brien and Kuehner [28] detailed observations over a three-month period of the adipocere formation on submerged human cadavers in order to determine if there was any correlation with the PMI. They found that temperature is the major determining factor in adipocere formation and they describe what they call the 'Goldilocks Phenomenon', meaning that adipocere formation is more likely when conditions are 'just right' but also concede that adipocere can form in almost any environment, making it difficult to apply to TSD estimates. This conclusion is echoed by Haglund & Sorg [20], who believe that adipocere as an indicator of PMI is unreliable as its formation is highly variable and dependant on the environment of submersion, the physical attributes of the remains and the presence of clothing, making any use of its formation to determine TSD very difficult to quantify to any degree of accuracy.

Variables unique to an aquatic environment

Generalisations about the process of decomposition can be made but without consideration of the environment of deposition they cannot be adjusted to suit the particular environment or quantified to any degree of accuracy. Water as an environment encompasses many different variables that will affect the process of decomposition.

Flotation/fluvial transportation

The way in which human remains interact with an aquatic environment will affect the process of decomposition. Variables such as depth, temperature, currents and flow patterns, water chemistry and substrate type all influence the movement of a body and the progression of decomposition. Due to the multiple variables involved, there is considerable disagreement in the literature regarding the typical behaviour of a dead human body when submerged in water.

Using data on 98 males from a previous study, Donoghue and Minnigerode [29] sought to determine if different oxygen lung capacities affected floating behaviour. They found that at full lung capacity all bodies floated but at a residual capacity (the approximate lung volume of a dead body) the vast majority sank. With the accumulation of putrefactive gases, the buoyancy of a body increases as the specific gravity of the body decreases and if water pressure allows, will surface. Once the remains have surfaced, they will continue to float until the putrefactive gases subside and they will gradually sink.

The depth of water will affect the likelihood of floatation. The deeper a body sinks, the amount of water pressure increases on the body and it may never resurface regardless of the level of buoyancy internally produced by putrefactive gases. In an experiment using a 26 kg pig euthanized by electrocution and placed in a marine environment, Anderson [30] observed that the pig did not re-float. The pig was submerged 94 m and tethered to the bottom to prevent it from being removed by currents or scavengers. The author states that there were few water currents, poorly oxygenated water and temperatures ranged from 9.5 to 9.8 °C. At this depth the pig would also be subjected to approximately 9.4 (Boyles Law) atmospheres of pressure. These variables would make floatation unlikely and according to Teather [31], it would be rare for a body at depths of 60 m or more to re-float.

Many controlled experiments in aquatic decomposition have forced submergence in their test models e.g. Refs. [32,33]. While this has enabled detailed data to be produced on submerged remains, it has not taken into account the floating behaviour of corpses and the different agents of destruction that a body is exposed to above the water line. In a specific scenario, for example of homicide where the perpetrators weigh the body down to prevent detection, or the body is snagged on underwater debris, then this completely submerged type of experiment may prove useful. However, an unhindered human body rarely remains submerged and will be exposed to the surface at some point [31].

As the specific gravity of a human body as a ratio of density to water is quite similar, any added weight or buoyancy will affect the way a body behaves. Clothing may trap air adding buoyancy whereas any attached weights on a body may decrease buoyancy. It has also been found that body fat ratio may have some effect on buoyancy [29]. While fresh water has a lower density than saltwater, a human body will still float but is more likely to float in saltwater environments. Salinity can retard bacterial action, slowing the decomposition rate but may also increase buoyancy exposing more of the carcass to air, increasing the decomposition rate.

In an early experiment, Tomita compared the floatation of dead mice to case reports of human bodies recovered from disasters at sea [34]. It was found that in saltwater at or about 20 °C or more, most bodies re-floated within 3 days and several floated from the outset but he also found that at a depth of 50 m or more and at lower temperatures floatation often did not occur or it was quite delayed. In one disaster, approximately half the bodies floated and half sank in waters with a temperature of approximately 14 °C. This level of variability lead Tomita to the conclusion that, while water temperature and pressure were highly influential, other factors such as cause of death (i.e. presence of water in the lungs or peri-mortem injuries) and ocean tides and currents played a role in body floatation or re-floatation. Overall, his findings demonstrated the variability in floatation of dead bodies in disaster scenarios.

The floating behaviour of a body will affect its movement in an aquatic environment. The transport potential of a floating body is significantly higher than one resting on the bed of the aquatic environment. As a body moves with the flow of water it may be subject to abrasion from obstructions in the water as well as the bed of the body of water. This may in turn cause tissue destruction and contribute to the decomposition process. Bodies in a fluid environment move in three dimensions as opposed to those found in terrestrial environments that have support on at least one facet of the body and generally remain static. A human body usually floats face down with its limbs hanging submerged in the water [21]. As such, the joints hanging lowest on the body will be mostly affected by the turbation of the water and may also drag along the bed of the water body causing abrasion and expediting both the decomposition and disarticulation process.

The distance covered by a floating body varies immensely and is dependent on currents and potential obstacles in the specific environment. In a study on the movement of 9 bodies along the coast of Portugal (2 suicides and 7 bus crash victims) Pampin and López-Abajo Rodrıguez [35] found that distances from the point of entry to recovery varied from 220 to 420 km. Two of the cases travelled 350 km in only 60 h. Along with the difficulties this poses for recovery, the movement would cause tissue destruction and contribute to the decomposition process as well as hamper identification.

The percentage of body mass above and below the water alters as the body sinks and floats depending on the phase of decay. When a body is floating, the decomposition process in water can produce different levels of tissue destruction on the parts submerged and the parts exposed to air. The modification of soft tissue can take on a hybrid appearance exhibiting signs commonly seen in dry environments above the water but also those seen in aquatic environments below (see Fig. 8.1). For example, if a body is floating in a fairly still environment, the parts of the body that are exposed to the air and not the water may be subject to desiccation. In dry environments some level of mummification may even present on those parts exposed even if the rest of the

FIG. 8.1 Pig carcass displaying signs of desiccation above the water line and signs of adipocere formation below. *Photo: F Gilbert.*

body remains submerged. However, the parts of the body that are constantly under the water will remain saturated and decompose without any level of desiccation and will potentially be preserved through adipocere formation.

Body coverings

The process of decomposition in water environments can be affected by clothing or other body coverings. Clothing or other coverings can protect the body from access by insects and other scavengers [36], as well as promote preservation in the form of adipocere formation [28,37]. In a study comparing the rate of adipocere formation on pig adipose tissue with or without various coverings, Notter and Stuart [37] found adipocere formation is accelerated when coverings are present when compared to the non covered samples. They also found that this acceleration is particularly evident when the coverings are made from natural materials.

Body coverings may insulate the body maintaining the body temperature and initially accelerating the decomposition process by affecting the rate of cooling and maintaining an environment suitable for micro-organisms. In contrast, materials like plastic can inhibit the levels of oxygen and bacterial action, slowing the process of decomposition [38]. Clothing also has the potential to trap air increasing buoyancy and affecting floating behaviour.

Water chemistry

The chemical composition of the aquatic environment will affect the process of decomposition. An aquatic environment with high bacterial content will accelerate decomposition rates whereas an environment with a low rate may have little effect. This is particularly evident in freshwater environments where bacteria levels are more likely to vary than saltwater environments, where bacterial action is retarded by salinity levels. Further, the bacteria responsible for decomposition cannot survive, let alone proliferate, at low or absent oxygen levels. These types of anaerobic conditions, such as those found at considerable water depth, will slow bacterial growth, and may foster preservation [39].

Scavenging

When access is available, human bodies can provide a nutrient rich substrate for a variety of vertebrate, invertebrate and microbial organisms. These organisms can then dramatically affect the decomposition process by enabling significant soft tissue loss. In an aquatic environment, many different species are opportunistic scavengers, and will take advantage of the introduction of a food source into their environment, including human bodies. For example, crustaceans are highly efficient scavengers. Large crustaceans such as crabs and lobsters are effective soft tissue removers capable of tearing through skin

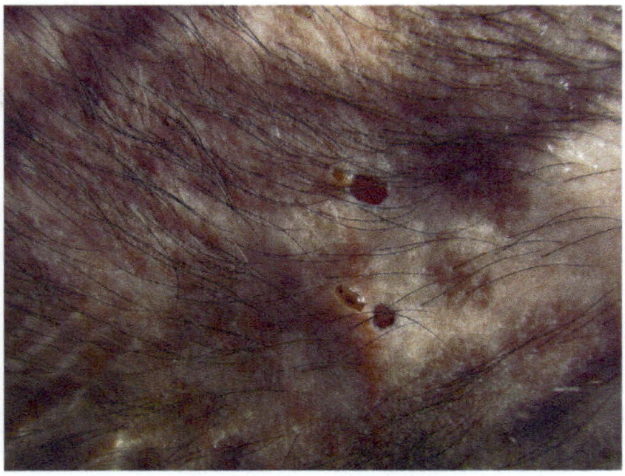

FIG. 8.2 Isopods creating characteristic bore holes on a pig submerged in a marine environment for 24 h. *Photo: F Gilbert.*

and accessing internal parts of the body. They are also common in both fresh and saltwater environments. Smaller crustaceans such as isopods (e.g. sea lice) will feed on carrion quickly when it is introduced to its environment causing round defects on the skin (see Fig. 8.2). They are often found in large numbers and can cause extensive damage. Fish have a tendency to feed on the easily accessible soft fleshy parts of a human body such as the lips and eyelids and will not tend to consume tougher parts of a body unless there is a wound or break in the skin. Other scavengers include starfish, mollusks and sharks, all of which will take full advantage of a food source being introduced to their environment and affect the progression and rate of decomposition.

Sealed underwater environments, such as air crashes or shipwrecks will prevent scavenging from large scavengers but small marine organisms such as arthropods and small fish may still succeed in reaching the bodies and cause significant damage [36]. Dumser and Turkay [25] compared the remains of two bodies found at depth (540–580 m) from two separate air crashes, one recovered in the Mediterranean Sea and the other in the Atlantic Ocean. The Atlantic remains had a PMI of 3 months and displayed complete skeletonisation whereas the Mediterranean remains had a PMI of only 34 days and were largely complete, with the only signs of skeletonisation on the skull. Despite the fairly substantial differences in PMI the authors attribute differences in the state of the remains to the specific composition of scavengers in the different environments.

Scavenging in aquatic environments is extremely variable. Some cases have been reported where vastly different levels of scavenging have occurred in the same environment and some cases where it has been completely absent despite the presence of known scavenging species [40,41]. As well as the soft tissue destruction, scavenging can increase bacterial penetration accelerating the decomposition process and subsequent skeletonisation and disarticulation.

Due to the relative accuracy of established terrestrially based entomological methods, several studies have attempted to establish improved estimates of time since death in aquatic environments by way of entomological analysis. In cases of remains found in terrestrial environments entomological analysis can be a reasonably accurate method of determining TSD (see Chapter 4, this volume). In aqueous environments, standard methods of entomological analysis do not generally apply. This is primarily due to the inability of the usual terrestrial TSD indicator, insects, to thrive underwater let alone establish colonies [33,42]. Terrestrially relevant entomological data should not be disregarded altogether as remains found in aqueous environments will generally float at some stage of decomposition, exposing areas of the carcass. This enables the usual indicator, insects, to feed and colonise on remains and even travel internally to the submerged portion of the carcass, affecting the decomposition process [20]. This may then allow some entomological estimation of the TSD but the specific context of the aqueous environment and the buoyancy behaviour of the carcass need to be considered to produce viable data.

Unlike terrestrial environments there are no aquatic insects that are purely carrion eaters. Aquatic insects rarely feed on carrion when it is introduced into their environment and do not generally exhibit any consistent let alone quantifiable feeding patterns [43]. In general it has been found that the level of soft tissue destruction by insects is minimal in submerged remains, when compared to insects in terrestrial environments and succession patterns are inconsistent due to fluctuating carcass buoyancy which makes entomological TSD estimates problematic and extremely difficult to quantify [44,45].

Anderson & Hobischak have conducted several different field experiments using pigs as analogues, to study decomposition and invertebrate activity in both salt and freshwater environments [32,46–48]. They have observed some patterns of decomposition that coincided with invertebrate activity but also point out that this is very environment specific. Most invertebrate fauna are opportunistic scavengers and will feed on remains when introduced into their environment but there is no real set pattern or timeframe in which this will occur. Variables such as depth, season, location, and temperature and water chemistry will all dictate the type and number of species present in the given aquatic environment and affect the decomposition process of introduced carrion.

Temperature

Water temperature is a principle determinant on the rate of the biological process of decomposition in aquatic environments [18,49]. The progression of decomposition will be inhibited by low water temperatures, slowing bacterial action whereas high water temperatures will accelerate the process. In an aquatic environment both water and ambient temperatures need to be considered as a floating body will be exposed to both.

Water temperatures decrease as water depths increase and there are generally significant water temperature differences between surface and bed waters [17]. Besides the process of decomposition in general, water temperature affects multiple variables in an aquatic environment such as floating behaviour, the presence of scavengers, water chemistry and preservation of remains. As it is generally accepted that temperature is the principle determinant for the process of decomposition, most research into decomposition explores temperature as a variable, regardless of the type of environment.

Research into aquatic decomposition and determining TSD

Perhaps the most common yet elusive topic of research in the forensic field has been the determination of PMI. In a death investigation this is one of the most important factors to establish as it has implications in establishing not only time of death but also victim identification, potential cause of death and in the case of a homicide establishing a time frame of potential suspects. Despite large quantities of research on the matter, there is still not (and may never be) one single technique that can be considered infallible and estimates at best, are only possible.

The number of studies on decomposition and its correlation to PMI conducted in terrestrial environments far outweighs those conducted in aquatic environments [33]. The following section will look at research detailing methods and experimentation that have been adapted from terrestrial studies for use in aqueous environments, as well as those developed almost exclusively to decomposition in aqueous environments. Research into decomposition in aqueous environments has gained some momentum over the past few decades. However, very few studies on aquatic decomposition have been attempted and a large percentage of research has been based on anecdotal data retrieved from coroners' reports.

Research into aquatic decomposition should ideally be studied in human subjects. However due to ethical and legislative restraints, negative public and media opinion and lack of available human cadavers, a large percentage of decomposition research is performed on animal analogues. A large percentage of research using human subjects is on analysis of autopsy and police reports retrospectively. This is generally based on photographs and anecdotal descriptions that may not provide adequate information and the researchers are often unable to personally examine the bodies. It also does not allow longitudinal studies in a controlled environment where the entire decomposition process might be observed. However, rigorously controlled experimental studies cannot account for all variables in a natural environment and may likely never be able to re-create a real-life scenario to any great degree of accuracy.

In the early postmortem period established techniques such as temperature changes (algor mortis) do provide relatively accurate PMI estimates. However, as the PMI increases, the accuracy of techniques declines, largely due to the multitude of extrinsic and intrinsic variables affecting the decomposition process. The following will review the relevant research directly applicably to determining TSD in aquatic environments with a focus on particular studies in the past 50 years that have influenced a variety of research.

The early processes of aquatic decomposition can be very similar to remains in terrestrial environments and it has often been found that "[e]arly sites of disappearance of soft tissue and exposure of bone in human bodies recovered from water parallel somewhat the sequence of soft tissue disappearance for bodies decomposing on land" [21: 812]. In decomposition studies, observational determination of a decomposition stage is often used as a basic guide in determining PMI. Stage systems to measure decomposition in terrestrial environments have been developed by several researchers [50,51].

In a similar manner to terrestrial studies, studies in aqueous decomposition are often separated into distinct stages of decomposition, with the stage of decomposition determined by the most advanced level of decomposition on a body. As in terrestrial studies, large variations exist in the number of decomposition stages used as well as the method of interpretation of each stage between different researchers. Decomposition stages used by researchers tend to follow a similar progression of commonly used terrestrial stages but are adapted to fit a very general aqueous environment. One of the most commonly utilised system of stages (or at least some variation of), are those established by Payne and King in 1972 [52].

Payne and King performed an experiment where they observed the decomposition and insect activity on the carcasses of 11 foetal pigs that they placed in small tubs of fresh water [52]. Through their observations they developed six stages of aqueous decomposition: Submerged Fresh, Early Floating, Floating Decay, Bloated Deterioration, Floating Remains and Sunken Remains. Despite Payne and Kings' observation that there was a significant amount of variability in aqueous decomposition, these stages are fairly rigid and make no real allowances for differing environments or the variability of submersion in remains.

The first stage of decomposition described by Payne and King [52] is 'Submerged Fresh' which is defined by the initial behaviour of the fresh carcass as sinking and ends when the carcass begins to bloat and rise to the surface. Payne and King note that while the majority of pigs behaved in this way, some of their specimens did float when initially placed in the water. The authors do not offer any alternative to this initial stage when floating occurred. Payne and King highlight the distinct lack of insects present on the carcasses in the 'Submerged Fresh' stage but if the carcasses had floated, there would be a difference in insect activity affecting the rate of decomposition. The 'Early Floating' and 'Floating Decay' stages are characterised by the initial maggot egg laying to hatching and the variety of fauna that contributed to decomposition during this time. Payne and King [52] describe the 'Bloated Deterioration Stage' as being from when increased maggot activity was evident, to when most of the maggot activity had ceased. The 'Floating Remains' stage was from when maggot activity ceased, to when the remains sank.

The final stage 'Sunken Remains' was deemed to be over when the parts of the pig could no longer be contained in the holder for weighing, and the end of the stage was thus arbitrarily determined. This method to ending the stage, and evidently the experiment, is extremely vague and does not allow for any variability of disarticulation or possible examination of a skeletal stage or any potential preservation. Payne and King do acknowledge that this stage was quite variable lasting from 10 to 30 days.

One significant problem from the outset of this experiment was that the pigs used had been frozen prior to submersion. The chemical composition of tissue that has been frozen alters, having a significant effect on the process of decomposition and making the remains "more susceptible to invasion by insects and microorganisms from the outside and aerobic decay of the skin and external surfaces" [53: 960]. The proliferation of internal bacteria will be delayed, and bacteria will have a greater effects on the course and manifestation of putrefaction of the outer body surface than on internal organs, altering the standard progression of decay (see also discussion in Chapter 5, this volume).

Payne and King also used the weight loss of the carcasses as corroborating data to clarify stages of decomposition. In decomposition studies weight is often a recorded variable to establish definitive points for decomposition stages [33,42]. Payne and Kings [52] found that their pigs increased in weight at what they classified as the Submerged Fresh and Early Floating Stages, however, the variability amongst the sample was pronounced and no definitive analysis in terms of weight loss could be made. Payne and King's experiment used foetal pigs in very shallow tubs of water, and this may have made weight loss/gain too small a variable to adequately record. They do not specify whether the amount of water that was naturally absorbed by the carcasses would have had some effect on weight as a measure of decomposition [47]. In the case of the discovery of human remains in an aquatic environment weight loss would only be useful if the weight of the human was known prior to deposition and if a consistent pattern of weight loss can be quantified.

The stages established by Payne and King [52] imply that decomposition occurs in an unambiguous and easily definable progression and the usefulness of such qualitative stages of decomposition has been contested [40,54]. Commonly used stages of decomposition do not account for differences within the stages or the potential for different body parts to display differing or multiple levels of decomposition at the same time, on the same body. The determination of differential body part decomposition is particularly important in aqueous environments where some portions of the remains may be exposed to air whilst floating and other portions may remain completely submerged causing them to be exposed to different agents of destruction.

In 1967, Reh, a German forensic pathologist, documented postmortem changes in bodies recovered from waterways. He developed a table to estimate the minimum time of immersion taking into account water temperature and signs of putrefaction [55]. Reh performed internal and external examinations of 277 human bodies recovered from the river Rhine along with other nearby rivers, lakes and ponds with a known postmortem interval. From his examinations Reh was able to identify 16 typical signs of putrefaction and developed a basic sequence for their appearance on the bodies and how this correlated to water temperature.

Reh recognised that several of his 16 signs of putrefaction were often taking place simultaneously and did not try to define an exact chronological sequence. He did, however, give a minimum time of immersion based on the traits present on the body and found that the more traits evident on body the more accurate the estimate should be. He also made it possible in some cases to estimate a maximum time by considering the signs of putrefaction that had not yet developed on the body. For example, if a body found within the average monthly temperature at the time of recovery in May, shows signs of loose nails but no gloving according to Reh's table, the time interval of immersion can be narrowed to between 5 and 10 days [56].

In 1977, Reh along with two colleges [18] re-tested his table on a new sample of 395 bodies recovered from essentially the same bodies of water and found that the results were valid with the initial table. They also state in this paper that in both studies they did not find any difference with the chronological development of the signs of putrefaction between stagnant and running water or between different bodies of water. Reh concluded that using the water temperature from the day of recovery and fitting it into the table to the nearest average water temperature was the most accurate method. However, this does not account for temperature fluctuation within the month or more importantly the temperatures in previous months if the body had been immersed for longer periods.

One noteworthy problem with Reh's method is that it only considers early signs of putrefaction. For example, in the data presented for the warmer month of July, all signs of putrefaction are between half a day and 3 days. This makes the table unusable for a body that has been in the water for longer than 3 days. Similar results exist in the other summer months with a maximum interval of 10 days [56]. No representation of later postmortem changes such as the extent of tissue degradation or bone exposure are represented in the sample, which may have given a greater timeframe with a larger sample. Another problem in this study is that the signs of putrefaction that are used are only given as brief descriptions. For example, the peeling of skin is not made clear as to the location or extent on the body, or if the timeframe refers to the absolute starting point regardless of extent or location. Discoloration is even more ambiguous and appears to refer to the initial onset of any discoloration on the body, but once again no description of type or location is given. As Reh performed the examinations himself, certainly more detailed descriptions were made, but do not appear to have been published.

In 2010 Doberentz and Madea [56] re-tested Reh's methods by looking retrospectively at the autopsy reports of 73 bodies with known postmortem intervals. The majority of the sample consisted of bodies recovered from the Rhine, with others from small rivers, ponds or swimming pools and appears to be a similar sample by way of location of recovery to Reh's. Doberentz and Madea found that Reh's table gave quite reliable estimates in 49 of the 73 cases. However, in 11 of the cases, Reh's table significantly underestimated time of immersion, and in 12 cases the table significantly overestimated time of immersion. The largest overestimation was 29 days longer than the reported missing time. The average water temperature of the Rhine is slightly higher than 40 years ago, which would account for some overestimation, but as per Reh's recommendations, if it has been situated within the closest average temperature it should be reasonably accurate.

While it must be kept in mind that Reh's table is focusing on minimum time of immersion in early putrefactive changes, Doberentz and Madea found that with water temperatures above 20° Celsius Reh's table is unreliable even in the early stages, as is also the case with longer periods of immersion as fluctuations in water temperature are not taken into account.

Despite the flaws in Reh's studies, he is reportedly the first person to prove a statistical correlation between putrefactive changes and water temperature, creating a practical method for estimating the minimum PMI of remains found in aquatic environments. Reh was also one of the first researchers to recognise that different signs of putrefaction can take place simultaneously and do not appear in a neat sequential process in aquatic environments. Unfortunately, the work of Reh and colleagues is often overlooked by the simple fact that it has only ever been published in German.

In 2005 Megyesi et al. [57] proposed that PMI could be determined using the entomologically devised Accumulated Degree Days (ADDs) method combined with a decomposition scoring method. ADD is a common method used for entomological estimations of time since death to determine the life cycle of insects found on a body by way of accumulated time and temperature. Using ADD takes into account temperature fluctuations over transpired time by summing the average daily temperature within the given timeframe. For example, if you have 10 days with an average daily temperature of 20°C that would give you an ADD of 200. Conversely, if you have 20 days with an average daily temperature of 10°C that would also give you an ADD of 200.

Megyesi et al. [57] used modified decomposition descriptions as developed by Galloway et al. [50] to create a Total Body Score (TBS). Megyesi et al.'s total body score system looks at different parts of the body independently as different areas of the body will exhibit different signs of putrefaction. Decomposition was scored in three areas of the body, the head and neck, the trunk and the limbs. A TBS score was produced by summing the scored decomposition on the three areas of the body rather than giving an overall score on the most advanced stage present in the body as a whole. They found that 80% of observed postmortem modifications quantified by the TBS system could be accounted for by ADD. The authors concluded that using this system allowed modelling of decomposition with accumulated temperature, not just time.

Megyesi's TBS system has been tested extensively (e.g. Refs. [45,58,59]), with varying levels of success. It has also been used in some aquatic decomposition studies with some adaptations to suit an aquatic environment. As previously mentioned, temperature is a major factor of decomposition in aqueous environments and both water and ambient temperatures need to be considered, which can be difficult in the case of obtaining retrospective data in a forensic case. The use of an accumulated degree days techniques to also include water temperature has been used by some researchers [28,40,60].

Heaton el al. [40] devised a system based on Megyesi et al.'s [57] Total Body Score (TBS) to quantify the progression of decomposition but they substituted the descriptions of decomposition to suit an aquatic environment and Accumulated Degree Days (ADDs) as a measure of time and temperature using water temperature instead of ambient temperature. In their study, Heaton et al. aimed to increase the accuracy of TSD estimates based on water based total body decomposition scores and the accumulation of water temperatures over time using ADD. The study used photographs and descriptions from case files, crime scene photographs and autopsy reports on a total of 187 human bodies recovered from a river in Scotland, a river in England and various canals in England with known postmortem intervals. To score the decomposition in each case the authors visually divided the bodies into three separate regions: the face (FADS), the body (BADS) and the limbs (LADS) and scored each separately according to their descriptive traits which were based on common terminology used by forensic pathologists. These descriptive stages are reasonably detailed and specific to the area of the body being looked at, and as opposed to Reh's signs of putrefaction they include late postmortem changes.

Once all three areas were scored in a numerical category that, as the authors describe would be an educated 'best fit', the scores were added together to produce a Total Aquatic Decomposition Score (TADS). Eight stages were used each for the face and body and nine for the limbs, meaning that the maximum TADS score would be 25. They then plotted the TADS against the known ADD and found a very strong relationship with which they developed a single linear regression model. One limitation that the authors acknowledge is that none of the cases used to create their model had a TADS score above 20, so once again the later stages decomposition have not been adequately represented.

One noteworthy aspect that is pointed out by the authors is that they also found no significant differences in decomposition on the remains between the waterways. These waterways would have their own unique combination of flora and fauna as well as differing currents and tides, but the authors found that time in the water and temperature were the variables that significantly affected the process of decay. They also mention that the pattern of decomposition observed did not follow the system of stages mentioned earlier developed by Payne and King [52].

One problem with this study, as is the case with all retrospective cases, is that the authors were not able to view the bodies themselves and had to rely on coroner and police reports, which did not always use the same descriptive terms and had varying levels of photographic documentation. This is a common problem with retrospective studies based on documented observations, but it is often the only source of information available. However, Heaton et al. were the first to attempt quantification of decomposition in an aquatic environment using quantified decomposition patterns and a quantified environmental factor (ADD).

In 2014 De Donno et al. [36], conducted a validation study on the Heaton et al. [40] TADS system. Their sample consisted of 68 bodies, 16 bodies found floating or submerged in shallow waters from the southern part of the Adriatic Sea and 52 bodies recovered from a shipwreck in the Otranto Canal (Adriatic Sea) that had sunk into deep cold water (approximately 800 m). The bodies from the shipwreck were contained within the wreck. They obtained water temperatures from the time of recovery and then retrospectively up until the presumed time of death for all bodies in the sample. Each of the bodies were evaluated by two examiners separately and assigned decomposition scores for three anatomical regions, head/neck, trunk and limbs based on the decomposition levels described in Heaton et al.'s [40] system to produce a TADS score. This was then plotted against ADD's derived from water temperatures.

In the remains recovered from the shipwreck, heavy clothing protected the bodies from scavenging activity and initial adipocere formation was on most clothed areas of the bodies, preserving them and preventing signs of later decomposition. This series was quite close to the ADD predicted scores using Heaton et al.'s method but preservation and animal activity affected the accuracy overall. Amongst the bodies found in shallow waters only one showed signs of complete saponification, with partial formation on a few of the others. This series showed a greater variability between the ADD and the predicted decomposition scores. The authors found that while Heaton et al. method did give some promising results overall, the great variability and complexity of aquatic environments and circumstances of remains makes determining PMI to any level of precision extremely difficult.

In 2017 van Daalen et al. [61] published research detailing an aquatic scoring method in salt water that was based on descriptions of specific aquatic decomposition traits referred to in the literature and Megyesi et al.'s [57] concept of a total body score (TBS) in the form of Total Aquatic Decomposition Score (TADS). Their scoring method differed from Heaton et al. [40] in some descriptive terms and the more distinct grouping of decomposition descriptions within the three body regions (Face, Body, Limbs). Using a sample of 38 cases scored by 12 participants from photographs, they found a strong correlation between the TADS and its predicted Postmortem Submersion Interval (PMSI), with 82% of the variation in PMSI predicted by the assigned TADS score. The authors point out several limitations in this study including, sample size and a lack of additional information that may have influenced decomposition such as floating behaviour. The authors also admit that temperature data could be of benefit in their model but the results they obtained do appear to validate their scoring method and the predictive model produced without the use of an ADD regression.

A study published in 2018 by Reijnen et al. [60], tested van Daalen et al.'s method on 58 freshwater cases and in this case tested against ADD. Their study again found strong correlation between TADS and PMSI and but also between the TADS and the ADD in bodies recovered from fresh water. However, this study did not include any bodies in the later stages of decomposition with high ADD's. As the authors recommend, future studies using this method would benefit from more cases with advanced decomposition and higher ADD's to validate the method.

The potential use of a variety of aquatic organisms to determine TSD has gained a lot of research attention in the past few decades. The development rate of the aquatic midge as indicators of submersion interval has been explored by Keiper et al. [62] and González Medina et al. [63]. Magni et al. [64] explored the growth rates of barnacles on a body to determine floating time. A handful of studies such as those by Haefner et al. [33] and Zimmerman and Walters [42] have explored the use of algal growth analysis as an alternative indicator of TSD. Haefner et al. [33] worked on the basis that a submerged body may act as a nutrient source for colonizing algae and by quantifying both the growth and diversity of algae on carrion, some estimate may be made in terms of PMI. According to these studies algal growth does appear to occur in a successional manner. However, various external factors will affect algal growth such as rainfall and water composition making it difficult to quantify.

The potential use of marine bacterial succession to determine time of submergence was explored by Dickson et al. [65]. The researchers conducted a series of experiments on pig heads deposited in a marine environment (Otago harbour) with the aim of researching any correlation between marine bacterial colonisation and PMSI. They found that some species of bacteria did colonise in a successional manner and have the potential to estimate time since submersion. In 2015 Benbow et al. [66] conducted a study using stillborn pig carcasses in a freshwater stream to measure aquatic bacterial communities using high throughput metagenomic sequencing and their correlation to PMSI. The researchers also found some evidence of bacteria succession that correlated to PMSI. Aquatic organisms are extremely habitat specific and much of this research is still in its infancy, but these approaches all have potential to contribute to determining the PMI of remains in aquatic environments.

Conclusions

Within the field of Forensic Taphonomy, one of the most ambiguous and rarely attempted areas of research is the study of decomposition in aquatic environments. This is largely due to the multitude of variables that can affect the process, and in the case of experimentation, the logistics of recreating or controlling an aquatic environment.

Overall, research into decomposition in aquatic environments has gained some momentum over the past few decades. However, very few studies or experiments of decomposition in purely aqueous environments have been conducted and have been limited to only a few specific environments. Compared to terrestrial studies, very little is known about the decomposition process in water. Aquatic decomposition provides a challenge as so much of the process is dependent on knowledge of each environment, and the multitude of variables that influence it. In terms of aiding forensic investigation in this area, very few attempts have been made to improve estimates of TSD, or to develop practical methods that may be applied to medico-legal investigations. While there may never be one single system to quantify PMI in aquatic environments that has global application, more thorough research into environmental variables and regional variation that affect the process of decay is essential if more comprehensive methods are to be developed.

Models of decomposition based on stages are too general and imply that decomposition occurs in an unambiguous and easily definable progression without consideration of environmental variables. While stage-based systems give practitioners a basic guide of what to expect in the process, they do not allow for variation. Attempts at using quantifiable traits of decay combined with quantified environment specific data are promising. However, more research is needed in order to determine which traits and which environmental variables are relevant to each unique aquatic context. While novel approaches, in isolation, can be limited in their contribution to TSD estimation, when combined with other research methods they may have the potential to provide insight into the complexities of aquatic decomposition.

This chapter has outlined the decomposition processes involved in aquatic environments, discussing the complexities of intrinsic and extrinsic variables unique to human remains recovered from water systems, and how they affect the process of decay. It has explored both the value, and limitations, of existing research in the field, focusing on pivotal studies that have influenced the, thus far, modest amount of research that has been conducted in this area.

References

[1] World Health Organisation. Global report on drowning: preventing a leading killer. Geneva, Switzerland: WHO Press; 2014.

[2] Catts EP, Goff ML. Forensic entomology in criminal investigations. Annu Rev Entomol 1992;37:253–72.

[3] Haglund WD. Applications of taphonomic models to forensic investigations [Ph.D. thesis]. University of Washington; 1991.
[4] Cotton GE, Aufderheide AC, Goldschmidt VG. Preservation of human tissue immersed for five years in fresh water of known temperature. J Forensic Sci 1987;32:6.
[5] Dix JD. Missouri's lakes and the disposal of homicide victims. J Forensic Sci 1987;32:806–9.
[6] Kahana T, Almog J, Levy J, Shmeltzer E, Spier Y, Hiss J. Marine Taphonomy: adipocere formation in a series of bodies recovered from a single shipwreck. J Forensic Sci 1999;44:897–901.
[7] Vass AA. Beyond the grave- understanding human decomposition. Microbiol Today 2001;28:190–2.
[8] Tsokos M. Postmortem changes and artifacts occurring during the early postmortem interval. In: Tsokos M, editor. Forensic pathology reviews, vol. 3. Totowa (NJ): Humana Press Inc; 2005. p. 183–238.
[9] Al-Alousi LM. A study of the shape of the post-mortem cooling curve in 117 forensic cases. Forensic Sci Int 2002;125:237–44.
[10] Althaus L, Henssge C. Rectal temperature time of death nomogram: sudden change of ambient temperature. Forensic Sci Int 1999;99:171–8.
[11] Henssge C. Precision of estimating the time of death by mathematical expression of rectal body cooling. Z Rechtsmed 1979;83:49–67.
[12] Baccino E, Cattaneo C, Jouineau CM, Poudoulec J, Martrille L. Cooling rates of the ear and brain in pig heads submerged in water: implications for postmortem interval estimation of cadavers found in still water. Am J Forensic Med Pathol 2007;28:80–5.
[13] Karhunen PJ, Goebeler S, Winberg O, Tuominen M. Time of death of victims found in cold water environment. Forensic Sci Int 2008;176:e17–22.
[14] Vanezis P, Trujillo O. Evaluation of hypostasis using a colorimeter measuring system and its application to assessment of the post-mortem interval (time of death). Forensic Sci Int 1996;78:19–28.
[15] Kaatsch HJ, Schmidtke E, Nietsch W. Photometric measurement of pressure-induced blanching of livor mortis as an aid to estimating time of death. Int J Leg Med 1994;106:209–14.
[16] Swift B. The timing of death. In: Rutty GN, editor. Essentials of autopsy practice. London: Springer; 2006. p. 189–214.
[17] Lunetta P, Modell JH. Macroscopical, microscopical, and laboratory findings in drowning victims: a comprehensive review. In: Tsokos M, editor. Forensic pathology reviews, vol. 3. Totowa (NJ): Humana Press Inc; 2005. p. 3–77.
[18] Reh H, Haarhoff K, Vogt CD. Die Schätzung der Todeszeit bei Wasserleichen (The estimation of the time of death of corpses recovered from water). Int J Leg Med 1977;79:261–6.
[19] Reh H. Über den frühpostmortalen Verlauf der Waschhaut an den Fingern. [On the early postmortal course of "washerwoman's skin" at the fingertips]. Z Rechtsmed 1984;92:183–8 [in German].
[20] Haglund WD, Sorg MH. Human remains in water environments. In: Haglund WD, Sorg MH, editors. Advances in forensic Taphonomy: method, theory and archaeological perspectives. Boca Raton: CRC Press; 2002. p. 201–18.
[21] Haglund WD. Disappearance of soft tissue and the disarticulation of human remains from aqueous environments. J Forensic Sci 1993;38:806–15.

[22] Ubelaker DH, Zarenko KM. Adipocere: what is known after over two centuries of research. Forensic Sci Int 2011;208:167–72.

[23] Yan F, McNally R, Kontanis EJ, Sadik OA. Preliminary quantitative investigation of postmortem adipocere formation. J Forensic Sci 2001;46:609–14.

[24] Forbes SL, Stuart BH, Dadour IR, Dent BB. A preliminary investigation of the stages of adipocere formation. J Forensic Sci 2004;49(3):1–9.

[25] Dumser TK, Turkay M. Postmortem changes of human bodies on the bathyal sea floor—two cases of aircraft accidents above the open sea. J Forensic Sci 2008;53(5):1049–52.

[26] Makristathis A, Schwarzmeier J, Mader RM, Varmuza K, Simonitsch I, Chavez JC, et al. Fatty acid composition and preservation of the Tyrolean iceman and other mummies. J Lipid Res 2002;43:2056–61.

[27] Komar DA. Decay rates in a cold climate region: a review of cases involving advanced decomposition from the medical examiner's office in edmonton, alberta. J Forensic Sci 1998;43:57–61.

[28] O'Brien TG, Kuehner AC. Waxing grave about adipocere: soft tissue change in an aquatic context. J Forensic Sci 2007;52:294–301.

[29] Donoghue ER, Minnigerode SC. Human body buoyancy: a study of 98 men. J Forensic Sci 1977;22:573–9.

[30] Anderson GS. Determination of elapsed time since death in homicide victims disposed of in the ocean. Ottawa (ON): Canadian Police Research Centre; 2008.

[31] Teather RG. Encyclopedia of underwater investigations. 2nd ed. Florida: Best Publishing Company; 2013. p. 197.

[32] Anderson GS, Hobischak NR. Decomposition of carrion in the marine environment in British Columbia, Canada. Int J Leg Med 2004;118:206–9.

[33] Haefner JN, Wallace JR, Merritt RW. Pig decomposition in lotic aquatic systems: the potential use of algal growth in establishing a postmortem submersion interval (PMSI). J Forensic Sci 2004;49:1–7.

[34] Tomita K. On putrefactions and floatations of dead bodies under water. Hiroshima J Med Sci 1975;24:117–52.

[35] Pampın JB, López-Abajo Rodrıguez BA. Surprising drifting of bodies along the coast of Portugal and Spain. Leg Med 2001;3(3):177–82.

[36] De Donno A, Campobasso CP, Santoro V, Leonardi S, Tafuri S, Introna F. Bodies in sequestered and non-sequestered aquatic environments: a comparative taphonomic study using decompositional scoring system. Sci Justice 2014;54(6):439–46.

[37] Notter SJ, Stuart BH. The effect of body coverings on the formation of adipocere in an aqueous environment. J Forensic Sci 2012;57(1):120–5.

[38] Pakosh CM, Rogers TL. Soft tissue decomposition of submerged, dismembered pig limbs enclosed in plastic bags. J Forensic Sci 2009;54:1223–8.

[39] Gill-King H. Chemical and ultrastructual aspects of decomposition. In: Haglund WD, Sorg MH, editors. Forensic Taphonomy: the postmortem fate of human remains. Boca Raton (FL): CRC Press; 1996. p. 93–108.

[40] Heaton V, Lagden A, Moffatt C, Simmons T. Predicting the postmortem submersion interval for human remains recovered from U.K. Waterways. J Forensic Sci 2010;55:302–3.

[41] Haglund WD, Sorg MH. Method and theory of forensic taphonomy research. In: Haglund WD, Sorg MH, editors. Forensic Taphonomy: the postmortem fate of human remains. Boca Raton (FL): CRC Press; 1996. p. 13–26.

[42] Zimmerman KA, Walters JR. The potential to determine a postmortem submersion interval based on algal/diatom diversity on decomposing mammalian carcasses in brackish ponds in Delaware. J Forensic Sci 2008;53:935–41.

[43] Barrios M, Wolff M. Initial study of arthropods succession and pig carrion decomposition in two freshwater ecosystems in the Colombian Andes. Forensic Sci Int 2011;212:164–72.

[44] Haskell ND, Williams RP. Use of aquatic insects in determining submersion interval. J Forensic Sci 1989;34:622–32.

[45] Simmons T, Adlam RE, Moffatt C. Debugging decomposition data—comparative taphonomic studies and the influence of insects and carcass size on decomposition rate. J Forensic Sci 2010;55:8–13.

[46] Anderson GS, Hobischak NR. Determination of time of death for humans discovered in saltwater using aquatic organism succession and decomposition rates. Ottawa (ON): Canadian Police Research Centre; 2002.

[47] Hobischak NR, Anderson GS. Time of submergence using aquatic invertebrate succession and decompositional changes. J Forensic Sci 2002;47:142–51.

[48] Hobischak NR. Freshwater invertebrate succession and decompositional studies on carrion in British Columbia. Master of pest management. Simon Fraser University; 1997.

[49] Petrik MS, Hobischak NR, Anderson GS. Examination of factors surrounding human decomposition in freshwater: a review of body recoveries and coroner cases in British columbia. Can Soc Forensic Sci J 2004;37:9–17.

[50] Galloway A, Bikby WH, Jones AM, Henry TE, Parkes BO. Decay rates of human remains in an arid environment. J Forensic Sci 1989;34:607–16.

[51] Rodriguez WC, Bass WM. Insect activity and its relationship to decay rates of human cadavers in east Tennessee. J Forensic Sci 1983;28:423–32.

[52] Payne JA, King EW. Insect succession and decomposition of pig carcasses in water. J Ga Entomol Soc 1972;7:153–62.

[53] Micozzi MS. Experimental study of postmortem change under field conditlons: effects of freezing, thawing, and mechanical injury. J Forensic Sci 1986;31:953–61.

[54] Fitzgerald CM, Oxenham M. Modelling time-since-death in Australian Temperate conditions. Aust J Forensic Sci 2009;41:27–41.

[55] Reh H. Anhaltspunkte für die Bestimmung der Wasserzeit. Dtsch Z für Gesamte Gerichtl Med 1967;59:235–45.

[56] Doberentz E, Madea B. Estimating the time of immersion of bodies found in water- an evaluation of a common method to estimate the minimum time interval of immersion. Rev Española Med Leg 2010;36:51–61.

[57] Megyesi MS, Nawrocki SP, Haskell NH. Using accumulated degree- days to estimate the postmortem interval from decomposed human remains. J Forensic Sci 2005;50:1–9.

[58] Myburgh J, L'abbé EN, Steyn M, Becker PJ. Estimating the postmortem interval (PMI) using accumulated degree-days (ADD) in a temperate region of South Africa. Forensic Sci Int 2013;229:165.e1–6.

[59] Moffatt C, Simmons T, Lynch-Aird J. An improved equation for TBS and ADD: establishing a reliable postmortem interval framework for casework and experimental studies. J Forensic Sci 2016;61:S201–7.

[60] Reijnen G, Gelderman HT, Oude Grotebevelsborg BFL, Reijnders UJL, Duijst-Heesters WLM. The correlation between the Aquatic Decomposition Score (ADS) and the post-mortem submersion interval measured in Accumulated Degree Days (ADD) in bodies recovered from fresh water. Forensic Sci Med Pathol 2018;14(3):301–6.

[61] van Daalen MA, de Kat DS, Oude Grotebevelsborg BF, Leeuwe R, Warnaar J, Oostra RJ, Duijst-Heesters WLM. An aquatic decomposition scoring method to potentially predict the postmortem submersion interval of bodies recovered from the North Sea. J Forensic Sci 2017;62:369–73.

[62] Keiper JB, Chapman EG, Foot BA. Midge larvae (Diptera: Chrionomidae) as indicators of postmortem submersion interval of carcasses in a woodland stream: a preliminary report. J Forensic Sci 1997;42:1074–9.

[63] González Medina A, Soriano Hernando Ó, Jiménez Ríos G. The use of the developmental rate of the aquatic midge *Chironomus riparius* (Diptera, chironomidae) in the assessment of the postsubmersion interval. J Forensic Sci 2015;60:822–6.

[64] Magni PA, Venn C, Aquila I, Pepe F, Ricci P, Di Nunzio C, Ausania F, Dadour IR. Evaluation of the floating time of a corpse found in a marine environment using the barnacle *Lepas anatifera* L. (Crustacea: Cirripedia: Pedunculata). Forensic Sci Int 2015;247:e6–10.

[65] Dickson GC, Poulter RT, Maas EW, Probert PK, Kieser JA. Marine bacterial succession as a potential indicator of postmortem submersion interval. Forensic Sci Int 2011;209:1–10. 2011.

[66] Benbow ME, Pechal JL, Lang JM, Erb R, Wallace JR. The potential of high-throughput metagenomic sequencing of aquatic bacterial communities to estimate the postmortem submersion interval. J Forensic Sci 2015;60:1500–10.

Chapter 9

Radiocarbon and amino acid racemization (AAR) and the time since death

Stewart J. Fallon[a], Colin V. Murray-Wallace[b]
[a]*Research School of Earth Sciences, Australian National University, Canberra, ACT, Australia;*
[b]*School of Earth, Atmospheric & Life Sciences, Faculty of Science, Medicine and Health, University of Wollongong, Wollongong, NSW, Australia*

Introduction

Understanding time since death is a critical component in missing person identification. Along with year-of-birth determination it can provide an age of the individual in order to compare with missing person databases. To determine time since death or year of birth a chronometer is needed. There are several chronometers inherent within the human body. All rely on the organic nature of human tissues and components. Two of these methods are Amino Acid Racemization (AAR) and radiocarbon dating (^{14}C dating). AAR uses the chemical decay of individual Amino acids derived from proteins, the blocks of life, whilst radiocarbon uses the radioactive decay of carbon-14 found in human tissue as a chronometer. In the following discussion both methods are described in detail including their usefulness and limitations in quantifying the time since death.

Traditional radiocarbon production

The formation of radiocarbon (^{14}C) starts with the premise that cosmic rays entering the upper atmosphere generate neutrons (see Fig. 9.1). These neutrons arrive on the order of ~ 2 neutrons cm^{-2} s^{-1} and interact with reactive Nitrogen atoms [1]. Nitrogen atoms can adsorb these neutrons. During this process, a proton is released resulting in the formation of a new element commonly termed ^{14}C, carbon-14 or radiocarbon. Approximately 2–3 ^{14}C atoms are generated per square centimetre per second and on an annual basis is equivalent to the production of approximately 7 kg of ^{14}C distributed globally in the upper atmosphere [2,3]. This extra neutron makes the nucleus unstable

Estimation of the Time since Death. https://doi.org/10.1016/B978-0-12-815731-2.00009-1

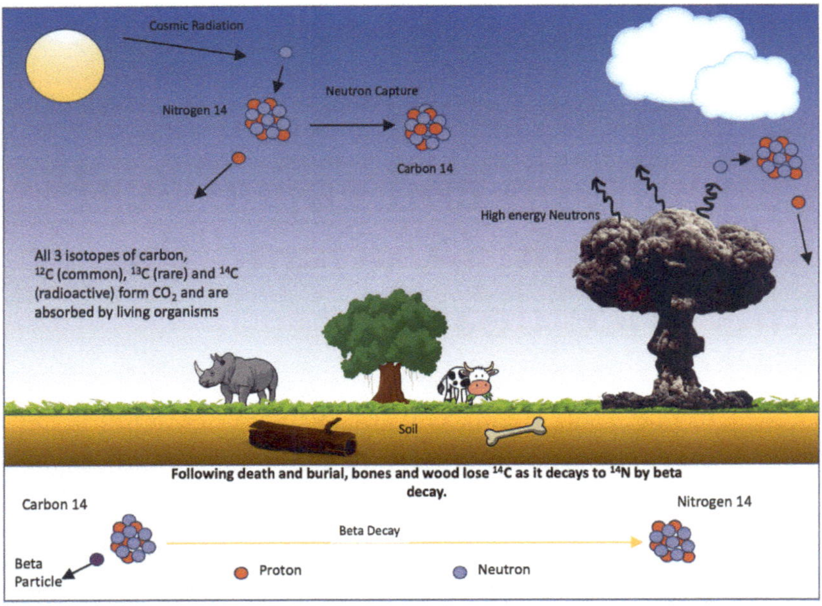

FIG. 9.1 Radiocarbon production both natural (cosmic ray flux) and human-induced (atmospheric nuclear weapon testing).

and radioactive compared with the stable isotopes of carbon (^{12}C and ^{13}C). Production of ^{14}C can vary due to cosmic ray flux, which in turn is influenced by the Earth's magnetic field. Radiocarbon returns to ^{14}N by beta decay. In the development of the radiocarbon method for dating, the radioactive decay of radiocarbon has been defined by two half-lives (the amount of time required for 50% of the atoms to decay back to ^{14}N). The first, termed the Libby half-life is 5568 ± 30 years [4] and continues to be used in the calculation of radiocarbon ages. The currently accepted half-life, however, termed Cambridge half-life is 5730 ± 40 years [5], and interestingly conforms with one of the first radiocarbon publications reporting the half-life to be 5720 ± 47 [6]. With production and decay essentially balancing out, a quasi-steady state is achieved in the atmosphere.

Atmospheric ^{14}C is rapidly oxidized to ^{14}CO [7] and $^{14}CO_2$ [8,9] joining the two stable carbon isotopes $^{12}CO_2$ and $^{13}CO_2$ and mixing into the global carbon cycle, entering plants, animals and humans [10]. Carbon enters plants as CO_2 directly through photosynthesis. In the case of animals and humans, the carbon can enter directly from eating the plant material or through a slightly longer and more complicated food chain. Fortunately, most carbon in animal/human diets will have been fixed in the last 1–2 years [11]. Thus, the ratio of $^{14}C/^{12}C$ in all living matter will continuously be set to near the current atmospheric $^{14}CO_2$ value [12,13]. When an organism (living matter) ceases to exchange $^{14}CO_2$ with the atmosphere the radioactive decay of ^{14}C takes over, thus the "clock" starts. This is the basis of radiocarbon dating.

Determining an age from a radiocarbon measurement

Radiocarbon was originally determined by measuring the radioactive beta decay of ^{14}C by either gas counting or liquid scintillation (using a chemical which emits light when hit by a beta particle; [14,15]). These methods required large sample masses of approximately 1 g of carbon. Today ^{14}C is mostly measured using accelerator mass spectrometry (AMS) [16]. AMS is considered faster and more precise as it measures the atomic mass ratios and does not need to wait for a radioactive decay event to occur to measure the ^{14}C. Sample mass is also decreased with routine measurement of 0.1−1 mg of carbon.

Before the measurement of residual radiocarbon, samples commonly undergo a variety of pre-treatment procedures to remove environmental contaminants absorbed within sample matrices during their burial history. The pre-treatment procedures isolate the indigenous carbon of interest. Following pre-treatment, samples are converted to CO_2 either by combustion or by evolution with acid if the material is carbonate. The CO_2 is purified to remove other unwanted gas species (e.g. water vapour, nitrogen, sulphur) and is then normally converted to graphite (pure carbon) deposited on iron which is then pressed into a sample holder for AMS measurement. Primary and secondary standards as well as background samples are produced in the same manner [17].

AMS radiocarbon dating relies on the measurement of the three carbon isotopes, ^{12}C, ^{13}C and ^{14}C and their ratios ($^{14}C/^{12}C$, $^{13}C/^{12}C$). In principle the $^{14}C/^{12}C$ ratio in a sample is all that is needed to compare with known age standards (the primary standard for radiocarbon dating is called Oxalic Acid I (OX-I), made from French sugar beets in 1955). However by measuring the $^{13}C/^{12}C$ the sample can be corrected for any mass dependent fractionation that takes place during uptake or in the measurement process itself [11]. The fractionation corrected ratio is then compared with the known age standard (OX-I) and this relative ratio is expressed as $F^{14}C$, which is the fraction of the sample compared with the value expected from 1950 [18], but can also be expressed as pMC (% Modern Carbon, with "Modern" defined as AD 1950).

A radiocarbon age can then be calculated using the Libby half-life of 5568 and Eq. (9.1). The unit is BP or 'before present', where 1950 is taken as the present.

$$\text{Radiocarbon age} = -8033 \ln(F^{14}C) \qquad (9.1)$$

Due to the variations in ^{14}C production over time (e.g. changes in cosmic ray flux) and the use of the incorrect half-life in Eq. (9.1), a radiocarbon age does not equal a calendar ages and calibration is required to calculate an age which approximates the calendar age. Since the discovery of ^{14}C production changes in the 1950s [18a] many geologic and environmental records have been collated to produce a radiocarbon calibration curves. These calibration curve consists of radiocarbon measurements made on independently dated archives, such as wood from tree rings, laminated sediments, corals and speleothems [19−22]. Calibration curves are non-linear with complex structure, and so various radiocarbon calibration programs (e.g. Calib, OxCal) have been produced to ease calculation of the calibrated probability distributions [23,24]. The most commonly accepted unit of calibrated radiocarbon dates is 'cal BP', although 'cal AD' is more appropriate for forensic cases. The probability distributions are not bell-shaped nor have a Gaussian distribution, and should be quoted as a probability range, for example 1968–1971 cal AD (95% probability).

"Bomb" production

A second form of ^{14}C production occurred in the 1950s–1960s. Atmospheric nuclear weapon testing produced additional ^{14}C. High energy neutrons produced in nuclear weapon tests acted on ^{14}N in a similar way as cosmic-ray derived neutrons to yield ^{14}C. The number of neutrons produced was sufficient to nearly double the concentration of atmospheric ^{14}C by 1963 (the cessation of testing due to the International nuclear test ban treaty). The increase in atmospheric ^{14}C was first observed in 1957 [25] and subsequently in human tissue in 1959 by Broecker and colleagues [26]. After the ban, the amount of $^{14}CO_2$ has rapidly decreased due to CO_2 exchange with the oceans and biosphere and dilution of ^{14}C by burning of ^{14}C free fossil fuels. The increase of ^{14}C in the atmosphere and subsequent decrease is termed the Radiocarbon Bomb Curve, or just Bomb Curve and has numerous forensic applications [27–44] (Fig. 9.2 bomb curve).

One significant issue to using the Bomb Curve to date material is that the curve has two sides. For example, a sample with a F14C value of 1.2 would correspond to 1960 and ~1986 (Fig. 9.2). Therefore, additional information or a second measurement from a different tissue is needed to determine whether the sample date is on the ascending or descending portion of the Bomb Curve.

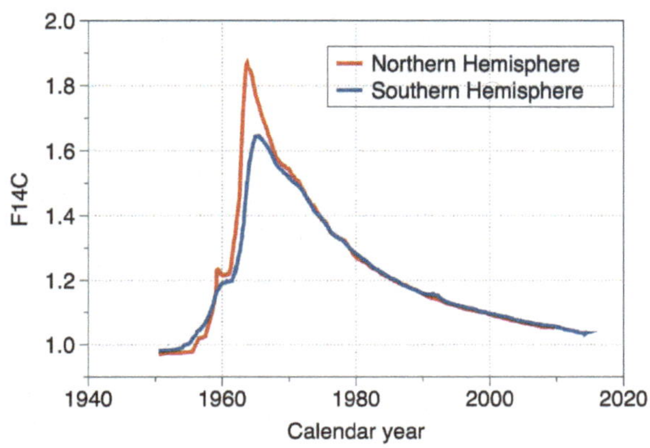

FIG. 9.2 $F^{14}C$ from the northern and southern hemisphere [45].

Because living matter constantly exchanges $^{14}CO_2$ with the atmosphere the $^{14}C/^{12}C$ ratio in living matter carbon will reflect the ratio at a given year. This has enabled the use of ^{14}C bomb curve or ^{14}C bomb pulse dating for determining the year of death or birth for forensic applications [28,34,39,43,44,46,47]. The following sections will discuss the incorporation of ^{14}C into human tissue, highlighting locations of rapid carbon turnover (useful to determine the year of death), slower turnover (e.g. carbon in bone collagen) and essentially zero carbon turnover (estimating the year of birth).

In order to utilize radiocarbon dating for time since death several questions need to be considered:

1. What material is available for analysis? (e.g. bone, teeth, hair, skin, blood)
2. Where does the carbon reside?
3. How did it get there?
4. When did it get there?

The radiocarbon content in human tissue is directly related to the atmospheric content at the time of tissue formation [48–50]. Therefore, understanding the rate of carbon turnover in different tissues is critical for accurate time determination. Carbon turnover consists of two main components: the time it takes for carbon from atmospheric CO_2 to enter the tissue reservoir (food to blood to tissue to bone); and the length of time the carbon resides in these reservoirs. Furthering knowledge of whether the carbon is continuously replaced, permanently stored or some combination of both is critical to the accurate quantification of time since 'death'. Tissues that exhibit rapid carbon turnover, the most reliable for time since death are first considered. Slower turnover of ^{14}C tissues and the resulting issues to determine year of death (time since death) are discussed, followed by consideration of tissues that exhibit "no" carbon turnover; these have scope for year of birth estimations.

Rapid carbon turnover (year of death)

It has been shown that the carbon residing in soft tissues such as blood, hair, nail and skin commonly lag the atmosphere by less than 1 year [26,48,50,51]. This is the length of time it takes atmospheric CO_2 to enter the food chain. Items such as vegetables, fruit and dairy produce have short transit times to consumption and are coupled closely to the atmospheric ^{14}C content [37]. In contrast, meat and fish contain older carbon and are offset from atmospheric $^{14}CO_2$ content [37]. Soft tissues (blood, nail, hair, skin) provide the most accurate time of death, but they are also the most susceptible to decay and therefore the first material to disappear.

Blood

Hodgins [37] measured blood $F^{14}C$, in a study of 36 individuals, born between 1913 and 1975 and dying in 2006. The $F^{14}C$ results from all individuals ($F^{14}C = 1.0607 \pm 0.0069$) was consistent with the atmospheric $^{14}CO_2$ during the year of their death in 2006 regardless of their year of birth (Fig. 9.3 inset). In a separate study, Spalding et al. [51], measured the DNA from the blood of two individuals in 2004 and their results showed that the $F^{14}C$ was consistent with the atmospheric ^{14}C content in 2004. Blood is an excellent choice to determine year of death, however, it also rapidly decays and is rarely available as a material to date.

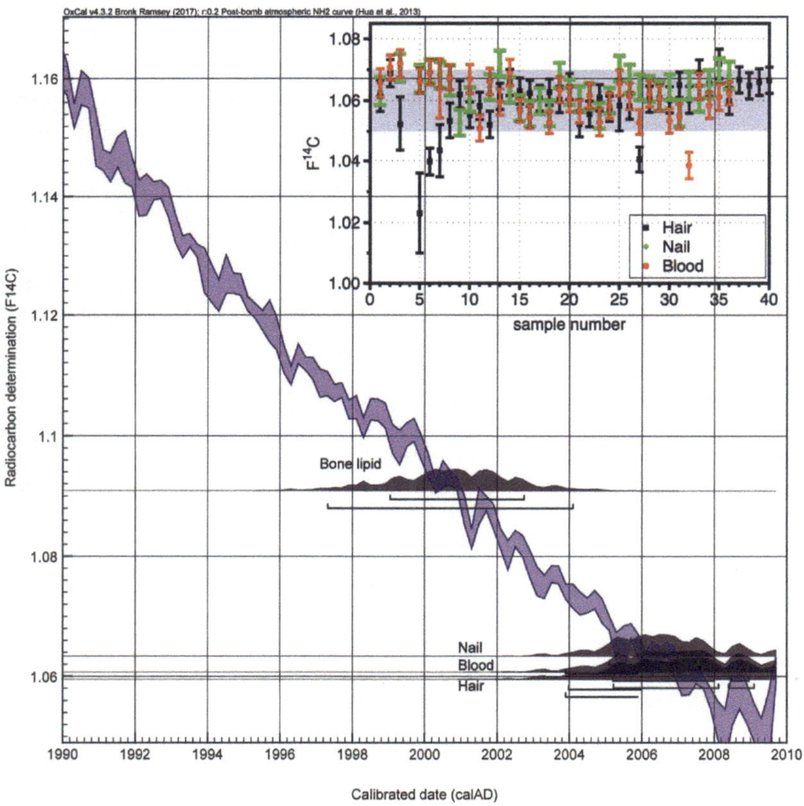

FIG. 9.3 Hodgins [37] average $F^{14}C$ data for blood, nail, hair and bone lipid calibrated using OxCal 4.3 [23] and the Northern Hemisphere zone 2 atmospheric radiocarbon curve [45]. Inset upper right shows the measurements on individuals (blood, hair, nails) from the Hodgins [37] study. All measurements aside from 4 hair and one blood are consistent with the atmospheric ^{14}C content at time of death. Bone lipid is offset from the atmosphere in 2006 indicating slower carbon turnover resulting in slightly older ages.

Nails and hair

Both nails and hair are made of the protein keratin and are continuously extruded from the body. Although they decay faster than skeletal tissues, they are more resistant to degradation than blood in the environment and therefore are more likely to be preserved. Previous studies have shown that nail and hair have $F^{14}C$ measurements consistent with the atmospheric ^{14}C content at the date of death [33,35,37,43,52,53]. Hodgins [37] also measured $F^{14}C$ in hair and nails from the same 36 individuals as the blood measurements. Aside from 4 hair measurements, all the measurements were consistent with the 2006 year of death (Fig. 9.3 inset). Both nails and hair are subjected to numerous cosmetic treatments during colouring and painting. Whilst nail material does not seem to be altered by these [54], hair treatments commonly include petrochemical (no ^{14}C) ingredients diluting the radiocarbon content [54] and amino acids in hair can be modified by bleaching and hair dyes [55]. Petrochemical ingredients contain little to no ^{14}C due to the extreme age of the material, this can therefore dilute the recorded $F^{14}C$ measured in the hair. De La Torre et al. [52], and Santos et al. [54], demonstrated clear ^{14}C depletions in scalp hair due to dilution of ^{14}C free carbon. This resulted in an age of ~4–5 years too old when compared with nails [54]. Hodgins [37] speculated that the 4 low hair $F^{14}C$ values in his study were probably due to cosmetic treatments (Fig. 9.3).

Puparia

Quite often soft tissue preservation of a body is poor, with full degradation of hair, nails and blood. A different source for determining time since death that has been proposed and used is the $F^{14}C$ content of insect pupal cases [37]. Insects will be feeding on the soft tissues and will therefore have the same $F^{14}C$ content as the time of death. Insect chitin is quite robust and has been found in numerous studies. Insect chitin has been dated to 40,000 cal BP illustrating its long-term preservation.

Slow carbon turnover

Bone can survive >50,000 years in the environment, as the protein collagen has minimal interaction/contamination with the environment. The high percentage of carbon within bone has rendered it a preferred material for radiocarbon dating of human remains in archaeological investigations. The carbon in bone collagen derives from atmospheric CO_2 in food via photosynthesis. Bone continues to remodel or turnover carbon throughout an individual's life providing an integration of carbon over the lifespan of an individual. Carbon turnover in bone is complex and slower than other items like hair, skin, and nails [33,36,37,42,56,57]. This slow turnover makes bone more difficult to use during forensic time periods. However, bone is the material most likely to be preserved. In order to use ^{14}C from bones to determine the time since death a complete understanding of the bone formation date and the carbon turnover rate of the bone is needed.

The carbon stored in the bone collagen can be anywhere from 10 to 30 years old depending on the type of bone and age of the individual [35,43,49,56,58]. There are two types of bone, cortical and trabecular, which remodel, or turnover, at different rates. Cortical bone, the dense outer surface of bones thickest in the shaft of the long bones, has a slower turnover than trabecular or spongy bone, which is more porous and usually found in the centre and the end of bones [59–62]. Therefore, a radiocarbon age estimate from trabecular bone should be closer to the time of death than cortical bone [42]. Having access to and dating both types of bone aids in determining whether you are ascending or descending the bomb curve, helping to better understand the time since death. Fig. 9.4 shows the radiocarbon collagen $F^{14}C$ variability in both cortical and trabecular bone from the same individuals studied by Hodgins [37] for blood, hair and nails.

Changes in turnover rate during life complicate the picture further. In a study of the cortical bone of femur, individuals <15 years old have approximately a 30% carbon turnover per year [56]. By 25 years of age this decreases to ~4% per year for both females and males [56]. Carbon turnover in bone decreases throughout life and circumstances, with most people nearing 80 years of age only having ~1%–2% carbon (collagen) turnover per year [56].

To refine the use of bone for time of death Hodgins [37] analysed lipids in bone which have a higher rate of carbon turnover. Hodgins [37] showed that $F^{14}C$ of bone lipids were significantly closer to the actual year of death than bone collagen, but still several years before the actual death (Figs 9.2 and 9.4). The $F^{14}C$ lipid values are more consistent than the bone collagen so can therefore aid in narrowing the date of death time window. Bone lipids should survive longer than the easily decaying soft tissues, but the longevity of bone lipids has not been studied.

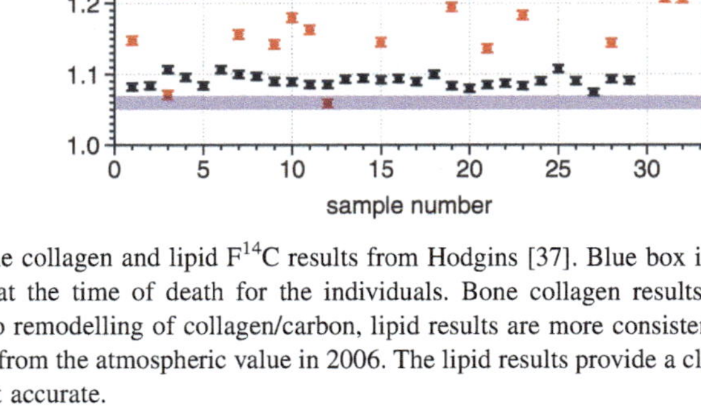

FIG. 9.4 Bone collagen and lipid $F^{14}C$ results from Hodgins [37]. Blue box is the atmospheric $F^{14}C$ in 2006 at the time of death for the individuals. Bone collagen results show significant variation due to remodelling of collagen/carbon, lipid results are more consistent showing a near constant offset from the atmospheric value in 2006. The lipid results provide a closer year of death but are still not accurate.

"No" carbon turnover (year of birth)

Teeth

Teeth have been widely used to determine the age of unidentified individuals. Traditional forensic anthropological age determination from teeth relies on examining different morphological characteristics and comparing them with the landmark study of Nolla [63]. Detailed studies of teeth formation in children have shown that each tooth forms at distinct times and can be used as a predictor of age [63,64]. Teeth are useful in forensic applications because they resist heat and chemical degradation more readily than bone [34]. Teeth are composed of 4 main parts: enamel, dentine, pulp cavity and cementum. Both enamel and dentin have been used for radiocarbon dating [27–29,32,34,37,40]. Enamel is the hardest substance in the body and it is formed in layers and lacks a cell structure, and therefore does not remodel during life [65]. Enamel formation takes place over several years but this formation time has been well characterized (see tables in Refs. [63,64]).

A year of birth determination is possible by measuring radiocarbon in the enamel carbonate (~0.7% Carbon). By placing the radiocarbon measurement ($F^{14}C$) on the atmospheric bomb curve a date is obtained (Fig. 9.2). Then the time in years corresponding to the enamel formation in the particular tooth is subtracted to derive the birth year [27,28]. In addition, a bone date can be used in conjunction with the enamel to determine whether the age falls on the early rising part of the bomb curve or the later falling portion [28,34]. Using literature results, the analytical uncertainty for determining the year of birth from enamel radiocarbon dating is 1.5 ± 1.5 years (Fig. 9.5, DOB enamel [27,28,34,37,40]).

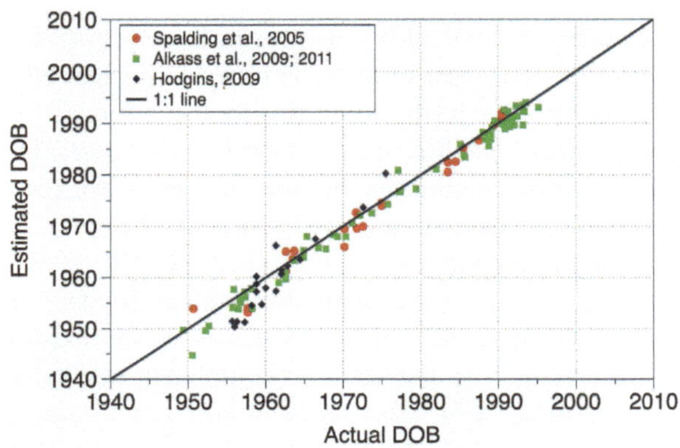

FIG. 9.5 Estimated date of birth using radiocarbon measured in tooth enamel vs. actual date of birth. *Data from Refs. [27,28,37,40].*

One potential problem when dating tooth enamel is diagenesis. In archaeological contexts radiocarbon dates on tooth enamel are always erroneously young, with at least 15% of the carbonate in some teeth being a recent contaminant [39,66,67], and no chemical pre-treatment is able to remove all contamination from enamel. Few studies have examined the mechanisms of enamel alteration in the burial environment, and it is unclear whether contamination could affect enamel over forensic timescales.

The collagen within dentine can also be used for radiocarbon dating. It is often favoured over enamel as collagen diagenesis is better understood due to the heavy utilisation of collagen in dating, stable isotope and proteomic studies in archaeology, and several pre-treatment protocols are able to successfully remove contaminants [34,37]. Early studies on dentine using AAR showed that age of dentine correlated to the age of the tooth, suggestive of no turnover throughout life [68]. Because of this study dentine was originally thought to be more reliable than enamel for year of birth determination [34]. Like enamel, dentine is formed in distinct periods and is deposited in layers. The outer layers in dentine can be several years older than the core dentine, resulting in an age bias [34]. If one is careful to sample defined layers this offset can be minimized [69].

Eye lens crystallines and petrous bone

Two other archives have also been discussed to determine the year of birth, eye lens proteins and the petrous bone [38,39,70]. The human eye lens grows rapidly *in utero* and during the first year of life [71]. The lens continues to grow throughout life but slows dramatically after early childhood [71]. The lens fibre cells once formed, are disconnected from blood vessels so remodelling should not occur [71]. Results from Lynnerup et al. [39], showed that radiocarbon content in eye proteins was able to estimate the year of birth to within 3 years (see Fig. 2 in Ref. [39]). However, these year of birth estimates were always after the actual year of birth. This highlights that eye lens growth continues for a period after birth. After developing a model to account for additional growth throughout life, their uncertainty decreased to ~1.5 years [39]. One major issue preventing the widespread use of eye lens crystallines dating is that the soft tissue in the eye easily degrades so sampling and measurement needs to take place soon after death [38,39].

The otic capsule containing the vestibulo-cochlear organs is found within the petrous or pars petrosal bone – the densest bone in the body [70]. The otic capsule is also formed *in utero* and becomes completely ossified at the time of birth [72], and it is thought to cease remodelling after the age of two (e.g. Refs. [73,74]). An isotope study of $\delta^{13}C$ and $\delta^{15}N$ in otic bone collagen and first molar dentine collagen showed no significant difference to each other but significant differences to femur collagen (slower turnover, a later time in a person's life) [70]. This suggests the petrous records the same environmental signal of early life as dentine and therefore should be appropriate for radiocarbon determination of year of birth. However, up to this point no detailed studies of radiocarbon in petrous bone have been undertaken. Additionally, the otic capsule is surrounded by other dense bone that is more likely to turnover like a femur or spongy bone, so this one bone could provide two time periods in order to understand which side of the bomb curve is the correct date.

Amino acid racemization

The potential of time-dependent amino acid racemization (epimerization) reactions for determining the time since death was anticipated by Hare and Mitterer [75]. They reported a D/L value of 0.15 for the ratio of the protein amino acid L-isoleucine to its non-protein counterpart, D-alloisoleucine (D-aile/L-ile) in the marine bivalve mollusc *Mercenaria* sp., independently dated at 1000 years. They also reported a D-aile/L-ile value of 0.53 for a *Mercenaria* shell of Upper Pleistocene age, independently shown to be older than 40 ka by radiocarbon dating. Hare and Abelson [76] subsequently reported higher concentrations of amino acids in the D-configuration (right-handed molecule) for several amino acids with increasing fossil age, in specimens of *Mercenaria* sp., and negligible racemization in a modern specimen of the species. Collectively these investigations highlighted the potential of amino acid racemization (epimerization) for assessing the time since death of organic remains and biominerals. Numerous reviews on the application of amino acid racemization in geochronology have since been published, illustrating the historical development of the method [77–88]. In addition, three seminal volumes have summarised the nuances and applications of amino acid racemization in geochronology [89–91].

Amino acid racemization has been used in a diverse range of research themes, predominantly in 'deep time' applications rather than in determining the time since death of recently deceased individuals. Applications have included assessments of the relative age and time equivalence of sedimentary deposits (stratigraphical correlation), determination of numeric ages of geological and archaeological successions based on the time since death of their preserved organic remains and biominerals [92], palaeotemperature studies [93], identification of reworked fossils [94], and for screening samples before undertaking radiocarbon, uranium-series or other dating methods [95]. The method has also been applied in determining the time elapsed since the death for materials younger than 500 years [96–98]. Amino acid racemization has also been used for determining the age at the time of death (biological age) based on the analysis of teeth [99], eye lenses [83], brain tissue [100], and long-lived corals [101] as well as the *ex vivo* determination of the age of bloodstains based on the analysis of red blood cells [102]. In the following discussion, the fundamental principles of amino acid racemization are reviewed in the context of evaluating the time since death. The factors influencing racemization in natural systems, the nature of racemization kinetics, and case studies illustrating the application of amino acid racemization are also reviewed.

The racemization reaction in natural systems

The α-amino carboxylic acids are non-volatile, organic molecules of low molecular mass (c. 100–200 Da) representing the structural components of proteins. Twenty protein amino acids commonly occur in the protein of living organisms, and many more are of diagenetic origin (non-protein amino acids). Amino acids are characterised by a centre of asymmetry at the α-carbon position, to which is attached an amino group (-NH_2), a carboxyl group (-COOH), a hydrogen atom (-H), and a hydrocarbon group (-R) (Fig. 9.6). Variation between amino acids results from the presence of different R-group side chains. Structurally, all amino acids except glycine contain at least one asymmetric central tetrahedral carbon atom. Amino acids are present in all living organisms as polymers linked together through covalent peptide bonds to form enzymes and structural material such as protein [77,87].

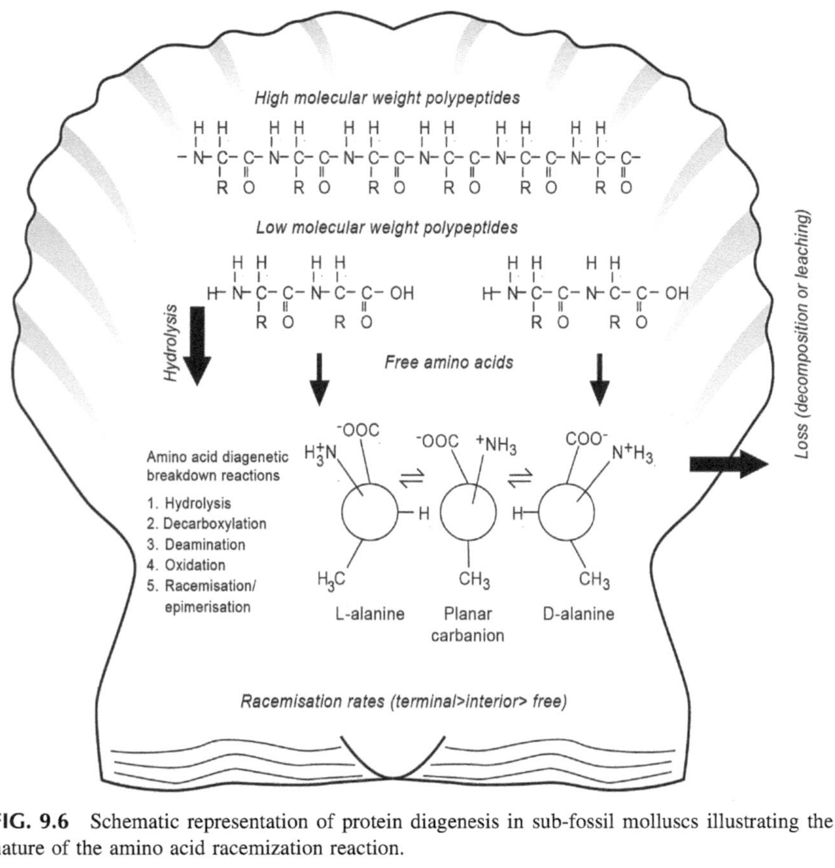

FIG. 9.6 Schematic representation of protein diagenesis in sub-fossil molluscs illustrating the nature of the amino acid racemization reaction.

During diagenesis, amino acids and their precursor peptides may undergo numerous reactions that include oxidation, decarboxylation, deamination, hydrolysis and racemization (epimerization; Fig. 9.4). In the protein of living organisms, amino acids are bound in peptides exclusively as left-handed molecules (L-amino acid: *laevorotatory*, in reference to rotating light in a left-handed direction in plane polarised light for a specific amino acid enantiomer). The exclusive presence of the L-form of amino acid in living organisms has been related to enzymic reactions inhibiting the formation of the non-superimposable mirror image, counterpart, D-enantiomer or diastereoisomer [80]. Following the cessation of protein formation, or the death of an organism, racemization of amino acids commences. The cessation of protein formation and the death of an organism are not necessarily contemporaneous, as racemization may occur in non-metabolically active tissue and biominerals during life, such as within eye lenses, teeth, and older, formerly active growth layers of marine molluscs and corals [82,83,96,99,101–104]. With the cessation of protein formation, the enzymic reactions that formerly maintained the disequilibrium condition cease (i.e. exclusively L-amino acids corresponding with an enantiomeric D/L value of $D/L = 0$) and amino acids then slowly and progressively interconvert from a left-handed molecule to a right-handed counterpart (D-amino acid: *dextrorotatory*). This process is termed racemization for amino acids with only one chiral carbon centre (i.e. enantiomers such as aspartic acid, glutamic acid and leucine) and epimerization for amino acids with two carbon centres (e.g. isoleucine and threonine).

The interconversion of L- to D-amino acids continues until equilibrium (i.e. $D/L = 1$) for enantiomers and approximately 1.3 for diastereoisomers, although a range of equilibrium values have been reported for the latter, between 1.25 and 1.4 [80]. Epimerization results in a chemically, not just optically different molecule as in the case of racemization and is therefore readily distinguished on conventional amino acid analysers, accounting historically for the popularity of isoleucine for quantifying the time since death [85,105]. The term racemization is therefore restricted to a change in configuration only at the α-carbon of an amino acid with only one chiral carbon atom [77]. The four commonly occurring diastereoisomers which undergo epimerization are isoleucine, threonine, hydroxyproline and hydroxylysine.

A mechanism for the amino acid racemization reaction was proposed by Neuberger [106], who suggested that the initial rate-limiting step in the reaction involves the removal (ionization) of the proton attached to the α-carbon atom. This creates a planar carbanion and is rapidly followed by the non-stereospecific re-addition of the proton from either side with equal probability of forming either the D- or L-enantiomer. The reaction is general-base catalysed, and any nucleophilic species may therefore initiate the reaction through removal of the α-proton. In aqueous solution, the nucleophile is the hydroxide ion (or H_2O) [77,107].

In aragonite and calcite biominerals derived from marine invertebrates, the residual protein occurs between mineral crystals (inter-crystalline amino acids) and at boundaries between coherent blocks within crystals (intra-crystalline amino acids [108]). In the history of amino acid racemization studies, the inter-crystalline fraction has more commonly been analysed. More recently, however, the intra-crystalline amino acid fraction, although of lower concentration has also been analysed in view of the possible diffusive loss of a portion of the inter-crystalline fraction, as well as potential sources of contamination [108–110]. The intra-crystalline amino acids are isolated by removing the inter-crystalline fraction commonly using a concentrated solution of sodium hypochlorite.

Amino acid racemization analyses are most commonly reported for the total hydrolysable amino acids, in which the measured D/L value is based on the extent of racemization in the residual protein breakdown products of a range of molecular weights. Fewer investigations have reported the extent of racemization for free amino acids. The measured D/L value tends to be higher for free amino acids than the total hydrolysable amino acids for a substantial portion of the reaction history. In the latter stages of the reaction history, however, the extent of racemization for both are similar. Although free amino acids show higher D/L values, their rate of racemization is slower than for the total hydrolysable amino acids.

In principle, all the protein amino acids and their non-protein counterparts can be analysed by gas chromatography and high-performance liquid chromatography. Details of the analytical methods and sample preparation for these methods are outlined elsewhere [111,112]. The amino acids commonly analysed include aspartic acid (Asp), leucine (Leu), glutamic acid (Glu), valine (Val) and the diastereoisomer isoleucine (ile). Aspartic acid is one of the fastest racemizing amino acids and therefore offers the greatest potential for determining the time of death over the past 1000 years. Leucine, glutamic acid, valine and isoleucine change configuration at a slower rate and accordingly provide the opportunity to date significantly older materials. The symbol Asx is used in reference to racemization of both aspartic acid and asparagine as the two acids cannot be distinguished chromatographically. In a similar manner, glutamic acid and glutamine are designated Glx.

Amino acid racemization and the time since death

Important considerations for the application of amino acid racemization in quantifying the time since death include analytical precision in the measurement of amino acid D/L values, the age-resolving power of the analytical method in relation to other potential sources of uncertainty (e.g. within-fossil and between-fossil amino acid D/L variability for sample populations from a single deposit or stratum), and the deviation of the derived numeric age from the 'true' age of the dated materials [113,114].

The possibility of mixed-age death assemblages (*thanatocenose* death assemblages [94]) as well as, for longer intervals of time, the influence of different magnitudes of diagenetic temperature on racemization rate associated with long-term climate change represent additional considerations for determining the time since death. The accuracy in determining the time since death will decrease with increasing fossil age, due to the higher uncertainty of the thermal history experienced by the dated materials, particularly over Quaternary timescales of several hundred thousand years involving multiple glacial cycles.

For recently deceased individuals, it is possible to directly determine their age at the time of death, in contrast to the time elapsed since death. This relates to individuals that have been deceased for only a few years. For example, Man et al. [100] noted the progressive accumulation of D-aspartic acid in the white matter of human brains for 10 individuals aged between 30 and 80 years. Aspartic acid, one of the fastest racemizing amino acids showed an increase from a D/L value of 0.05 in individuals aged 30 to a D/L value of 0.25 for an individual aged 80 at the time of death. In a similar manner, aspartic acid racemization has been noted in human eye lenses during ageing and cataract formation [115]. In an investigation examining the extent of aspartic acid racemization in 17 individuals, Masters et al. [115] noted that D/L values increased from a value of 0.047 for a 3-year-old lens to a D/L of 0.171 for a 76 year-old-lens. Griffin et al. [99] reported the extent of aspartic acid racemization (Asx – aspartic acid and asparagine) in the soluble enamel of human teeth and concluded that it should be possible to determine the biological age of an individual at death to within ±8.7 years at the 2-sigma level (95% confidence).

For biological materials that have been deceased for several tens of years, the continued racemization reaction renders it unable to determine the age of an individual at the time of death (biological age), and the method is then only capable of quantifying the time since death. Accordingly, the time elapsed during the formation of successive growth bands within a fossil shell for example, cannot be resolved from the time elapsed since death, particularly for shells that died several hundred to thousands of years ago. Although the exact timing of the transition from quantifying the biological age of an individual at the time of death, to only resolving the time elapsed since death is difficult to define rigorously, it is most likely within 20–50 years following the death of an individual [99]. Variations in the timing of this transition relate to the age-resolving power of amino acid racemization, a function of the spatial resolution of sampling biological remains, and the rate of racemization of the specific amino acid of interest, as rates of racemization (epimerization) differ for each amino acid [116]. This does not, however, affect the accuracy of defining the time since death (i.e. deviation from 'true age'), in view of the overall analytical uncertainty inherent in the method. Several factors influence the accuracy of amino acid racemization-derived ages of the time since death and include uncertainty in the measurement of amino acid D/L values, a transition from a stable body temperature during life (e.g. 37 ± 0.7 °C for human body temperature) to a more variable temperature regime affecting *post-mortem* racemization, and uncertainties relating to the Arrhenius equation (see later discussion). In temperate climates, the *post-mortem* temperature history is likely to be lower than body temperature, resulting in a significant reduction in racemization rate. Griffin et al. [99] note that at a burial temperature of 10 °C, a 40-fold reduction in reaction rate comparable to an Activation Energy (Ea) of 106 kJ/mol. In warmer climates less change is evident in reaction rate, especially given the disproportionate influence of higher summer temperatures on racemization rate.

Calculation of an age uncertainty term, associated with an amino acid racemization-derived numeric age, involves accounting for all the potential sources of uncertainty in the transformation of an amino acid D/L value to a numeric age. Early studies tended only to incorporate the temperature function as a source of uncertainty and calculated ages using the integrated rate expression which assumes linear-first order racemization kinetics [117]. Using this approach, the associated age uncertainty tended only to account for uncertainties associated with diagenetic temperatures. Other parameters, however, contributing to the uncertainty of the time since death using amino acid racemization include the uncertainty in the independently-derived age for calculating the forward rate constant of racemization, uncertainty of the *postmortem* temperature history, and amino acid D/L variability in replicate samples from the sedimentary deposit. One approach to account for all the potential uncertainties involves calculating the square root of the sum of the squares of all uncertainties expressed in years (i.e. $\sqrt{a^2 + b^2 + c^2}$).

The rationale for applying amino acid racemization reactions for defining the time since death is the wide range of organic remains that may be analysed, the small sample mass required for analysis (mg), the speed of analysis and the potential to define the time since death over a wide age range (tens of years to several hundred thousand years).

Given the temperature-dependence of amino acid racemization reactions, the age range of the method for determining the time since death, defined as the attainment of an equilibrium D/L value of 1, will vary spatially in accordance with contrasting diagenetic temperature histories. Results from Arctic regions with current mean annual temperatures in the range of −12 to −7 °C indicate that equilibrium may be attained within 10 million years from the onset of racemization [118]. In contrast, equilibrium is achieved significantly faster in temperate and tropical environments. Bowen et al. [119] report near equilibrium D/L values for the diastereoisomer isoleucine (D/L of 1.22 ± 0.08) in specimens of the fossil mollusc *Tawera spissa* from the Butlers Shell Conglomerate, Castlecliff Beach, Wanganui Basin, New Zealand (CMAT 13.5 °C) independently assigned to Marine Isotope Stage 31 (1.06−1.08 Ma). Near-equilibrium values for the extent of isoleucine epimerization in molluscs of last interglacial age (125 ka) have been reported from an emergent reef terrace on the Huon Peninsula, Papua New Guinea, with a current mean annual temperature of 28 °C, and as a corollary, significantly higher diagenetic temperatures than experienced by the fossil shells from the Wanganui Basin [120].

Parameters that influence racemization in natural systems

Although the racemization reaction is sensitive to several environmental parameters, some of these variables may be less significant in particular field contexts and will depend on the nature of the host matrix to the residual protein, and the environment in which the material is buried. For example, although pH and clay mineral catalysis are known to influence racemization [121], the aragonitic or calcitic matrix of marine and terrestrial mollusc shells, generally represents a highly protective microenvironment for the retention of indigenous protein residues.

Broadly in order of significance, the parameters which may influence racemization in natural systems include: (1) the *postmortem* (diagenetic) temperature history experienced by the material of interest; (2) the fossil genus, and structure and composition of the host matrix; (3) moisture regime; (4) hydrolysis state of the peptide residues and their susceptibility to breakdown during diagenesis; and (5) pH and clay mineral catalysis.

An important distinction arises concerning the *rate* and *extent* of amino acid racemization. Some processes may determine the measured extent rather than the rate of racemization with significant implications for assessing the time since death. For example, whilst the presence of water within the microenvironment of protein residues has been shown to accelerate racemization [107], it can also provide a mechanism for the diffusive loss of amino acids from fossil matrices (e.g. the preferential loss of amino acids bound in low molecular weight peptides and free amino acids). This is particularly evident where regular changes in the moisture content of sediments and soils occur within the near-surface environment. Fossils obtained from such contexts may be physically degraded, recrystallized or have chalky surfaces which crumble readily. Such poorly preserved fossils characteristically show lower reproducibility in the extent of racemization for within- and between-fossil D/L values, particularly for the total hydrolysable amino acids. In addition, such materials are likely to display a lower extent of racemization for the total hydrolysable amino acids and therefore yield younger apparent ages.

Post-mortem (diagenetic) temperature history

The most significant parameter influencing the racemization of amino acids in natural systems is the *postmortem* temperature history, also termed diagenetic temperature history in the context of longer geological and archaeological records [80,85]. The *postmortem* temperature history refers to the integrated kinetic effect on racemization of all temperatures, biological materials have experienced since the onset of racemization to the time of sample collection and determination of amino acid D/L value. Prolonged temperature changes over timescales of thousands of years have an exponential influence on racemization rate. For every 1 °C increase in temperature, the racemization rate will increase by approximately 20% [122]. Accordingly, racemization rates double for every 5 °C increase in temperature, a phenomenon predicted by the Arrhenius equation;

$$\ln(k) = \ln(A) - E_a/RT$$

where k is the rate of racemization, A is the frequency factor ($year^{-1}$), Ea is the energy of activation (kJ/mol), R is a gas constant (0.008314 kJ/mol) and T is the absolute temperature [123]. The sensitivity of the amino acid racemization reaction to temperature is further illustrated by theoretical calculations which reveal that aspartic acid will undergo ten times the extent of racemization in 1000 years at 25 °C than in 2000 years at 12.5 °C [79].

As temperature is a major consideration in the determination of the time since death using amino acid racemization, it is imperative that samples are obtained from deeply-buried contexts (i.e. $\geq$1 m). This will significantly reduce the influence of seasonal temperature extremes, so that the extent of racemization measured in biological remains primarily reflects temperatures associated with long-term climate change. The effective diagenetic temperature (EDT) represents the integrated kinetic effect of all temperatures a sample has experienced during diagenesis, from the death of the organism and its incorporation within a sedimentary deposit, to the time of sampling. The EDT therefore represents the temperature parameter of interest in diagenetic racemization. The EDT will always be higher than the average temperature biological remains have experienced during diagenesis, due to the exponential relationship between temperature and racemization rate. This is because higher summer temperatures disproportionately influence the rate of racemization as predicted by the Arrhenius equation.

From an archaeological and forensic perspective there is the further question of whether the materials for analysis have been burnt. Here, issues such as the intensity and duration of the heating event are important. For example, a short-term heating event from a low intensity fire might have a negligible influence on the extent of racemization for archaeological materials that are several thousand years old at the time of sampling. In contrast, modern materials subjected to heating will show evidence of accelerated racemization with respect to age. Besides obvious physical signs of fire such as associated charcoal and carbonised surfaces of samples, further evidence for heating events may include unusually high extents of racemization with age, and rapid loss of unstable amino acids such as threonine and serine.

Fossil genus and matrix

Early investigations of the extent of amino acid racemization in fossil foraminifers from deep sea cores suggested that different rates of racemization were evident at the species-level [124]. Subsequent studies found that this phenomenon is actually expressed at the genus level and relates specifically to the original composition of the residual protein [81,125]. Accordingly, amino acids bound in polypeptides with stable peptide-linkages will undergo slower rates of racemization than for amino acids within peptides more susceptible to cleavage of peptide bonds. This is because more time is required for hydrolysis reactions to break down more stable polypeptides, so that amino acids located in newly created terminal positions of smaller peptides may undergo racemization. Thus, there is a clear relation between fossil genus, rates of hydrolysis and rates of racemization. Wehmiller [81] noted a strong correspondence between rates of racemization in different mollusc genera and the classical taxonomic subdivision of the phylum mollusca. Miller and Brigham-Grette [125] identified broad groups of fossil molluscs based on contrasting rates of isoleucine epimerization. They found that gastropods appear to be characterised by slow to moderate epimerization rates while pelecypods showed moderate to fast rates of epimerization.

Contrasting rates of racemization at the genus-level are evident for the marine molluscs *Anadara trapezia* and *Notospisula trigonella* as revealed in a pyrolysis experiment conducted at 110 °C over a period of 100 days [98] (Fig. 9.7). The pyrolysis experiment was undertaken on modern individuals and simulates the trend of racemization expected over a period of tens of thousands of years.

Rates of amino acid racemization also appear to vary depending on the composition and structure of the host matrix to the residual protein. Rates of racemization appear to be fastest in molluscs with slower rates documented for bones and wood [126].

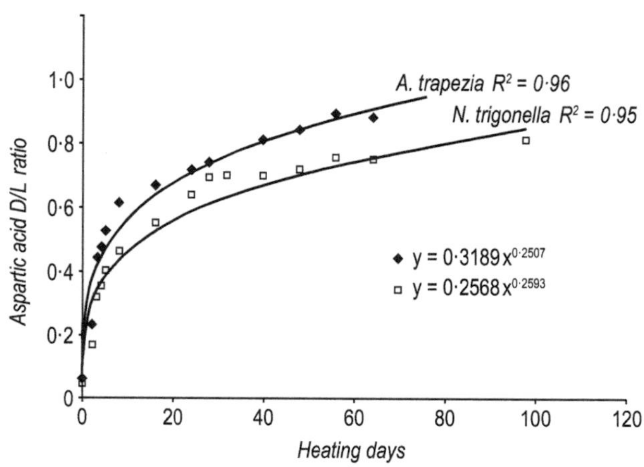

FIG. 9.7 The extent of amino acid racemization (total hydrolysable amino acids) in modern specimens of the marine molluscs *Anadara trapezia* and *Notospisula trigonella* induced by an isothermal heating experiment at 110 °C for a period of approximately 100 days. The non-linear nature of racemization kinetics is evident in this plot and is characteristic of the kinetics observed in fossil molluscs and many other biominerals.

Moisture regime

The presence or absence of water within sedimentary deposits has been directly related to the observed extent of racemization. The very low extent of racemization in bones from the La Brea asphalt deposits, California, has been attributed to the anhydrous nature of the sedimentary environment [127]. Samples that are permanently below the water table and hence remain in an aqueous environment during diagenesis, less commonly present a major difficulty for amino acid racemization dating, in contrast to fossils that have experienced substantial fluctuations in moisture regime.

The moisture regime is significant for not only influencing the rate, but also the measured extent of amino acid racemization, particularly for the total hydrolysable amino acids. Repeated alternate wetting and drying may promote *in situ* leaching of amino acids from fossils. In particular, the preferential loss of labile, highly racemized amino acids bound in lower molecular weight peptides, as well as free amino acids, is more likely to occur in these conditions, particularly for the inter-crystalline fraction. This will have the effect of yielding a lower extent of racemization for the total hydrolysable amino acids, as the D/L values will be preferentially influenced by the lower extent of racemization in the higher molecular weight peptides remaining within fossils. The magnitude of this effect is likely to be more evident in younger materials of Holocene age (<11.7 ka), as within only a few thousand years from the onset of racemization, natural hydrolysis will have broken down the majority of large peptides to smaller molecules [128]. If such results are taken at face value, they would suggest an erroneously younger age. Fossils that show the effect of diffusive loss of amino acids (leaching) generally show poorly concordant D/L values in replicate measurements from multiple fossil specimens for the total hydrolysable amino acids, but better reproducibility for the free amino acid fraction.

Hydrolysis state of peptide residues

Rates of racemization also vary according to the location of amino acids within peptide chains [129]. Accordingly, the relative rates of racemization follow the relation:

$$NH_2\text{- terminal} > \text{diketopiperazine} \gg \text{COOH-terminal} \sim= \text{interior positions} \sim= \text{free amino acids}$$

Diketopiperazine forms when free COOH and free alpha NH_2 groups of a dipeptide join to form a cyclic structure. As the majority of laboratories report results only for the total hydrolysable amino acids, the above relation is not immediately evident. Thus, the D/L value for each amino acid reported for the total hydrolysable amino acids represents the integrated effect of all D/L values of amino acids within peptide residues of contrasting molecular weight. Knowledge of this relation, however, assists with the interpretation of the complex nature of racemization kinetics in natural systems and in assessments of the diagenetic integrity of the retained protein residue within fossils. In particular, analysis of free amino acids and the total hydrolysable amino acids from the same HCl-digested sample, in association with measurements of their concentrations, permit an assessment of the integrity of the fossil matrix in retaining indigenous protein residues [130].

Clay mineral catalysis and pH

Although clay mineral catalysis and pH are known to influence racemization, for many natural matrices such as aragonitic or calcitic shells, teeth, and wood, these variables are less significant for most sedimentary deposits and are unlikely to influence quantifying the time since death. The calcium carbonate matrix of shells prevents catalytic surface effects from clays such as montmorillonite from affecting racemization. In addition, the range of pH typically experienced in natural and anthropogenic formed deposits (pH 5–9) appears not to influence amino acid racemization within fossils [107]. In pyrolysis experiments at 110 °C in a pH 10 buffer, the rate of racemization increased in lacustrine ostracods and leached more highly racemized free amino acids into the buffer solution, revealing that extreme pH conditions may have some effect on racemization in natural systems [131].

In summary, several parameters may potentially influence the racemization of amino acids in natural systems. Despite this, with careful sampling, especially in terms of the site context of the material subject to dating, it is possible to derive either relative or numeric ages that will assist in determining the time since death.

Amino acid racemization kinetics

Since the earliest amino acid racemization studies, considerable attention has focused on the nature of racemization reaction kinetics in organic remains so that reliable assessments may be made of the time since death. The kinetics of amino acid racemization reactions have been defined empirically, based on the analysis of fossils from geological and archaeological deposits of known age, as well as independently derived numeric ages from other geochronological methods, on the same materials dated by amino acid racemization, as well as the results of pyrolysis experiments. In the latter, high temperature heating experiments under isothermal conditions, attempt to simulate kinetic trends that would normally occur at ambient temperatures over longer timescales, characteristically tens to thousands of years [98,132]. The pyrolysis experiments which model racemization kinetics implicitly assume that the kinetics evident at high temperatures reflects racemization under ambient, diagenetic conditions over longer periods. Such experiments may involve heating several aliquots of a sample for successive time intervals, commonly at 110 °C over a period of up to 120 days [121], although shorter term heating experiments at higher temperatures have also been undertaken (e.g. 24 days at 140 °C [133]).

The interconversion (racemization or epimerization) of amino acids has been described as a first-order reaction [77,78,80]. In general terms the reaction is represented thus;

$$\text{L-amino acid} \underset{k_2}{\overset{k_1}{\leftrightarrow}} \text{D-amino acid}$$

where k_1 and k_2 are the first-order rate constants for the interconversion of L- and D-amino acids. For enantiomeric amino acids $k_1 = k_2$ and accordingly $K' = 1$. For diastereoisomers such as L-isoleucine/D-alloisoleucine, $k_1 \neq k_2$ and the forward rate constant k_1 is greater than the reverse rate constant k_2 ($k_1/k_2 = 1.3$ and $K' = 0.77$). The rate law for the interconversion of amino acids is;

$$-d(L)/dt = k_1(L) - k_2(D)$$

where (L) is the concentration of the L-amino acid and (D) the concentration of the D-amino acid. Integration with age of the material of interest (t) gives;

$$\ln[1 + (D/L)]/[1 - K\text{^}'(D/L)] - \ln[1 + (D/L)]/[1 - K\text{^}'(D/L)]_{to} = (1 + k\text{^}')\cdot KL\cdot t$$

where $K' = KD/KL = 1/Keq$ and is the reciprocal of the equilibrium constant [80]. The second term [t_o] on the right-hand side of the above equation is a correction for any D-amino acids in the sample at the time of death, and the small amount of racemization induced in the acid hydrolysis step in sample preparation for the total hydrolysable amino acids (e.g. heating at 110 °C in 7 mol/L HCl for 22 h). This correction is normally evaluated by analysis of modern samples (i.e. alive at the time of collection).

Some have attempted to define the amino acid racemization reaction in terms of a 'half-life' (τ) defined as when 25% of the L-isomer has converted to the D-configuration [80]. The general expression for half-life (τ) derived from the rate law is;

$$\tau = \ln_2/k_1 + k_2$$

Given the temperature dependence of racemization reactions, the duration of a half-life may range from 10^4 to 10^6 years. Although not widely used, this relation is useful for defining the potential age range of the amino acid racemization method for a given field area.

Attempts to define the nature of amino acid racemization kinetics in biological materials have included models based on extended-linear kinetics [134,135], non-linear kinetics [81], natural logarithmic curve fits [136] and a model based upon apparent parabolic kinetics [111,137].

The majority of biological materials display non-linear racemization kinetics in the later stages of diagenetic racemization. Characteristically, depending on diagenetic temperature, fossil genus, and the amino acid of interest, linear reaction kinetics are observed to a D/L value of 0.3–0.5 [137]. The initially rapid linear rate of racemization is followed by a progressive decline in the rate of racemization and subsequently a second, broadly linear component of racemization approximately ten times slower than the initial linear rate [138] (Fig. 9.8). The change in the observed kinetics of racemization relate to the interplay of differential rates of hydrolysis over time and its effect on observed racemization rate. In the early *post-mortem* stages of diagenesis, the extent of racemization is largely determined by the reaction at the terminal positions of peptides. As the rate of racemization is slower in free amino acids than at the terminal- or interior-positions of peptides, the overall rate of racemization for the total hydrolysable amino acids will significantly decrease as natural hydrolysis produces more free amino acids during later diagenesis. Thus, in the later stages of diagenesis, the rate of racemization observed for the total hydrolysable amino acids is dominated by the rate of free amino acid racemization.

A model of 'apparent parabolic kinetics' for the observed pattern of amino acid racemization in foraminifera from deep sea cores was proposed by Mitterer and Kriausakul [137] based on a review of published literature. The

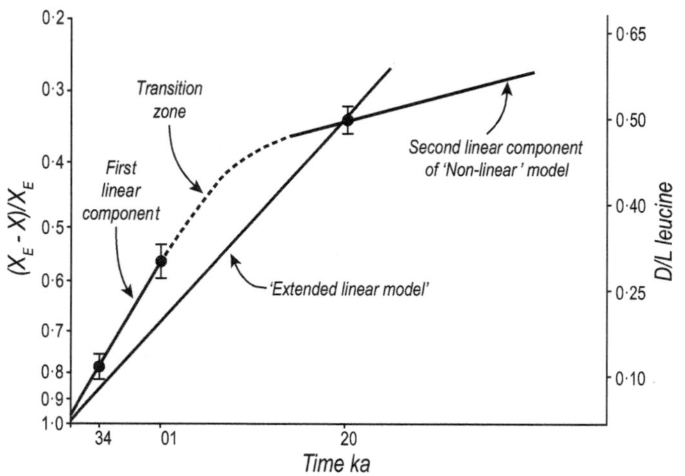

FIG. 9.8 Alternative models for describing the kinetics of racemization in natural systems plotted in a logarithmic (base 10) format. The majority of biological remains appear to follow non-linear kinetics. $X = D/(D + L)$ at any time T, and $X_E = X$ at equilibrium. For enantiomers $X = 50$ which is equivalent to the expression $\ln\ [(1 + D/L)/(1 - k' \cdot (D/L))]$. The 'non-linear' kinetic model is characterised by two essentially linear kinetic segments separated by a transition zone. The second linear component is approximately 10× slower than the first linear component. In the 'extended-linear' kinetic model, linear kinetics extend to a leucine D/L value of approximately 0.55. This graphical format has traditionally been used because if racemization conforms to simple first-order kinetics, the reaction pathway would be defined by a *straight line*. Leucine D/L values are for the bivalve marine mollusc *Katelysia* sp., from southern Australia [114] and illustrate the non-linear nature of racemization kinetics in this genus. Uncertainty terms indicate between-shell D/L variation.

results revealed a high level of association ($R \geq 0.95$) in the extent of isoleucine epimerization with the square root of age when plotted in a linear format, indicating that the kinetics could be described by a parabolic model from the onset of the reaction to a D-aIle/L-Ile value of 1. Parabolic kinetics have also been shown to apply to the enantiomeric amino acids leucine (LEU) and valine (VAL) in the marine mollusc *Katelysia rhytiphora* from southern Australia [111].

Using the parabolic model, the time since death (tsd) can be determined from the following equation;

$$\text{tsd} = [(D/L)_s - (D/L)_{to}/Mc]^2$$

where $(D/L)_S$ is the extent of amino acid racemization (epimerization) in the organic remains or fossil of unknown age, $(D/L)_{to}$ is the extent of racemization in a modern equivalent, and Mc is the slope representing the rate of racemization. The slope Mc is defined as;

$$Mc = (D/L_f - D/L_{to})/t^{1/2}$$

where D/L_f is the extent of racemization in an independently dated biomineral, D/L_{to} is the extent of racemization in a modern equivalent of the independently dated specimen, and $t^{1/2}$ is the square root of the age of the independently dated biomineral D/L_f. Forcing the line through the origin, accounts for the small amount of racemization induced in the hydrolysis procedure of sample preparation for the total hydrolysable amino acids. Depending on the amino acid of interest and its specific rate of racemization, the modern value may range from approximately 0.03 for valine to 0.06 for aspartic acid.

The parabolic racemization kinetic model has been used for establishing the time since death for a range of carbonate biominerals including aragonitic fossil molluscs of Holocene age [98], foraminifers of Pleistocene age [139] and bioclastic, skeletal carbonate sand particles from Pleistocene aeolianite, coastal barrier landforms [92]. In the case of the Holocene fossil bivalve mollusc *A. trapezia*, apparent parabolic kinetic ages for the time since death have been reported from <50 to approximately 5750 years and has involved calibration by numerous radiocarbon ages [98] (Fig. 9.9).

Extended-linear kinetics have been reported for isoleucine epimerization in Emu (*Dromaius novaehollandie*) eggshells to an aile D/L value of 1, although an initial period of non-linear kinetics was evident in pyrolysis experiments, equivalent to a period of approximately 10 years at 20 °C corresponding to an D-aile/L-ile D/L value of 0.0003 [109].

Applications of amino acid racemization in studies of the time since death

Time equivalence and relative ages of biological remains

The simplest application of amino acid racemization involves the comparison of amino acid D/L values from multiple individuals within a sedimentary

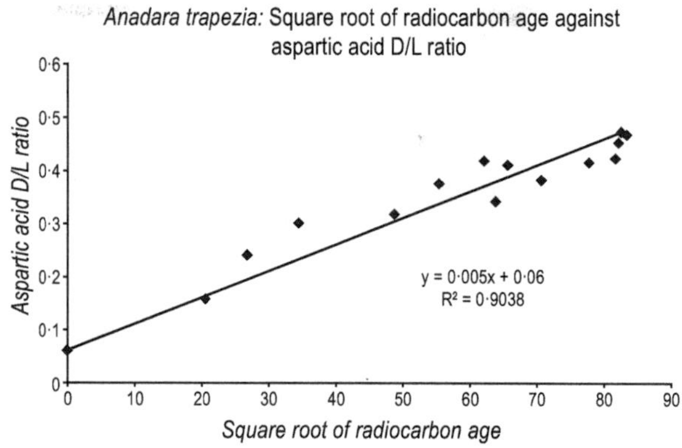

FIG. 9.9 The extent of aspartic acid racemization (total hydrolysable amino acids) in the fossil mollusc *Anadara trapezia* plotted against the square root of radiocarbon age, expressed in sidereal years, illustrating the apparent parabolic racemization kinetics evident in this mollusc species.

deposit. For a sample population collected from a discrete space, given that the materials are likely to have experienced a similar temperature history during burial, the method can be used to confirm age equivalence or establish differences in age for multiple individuals. This application of amino acid racemization does not require a detailed knowledge of the thermal history of the site and can also quickly identify older materials introduced to the site by time-averaging and physical reworking processes. In this context, amino acid racemization is a valuable tool in taphonomic investigations.

At a larger spatial scale, amino acid racemization may be applied in demonstrating the time-equivalence of biological materials and fossils over wider geographic regions. This approach has been used for assisting in the mapping of the spatial distribution of coastal geological successions of last interglacial age (125 ka) based on the extent of amino acid racemization in fossil marine molluscs [140,141]. In this approach to stratigraphical correlation, the extent of amino acid racemization in the fossils is plotted against the current mean annual temperature of each site investigated. As diagenetic temperature is the dominant parameter influencing racemization rate, plotting the extent of amino acid racemization against current mean annual temperature provides a framework for evaluating the data. Fossils of equivalent age, when depicted on a linear plot of temperature, will define an exponential trend and accordingly demonstrate their time-equivalence (Fig. 9.10).

Numeric ages

The determination of numeric ages by amino acid racemization, representing the time since death, may be undertaken by calibrating the rate of racemization with an independent dating method such as radiocarbon or uranium-series dating and applying the parabolic kinetic model to derive ages for samples

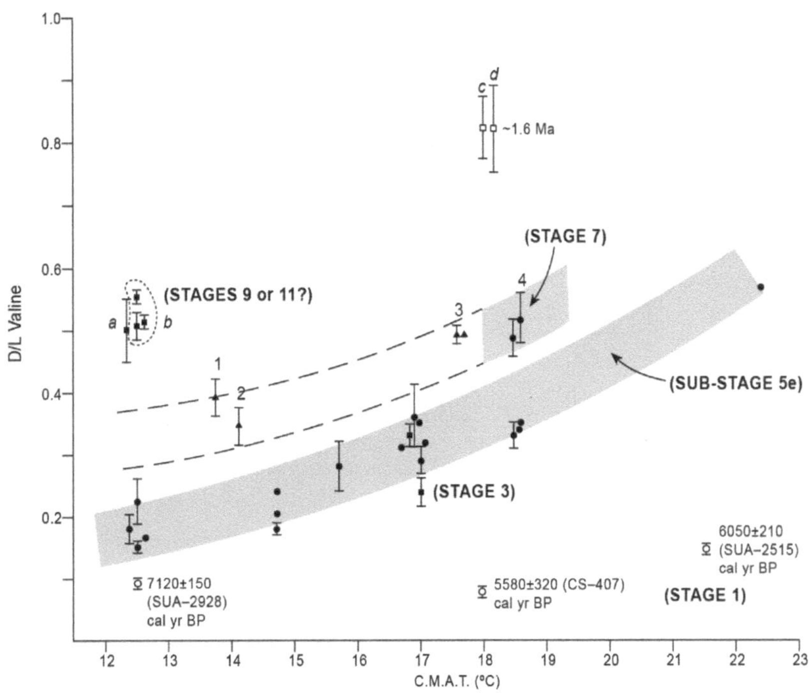

FIG. 9.10 The extent of valine racemization (total hydrolysable amino acids) in fossil marine molluscs of contrasting ages from southern Australia. The shaded Sub-stage 5e envelope refers to shells of last interglacial age (132–118 ka). The data are plotted against current mean annual air temperature.

of unknown age. Once the rate of racemization has been determined, the ages of other biominerals from the same local environment, that experienced similar *post-mortem* temperatures, can be determined for stratigraphically related or younger materials. Commonly this approach may involve the use one or more independent ages, as well as the extent of racemization in a modern biomineral, to determine the rate of racemization. This analytical protocol has been used for the dating of sub-fossil marine molluscs (*A. trapezia* and *N. trigonella*) of Holocene age from south-eastern Australia, to construct palaeosea-level curves and quantify rates of sedimentation in estuarine and lacustrine environments [98,142].

The determination of the amino acid racemization forward rate constant involves analysing a sub-sample of a biomineral also dated by the radiocarbon method. Another approach has involved analysing amino acids within the acid residue of the CO_2 evolution procedure in radiocarbon sample preparation of carbonate biominerals [143]. Independent ages from portions of the radiocarbon timescale in which there is a unique solution in their calibration to sidereal years, rather than potentially several radiocarbon ages of differing probability, is preferred for the calculation of a racemization rate constant.

This analytical protocol also enables amino acid racemization numeric ages to be assigned to biominerals that formed within the past 500 years. This time interval has been problematic to date by radiocarbon in view of statistically resolving ages from modern, as well as the challenges arising in uniquely calibrating radiocarbon ages to sidereal years. The necessity of independent geochronological calibration becomes less critical in instances where a large geochronological constrained amino acid data base has been established for a specific geographical region.

Identification of time-averaged and reworked materials and mixed-aged populations

The time-averaging and reworking of fossils and biominerals commonly occurs within sedimentary environments, particularly those in higher energy systems with deep-profile taphonomically-active zones. The taphonomically-active zone refers to the depth down a sedimentary profile from the sediment-water or sediment-atmosphere interface subject to continued reworking and bioturbation. With continued sediment deposition, the lower portion of the profile becomes 'fossilised' and no longer subject to disturbance and the taphonomically-active zone progressively moves upwards, resulting in the lower portions of the sediment profile no longer subjected to reworking. In this sense, the taphonomically-active zone represents a palimpsest environment, characterised by the time-averaging of biota with the physical intermixing of biological remains of different ages that were not alive at the same time. A time-averaged sedimentary profile is considered to have formed over a continuous period of time and to have preserved fossils of differing age that during life did not overlap in time [144]. This contrasts with sedimentary successions that preserve reworked fossils of substantially different age to the host sediments. The extent of amino acid racemization in biominerals provides an opportunity to quantify the magnitude of time-averaging and reworking of sedimentary materials.

A particularly effective application of amino acid racemization has been in taphonomic studies to assess the magnitude of age difference in time-averaged successions as well as the extent of reworking of fossils in different sedimentary environments. This is particularly important in some field contexts as reworked biological materials may not immediately be evident based on their preservation state.

In a comprehensive study, Wehmiller et al. [145] examined the extent of isoleucine epimerization in molluscs (predominantly *Mercenaria* sp.) from 21 beaches between New Jersey and Florida. The study was undertaken to determine the magnitude of reworking of marine shells along the coastal plain, to quantify the residence time of shells in these littoral environments and to assess the implications for dating coastal deposits from the Atlantic Coastal Plain. The study focused on reworking of shells from older interglacial deposits into younger interglacial deposits, as the amino acid racemization method, with the exception of the present, Holocene interglacial, is unable to resolve time within older interglacials, such as the last interglacial Maximum (Marine Isotope Substage 5e – 132–118 ka ago). Wehmiller et al. [145] showed that based on the epimerization data there was a direct correlation between the blackening of *Mercenaria* sp. shells and their older inferred ages. They also concluded that approximately 60% of the shells collected from the modern beach surfaces of the Atlantic Coastal Plain were derived from a Pleistocene source.

In an investigation of fossil marine molluscs from cores collected offshore from Sydney, on the continental shelf in south-eastern Australia, variable degrees of sediment and fossil reworking was noted based on the extent of amino acid racemization [94] (Fig. 9.11).

Three cores collected in contrasting water depths revealed different magnitudes of sediment reworking, which relate to the location of the core sites to a sea level of approximately 125 m below present during the Last Glacial Maximum some 20 ka ago. Core VC#134 was collected in a present water depth of 150 m at a site that has always remained under water and as a result shows minimal evidence for reworking. The extent of alanine and valine racemization increases down-core as a step function indicating three discrete packages of sediment of progressively increasing age (Fig. 9.11). In core VC#121 collected in a present water depth of 139 m there is some evidence of sediment reworking and time-averaging of fossils as shown by the higher D/L values at 0.99 m and 1.55 m down core, compared with the underlying fossil molluscs at 1.85 and

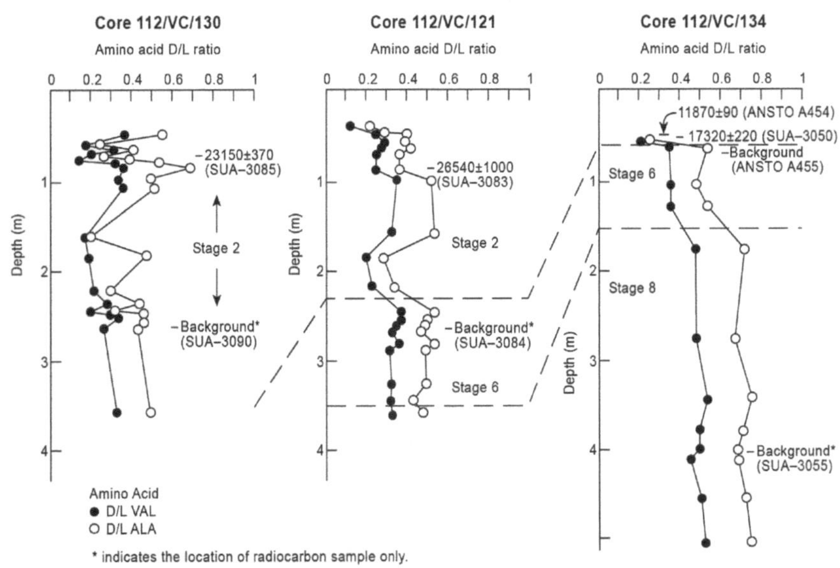

FIG. 9.11 The extent of alanine and valine racemization (total hydrolysable amino acids) in fossil marine molluscs from the continental shelf of south-eastern Australia. The marine sediments reveal varying degrees of sediment reworking and time-averaging of fossils based on the extent of racemization.

2.16 m (Fig. 9.9). Core VC#130 collected in a present water depth of 123 m is located, in principle, very close to the position of the Last Glacial shoreline and accordingly the sediment package shows the highest degree of sediment reworking and time-averaging of fossil molluscs (Fig. 9.11). Collectively, these two studies illustrate the utility of amino acid racemization in quantifying the time-averaging and reworking of biogenic remains.

Palaeotemperatures and exhumation

Subaerial exposure of sub-fossils for a lengthy portion of their *post-mortem* history is also a significant consideration in the application of amino acid racemization for defining the time since death. Given the exponential relationship between diagenetic temperature and reaction rate, high summer temperatures will disproportionately influence the rate of racemization in subaerially-exposed sub-fossils, resulting in a significantly higher extent of racemization than would be obtained if the material had remained continuously buried for the same period. In this regard, the extent of amino acid racemization with time will require calibration by an independent dating method such as radiocarbon on the same materials to determine the time since death and the duration of subaerial exposure. For example, specimens of the marine bivalve mollusc *Katelysia peronii* from the land surface on a beach ridge at Smoky Bay, South Australia, with a marine reservoir-corrected and calibrated radiocarbon age of 450 ± 80 yr cal BP (CS-416) had undergone a higher extent of racemization (D/L ASP of 0.31 ± 0.01) than in *K. rhytiphora* in 7370 ± 180 yr cal BP (CS-450) buried by 1.8 m of sediment (D/L ASP 0.23) from the same geographic region [146]. In some circumstances, however, the disproportionately high extent of racemization relative to inferred or independently determined age may assist in assessing if materials have been exhumed and then re-buried. Caution is required in selecting a calibration sample to ensure that it has remained buried for its entire diagenetic history to avoid ambiguous results.

Estimating the time since death over the past 500 years

In a pilot study Goodfriend et al. [101] examined the extent of aspartic acid racemization in a 350-year time series of samples from a living coral, *Porites australiensis* from the Great Barrier Reef, Queensland, Australia. Although aspartic acid has long been known as one of the fastest racemizing amino acids, the study revealed that aspartic acid racemization in *P. australiensis* is the fastest of any amino acid in any currently analysed biomineral. They noted that the initial rate of racemization was equivalent to 0.6% per year but slowed to 0.04% per year in the older growth bands of the corals. The aspartic acid D/L values ranged between 0.05 for 1985 CE to D/L 0.26 for 1632 CE. The mean annual sea surface temperature for the sample site is 24.3 °C. Goodfriend et al. [101] suggested that the extent of aspartic acid racemization could be used as a method to assess if some corals of interest have missing growth bands. In a similar study, Goodfriend et al. [96] used the extent of aspartic acid racemization to examine growth rates and longevity of the slit shell *Entemnotrochus adansonianus*, a living fossil which frequents the upper part of continental slope environments. Based on the racemization results they concluded that these gastropods have life spans averaging six years, similar to littoral taxa.

Conclusions

Time-dependent amino acid racemization reactions have been widely used in determining the time since death of a range of biological materials, as well as defining the biological age of materials at the time of death for recently deceased individuals. Historically, the majority of applications of amino acid racemization have involved the analysis of biogenic remains that died several tens of thousands of years ago. Although fewer studies have attempted to define the time since death for biogenic remains that died within the past 500 years, application of the fast racemizing acid, aspartic acid, shows considerable promise in assigning numeric ages in this time interval. The calculation of numeric ages based on the extent of amino acid racemization requires calibration by an independent method of dating such as radiocarbon or uranium-series. Once a forward rate constant for the reaction has been determined, the ages of multiple individuals can be determined, providing insights into the dynamics of different sedimentary environments. Calibration of amino acid racemization rate also enables the method to be applied in palaeothermometry, as well as examining the nuances of time-averaging of sedimentary deposits and the recognition of reworked materials.

Acknowledgements

CVM-W acknowledges funding from the Australian Research Council over many years as well as financial support from *GeoQuest Research Centre*, University of Wollongong. The manuscript was read at draft stage by Dr Terry Lachlan.

References

[1] Korff SA, Danforth WE. Neutron measurements with boron-trifluoride counters. Phys Rev 1939;55(10):980.

[2] Damon PE, Lerman JC, Long A. Temporal fluctuations of atmospheric C-14 - causal factors and implications. Annu Rev Earth Planet Sci 1978;6:457–94.

[3] Suess HE. Secular variations of cosmic-ray-produced carbon 14 in atmosphere and their interpretations. J Geophys Res 1965;70(23):5937.

[4] Anderson EC, Libby WF. World-wide distribution of natural radiocarbon. Phys Rev 1951;81(1):64–9.

[5] Godwin H. Half-life of radiocarbon. Nature 1962;195(4845):984.

[6] Arnold JR, Libby WF. Age determinations by radiocarbon content; checks with samples of known age. Science 1949;110(2869):678–80.

[7] Pandow M, Mackay C, Wolfgang R. The reaction of atomic carbon with oxygen - significance for the natural radio-carbon cycle. J Inorg Nucl Chem 1960;14(3–4):153–8.

[8] Bronk Ramsey C, Brenninkmeijer CAM, Jöckel P, Kjeldsen H, Masarik J. Direct measurement of the radiocarbon production at altitude. Nucl Instrum Methods Phys Res Sect B Beam Interact Mater Atoms 2007;259(1):558–64.

[9] Lelieveld J, Brenninkmeijer CAM, Joeckel P, Isaksen ISA, Krol MC, Mak JE, et al. New directions: watching over tropospheric hydroxyl (OH). Atmos Environ 2006;40(29):5741–3.

[10] Anderson EC, Libby WF, Weinhouse S, Reid AF, Kirshenbaum AD, Grosse AV. Radiocarbon from cosmic radiation. Science 1947;105(2735):576.

[11] Ramsey CB. Radiocarbon dating: revolutions in understanding. Archaeometry 2008;50(2):249–75.

[12] Libby WF. Chicago radiocarbon dates 3. Science 1952;116(3025):673–81.

[13] Libby WF, Anderson EC, Arnold JR. Age determination by radiocarbon content - world-wide assay of natural radiocarbon. Science 1949;109(2827):227–8.

[14] Kromer B, Munnich KO. Co_2 gas proportional counting in radiocarbon dating - review and perspective. Radiocarbon after four decades. 1992. p. 184–97.

[15] Povinec P, Polaskova H, Sivo A, Usacev S, Burchuladze AA, Eristavi IV, et al. Techniques for high accuracy radiocarbon measurements .1. Gas proportional counting. Radiochem Radioanal Lett 1978;33(1–2):67–76.

[16] Nelson DE, Korteling RG, Stott WR. Carbon-14: direct detection at natural concentrations. Science 1977;198(4316):507–8.

[17] Gupta SK, Polach HA. Radiocarbon dating practices at ANU. Australian National University; 1985. 187 p.

[18] Reimer PJ, Brown TA, Reimer RW. Discussion: reporting and calibration of post-bomb C-14 data. Radiocarbon 2004;46(3):1299–304.

[18a] de Vries HL. Variation in concentration of radiocarbon with time and location on Earth. Proc Koninkl Ned Akad Wetenschap 1958;**61**:94–102.

[19] Hogg A. SHCal13 southern Hemisphere calibration, 0–50,000 Years cal BP. Radiocarbon 2013;55(4):1889–903.

[20] Reimer PJ, Baillie MGL, Bard E, Bayliss A, Beck JW, Blackwell PG, et al. Intcal09 and Marine09 radiocarbon age calibration curves, 0-50,000 Years cal bp. Radiocarbon 2009;51(4):1111–50.

[21] Reimer PJ, Bard E, Bayliss A, Beck JW, Blackwell PG, Ramsey CB, et al. Selection and treatment of data for radiocarbon calibration: an update to the international calibration (intcal) criteria. Radiocarbon 2013;55(4):1923–45.

[22] Stuiver M, Reimer PJ, Bard E, Beck JW, Burr GS, Hughen KA, et al. INTCAL98 radiocarbon age calibration, 24,000–0 cal BP. Radiocarbon 1998;40(03):1041–83.

[23] Bronk Ramsey C. Bayesian analysis of radiocarbon dates. Radiocarbon 2009;51(01):337–60.

[24] Stuiver M, Reimer PJ. Extended 14C data base and revised CALIB 3.0 14C age calibration program. Radiocarbon 1993;35(1):215–30.

[25] Rafter TA, Fergusson GJ. Atom bomb effect - recent increase of carbon-14 content of the atmosphere and biosphere. Science 1957;126(3273):557–8.

[26] Broecker WS, Schulert A, Olson EA. Bomb carbon-14 in human beings. Science 1959;130(3371):331–2.

[27] Alkass K, Buchholz BA, Druid H, Spalding KL. Analysis of 14C and 13C in teeth provides precise birth dating and clues to geographical origin. Forensic Sci Int 2011;209(1–3):34–41.

[28] Alkass K, Buchholz BA, Ohtani S, Yamamoto T, Druid H, Spalding KL. Age estimation in forensic sciences. Mol Cell Proteom 2009;9(5):1022–30.

[29] Alkass K, Saitoh H, Buchholz BA, Bernard S, Holmlund G, Senn DR, et al. Analysis of radiocarbon, stable isotopes and DNA in teeth to facilitate identification of unknown decedents. PLoS One 2013;8(7):e69597.

[30] Brock F, Cook GT. Forensic Radiocarbon Dating of Human Remains: The Past, the Present, and the Future. Archaeol Environ Sci 2016;**1**(1):3–16.

[31] Buchholz BA, Alkass K, Druid H, Spalding KL. Bomb pulse radiocarbon dating of skeletal tissues. Elsevier; 2018. p. 185–96.

[32] Buchholz BA, Spalding KL. Year of birth determination using radiocarbon dating of dental enamel. Surf Interface Anal 2010;42(5):398–401.

[33] Calcagnile L, Quarta G, Cattaneo C, D'Elia M. Determining 14C content in different human tissues: implications for application of 14C bomb-spike dating in forensic medicine. Radiocarbon 2013;55(3):1845–9.

[34] Cook GT, Dunbar E, Black SM, Xu S. A preliminary assessment of age at death determination using the nuclear weapons testing 14C activity of dentine and enamel. Radiocarbon 2006;48(03):305–13.

[35] Geyh MA. Bomb radiocarbon dating of animal tissues and hair. Radiocarbon 2001;43(2B):723–30.

[36] Handlos P, Svetlik I, Horackova L, Fejgl M, Kotik L, Brychova V, et al. Bomb peak: radiocarbon dating of skeletal remains in routine forensic medical practice. Radiocarbon 2018;60(4):1017–28.

[37] Hodgins GWL. Measuring atomic bomb-derived 14 C levels in human remains to determine year of birth and/or year of death NCJRS Report 227839, US Department of Justice. 2009.

[38] Kjeldsen H, Heinemeier J, Heegaard S, Jacobsen C, Lynnerup N. Dating the time of birth: a radiocarbon calibration curve for human eye-lens crystallines. Nucl Instrum Methods Phys Res Sect B Beam Interact Mater Atoms 2010;268(7–8):1303–6.

[39] Lynnerup N, Kjeldsen H, Heegaard S, Jacobsen C, Heinemeier J. Radiocarbon dating of the human eye lens crystallines reveal proteins without carbon turnover throughout life. PLoS One 2008;3(1):e1529.

[40] Spalding KL, Buchholz BA, Bergman L-E, Druid H, Frisén J. Age written in teeth by nuclear tests. Nature 2005;437(7057):333–4.

[41] Taylor R, Myers Suchey J, Payen L, Slota P. The use of radiocarbon (^{14}C) to identify human skeletal materials of forensic science interest. Undefined 1989;34(5):1196–205.

[42] Ubelaker DH, Buchholz BA, Stewart JEB. Analysis of artificial radiocarbon in different skeletal and dental tissue types to evaluate date of death. J Forensic Sci 2006;51(3):484–8.

[43] Wild EM, Arlamovsky KA, Golser R, Kutschera W, Priller A, Puchegger S, et al. C-14 dating with the bomb peak: an application to forensic medicine. Nucl Instrum Methods B 2000;172:944–50.

[44] Zoppi U, Skopec Z, Skopec J, Jones G, Fink D, Hua Q, et al. Forensic applications of C-14 bomb-pulse dating. Nucl Instrum Methods B 2004;223:770–5.

[45] Hua Q, Barbetti M, Rakowski AZ. Atmospheric radiocarbon for the period 1950-2010. Radiocarbon 2013;55(4):2059–72.

[46] Buchholz BA, Spalding KL, Bergman LE, Druid H, Frisen J. ANYL 165-Forensic dating of dental enamel with bomb-pulse radiocarbon. Abstr Pap Am Chem Soc 2006;232.

[47] Ubelaker DH. Artificial radiocarbon as an indicator of recent origin of organic remains in forensic cases. J Forensic Sci 2001;46(6):1285–7.

[48] Harkness DD, Walton A. Carbon-14 in biosphere and humans. Nature 1969;223(5212):1216.

[49] Harkness DD, Walton A. Further investigations of transfer of bomb C-14 to man. Nature 1972;240(5379):302.

[50] Libby WF, Berger R, Mead JF, Alexander GV, Ross JF. Replacement rates for human tissue from atmospheric radiocarbon. Science 1964;146(3648):1170–2.

[51] Spalding KL, Bhardwaj RD, Buchholz BA, Druid H, Frisén J. Retrospective birth dating of cells in humans. Cell 2005;122(1):133–43.

[52] De La Torre HAM, Ormsby KM, Fuller BT, Santos GM. 14C measurements elucidate isotopic differences between nails and hair in modern humans. Radiocarbon 2014;56(1):53–65.

[53] Nydal R, Lövseth K, Syrstad O. Bomb 14C in the human population. Nature 1971;232(5310):418–21.

[54] Santos GM, De La Torre HAM, Boudin M, Bonafini M, Saverwyns S. Improved radiocarbon analyses of modern human hair to determine the year-of-death by cross-flow nanofiltered amino acids: common contaminants, implications for isotopic analysis, and recommendations. Rapid Commun Mass Spectrom 2015;29(19):1765–73.

[55] Robbins CR, Kelly C. Amino acid analysis of cosmetically altered hair. J Soc Cosmet Chem 1969;20(9):555.

[56] Hedges REM, Clement JG, Thomas CDL, O'Connell TC. Collagen turnover in the adult femoral mid-shaft: modeled from anthropogenic radiocarbon tracer measurements. Am J Phys Anthropol 2007;133(2):808–16.

[57] Ubelaker DH, Thomas C, Olson JE. The impact of age at death on the lag time of radiocarbon values in human bone. Forensic Sci Int 2015;251:56–60.

[58] Stenhouse MJ, Baxter MS. The uptake of bomb 14C in humans. In: Berger R, Suess HE, editors. Radiocarbon dating. Berkeley: University of California Press; 1979. p. 324–41.

[59] Babraj JA, Smith K, Cuthbertson DJ, Rickhuss P, Dorling JS, Rennie MJ. Human bone collagen synthesis is a rapid, nutritionally modulated process. J Bone Miner Res 2005;20(6):930–7.

[60] Enlow DH. Principles of bone remodeling; an account of post-natal growth and remodeling processes in long bones and the mandible. Springfield (IL): Thomas; 1963. p. 131.

[61] Manolagas SC, Jilka RL. Bone marrow, cytokines, and bone remodeling. Emerging insights into the pathophysiology of osteoporosis. N Engl J Med 1995;332(5):305–11.

[62] Parfitt AM. Targeted and nontargeted bone remodeling: relationship to basic multicellular unit origination and progression. Bone 2002;30(1):5–7.

[63] Nolla CM. The development of the human dentition. ASDC J Dent Child 1960;27:254–66.

[64] Bolaños MV, Manrique MC, Bolaños MJ, Briones MT. Approaches to chronological age assessment based on dental calcification. Forensic Sci Int 2000;110(2):97–106.

[65] Mays S. The archaeology of human bones. London, New York: Routledge; 1999. p. 242.

[66] Grün R, Abeyratne M, Head J, Tuniz C, Hedges REM. AMS 14C analysis of teeth from archaeological sites showing anomalous esr dating results. Quat Sci Rev 1997;16(3–5):437–44.

[67] Hedges REM, LeeThorp JA, Tuross NC. Is tooth enamel carbonate a suitable material for radiocarbon dating? Radiocarbon 1995;37(2):285–90.

[68] Helfman PM, Bada JL. Aspartic acid racemisation in dentine as a measure of ageing. Nature 1976;262(5566):279–81.

[69] Ritz S, Schutz HW, Schwarzer B. The extent of aspartic acid racemization in dentin: a possible method for a more accurate determination of age at death? Z für Rechtsmed 1990;103(6):457–62.

[70] Jorkov ML, Heinemeier J, Lynnerup N. The petrous bone–a new sampling site for identifying early dietary patterns in stable isotopic studies. Am J Phys Anthropol 2009;138(2):199–209.
[71] Bebe DC. The lens. In: Kaufman PL, Alm A, editors. Adler's physiology of the eye. St. Louis: Mosby Inc.; 2003. p. 117–58.
[72] Jeffery N, Spoor F. Prenatal growth and development of the modern human labyrinth. J Anat 2004;204(2):71–92.
[73] Frisch T, Overgaard S, Sørensen MS, Bretlau P. Estimation of volume referent bone turnover in the otic capsule after sequential point labeling. Ann Otol Rhinol Laryngol 2000;109(1):33–9.
[74] Sørensen MS, Bretlau P, Josrgensen MB. Bone repair in the otic capsule of the rabbit. Acta Otolaryngol 1992;112(6):968–75.
[75] Hare PE, Mitterer RM. Nonprotein amino acids in fossil shells, vol. 65. Carnegie Institution of Washington Yearbook; 1967. p. 362–4.
[76] Hare PE, Abelson PH. Racemization of amino acids in fossil shells, vol. 66. Carnegie Institution of Washington Yearbook; 1968. p. 526–8.
[77] Schroeder RA, Bada JL. A review of the geochemical applications of the amino acid racemization reaction. Earth Sci Rev 1976;12:347–91.
[78] Dungworth G. Optical configuration and the racemisation of amino acids in sediments and fossils – a review. Chem Geol 1976;17:135–53.
[79] Davies WD, Treloar FE. The application of racemisation dating in archaeology: a critical review. Artefact 1977;2:63–94.
[80] Williams KM, Smith GG. A critical evaluation of the application of amino acid racemization to geochronology and geothermometry. Orig Life 1977;8:91–144.
[81] Wehmiller JF. Relative and absolute dating of Quaternary molluscs with amino acid racemization: evaluation, applications and questions. In: Mahaney WC, editor. Quaternary dating methods. Amsterdam: Elsevier Science Publishers; 1984. p. 171–93.
[82] Masters PM. Amino acid racemisation dating – a review. In: Zimmerman MR, Angel JL, editors. Dating and age determination of biological materials. London: Croom Helm Press; 1986a. p. 39–58.
[83] Masters PM. Age determination of living mammals using aspartic acid racemisation in structural proteins. In: Zimmerman MR, Angel JL, editors. Dating and age determination of biological materials. London: Croom Helm Press; 1986b. p. 270–83.
[84] Murray-Wallace CV. A review of the application of the amino acid racemisation reaction to archaeological dating. Artefact 1993;16:19–26.
[85] Rutter NW, Blackwell B. Amino acid racemization dating. In: Rutter NW, Catto NR, editors. Dating methods for Quaternary deposits. Geological Association of Canada; 1995. p. 125–64. Geotext 2.
[86] Wehmiller JF, Miller GH. Aminostratigraphic dating methods in Quaternary geology. In: Noller JS, Sowers JM, Lettis WR, editors. Quaternary geochronology: methods and applications, vol. 4. Washington (DC): American Geophysical Union, Reference Shelf; 2000. p. 187–222.
[87] Miller GH, Clarke SJ. Amino-acid dating. In: Elias SA, editor. Encyclopedia of quaternary science. Amsterdam: Elsevier; 2007. p. 41–52.
[88] Miller GH, Kaufman DS, Clarke SJ. Amino acid dating. In: Elias SA, Mock CJ, editors. Encyclopedia of Quaternary Science. 2nd ed. Oxford: Elsevier; 2013. p. 37–48.
[89] Hare PE, Hoering TC, King Jr K. In: Biogeochemistry of amino acids. New York: John Wiley and Sons; 1980. p. 558.

[90] Goodfriend GA, Collins MJ, Fogel ML, Macko SA, Wehmiller JJ. In: Perspectives in amino acid and protein geochemistry. New York: Oxford University Press; 2000. p. 366.
[91] Amino acid racemizationPenkman K, Kaufman DS, editors. Quat Geochronol 2013;16:1−198.
[92] Murray-Wallace CV, Brooke BP, Cann JH, Belperio AP, Bourman RP. Whole-rock aminostratigraphy of the Coorong Coastal Plain, South Australia: towards a 1 million year record of sea-level highstands. J Geol Soc 2001;158:111−24. London.
[93] Reichert KL, Licciardi JM, Kaufman DS. Amino acid racemization in lacustrine ostracodes, part II: paleothermometry in Pleistocene sediments at Summer Lake, Oregon. Quat Geochronol 2011;6:174−85.
[94] Murray-Wallace CV, Ferland MA, Roy PS, Sollar A. Unravelling patterns of reworking in lowstand shelf deposits using amino acid racemisation and radiocarbon dating. Quat Sci Rev 1996;15:685−97.
[95] Simonson AE, Lockwood R, Wehmiller JF. Three approaches to radiocarbon calibration of amino acid racemization in *Mulinia lateralis* from the Holocene of Chesapeake Bay, USA. Quat Geochronol 2013;16:62−72.
[96] Goodfriend GA, Kashgarian M, Harasewych MG. Use of aspartic acid racemization and post-bomb ^{14}C to reconstruct growth rate and longevity of the deep-water slit shell *Entemnotrochus adansonianus*. Geochem Cosmochim Acta 1995;59:1125−9.
[97] Murray-Wallace CV, Colley SH. Amino acid racemisation and radiocarbon dating of a contact period midden, Greenglade rockshelter, New South Wales. Archaeol Ocean 1997;32:163−9.
[98] Sloss CR, Murray-Wallace CV, Jones BG, Wallin JT. Aspartic acid racemisation dating of mid-Holocene to recent estuarine sedimentation in New South Wales, Australia: a pilot study. Mar Geol 2004;212:45−59.
[99] Griffin RC, Moody H, Penkman KEH, Collins MJ. The application of amino acid racemization in the acid soluble fraction of enamel to the estimation of the age of human teeth. Forensic Sci Int 2008;175:11−6.
[100] Man EH, Sandhouse ME, Burg J, Fisher GH. Accumulation of D-aspartic acid with age in the human brain. Science 1983;220(4604):1407−8.
[101] Goodfriend GA, Hare PE, Druffel ERM. Aspartic acid racemization and protein diagenesis in corals over the last 350 years. Geochem Cosmochim Acta 1992;56:3847−50.
[102] Arany S, Ohtani S. Age estimation of bloodstains: a preliminary report based on aspartic acid racemization rate. Forensic Sci Int 2011;212:e36−9.
[103] Arany S, Ohtani S. Age estimation by racemization method in teeth: application of aspartic acid, glutamate, and alanine. J Forensic Sci 2010;55(3):701−5.
[104] Kalíková K, Šlechtová T, Tesařová E. Enantiomeric ratio of amino acids as a tool for determination of aging and disease diagnostics by chromatographic measurement. Separations 2016;3(30):1−18. https://doi.org/10.3390/separations 3040030.
[105] Bada JL, Zhao M, Steinberg S, Ruth E. Isoleucine stereoisomers on the Earth. Nature 1986;319:314−6.
[106] Neuberger A. Stereochemistry of amino acids. Adv Protein Chem 1948;4:298−383.
[107] Bada JL. Racemization of amino acids. In: Barrett GC, editor. Chemistry and Biochemistry of amino acids. Chapman and Hall; 1985. p. 399−414.
[108] Sykes GA, Collins MJ, Walton DI. The significance of a geochemically isolated intracrystalline organic fraction within biominerals. Org Geochem 1995;23:1059−65.
[109] Miller GH, Hart CP, Roark EB, Johnson BJ. Isoleucine epimerization in eggshells for the flightless Australian birds, *Genyornis* and *Dromaius*. In: Goodfriend GA, Collins MJ,

Fogel ML, Macko SA, Wehmiller JF, editors. Perspectives in amino acid and protein geochemistry. New York: Oxford University Press; 2000. p. 161–81.

[110] Penkman K, Kaufman DS, Maddy D, Collins MJ. Closed-system behaviour of the intra-crystalline fraction of amino acids in mollusc shells. Quat Geochronol 2008;3:2–25.

[111] Murray-Wallace CV, Kimber RWL. Further evidence for apparent 'parabolic' racemization kinetics in Quaternary molluscs. Aust J Earth Sci 1993;40:313–7.

[112] Kaufman DS, Manley WF. A new procedure for determining enantiomeric (D/L) amino acid ratios in fossils using reverse phase liquid chromatography. Quat Sci Rev 1998;17:987–1000.

[113] Murray-Wallace CV, Kimber RWL. Evaluation of the amino acid racemization reaction in studies of Quaternary marine sediments in South Australia. Aust J Earth Sci 1987;34:279–92.

[114] Murray-Wallace CV. Aminostratigraphy of Quaternary coastal sequences in southern Australia – an overview. Quat Int 1995;26:69–86.

[115] Masters PM, Bada JL, Zigler JS. Aspartic acid racemisation in the human lens during ageing and in cataract formation. Nature 1977;268:71–3.

[116] Lajoie KR, Wehmiller JF, Kennedy GL. Inter- and Intrageneric trends in apparent racemization kinetics of amino acids in Quaternary mollusks. In: Hare PE, Hoering TC, King Jr K, editors. Biogeochemistry of amino acids. New York: John Wiley and Sons; 1980. p. 305–40.

[117] Bada JL, Schroeder RA, Carter GF. New evidence for the antiquity of Man in North America deduced from aspartic acid racemization. Science 1974;184:791–3.

[118] Wehmiller JF. A review of amino acid racemization studies in Quaternary mollusks: stratigraphic and chronologic applications in coastal and interglacial sites, Pacific and Atlantic coasts, United States, United Kingdom, Baffin Island, and tropical islands. Quat Sci Rev 1982;1:83–120.

[119] Bowen DQ, Pillans B, Sykes GA, Beu AG, Edwards AR, Kamp PJJ, Hull AG. Amino acid geochronology of Pleistocene marine sediments in the Wanganui Basin: a New Zealand framework for correlation and dating. J Geol Soc 1998;155:439–46. London.

[120] Hearty PJ, Aharon P. Amino acid chronostratigraphy of late Quaternary coral reefs: Huon Peninsula, New Guinea, and the Great Barrier Reef, Australia. Geology 1988;16:579–83.

[121] Orem CA, Kaufman DS. Effects of basic pH on amino acid racemization and leaching of freshwater mollusc shell. Quat Geochronol 2011;6:233–45.

[122] McCoy WD. The precision of amino acid geochronology and palaeothermometry. Quat Sci Rev 1987;6:43–54.

[123] Clarke SJ, Murray-Wallace CV. Mathematical expressions used in amino acid racemisation geochronology – a review. Quat Geochronol 2006;1:261–78.

[124] King K, Neville C. Isoleucine epimerization for dating marine sediments: importance of analysing monospecific foraminiferal samples. Science 1977;195:1333–5.

[125] Miller GH, Brigham-Grette J. Amino acid geochronology: resolution and precision in carbonate fossils. Quat Int 1989;1:111–28.

[126] Pillans B. Amino acid racemisation dating: a review. In: Ambrose W, Duerden P, editors. Archaeometry: an Australasian perspective. Canberra: Australian National University; 1982. p. 228–35.

[127] McMenamin MAS, Blunt D, Kvenvolden KA, Miller SE, Marcus LF. Amino acid geochemistry of fossil bones from Rancho La Brea asphalt deposits, California. Quat Res 1982;18:174–83.

[128] Kimber RWL, Griffin CV. Further evidence of the complexity of the racemization process in fossil shells with implications for amino acid racemization dating. Geochem Cosmochim Acta 1987;51:839–46.

[129] Mitterer RM, Kriausakul N. Comparison of rates and degrees of isoleucine epimerization in dipeptides and tripeptides. Org Geochem 1984;7:91–8.

[130] Murray-Wallace CV, Belperio AP. Identification of remanié fossils using amino acid racemisation. Alcheringa 1994;18:219–27.

[131] Bright J, Kaufman DS. Amino acids in lacustrine ostracodes, part III: effects of pH and taxonomy on racemization and leaching. Quat Geochronol 2011;6:574–97.

[132] Tomiak PJ, Penkman KEH, Hendy EJ, Demarchi B, Murrells S, Davis SA, McCullagh P, Collins MJ. Testing the limitations of artificial protein degradation kinetics using known-age massive *Porites* coral skeletons. Quat Geochronol 2013;16:87–109.

[133] Ortiz JE, Sánchez-Palencia Y, Gutiérrez-Zugasti I, Torres T, González-Morales M. Protein diagenesis in archaeological gastropod shells and the suitability of this material for amino acid racemisation dating: *Phorcus lineatus* (de Costa, 1778). Quat Geochronol 2018;46:16–27.

[134] Kvenvolden K. Advances in the geochemistry of amino acids. Annu Rev Earth Planet Sci 1975;3:183–212.

[135] Kvenvolden K, Blunt DJ, Clifton HE. Amino-acid racemization in Quaternary shell deposits at Willapa Bay, Washington. Geochem Cosmochim Acta 1979;43:1505–20.

[136] Wehmiller JF, Belknap DF, Boutin BS, Mirecki JE, Rahaim SD, York LL. A review of the aminostratigraphy of Quaternary mollusks from United States Atlantic Coastal Plain sites. In: Easterbrook DJ, editor. Dating Quaternary sediments. Geological Society of America; 1988. p. 69–110. Special Paper 227.

[137] Mitterer RM, Kriausakul N. Calculation of amino acid racemization ages based on apparent parabolic kinetics. Quat Sci Rev 1989;8:353–7.

[138] Wehmiller JF. United States Quaternary coastal sequences and molluscan racemization geochronology – what have they meant for each other over the past 45 years? Quat Geochronol 2013;16:3–20.

[139] Blakemore A, Murray-Wallace CV, Westaway KE, Lachlan TJ. Aminostratigraphy and sea level history of the Pleistocene Bridgewater Formation, Mount Gambier region, southern Australia. Aust J Earth Sci 2015;62:151–69.

[140] Kennedy GL, Lajoie KR, Wehmiller JF. Aminostratigraphy and faunal correlations of late Quaternary marine terraces, Pacific Coast, USA. Nature 1982;299:545–7.

[141] Murray-Wallace CV, Belperio AP, Picker K, Kimber RWL. Coastal aminostratigraphy of the last interglaciation in southern Australia. Quat Res 1991;35:63–71.

[142] Sloss CR, Murray-Wallace CV, Jones BG. Holocene sea-level change on the southeast coast of Australia: a review. Holocene 2007;17:999–1014.

[143] Murray-Wallace CV, Bourman RP. Direct radiocarbon calibration for amino acid racemization dating. Aust J Earth Sci 1990;37:365–7.

[144] Flessa KW. Time-averaging. In: Briggs DEG, Crowther PR, editors. Palaeobiology II. Oxford: Blackwell Science; 2001. p. 292–6.

[145] Wehmiller JF, York LL, Bart ML. Amino acid racemization geochronology of reworked Quaternary mollusks on U. S. Atlantic coast beaches: implications for chronostratigraphy, taphonomy and coastal sediment transport. Mar Geol 1995;124:303–37.

[146] Murray-Wallace CV, Kimber RWL, Belperio AP. Holocene palaeotemperature studies using amino acid racemization. Aust J Earth Sci 1988;35:575–7.

Chapter 10

The development of grading systems to determine human decomposition: Total Body Scoring of decomposed human bodies in indoor settings

Jarvis Hayman, Marc Oxenham
School of Archaeology and Anthropology, Australian National University, Canberra, ACT, Australia

Introduction

Immediately following death, during the stage of body cooling and before autolysis becomes established, it is now well recognised that the two most reliable methods of estimating the time since death are firstly, the recording of body temperature together with the use of Hennsge's Nomogram and secondly, the measurement of vitreous potassium levels (see especially Chapter 2 and 3, this volume). Both methods have a recognised error rate. Once the stage of autolysis begins and progresses to active and then advanced decay of soft tissues and body organs, the estimation of the time since death becomes increasingly more difficult and the error rate increases with the time since death.

Statistical data concerning decomposed human bodies is difficult, if not impossible, to obtain because of the lack of compilation of national or even regional statistics. Australia is fortunate to have a statistical data base, the National Coronial Information System (NCIS) based at the Victorian Institute of Forensic Medicine in Melbourne which collects and collates data about all death investigations conducted by a Coroner in Australia and New Zealand. The purpose of the investigation is to determine the identity of the deceased and the cause of death and where appropriate, to make recommendations to prevent similar deaths from occurring. The NCIS database contains both coded and non-coded data as well as searchable legal, medical and scientific reports such as the coroner's finding, postmortem report, toxicology report and police

Estimation of the Time since Death. https://doi.org/10.1016/B978-0-12-815731-2.00010-8

summary of death report. As far as possible the data is nationally standardised. The data base is secure, but a search was ethically approved and statistics were compiled for the years 2000–10 [1]. This revealed that the majority of human bodies found decomposing and decomposed in the south eastern states of Australia and the Northern Territory were found indoors in houses and units. From this data a model was formulated for the estimation of the postmortem interval in decomposed bodies found indoors in Australian conditions.

With respect to the concept that it is informative to know where we have come from in order to know where we are going, the aim of this chapter is to provide a historical overview of research in this area, followed by a discussion of the more recent work into the development of body scoring systems.

The evolution of grading systems to determine decomposition in human bodies

Sung Tz'u, a 13th century Sung dynasty legal official and death investigator in China, was the first recorded person to recognise that the rate of human decomposition varied depending on environmental temperature. He noted; "[i] n extremely cold weather, five days is equivalent to one day in a time of great heat, and half a month the equivalent of three or four extremely hot days" [2]. In the age of enlightenment, an intellectual and philosophical movement that dominated the world of ideas in Europe during the 18th century, René - Antoine Ferchault de Réaumur was the first recorded scientist in the modern era to recognise the effect of temperature variations on the rate of progression of a natural system [3]. While studying the relationship between rates of growth of insects and temperature, he attempted to compute the rate of growth to temperature in a regular geometric progression. When he failed to do so, he recognised that there were other factors other than temperature, such as disease, parasites, predators and variable weather patterns which influenced rates of growth. Considering the effect of temperature on the rate of human decomposition, while it would seem to be the major factor affecting the rate, the conundrum has been how to factor in the many other variable factors such as moisture, location of the body, insect predation, wounding to the body and scavenging in the development of a model to narrow down the estimation of the time since death.

In the 19th century research centred mainly on describing the condition of exhumed bodies. In a remarkable paper for its time, and whose authors deserve better recognition, Matthieu Joseph Bonaventure Orfila, a Professor of Medicine in Paris and his colleague, Octave Lesueur, a Doctor of Medicine, published "Traité des Exhumations Juridiques et considerations sur les changemens physique que les cadavres éprouvent en se pourrissant dans la terre, dans l' eau, dans les fosses d'aissance et dans le fumier." ("*Treatise on Legal Exhumations and on the physical changes that corpses experience in rotting in the soil, water, pits and manure.*") [4].

The decomposition of twenty-one bodies dragged from the Seine in the 1820s, is described in great detail and includes descriptions of skin changes at the time of removal from the river, after exposure to air and after varying periods of immersion. Saponification is described as are the varying effects of age, sex, state of health and how in the obese, saponification occurs more rapidly. Orfila recognised that bodies in stagnant water decomposed faster than those in running water and that temperature made a difference to the rate of decomposition. The decomposition of internal organs and connective tissues is also described. Carrying out further research, Orfila buried the bodies of newborn infants who had died, in cesspits and in manure and studied and described the changes that occurred over several months. There are chapters comparing the decomposition process on bodies found in these environments and on decomposition changes in the digestive tract, a phenomenon which had long confounded pathologists. Finally, there is a chapter on the usefulness of autopsies on decomposed bodies as an aid to medico-legal diagnoses, particularly with regard to age, sex and identity and its usefulness in poisonings, infanticide and wounding. Many examples of cases are described in order to refute the commonly held belief at that time that autopsies on decomposed bodies were of no scientific use. Although Orfila made no attempt to estimate the time since death, nevertheless it is remarkable research for the period and not until more than a century later would similar research be carried out.

The first attempts at staging decomposition in human bodies were carried out by entomologists studying the succession of flies and insects inhabiting a cadaver in order to determine which group of insects inhabited the body at varying times after death. In 1894, J.P. Mégnin, a French army surgeon published a book; "La faune des cadavres: application de l'entomologie a la médecine légale." ("*The fauna of corpses: application of entomology to forensic medicine.*") [5]. Mégnin is often attributed as being the first research scientist to attempt to classify human decomposition but he did this by default. His detailed research describes the species of flies, insects, beetles and mites that inhabit a decomposing corpse over time and he is often quoted as describing eight stages of decomposition when in fact he describes eight "squads" or groups of insect species descending on the corpse over the time a human body was decomposing. In order to correlate the time at which each of these groups arrived on the corpse, he found it necessary to describe the stages of decomposition.

The first group inhabits a freshly dead body until fatty acid formation occurs. The second group arrives when the body exudes fluid and decomposition odours. The third group arrives three to six months after death when the volatile fatty acids dry up. In this context he recognises the differing rate of decomposition in bodies becoming mummified in the rarefied atmosphere of mountain tops and in hot dry desert conditions, compared with those bodies decomposing in graves when fatty acids are slower to dissipate and when adipocere can form. Between three and six months, caseation can occur, when the fourth group then arrives. The fifth group consisting of Diptera and beetles arrives when ammoniacal fermentation of the caseous material produces a blackish liquefaction of the animal matter. The insects of the sixth group, mainly mites, arrive between four to eight months and he attributes them to completing the desiccation or mummification process. The seventh group arrives between one and three years and the eighth group after that time, converting the corpse to debris.

In 1896 and 1897, M.G. Motter studied 150 disinterred bodies in and around Washington DC with the purpose of ascertaining the condition of the bodies at varying times after burial and the insects associated with them [6]. Commenting on Mégnin's study Motter [6] states that his findings had been accepted by the French courts, legal decisions made and sentences imposed as a result of them. However, he states [6: 228] that, with regard to using insect successions to estimate the time since death;

> *I am thoroughly convinced that we cannot, as yet, make any broad, universally applicable generalisations on this subject. The field is far too broad, the important and modifying factors are far too numerous and conflicting, the conditions vary far too widely to be thus comprehended in any concise, unqualified formula. The only conclusion I can reach, as the result of my studies thus far, is that it is not safe to draw any conclusion at all.*

Motter also made some relevant observations regarding the conditions of the bodies. He lists some of the conditions affecting the progress and process of decomposition as; age, sex, race, character and duration of the disease process, mode of death, the season of the year at which this occurs as well as the temperature of the sick room. Also listed are the manner of cleaning, embalming and clothing the body, the type of coffin, the depth of the grave and character of the soil used to fill the grave including its temperature, moisture content and physical and chemical characteristics. Lastly, the general physical, climatic and meteorological conditions of the cemetery are also important and that each case would seem to be a law unto itself. Indeed, he states that "so varied and so numerous are the modifying conditions and circumstances that it is impossible to say, definitely and absolutely, what is the exact order of disappearance of the several organs and tissues." [6:203].

The very interesting observations from these studies were not to be repeated until the 1980s and no further attempts were made to classify the stages of decomposition until Fuller's study in 1934 [7]. This hiatus in research was possibly because of the intervention of two World Wars and the Great Depression of the 1920s. In 1934, Fuller, working with sheep and cat carcasses, divided decomposition into three stages. Howden, in an unpublished thesis and working with partial and entire carcasses of an assorted variety of animals, recognised two stages [8]. Reed, in 1958, seems to be the first to define a more descriptive scale of decomposition with defined durations when he studied insect successions on dog carcasses in Tennessee [9].

Reed recognised four stages; 1. Fresh stage starting at death and continuing until bloating occurred, usually after one day; 2. Bloated stage. This ended when bloating ceased to be evident. The time period varied, being rapid in summer and slower in colder weather; 3. Decay Stage. This began when bloating had ceased and ended when the carcass had dried out; 4. Dry stage. Reed found the limits of this stage more difficult to define but it began when only small amounts of decaying tissue remained and ended when no carrion fauna remained.

Bornemissza, studying the arthropod succession on dead and decomposing guinea pigs, recognised five stages; 1. Initial Decay stage, 2. Putrefaction stage, 3. Black Putrefaction stage, 4. Butyric Fermentation stage and 5. Dry Decay stage [10]. He also found that the rate of decomposition was largely dependent on climatic and seasonal conditions as well as the type of soil.

In a seminal study in 1965, Payne researched decomposition in animals with and without insect access [11]. After finding that decomposition in small animals such as frogs, toads, mice, shrews, rats, and chipmunks was too rapid to allow the detailed study of insect succession and the feathers in chickens caused problems in recognition and estimation of insects, he found baby pigs more suitable for the study. Recognising decomposition as a continuous process, he described in detail six stages of decomposition when the various insects were attracted to the carcasses: fresh, bloated, active decay, advanced decay, dry, and remains. He found a defined insect succession at each stage of decomposition and that carcasses exposed to insects decomposed more rapidly. In carcasses that were kept free of insects, he defined different descriptive stages with the time interval for each stage. These were 1. Fresh: 1-1½ days; 2. Bloating and Decomposition: 8 days; 3. Flaccidity and Dehydration: 6 days; 4. Mummification stage: up to 2 months; 5. Desiccation and Dehydration: unknown. As well as staging decomposition, Payne also seems to have been the first to attempt to correlate the stages with the variables of environmental temperature, insects and moisture. In 1983, Rodriguez and Bass used human cadavers in their study of insect activity and its relationship to decomposition [12]. They used Reed's 1958 description of four stages [9].

Apart from the studies of Payne [11] and Rodriguez and Bass [12] all studies attempting to stage decomposition until the 1980s were by entomologists trying to correlate the various stages of decomposition with the varying species of flies and insects inhabiting carcasses. Galloway and colleagues seem to have been the first to attempt decomposition staging in human bodies for purposes other than insect succession staging [13]. They carried out a retrospective study of autopsy reports, forensic anthropological reports and photographs in 189 cases of human remains found in the arid, dry conditions of Arizona, where the date when they were last seen alive until recovery of remains occurred was known, thus providing a time for the postmortem interval (PMI). The authors acknowledged that because of the retrospective nature of the study and that the staging of many cases relied on photographic records, certain errors and inaccuracies were possible and that it was probable that the PMI was overestimated in many cases. Five stages of decomposition were recognised in this study; 1. Fresh; 2. Early Decomposition; 3. Advanced Decomposition; 4. Skeletonisation; and 5. Extreme Decomposition. Within each stage, subcategories were recognised, up to six different subcategories within some of the stages. The location of the body was noted to be important regarding the rate of decomposition; bodies found in the open decomposed faster than those that were buried or found indoors, those found at higher levels and in colder seasons decomposed more slowly, but no conclusion could be made about those found in water as the number of cases in this location were too few in number. Data were collected regarding the amount of clothing on bodies, sex, age and racial affinity. An approximate time sequence of the stages of decomposition was calculated and the factors accelerating or slowing the process recognised such as insect access, season of the year, temperature, moisture and humidity and carnivore scavenging. This was an important study as it was the first carried out to quantify the stages of human decomposition and to iterate the probable factors influencing its rate.

Vass and colleagues introduced the concept of accumulated degree days (ADDs) into decomposition research, in order to standardise temperature accumulation over time and with the purpose of using it to estimate the PMI [14]. They based their definition of ADDs on that of Edwards and colleagues as being the sum of the average daily temperatures in degrees Centigrade above 0 °C for however many days the corpse had been decomposing [15]. Seven decomposing cadavers were placed face down on soil at various times of the year and the quantitative amounts of volatile fatty acids (VFAs), as well as cations and anions released into the soil below the bodies, were measured. They found that butyric, valeric and propionic acids were most suitable for analysis and that only seven ions (sodium, chloride, ammonium, potassium, calcium, magnesium and sulphate) leaching from the cadaver, were stable enough in the soil to enable analysis. Maximum and minimum temperatures of the environment every three days in summer and autumn and weekly in winter were recorded as well as insect activity. The stages of body decomposition were based on that of Reed (1958) i.e. four stages of fresh, bloated, decay and dry [9]. Vass and colleagues noted that two variables, soil moisture and body weight, were important in determining the concentration of VFAs in soil solution [14]. Once these two factors were standardised and considered the most important factor determining the speed of VFA concentration was temperature. It was noted that bodies decomposed more slowly in cooler temperatures compared with warmer temperatures. By equating the concentration of VFAs in soil solution beneath the corpse with the amount of accumulated degree days, an estimation of the time since death could be given as they calculated that soft tissue decomposition ceased after 1285 ± 110 ADDs.

Vass and colleagues' [14] definition of ADDs varies somewhat from the definition of Degree Days that Edwards and colleagues [15] introduced. The latter authors proposed a "Temperature Development Unit" for insect development because they had noted that temperature controlled insect development from fertilisation of the egg to maturity and this process occurred within the limits of upper and lower temperature thresholds. Insects are cold blooded organisms. If the temperature rises, then insect development may be more rapid and conversely development occurs more slowly at lower temperatures. Eventually the required amount of heat is accumulated and insect development is completed. Edwards et al. [15: 5] stated that "*a Degree Day is the amount of biological activity caused by 1 degree above threshold for 1 day.*" It is implicit in this definition of Degree Days that there is a clear temperature threshold below and above which insect development doesn't occur but in Vass and colleagues' [14] definition there is no clear threshold, either above or below which decomposition ceases. Human body decomposition is a dynamic process with no defined temperature limit above or below which it ceases. Regarding the lower threshold, Vass and colleagues [14] state that it is difficult to determine the time since death because below 4 °C greater concentrations of longer chained VFAs are released and even below 0 °C decomposition will occur because of the increased concentrations of salt in the human body. Therefore, Vass and colleagues [14] arbitrarily decided that any decomposition below 0 °C would have ceased in order to avoid subtracting days from the time since death estimate. No attempt was made in this study to equate the time since death with the stage of body decomposition as the seven bodies were deposited at various times of year and therefore, they were exposed to widely different temperature variations.

A further study by Vass and colleagues in 2002 analysed the chemical markers associated with the decomposition of human remains in order to identify time dependent biomarkers of decomposition [16]. It was hoped that the biomarkers could be equated with the various stages of decomposition and would therefore enable an estimation of the time since death. Eighteen cadavers were placed in various contexts at a body decomposition facility over a four-year period and various chemical compounds in the heart, lung, brain, kidney, liver, and muscle associated with decomposition were analysed. The contexts included on top of soil, in polyethylene body bags; some were fresh from morgue storage, while others had been stored for some time. Various amino acid and other chemical biomarkers were analysed from the various body organs over varying periods of time. Complex models were produced of the concentration of the chemicals released from the various body organs, the concentrations correlating with various times after death thus giving an estimate of the time since death. The algorithms were complex and difficult to use in general forensic analysis. The important facts to arise from this study were the reported accuracy of the VFA method of determining time since death (TSD) in pre-skeletonised remains which was ± 2 days and in skeletonised remains it was ±2 weeks. It was also found that Accumulated Degree Days were no longer sufficiently accurate to describe the narrowing time since death intervals which were equated with the appearance of the various chemicals. Therefore, Cumulative Degree Hours were introduced and defined as the average temperature in degrees Centigrade for each 12 h interval cumulatively added. Temperature data were obtained from the nearest National Weather Service Station.

Present research into human Total Body Scoring systems

In 2007, Henssge and Madea, in a paper outlining progress in estimation of the time since death up to that time, stated;

> *[t]hus, most methods proposed for estimation of the time since death are of only academic interest since they describe just post-mortem changes. They only gain practical relevance if the following criteria are fulfilled: quantitative measurement, mathematical description, taking into account influencing factors quantitatively, declaration of precision and proof of precision on independent material [17:183].*

In 2005, an important study foreshadowing this principle was published by Megyesi and colleagues [18]. The study recognised that soft tissue decomposition was a sequential process with numerous small changes occurring throughout and it was the first study to quantify human decomposition independently rather than as a function of some other quantifiable process. An attempt was made to correlate the qualitatively described stages with a quantitative point value system assigned to each stage. Sixty-eight cases of human remains were examined, taken from forensic case files in many states throughout the USA and which had a wide range of environmental conditions e.g. Texas, Florida, and New York. They also came from several contexts such as outside in the shade and in the sun, indoors, clothed and unclothed. All cases showed evidence of insect access but only cases with a known PMI of up to 1 year were chosen and the time when death had occurred was known in all cases. The state of decomposition was assessed and quantitatively staged from photographs of the remains. Four broad categories of decomposition were described; 1. Fresh; 2. Early Decomposition; 3. Advanced Decomposition; 4. Skeletonisation. Within each stage, point values were allocated to various stages of the decomposition process, up to 5 points in some of the stages. Because it was recognised that different parts of the body decomposed in a different manner, the body was divided into three parts, 1. Head and Neck, 2. Trunk and 3. The Limbs. Scoring was made for each of the three parts for each body which, when summated, gave a Total Body Score (TBS).

Megyesi and colleagues [18] also recognised that previous studies had equated decomposition with only the passage of time when the more important variable affecting the process was temperature. To achieve the quantification of temperature with time they used Accumulated Degree Days (ADDs) but they defined these more accurately than Edwards, Chaney and Bergman [15] and Vass et al. [14]. Recognising that the higher the temperature the faster decomposition occurred and that below a certain temperature the process ceased, they calculated ADDs as the average of the maximum and minimum air temperatures for each day that the body was decomposing, taken from the nearest National Weather Service Station. Because there was no evidence to determine the temperature below which decomposition ceased, 0 °C was taken as the base level and ADDs were calculated by summating all average daily temperatures above 0 °C from death until discovery.

The quantitative analysis plotted TBS as the dependent variable against PMI and ADD as the independent variables. The relationships were not linear but, by log transforming both the ADD and PMI and squaring the TBS, an effective linear relationship was found, from which an equation could be produced. To find the PMI for any given case, the TBS would be calculated and this figure then substituted in the equation to calculate the figure for ADD. Once the ADD was known, the PMI could be calculated. Megyesi et al. [18] stressed that the study only accounted for accumulated time and temperature as the main variables affecting decomposition and that other variables such as animal scavenging, sunlight, rainfall, and clothing might not be possible to quantify. Over 80% of the observed variation in human decomposition could be accounted for by the combination of elapsed time and temperature as reflected in ADDs.

Megyesi and colleagues [18] admitted that this was only a preliminary study and was retrospective. The method of Total Body Scoring and of calculating ADDs are open to criticism but unfortunately this has not stopped other researchers using both systems without modifications. The first criticism is that the TBS was calculated from many human remains taken from a wide variety of geographical environments and contexts without accounting for this type and degree of variability. Secondly, the scoring was compiled from photographs of the bodies, some not complete, some clothed, some not clothed and in various contexts rather than by direct observation and assessment of the bodies. The method of calculating ADDs is also open to criticism on several points. Despite these criticisms the study by Megyesi et al. [18] has prompted researchers to pursue quantitative methods of determining the PMI in a variety of environments and contexts [19–25].

Fitzgerald and Oxenham proposed a different method of determining the TBS when they devised a Degree of Decomposition Index (DDI) while studying the differential decomposition of two pigs, one in full sunlight and the other in semi-shade [20]. The DDI was a numerical scale of the decomposition process which incorporated three other devised scales; those of Rodriguez and Bass [12], Galloway et al. [13] and Megyesi et al. [18]. The derivation of the DDI was based on the method of Megyesi et al. [18] which used decomposition categories independently on separate body parts. Temperature and humidity were recorded close to each carcass while decomposing and it was proved that decomposition was significantly different in the two environments. The pig decomposing in full sunlight decomposed faster in the initial stages than the pig in shade but both reached the skeletal stage about the same time. The DDI, plotted against TSD, in days, for both carcasses was compared with the decomposition scales of Rodriguez and Bass [12] and of Galloway et al. [13] and found to be more closely related to that of Rodriguez and Bass but not at all to that of Galloway et al. [13]. It was also much smoother and more gradual than either of the other methods. There were no statistical differences in the DDI of either carcass and when the DDI was plotted against the log transformed TSD, a linear relationship was produced which indicated a very strong relationship between the DDI and TSD, TSD accounting for 95% of the variation in decomposition between the carcasses. Fitzgerald and Oxenham [20] concluded that TSD was not only a measure of transpired time, but it also incorporated environmental variables specific to the TSD such as the variables of temperature and humidity but without quantifying them whereas ADD, as described by Megyesi et al. [18], also quantified temperature and humidity during the decomposition period for a specific site when those quantities were known. However, there were issues with the use of ADDs retrospectively as shown by Dabbs [26], Archer [27] and Johnson et al. [28].

In 2016 Hayman and Oxenham developed a different method of Total Body Scoring after researching the Australian National Coronial Information System (NCIS) Data Base [25]. This unique system has recorded the details of all cases reported to Australian coroners since the year 2000. By examining over 4000 cases of decomposed bodies, mainly in the temperate eastern states but also the tropical Northern Territory, it was found that over 70% were found indoors in houses and units. These were narrowed down to 239 cases where the time since death (TSD) could be accurately determined from police and coroners' reports. As pathologists' reports are standardised, it was possible to determine that certain organs decomposed in a gradual and easily described manner which correlated with the passage of time. These were the brain, the spleen, the heart and the liver. By allocating a numerical score to the descriptive stages of decomposition of each of these organs, together with a numerical score of the external body appearance, it was possible to derive a TBS when the values were summated. It was found that estimating the TBS up to 14 days postmortem was reliable but after that time the estimation of TBS and of TSD became unreliable. ADDs were calculated from the nearest Bureau of Meteorological weather station but because these were too distant from body discovery sites in rural areas, only decomposed bodies found in large state capital cities close to weather stations were considered for statistical analysis. Several temperature and humidity parameters as well as ADDs and a new concept, Accumulated Humidity Days (AHDs), were determined for the length of time during which bodies were decomposing but the correlation between these parameters and the TSD was found to be too weak to continue exploring them. However, the correlation between the TSD and the TBS in all states was very strong. Models were developed for each state to estimate the TSD of decomposed bodies up to 14 days (Table 10.1). Beyond this time period the models became less reliable. In all states 94% −96% of the TSD could be accounted for by the TBS. There was no indication of the cause of the remaining 4%−6% but it was found that the TSD was shorter for the same TBS value in the tropical Northern Territory than in the more temperate southern states, indicating that the higher temperature played an important part in accelerating the decomposition process. It was also found that the External Body Score (EBS) gave a close approximation of the TSD which would be a useful estimate while awaiting an autopsy to give a TBS.

No new methods of body scoring systems seem to have been developed but further studies have been carried out in attempts to improve upon the existing systems especially the Megyesi et al. system [18]. Further problems remaining to be researched and improved upon are; 1. The accuracy of temperature measurements during the time a body is decomposing and the statistical correlation of temperature measurements with the TSD; 2. The inter-observer reliability of scoring systems for the TBS; 3. Which TBS system gives the best results?; 4. Will it be possible to develop a "universal formula" for the estimation of TSD?

The problem of accurate temperature recording

Entomologists have long recognised the difficulty of measuring temperature and humidity when assessing the growth cycle of insects and their use in assessing the temporal degree of decomposition. Catts [29] commented that

TABLE 10.1 Formulae for estimating the time since death (TSD) in each state.

Region	TSD equation
New South Wales	= −2.138 + (0.624 × TBS)
Victoria	= −5.278 + (0.917 × TBS)
Tasmania	= −2.968 + (0.614 × TBS)
Northern Territory	= −0.840 + (0.345 × TBS)
Total all states	= −2.977 + (0.668 × TBS)
Southern states only	= −3.343 + (0.733 × TBS)

the use of temperature recordings from a weather station some distance from the corpse, and even from one close by, may not be valid because even although gross weather conditions may be similar, microhabitat conditions might differ considerably and may not be comparable. Archer [27] noted that there were no data examining the accuracy of correlating relationships between body discovery sites and weather station temperature measurements in the retrospective estimation of temperatures when the body lay in situ and that there were also no data on whether regression relationships between body discovery sites and weather stations were likely to vary over time. In this context Archer [27] researched the correlation regarding the effect of temperature differences between body discovery site and the length of time after body removal. Six hypothetical body discovery sites were chosen within a 5 km radius of the main Melbourne Regional Office (MRO) official recording station. Data loggers at these sites recorded temperatures for seven consecutive days then a further four periods of 10 days each. The temperature records were then compared with the MRO temperature records for the same periods. It was found that the mean estimated temperatures for the recording periods at the various sites varied greatly but statistically correcting them usually provided a more accurate representation of site temperatures during the period the body remained in situ, than uncorrected data, regardless of time after body removal. However, the degree of improvement was highly variable between correlation periods.

Johnson et al. [28], expanding on Archer's [27] work, published further research examining additional factors affecting ambient temperature corrections of weather station data in forensic entomology. Ambient temperature data were collected from 16 hypothetical body discovery sites in two different states in Australia, in two different seasons, and across several geographical regions. They were then compared with temperature data from the nearest weather station which were all within 15 km of the body discovery sites. The accuracy of retrospective weather data collection was tested by four experiments: firstly, to test the length of the correlation period; secondly, to test the distance between body discovery sites and weather stations; thirdly, to test the periodicity of ambient temperature measurements; and finally, to assess statistical correlation accuracy in casework scenarios. Their results showed that correlation resulted in a significant improvement over raw weather data regardless of the length of the correlation period, improving the accuracy of body site discovery temperature estimation by more than 1(±0.5 °C) in 96% of correlations [28]. Secondly, there was no effect of distance on the accuracy of correlations for either experimental season. Thirdly, results suggested that 30-min and 3-hourly temperature measurement intervals provided improvement over raw weather data, but twice-daily measurements did not. Lastly, when assessing correlation accuracy in casework scenarios, the greater the difference between the average weather station temperatures for the in situ body period and the average weather station temperatures for the correlation period, the greater was the accuracy. In those cases where the accuracy was not good, it was made acceptable by extending the duration of the correlation period. Johnson and colleagues [28] concluded that retrospective ambient temperature correction of weather station temperature was a robust technique, the accuracy of which was not affected by season, the length of the correlation period, or distances up to 15 km between the site of body discovery and the weather station. The accuracy, however, was diminished if there was >5 °C difference between weather station, body in situ, and correlation data. Extending the length of the correlation period from 2 to 5 days could overcome this error and in fact the authors recommended the collection of correlation data for 10 days when possible, and at intervals not longer than every 30 min or 3 h.

Dabbs compared the differences in temperature data between a decomposition site at Farmington, Arkansas and two National Weather Service (NWS) stations, 5.7 and 9.9 km away over a 154 day period [26]. Statistically corrected data showed that the NWS station closest to the decomposition site had an average absolute temperature difference of 2 °C while the average absolute difference between the decomposition site and the NWS station further away was 1 °C. PMI was calculated in days for TBS ranging from 3 to 27 using the equation published by Megyesi and colleagues [18] to calculate ADDs. Dabbs found that the average difference in the PMI estimate between the decomposition site and the nearest NWS station was 5.8 days while that between the decomposition site and the furthest NWS station was 3.55 days. Dabbs concluded that blind utilisation of temperature data from the nearest NWS station to the decomposition site was inappropriate and secondly that it was necessary to develop a protocol to test for agreement between a decomposition site and the nearest NWS site before estimation of PMI in forensic cases.

Dabbs carried out further research to examine the long term correlation of site-specific and NWS temperature data in order to assess the usefulness of simple mean difference adjustments and regression adjustments to correct retrospectively collected NWS data for use as a site-specific temperature model in the estimation of PMI over a long time span [30]. Dabbs used data collected from 15 widely scattered sites over the mid-west and north east part of the USA over a 13 month period. The results of the study revealed that correction of NWS temperature data using either regression or simple mean difference adjustment was not a robust technique for the long term frame, over months, typically found in forensic anthropology studies. Dabbs [30] strongly recommended that investigators using quantitative methods of estimating the PMI, incorporating temperature data, should consider using uncorrected retrospectively collected NWS temperature data for time periods concurrent with the decomposition data but ensure margins of standard error were sufficient to accommodate the use of that data. The data could be from NWS stations within 15.3 km of the decomposition site but not necessarily limited to the closest site as a site further away may be a better fit to the model. These studies would indicate that the method of collecting temperature data for any quantitative decomposition model seems to be unresolved.

Inter-observer reliability of body scoring systems

Recent research has shown that inter-observer reliability of body scoring systems can be statistically reliable. Nawrocka et al. [31] conducted a study using 120 students of law, medicine and biology who had undergone training in the use of a TBS system based on that of Galloway et al. [13]. After training they were asked to quantify decomposition from 12 digital photographs of pig carcasses. Results collected and statistically adjusted indicated that the TBS scale, when used by different people, gave homogeneous results irrespective of the user qualifications. It was also found that scores in the early stages of decomposition which showed a mosaic of changes and those in the advanced stage were less accurately scored. The researchers also noted that scoring by the percentages method such as that used by Vass, led to inconsistencies among observers [32].

Dabbs et al. compared the scoring of human decomposition from digital images to scoring using direct observations [33]. Sixteen observers who had been previously trained to collect decomposition data and who worked at three decomposition facilities, scored the level of decomposition in 59 digital observation packages using the Megyesi et al. TBS method [18]. 13 cadavers with a TSD between 2 and 186 days were laid out in a supine position on the ground outdoors at a decomposition facility, either naked or lightly clothed. The researchers found no statistical difference between TBS scoring from digital images and direct observation when corrected statistically. They did find, however, that bodies in the early stages of decomposition were scored higher from digital images than by direct observation and that observers with less than 1 years' experience were less reliable in their TBS scoring of digital images compared with direct observation.

Which Total Body Scoring system gives the best results?

If a quantitative TBS System is to be used by all researchers it must be standardised, accurate and as simple as possible in the description of the quantification of the different phases of decomposition in order to reduce the error rate when used in practice by different anthropologists. It should also be recognised that decomposition is a dynamic process involving all the body organs and not just the external appearance, the most obvious manifestation of it. The beginning and the end of each phase has to be as descriptively accurate as possible in order to be understood by all observers and the time period of each phase has to be correlated with the variables which affect its progression, the main ones being temperature, humidity, insect effects, and environmental variables.

The early scoring methods such as that used by Reed [9] and Payne [11] were descriptive only and not quantitative, giving no clear indication as to when each stage began or ended, even although Payne indicated the number of days each stage lasted. The percentage method was suggested by Vass who states that it should be done by a qualified investigator with input from a Medical Examiner or Forensic Anthropologist [32]. It should incorporate an assessment of the environmental air temperature with warm defined as being greater than 12 °C as flies do not fly or oviposit on a corpse this temperature and cold being less than 12 °C, no decomposition occurring below 0 °C. This method, however, is very subjective with no defined limits from which the decomposition percentage is being determined. The first quantitative method of Galloway et al. [13] was a retrospective study compiled from case files from a number of different contexts and environments and it did not account for the large number of variables causing decomposition. However, it did, for the first time, introduce a detailed method of staging the decomposition process. The method of Megyesi et al. was the first to incorporate the main variables of temperature and time, as expressed by accumulated degree days, in a specific mathematical formula [18]. This study, as stated previously was a retrospective one using photographs of bodies from a wide variety of geographical environments and contexts and in varying degrees of dress and undress. This makes its accuracy dubious. Indeed Megyesi et al. state that much more can be done to refine their method such as only using it on adult sized remains, and that it should be tested by multiple practitioners and in a variety of climates [18]. Moffat et al. [24: S206] recognised the shortcomings of the Megyesi et al. [18] method, stating; "entomologically derived PMI estimates were given too much credence when employed as precise reference data, statistical assumptions were erroneous and other errors arose through rounding and use of an inappropriate temperature scale in the worked example." Moffat et al. produced a new mathematical formula incorporating $\log_{10}$ ADD and a scale of TBS scores from 0 to 32 with upper and lower limits, to more accurately estimate the TBS [24].

The method devised by Fitzgerald and Oxenham, although it found that TSD accounted for the majority of variation in decomposition when the DDI was used and it produced mathematical models for the decomposition of the two pigs, is too narrow in its scope to be generally used without much more research [20]. The mathematical models developed by Hayman [1] and Hayman and Oxenham [25] also found that TSD incorporated not only the passage of time but also accounted for the majority of the variation in decomposition. However, these models are specific to the indoor environment and require an autopsy for greater accuracy. They remain to be tested by further research.

Is a universal formula for estimating the TSD possible?

A quantitative mathematical model for the estimation of the TSD in decomposed human bodies has been the ultimate goal of researchers since Megyesi and colleagues [18] first proposed a quantitative model and since Henssge and Madea [17] emphasised the need for quantitative rather than qualitative research. In 2011, Arpad Vass proposed two such universal models, one for buried bodies and one for decomposed bodies found on the surface, based on twenty years of research at the University of Tennessee's Anthropology Research Facility at Knoxville [32]. The models incorporated the four major factors affecting decomposition, namely temperature, moisture, the partial pressure of oxygen and the previously discovered fact that soft tissue decomposition ends at 1285 ± 110 ADDs [14].

The first model, for decomposed bodies found on the surface, i.e. in aerobic conditions in days is;

$$\text{PMI aerobic} = \frac{1285 \times (\text{decomposition}/100)}{0.0103 \times \text{temperature} \times \text{humidity}}$$

where:

1285 is a constant, representing the empirically determined ADD value at which volatile fatty acid (VFA) liberation from soft tissue ceases.

Decomposition is a single value, or range, between 1 and 100, representing the best estimation of the extent of total body soft tissue decomposition.

0.0103 is a constant, representing an empirically determined measure of the effect of moisture on decomposition rates.

Temperature is the value in degrees Celsius (°C) of either the average temperature at the site on the day the corpse was discovered or the average temperature over a period of time.

Humidity is a value between 1 and 100, representing either the average humidity at the site on the day the corpse was discovered or the average humidity over a period of time.

The requirements for this model are that the body must be found above ground and in the pre-skeletonised stage with soft tissue present. It must be at least 1 day old, free from damage by carnivores or dismemberment and the temperature must be above 1 °C and with little or no adiopocere on the corpse. The estimate of decomposition is a percentage which should be judged by an experienced investigator. The figure, 0.0103, represents a line with a slope of 0.0103 which is derived by observing the effect of humidity on the rate of decomposition over a decade at the Anthropology Research Facility.

The second model for human bodies found buried, i.e. in anaerobic conditions, in days, is;

$$\text{PMI anaerobic} = \frac{1285 \times \left(\frac{\text{decomposition}}{100}\right) \times 4.6 \times \text{adipocere}}{0.0103 \times \text{temperature} \times \text{soil moisture}}$$

where:

1285 is a constant, representing the empirically determined BADD value (burial accumulated degree days) at which volatile fatty acid (VFA) liberation from soft tissue ceases.
Decomposition is a value, or range, between 1 and 100, representing the best estimation of the extent of total body soft tissue decomposition.
4.6 is a constant which represents a slowdown in the rate of decomposition due to a lack of oxygen.
Adipocere is an arbitrarily devised multiplicative value based on the % adipocere estimated to be associated with the corpse.
0.0103 is a constant, representing an empirically determined measure of the effect of moisture on decomposition rates.
Temperature is the value in degrees Celsius (°C) of the soil temperature in the grave vault at the time of excavation and at the level of the corpse (or the average temperature over a period of time).
Soil moisture is a value between 1 and 100, representing the soil moisture at the site on the day the corpse was discovered (or the average over a period of time).

The requirements for the second model are that the body should be buried between 0.46 and 1.07 m deep, undergoing anaerobic decomposition in the pre-skeletonised phase with ground temperature above 0 °C. The percentage of decomposition, soil moisture and adipocere tissue present should be estimated and the burial should not be in an area heavily saturated with water. Vass claimed that these models worked well in the geographical area of the mid to eastern United States where humidity, soil moisture and type and vegetation were similar and he also claimed to have applied the models to many cases worldwide with "remarkable success" [32].

In 2015, Cockle and Bell attempted to verify the accuracy of these models by examining 118 outdoor corpses taken at random from a group of 7328 Canadian death investigations but selected by the quality of data and photographs and the availability of a known PMI [34]. 96 cases were found on the surface and 22 cases buried in clandestine graves. Cases were from a number of Canadian Provinces. The stage of decomposition was classified quantitatively by one person from crime scene and autopsy photographs using a scale from 1 to 8. Climate data was obtained for the PMI from the Canadian National Climate Data and Information Archive, temperature and humidity data being taken from the geographically nearest weather station. ADDs were calculated for each case using the method of Megyesi et al. [18]. A subset of 42 cases were selected from the 96 outdoor cases to test the ability of the Universal Formula [32] in surface bodies. 36 of the cases met Vass's criteria of having a PMI greater than 1 day, no scavenging, not being exposed to freezing temperatures and with no adipocere formation. A further 6 cases with longer PMIs, exposed to freezing temperatures were selected to determine if cold temperatures had any impact on the accuracy of the formula. In order to convert the 8 decomposition stages into a percentage, each stage was multiplied by 12.5.

Vass's formula for buried bodies requires soil moisture and temperature on the day of the body's discovery to be recorded [32]. These values were unavailable in this study. However, Vass's value of 4.6 used to represent the slowdown in the rate of decomposition due to lack of oxygen in buried bodies, was able to be tested [32]. The study results showed that Vass's formula [32] for decomposition of surface bodies either overestimated the PMI in Canada in warmer temperatures or underestimated bodies exposed to colder temperatures. It also found that the ratio of 4.6 used in the formula for buried bodies, could not be validated, leading to the conclusion that PMI estimations for cases in Canada using the formula would produce inaccurate results. Therefore, the idea of universality was also not supported. Cockle and Bell postulated that the reasons for these results could be that not all variables contributing to the rate of decomposition had been identified and that these variables may differ from one geographical region to another [34]. The authors concluded that understanding the variables which affect human decomposition may be more complex than previously thought.

The only other known study conducted to test the Universal equation of Vass [32] was carried out by Maile et al. [35]. A total of 19 decomposed human bodies were investigated where the PMI was known. 10 were located in the city of Honolulu, Hawaii and 9 in Lancaster County Nebraska. Nebraska has a cold climate with hot summers and a lack of a dry season while Honolulu has a tropical climate. Data loggers were used to record temperature and humidity at each death scene, in Nebraska they remained in situ for 120 min with recordings every minute while in Honolulu they remained in situ for 60 min with recordings taken every 30 s. In order to estimate the percentage decomposition, an estimate of the soft tissue mass loss was made quantitatively associated with the scale; Fresh (0.1%–5% loss of soft tissue mass), Bloat (5%–10%), Active Decay (10%–50%) and Advanced Decay (>50%). Because soft tissue mass loss estimation is difficult, subjective and inexact, a range of percentages rather than a single figure was employed. Two researchers estimated each percentage and their estimates were then averaged. The mean temperature in Nebraska was 24.6 ± 0.9°C and in Honolulu it was 25.3 ± 0.6 °C. The mean humidity in Nebraska was 46.3% ± 7.4% and in Honolulu it was 67.8% ± 2.4%.

Statistical analysis revealed that in all cases the estimated PMI was consistent with the known PMI using Vass's [32] formula for bodies found on the surface whereas in only 6 out of the 10 cases in Honolulu did the estimated PMI fall within the range of the known PMI. Two significant differences between the Nebraska cases and the Honolulu cases emerged, firstly the relative humidity in Nebraska was significantly less than in Honolulu and secondly, soft tissue mass loss was significantly less in Nebraska than in Honolulu. Inaccurate results in Honolulu were associated with much greater soft tissue mass loss and occurred in cases with a PMI greater than 5 days. The authors concluded that the Vass [32] formula for estimating PMI in decomposed bodies found on the surface was sufficiently accurate to estimate the PMI when it was ≤ 5 days. However, both the Cockle and Bell [34] and the Maile et al. [35] study overestimated the known PMI. One explanation might be the difficulty in estimating soft tissue mass loss. Both studies used different methods and it was suggested that a standard protocol for estimating soft tissue mass loss might help. A further explanation for the inaccuracy of PMI estimation could be the climatic differences between death scenes. Many studies of PMI estimation lose accuracy as decomposition progresses, the reason being that many temporary processes designed for various stages of decomposition are used which are relevant only for that transient stage of decomposition. The authors proposed that further research be conducted to increase the dataset and establish a standardised visual reference guide for estimating soft tissue loss.

Conclusion

It is only in the last 30 years that quantitative estimation of human body decomposition has been attempted and only in the last decade or so that attempts have been made to correlate this estimation with the main variables affecting the rate of decomposition, temperature and humidity. However, the context in which a decomposing body is found also has a profound effect on the rate and nature of the process. There is a marked difference in the decomposition of bodies found decomposing on the surface outside than those inside a house or apartment and again between those that are buried and those found in water. In all these contexts there is also a marked difference in the rate between geographical and climatic regions. Bodies in all these contexts decompose faster in tropical regions than in temperate regions. Yet again altitude affects the rate of decomposition; bodies found at high altitude may be very slow to decompose, if at all, as they may be found mummified, thus halting the process of decomposition. Bodies in hot dry desert environments may also mummify before decomposition is complete. Descriptions of the various stages of decomposition of the external appearance of a body and correlation with the simultaneous decomposition of relevant internal organs is promising but to date no further research has been carried out in this field. A quantitative scale of decomposition has been shown to be possible, but the description of the various stages must be more clearly defined and narrowed down. Models should be developed for each context and regional area. With the increasing establishment of human body decomposition facilities in many parts of the world, this may be possible in the future. However, there remains the problem of correlating the many variables affecting decomposition with the description of the rate at which it progresses. Statistical analysis is difficult at present, but it may be possible in the future, not only with the development of quantum computing but first and foremost in the compilation of accurate records of all human bodies found decomposed. Australia is unique in this respect in its establishment of the National Coronial Information System in the year 2000. At the present time research in the field seems to be stagnant with many projects focussing on fringe questions rather on the key question of how to more accurately estimate the time of death in human bodies found decomposed. Perhaps it is time for some lateral thinking on this important issue.

References

[1] Hayman J. Towards a more accurate estimation of the time since death in human bodies found decomposed in Australian conditions [Ph.D. thesis]. Canberra: Australian National University; 2013.

[2] McKnight BE. The washing away of wrongs: forensic medicine in thirteenth century China. Ann Arbor: University of Michigan; 1981.

[3] Réaumur RAF. Observations du thérmomètre faites à Paris pendant l'année 1735, comparées avec celles qui ont été faites sous la ligne; à l'Isle de France, à Alger et en quelques-unes de nos Isles de l'Amérique. Mémoires de l'Académie des Sciences; 1735. p. 545–76.

[4] Orfila MJB, Lesueur O. Traité des Exhumations Juridiques et considerations sur les changemens physique que les cadavres éprouvent en se pourrissant dans la terre, dans l' eau, dans les fosses d'aissance et dans le fumier, vol. 2; 1831.

[5] Mégnin JP. La Faune des Cadavres. Application d'Entomologie à la Médecine Légale. Paris: Gauthier et fils; 1894.

[6] Motter MG. A contribution to the study of the fauna of the grave. J NY Entomol Soc 1898;6(4):201–31. Dec 1898.

[7] Fuller ME. Insect inhabitants of carrion: a study in animal ecology. Aust Counc Sci Ind Res Bull 1934;82:1–62.

[8] Howden AT. The succession of beetles on carrion [Unpublished thesis]. Raleigh (NC): North Carolina State College; 1950.

[9] Reed HB. A study of dog carcass communities in Tennessee with special reference to the insects. Am Midl Nat 1958;59(1):213–45.

[10] Bornemissza GF. An analysis of arthropod succession in carrion and the effect of its decomposition on the soil fauna. Aust J Zool 1957;5(1):1–12.

[11] Payne JA. A summer carrion study of the baby pig *Sus scrofa* Linnaeus. Ecology 1965;46(5):592–602.

[12] Rodriguez WC, Bass WM. Insect activity and its relationship to decay rates of human cadavers in east Tennessee. J Forensic Sci 1983;28(2):423–32.

[13] Galloway A, et al. Decay rates of human remains in an arid environment. J Forensic Sci 1989;34(3):607–16.
[14] Vass AA, et al. Time since death determinations in human cadavers using soil solution. J Forensic Sci 1992;37(5):1236–53.
[15] Edwards R, Chaney B, Bergman M. Temperature developmental units for insects. Pest Crop Newslett 1987;2:5–6. Purdue Univ.
[16] Vass AA, et al. Decomposition chemistry of human remains: a new methodology for determining the post-mortem interval. J Forensic Sci 2002;47(3):542–53.
[17] Henssge C, Madea B. Estimation of the time since death. Forensic Sci Int 2007;165:182–4.
[18] Megyesi MS, Nawrocki SP, Haskell NH. Using accumulated degree days to estimate the post-mortem interval from decomposed human remains. J Forensic Sci 2005;50(3):1–9.
[19] Adlam RE, Simmons T. The effect of repeated physical disturbance on soft tissue decomposition - are taphonomic studies an accurate reflection of decomposition? J Forensic Sci 2007;52(5):1007–14.
[20] Fitzgerald CM, Oxenham M. Modelling time-since-death in Australian temperate conditions. Aust J Forensic Sci 2009;41(1):27–41.
[21] Michaud J-P, Moreau G. A statistical approach based on accumulated degree-days to predict decomposition-related processes in forensic studies. J Forensic Sci 2011;56(1):229–32.
[22] Myburgh J, et al. Estimating the post-mortem interval (PMI) using accumulated degree days (ADD) in a temperate region of South Africa. Forensic Sci Int 2013;229. 165.e1-165.e6.
[23] Suckling JK. A longitudinal study on the outdoor human decomposition sequence in central Texas [MSc thesis]. Texas State University; 2011.
[24] Moffatt C, et al. An improved equation for TBS and ADD: establishing a reliable postmortem interval framework for casework and experimental studies. J Forensic Sci 2016;61(S1):201–7.
[25] Hayman J, Oxenham M. Estimation of the time since death in decomposed bodies found in Australian conditions. Aust J Forensic Sci 2016;48(2):171–85.
[26] Dabbs GR. Caution! All data are not created equal: the hazards of using National Weather Service data for calculating accumulated degree days. Forensic Sci Int 2010;202:e49–52.
[27] Archer MS. The effect of time after body discovery on the accuracy of retrospective weather station ambient temperature corrections in forensic entomology. J Forensic Sci 2004;49(3):1–7.
[28] Johnson AP, Wallman JF, Archer MS. Experimental and casework validation of ambient temperature corrections in forensic entomology. J Forensic Sci 2012;57(1):215–21.
[29] Catts EP. Problems in estimating the postmortem interval in death investigations. J Agric Entomol 1992;9(4):245–55.
[30] Dabbs GR. How should forensic anthropologists correct national weather Service temperature data for use in estimating the postmortem interval? J Forensic Sci 2015;60(3):581–7.
[31] Nawrocka M, et al. Inter-rater reliability of total body score – a scale for quantification of corpse decomposition. J Forensic Sci 2016;61(3):798–802.
[32] Vass AA. The elusive post-mortem interval. Forensic Sci Int 2011;204:34–40.
[33] Dabbs GR, et al. Comparing the scoring of human decomposition from digital images to scoring using on-site observations. J Forensic Sci 2017;62(5):1292–6.
[34] Cockle DL, Bell LS. Human decomposition and the reliability of a "Universal" model for post mortem interval. Forensic Sci Int 2015;253. 136.e1-136e9.
[35] Maile AE, et al. Toward a universal equation to estimate post-mortem interval. Forensic Sci Int 2017;272:150–3.

Chapter 11

The future of taphonomic research

Giovanna M. Vidoli[a], Melanie M. Beasley[b], Lee Meadows Jantz[a], Joanne Bennett Devlin[a], Dawnie Wolfe Steadman[a]

[a]*Forensic Anthropology Center, Department of Anthropology, University of Tennessee, Knoxville, TN, United States;* [b]*Department of Anthropology, Purdue University, West Lafayette, IN, United States*

Introduction

Taphonomic research expanded greatly with the establishment of the first human decomposition facility in 1981, in Knoxville, Tennessee. The Anthropology Research Facility (ARF) and the associated Body Donation Program offers the opportunity to systematically observe and research human decomposition and associated taphonomic changes. Initial research at the ARF focused on morphological changes as a way to describe visual aspects of decomposition [1,2]. This initial research was followed by establishing methods to estimate postmortem interval (PMI) and time since death. This early research laid the foundation for more systematic studies with large sample sizes that incorporated new technologies. In this chapter, we focus on the future of taphonomic research and areas of potential growth.

Time since death

The estimation of time since death in forensic cases relies on the state of decomposition at the time of body discovery, a snapshot in time that may hold few clues as to the multitude of post depositional processes that lead to the observed condition of the remains. While ultimately the question investigators want to answer is when the person died, the first question the anthropologist must answer is, "what are the confluence of factors that led to the observed state of decomposition?"

Initial studies at the ARF focused on the first exhaustive descriptions of the human decomposition process compared with animal decomposition, and immediately demonstrated the complexities of the process [1,2]. The multitude of variables outlined by Mann and colleagues intersect, interfere with and co-opt each other in ways that are not straight-forward or easily interpretable

Estimation of the Time since Death. https://doi.org/10.1016/B978-0-12-815731-2.00011-X

[1]. Depending on environmental conditions, decomposition can occur rapidly with skeletonisation developing in a short time or there may be long periods of stasis punctuated by brief periods of change. It is only through systematic studies of decomposition occurring over long time periods that the nature of these interactions can be understood in a manner in which the PMI can be more accurately determined. Decomposition does not have a linear relationship with time since death and is not even unidirectional (e.g., when mummified tissue rehydrates and begins to decompose again). The large number of variable factors involved in decomposition and the development of new technologies has not only stimulated research at the ARF but has led to the establishment of new facilities to study human decomposition in other parts of the world and in different environments.

PMI in skeletonised remains

Estimation of the postmortem interval (PMI) from skeletonised remains is notoriously difficult and current methods employed by forensic anthropologists and pathologists to estimate PMI from skeletal remains are largely based on qualitative data (see Chapter 7, this volume, for a detailed discussion of this topic). For instance, researchers at the ARF follow a five-stage model of decomposition: fresh, bloat, active decomposition, skeletonisation and skeletal decay [3]. The timeline of each stage is loosely defined in days, weeks or months. Other data has helped determine the length of time of each stage but these are far from precise. For example, controlled taphonomic studies at the ARF have shown that grey squirrels generally do not gnaw human bones until 30 months postmortem allowing some insight into the long term PMI of skeletal elements [4]. Therefore, simply the *presence* of rodent gnawing could provide information about the PMI. Again, research at Texas State University has demonstrated that skeletonisation of a newly placed body can take place within a few hours after the onset of vulture activity, although there was a lag of over 30 days before scavenging began [5]. As another example, macroscopic changes to bone exposed to environmental elements such as water or sun will eventually exhibit taphonomic changes including bone bleaching, staining and exfoliation of the outer cortical bone. These distinctive traits are used to establish large time interval estimates that can range from years to decades but are largely subjective [6,7]. In an attempt to improve objectivity, Sauerwein examined the patterning, timing, and properties of bone staining and colour changes for use in PMI estimation [6]. Using a colour scanner, photographs, and soil samples, he concluded that staining patterns did not provide reliable time since death estimates [6].

TBS approaches and the PMI

Megyesi and colleagues' Total Body Scoring method (TBS) provided an excellent attempt to produce time since death estimations but the method is imprecise and assumes a unidirectional decomposition process (see Chapter

10, this volume, for a detailed discussion of this topic) [8]. The TBS model describes mathematically quantified observations of decomposition patterns for three areas of the body; the head and neck, all four limbs, and the trunk. A score is determined for each region and then summated as a total body score. The equation used to predict accumulated degree days (ADDs) has an error range of ±388 ADD. During a Knoxville, Tennessee, summer with average temperatures of 77 °F (25 °C), that is an error of ±15 days with one standard deviation. During the winter, in Knoxville, Tennessee, average daily temperatures are 41 °F (5.1 °C), an error rate of ±77 days with one standard deviation. The future challenge will be to more accurately estimate the PMI in skeletal remains taking into consideration all the variable factors involved.

Microscopic and biochemical approaches to the PMI

With the significant contributions of new technologies, particularly mass spectrometry, advanced microscopy (e.g., micro CT, synchrotron), molecular genetics, as well as research data concerning microbiomes (see Chapter 6, this volume), anthropologists will be better equipped to examine the microstructure of bone and collagen in order to estimate the PMI of skeletal remains. The determination of postmortem skeletal microstructure, using histological techniques, has been used to examine the taphonomic effects in bone but PMI estimates are not very accurate because of variations caused by microbial activity [9,10]. Colonisation by microorganisms can occur relatively quickly after death, within 30 days, and has been shown to be detectable after postmortem intervals of several years [11,12].

A current study employing tandem mass spectrometry is sampling the bones of 20 donors over a decomposition period of two years at the ARF as well as bone from skeletons that have been accessioned into the skeletal collection for the past 30 years. This will allow longitudinal testing of the microstructure of bone over a range of PMIs. The research is examining the proposal that osteocytes, bone cells, housed in the trabecular bone may retain marrow longer than cortical bone. As a result, lipid extraction, in addition to measuring the percentage of collagen and osteocalcin protein, may be a feasible method to estimate the time since death of skeletonised remains. This research follows a recent project which targeted lipidomics and metabolomics assays of muscle tissue collected throughout the decomposition process and which demonstrated that cell membrane phospholipids, particularly glycerophospholipids, are reliable biomarkers of PMI [13].

In addition to lipid and collagen, recently completed research led by the University of Colorado, is exploring the microbiome of decaying human bone to estimate the PMI during the extended postmortem period. Recent studies have documented the changes in microbial communities on, in, or under decomposing human subjects [14–19]. Collectively these studies reveal general patterns of microbial succession during decomposition with varying postmortem intervals. Previous research explored bacterial communities in ribs from partially skeletonised to dry remains of 12 individuals from the ARF [16]. This research demonstrated that ribs represent a relatively closed habitat with a microbial community that undergoes predictable changes after death. Following on from this research, studies are in progress to further investigate changes in microbial communities in bone in order to estimate prolonged PMIs [20].

Stable isotopes and the PMI

In addition to microbial communities, the use of isotopes is showing promise as a method of estimating the PMI. Stable isotope analysis capitalizes on the use of stoichiometric models to understand how elements in the landscape move throughout an entire ecological system, creating unique "fingerprints" of elements within a habitat and the resulting incorporation of the elements into human biological tissues. Previous research has demonstrated the usefulness of multiple stable isotopes to identify the region of origin and/or dietary patterns in border-crossers' deaths from Mexico [21], US soldier war-dead from the Vietnam conflict [22], the identification of a US airman's remains recovered in Laos [23], and distinguishing between Americans and Southeast Asians from WWII [24]. With the early success and application in forensic anthropology of stable isotope analysis for geolocation information of unknown remains, there are other questions that stable isotopes have the potential to address. Specifically, how might stable isotopes be used in innovative applications to determine the PMI?

Current research at the FAC is exploring how systematic alteration to stable nitrogen isotope ($\delta^{15}N$) values during decomposition can be used to estimate the PMI [25]. It is necessary to understand two basic principles: (1) what a $\delta^{15}N$ value is measuring and (2) what is happening to nitrogen during muscle tissue decomposition. Nitrogen has two stable isotopes with different masses, a heavy (^{15}N) and a light (^{14}N) isotope. In a chemical reaction the isotopes with different masses will react at different speeds resulting in a preferential selection of one isotope (^{14}N) compared with the other (^{15}N). During decomposition of muscle tissue (i.e., putrefaction), the breakdown of amino acids produces a variety of volatile compounds, including ammonia (NH_3) and lesser amounts of two other nitrogenous gases, cadaverine ($NH_2(CH_2)_5NH_2$) and putrescine ($NH_2(CH_2)_4NH_2$). As putrefaction progresses, the chemical reactions producing the nitrogenous gases will preferentially incorporate the light isotope (^{14}N) because it will react faster in a chemical reaction, resulting in an enrichment of the heavy isotope (^{15}N) in the remaining muscle tissue. The result, as putrefaction progresses, will be a higher concentration of $\delta^{15}N$ compared with the concentration of $\delta^{15}N$ in fresh muscle tissue (Fig. 11.1). Initial results from pilot data follow the hypothesis outlined in Fig. 11.1 for systematic increase in $\delta^{15}N$ values as putrefaction progresses.

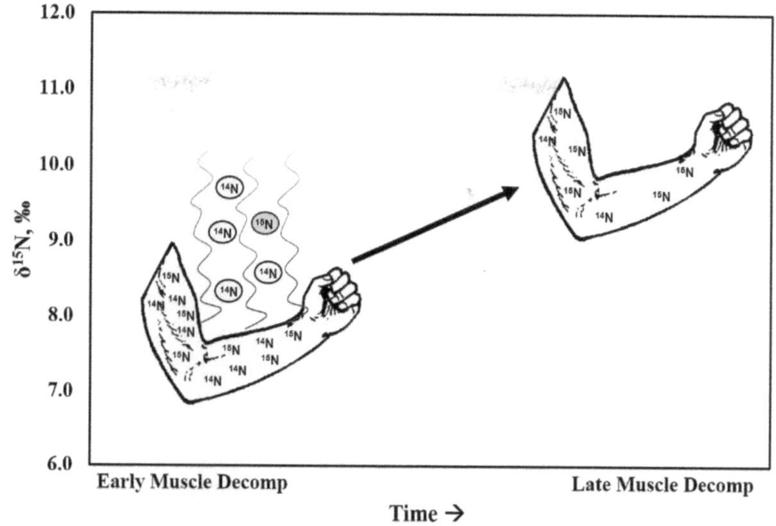

FIG. 11.1 Hypothesised change in $\delta^{15}N$ values as putrefaction progresses during human muscle decomposition.

These two research projects demonstrate that in order to fully understand late postmortem changes, the future of taphonomic research will depend on the collaboration of scientists with a range of expertise and in a number of fields.

Variation in decomposition

More accurate PMI estimates with a smaller standard error than can be determined by a TBS will be necessary for the criminal justice system. In order to increase the accuracy of PMI estimates, dedicated research is needed to better understand the variable factors involved in decomposition. For many years, decomposition research has focused on the external ecological factors involved (e.g., temperature, insects, scavenging) but new research is now concentrating on how intrinsic components of the body also affect the decomposition of the cadaver [17,26,27]. Moreover, recent studies have involved common animal carrion species in order to assess whether their interference with animal decomposition can be compared with their interference with human decomposition.

For the past several decades a prevailing, though untested, assumption was that interspecific variation in carrion decomposition was minimal such that pigs, rabbits, guinea pigs and many other animals could be reliably substituted for human cadavers. The advantage of using animal proxies is that greater sample sizes can be used and there is no necessity for secure land, as is required in a human body donation facility. Pigs (*Sus scrofa*), in particular, were considered a useful proxy for human remains when considering body weight, hairlessness, and skin thickness. While one study compared two pigs to one human and found similar species of arthropod succession at the ARF [28], a large-scale study was thought to be necessary in order to compare PMI estimates where carrion species were involved and to evaluate multiple variables. A two-year project that compared decomposition patterns and rates of 45 humans, pigs and rabbits placed at the ARF in three separate seasonal trials provided some information as to how and why choice of carrion species is important to address specific decomposition questions. Five of each species were simultaneously placed during summer, winter and spring. The TBS method was applied to each subject throughout the decomposition period and was found to yield ADD estimates that were not only very different from known PMIs but were also different within the same species despite the same external environment [29]. For example, pigs were more likely to be colonised by maggots earlier and more completely than humans, which increases their decomposition rate in the summer, while humans were more likely to be scavenged [30]. Other species-specific factors that could be researched in the future are microbial loading, dietary variation (farm-fed rabbits and pigs have homogenous, restricted diets compared to humans) and body composition.

As the FAC began to do more research involving large trials of human donors (five or more donors placed at the same time in the same microenvironment) in order to study interspecific variation, modified TBS methods or microbiomes, it became clear that the external environment could not explain all of the variation observed in human decomposition. While one human donor in a trial of five subjects may exhibit expected insect colonisation and succession, another donor placed simultaneously only five meters away may have little or no insect activity while another may be heavily scavenged and others may not be touched. The intrinsic environment of the body itself may have a greater effect on the extrinsic factors controlling decomposition, for example soil microbes, insects and scavengers, than previously thought. A recent research study by Hayman and Oxenham evaluated two human subjects that differed in medical treatment before death (one had cancer and was undergoing chemotherapy and antibiotic therapy at the time of death while the other subject had diabetes and died of an acute myocardial infarction) [31]. While the external conditions were similar for the two donors at the time of placement, insects did not access the body of the cancer donor and overall decomposition was much slower. Insect and scavenger preference and avoidance of donors has also been observed at the ARF. In 2015, four donors were placed simultaneously at the ARF in the summer, three of whom who had cancer but only one who had received radiation and chemotherapy treatments. The donor who had received treatments had delayed insect activity and was avoided by scavengers compared to the others who exhibited the expected decomposition patterns and rates for the season. This delay in oviposition will result in erroneous PMI estimates if it is assumed that oviposition should always have occurred soon after death.

Considering that methods to estimate the postmortem interval have been developed based on entomological data [32–34], as well as morphological changes to the body [8], and new methods are being developed on microbial data, it is necessary to establish the parameters by which drugs in the human body influence the macro- and micro-decomposers found at death scenes. Thus, a new study was recently launched at the ARF to study the relationship between drug metabolites in the decomposer communities and how this affects PMI rates in approximately 100 donors. This systematic study will correlate the reasons why scavengers choose to consume body tissues in bodies with different documented diseases, treatments, and with multiple drugs in their systems. At the same time fly oviposition timing and location will be documented, as well as maggot metabolomics that will hopefully reveal which human-derived drugs are being ingested and which may affect maggot development. Enteric and soil microbes will be studied to assess relative community taxonomy and activity in response to human drug metabolomic loading. It is hoped that this research involving drugs and disease in decomposing bodies will increase the understanding of other intrinsic parameters that might influence decomposition rates.

As discussed above, a TBS has provided a much-needed quantitative method of determining the PMI but the standard error is high, the technique is imprecise and still suffers from subjectivity in the scoring. The goal of a recently completed project was to simplify and standardise decomposition observations, to maximize agreement among observers and to reduce bias [35,36]. The standardisation of decomposition observations was accomplished through the development of a list of easily identified traits across 16 body regions that were recorded as present or absent. The addition of a scavenging observation added the ability to document rapid tissue loss due to animal activity. This study improved on the deficiencies of the Megyesi et al. TBS method [8] in that it used empirical longitudinal data from donors with known PMI rather than photographs that had minimal temporal or contextual control. By placing multiple human donors at the same time in the same environment, direct observation of variation within and among individuals provided an associated prediction interval. The trait scores were then converted to an associated weighted score that reduced bias and increased observer agreement. Finally, the inclusion of GIS (geographic information system) techniques allowed for both the visualization and quantification of decomposition patterns through time with the use of heat maps and hot spot analysis. Random forest models were created from all these data (all regions) and on individual regions. The models were created using known ADD as a function of each of the binary observations. The random forest model then predicted estimated ADD scores for the entire dataset, which could then be used to work backwards to estimate the time since death for an individual. The models created will be incorporated into a graphical user interface (GUI) that will be available as a downloadable application on a tablet or smartphone. This will allow practitioners to score each of the observations for a decomposing body and be provided with an estimated ADD point estimate and associated prediction interval.

The completed project elucidated several important outcomes for postmortem interval estimation. First, the addition of scoring individual, discrete traits, without any weight associated with it during collection allowed for less bias, especially from practitioners that do not have much experience with decomposition. This was especially important because there were no instructions on which part of the composite observations in Megyesi et al. should be given more weight [8]. Second, scavenging activity greatly accelerated decomposition around the scavenged region. However, more precise observations are necessary. Adding in observations such as "colour changes in distal aspect" or "colour changes in proximal aspect" will aid in capturing more variability in limb decomposition, especially in the earlier stages of decomposition.

Unanswered questions

Taphonomic research has expanded in the past 30 years to provide new glimpses into microenvironments in the soil, in the body, and even within cells that may be useful in developing new PMI techniques. However, it is important to continue research into decomposition macro environments in order to provide the medicolegal community with more precise postmortem intervals in different environments. Much of the research conducted at body farms stems directly from law enforcement cases. The FAC receives weekly calls from law enforcement around the world enquiring about the condition of a decomposed body, or what quantity of a skeleton would remain, considering a particular environment or period of time (e.g., in the water for a year). One example concerns hanging. Police found that the appearance of bodies of hanging victims in Tennessee did not appear similar to the literature describing bodies of donors used in research at the Body Farm where the donors had been laid on the ground surface or buried. Wilson-Taylor and Dautartas conducted a study on hanging individuals and found differences in decomposition patterns and rates that were possibly due to the absence of the ground-body interface and maggot behaviour, but this research needs to be repeated with a larger sample size and expanded to include more entomological data [37].

Another depositional environment for which little systematic research has been conducted on human remains is in water (see Chapter 8, this volume, for a detailed discussion of this topic). Decomposition in aquatic environments varies depending on the salinity, oxygen levels, currents, and temperature of the water [38,39] and therefore the environments are difficult to recreate. However, even limited research with porcine remains has demonstrated the importance of aquatic fauna and microorganisms that requires additional study [40]. Fluvial environments are especially challenging to research when considering that human remains may disarticulate and possibly travel over hundreds of miles. A current study is examining the transport of bodies on fluvial waterways with mannequins, although non-biological materials cannot replicate the effect of water on decomposition and body disarticulation [41]. Finally, the effect of burning on bodies when estimating an accurate postmortem interval is currently unknown and controlled studies using some of the methods mentioned above, including microbes or tissue sampling, could provide medicolegal personnel additional information in complex forensic cases.

Conclusions

This chapter demonstrates the commitment of taphonomic researchers to work with the law enforcement and medicolegal communities to better estimate the PMI and the necessity to obtain human donors as study subjects. Ideally, taphonomic studies should be repeated at many human decomposition facilities in order to ensure robust methods of validation prior to applications in forensic casework. In addition, the future of taphonomic studies lies in working with many scientific disciplines and in many different facilities which research decomposition in order to gain a more complete understanding of how the human body is affected, not only after death but also after the remains have skeletonised.

References

[1] Mann RW, Bass WM, Meadows L. Time since death and decomposition of the human body: variables and observations in case and experimental field studies. J Forensic Sci 1990;35(1):103–11.

[2] Rodriguez W, Bass WM. Insect activity and its relationship to decay rates of human cadavers in east Tennessee. J Forensic Sci 1983;28:423–32.

[3] Marks MK, Love JC, Dadour IR. Taphonomy and time: estimating the postmortem interval. In: Steadman DW, editor. Hard evidence: case studies in forensic anthropology. 2nd ed. Upper Saddle River (NJ): Prentice Hall; 2009. p. 165–78.

[4] Klippel WE, Synstelien JA. Rodents as taphonomic agents: bone gnawing by brown rats and gray squirrels. J Forensic Sci 2007;52(4):765–73.

[5] Spradley MK, Hamilton MD, Giordano A. Spatial patterning of vulture scavenged human remains. Forensic Sci Int 2012;219(1–3):57–63.

[6] Sauerwein K. The sequence of bone staining and its applications to the postmortem interval [MA thesis]. San Marcos: Department of Anthropology, Texas State University; 2012.

[7] Behrensmeyer AK. Taphonomic and ecologic information from bone weathering. Paleobiology 1978;4(2):150–62.

[8] Megyesi MS, et al. Using accumulated degree-days to estimate the postmortem interval from decomposed human remains. J Forensic Sci 2005;50(3):618–26.

[9] Cappela A, Gibelli D, Muccino E, Scarulla V, Cerutti E, Caruso V, Sguazza E, Mazzarelli D, Cattaneo C. The comparative performance of PMI estimation in skeletal remains by three methods (C-14, luminol test and OHI): analysis of 20 cases. Int J Leg Med 2015;132:1215–24.

[10] Hackett CJ. Microscopical focal destruction (tunnels) in exhumed human bones. Med Sci Law 1981;21:243–65.

[11] Damann FE. Human decomposition ecology at the University of Tennessee anthropology Research facility [Ph.D. dissertation]. Department of Anthropology, University of Tennessee; 2010.

[12] Emmons AL, Mundorff AZ, Keenan SW, Davoren J, Andronowski JM, Carter DO, DeBruyn JM. Patterns of microbial colonization of human bone from surface-decomposed remains. BioRxiv 2019:664482.

[13] Langley N, Wood P, Steadman D. Postmortem interval determination-A metabolomics/lipidomics approach. Forensic Anthropol 2019. https://doi.org/10.5744/fa.2019.1011 (in press).

[14] Hyde ER, Haarmann DP, Lynne AM, Bucheli SR, Petrosino JF. The living dead: bacterial community structure of a cadaver at the onset and end of the bloat stage of decomposition. PLoS One 2013;8(10):e77733.

[15] Tuomisto S, Karhunen PJ, Pessi T. Time-dependent post mortem changes in the composition of intestinal bacteria using real-time quantitative PCR. Gut Pathog 2013;5(1):35.

[16] Damann FE, Williams DE, Layton AC. Potential use of bacterial community succession in decaying human bone for estimating postmortem interval. J Forensic Sci 2015;60(4):844–50.

[17] Cobaugh KL, Schaeffer SM, DeBruyn JM. Functional and structural succession of soil microbial communities below decomposing human cadavers. PLoS One 2015;10:e0130201.

[18] Javan GT, Finley SJ, Can I, Wilkinson JE, Hanson JD, Tarone AM. Human thanatomicrobiome succession and time since death. Sci Rep 2016;6:29598.

[19] Metcalf JL, Xu XX, Weiss S, Lax S, Van Treuren W, Hyde ER, Song SJ, Amir A, Larsen P, Sangwant N, Haarmann D, Humphrey GC, Ackermann G, Thompson LR, Lauber C, Bibat A, Nicholas C, Gebert MJ, Petrosino JF, Reed SC, Gilbert JA, Lynne AM, Bcheli SR, Carter DO, Knight R. Microbial community assembly and metabolic function during mammalian corpse decomposition. Science 2016;351(6269):158–62.

[20] Deel HL, Belk AD, Lynne AM, Bucheli SR, Zhenjiang ZX, Damann FE, Carter DO, Knight R, Metcalf JL. Estimating postmortem interval (PMI) using microbial succession in human cadaver rib bones. In: Paper presented at the 71st annual meeting of the American Academy of Forensic Sciences, Baltimore, MD, February 21, 2019; 2019.

[21] Juarez CA. Strontium and geolocation, the pathway to identification for deceased undocumented Mexican border-crossers: a preliminary report. J Forensic Sci 2008;53:46–9.

[22] Regan LA. Isotopic determination of region of origin in modern peoples: applications for identification of U.S. war-dead from the Vietnam conflict [Unpublished Ph.D. dissertation]. University of Florida; 2006.

[23] Holland TD, Berg GE, Regan LA. Identification of a United States airman using stable isotopes. In: Proceedings of the 64th annual meetings of American Academy of Forensic Sciences, Atlanta, vol. 18; 2012. p. 420–1.

[24] Bartelink EJ, Berg GE, Beasley MM, Chesson LA. Application of stable isotope forensics for predicting region-of-origin of human remains from past wars and conflicts. Ann Anthropol Pract 2014;38(1):124–36. Special volume (invited): "Practicing forensic anthropology: a human rights approach to the global problem of missing and unidentified persons".

[25] Beasley MM, Lesnik J, McKee H, Steadman DW. Using stable nitrogen isotope ratios from human muscle tissue for postmortem interval (PMI) estimation. In: Proceedings of the 71st annual meetings of American Academy of Forensic Sciences, Baltimore, vol. 25; 2019. p. 108 (A61).

[26] Carter DO, Metcalf JL, Bibat A, Knight R. Seasonal variation of postmortem microbial communities. Forensic Sci Med Pathol 2015;11:202–27.

[27] Fancher JP, Aitkenhead-Peterson JA, Farris T, Mix K, Schwab AP, Wescott DJ, Hamilton MD. An evaluation of soil chemistry in human cadaver decomposition islands: potential for estimating postmortem interval (PMI). Forensic Sci Int 2017;279:130–9.

[28] Schoenly KG, Haskell NH, Hall RD, Gbur JR. Comparative performance and complementarity of four sampling methods and arthropod preference tests from human and porcine remains at the Forensic Anthropology Center in Knoxville, Tennessee. J Med Entomol 2007;44:881–94.

[29] Dautartas A, Kenyhercz MW, Vidoli GM, Meadows Jantz L, Mundorff A, Steadman DW. Differential decomposition among pig, rabbit, and human remains. J Forensic Sci 2018;63(6):1673–83.

[30] Steadman DW, Dautartas A, Kenyhercz MW, Jantz LM, Mundorff A, Vidoli GM. Differential scavenging among pig, rabbit, and human subjects. J Forensic Sci 2018;63(6):1684–91.

[31] Hayman J, Oxenham M. Peri-mortem disease treatment: a little known cause of error in the estimation of the time since death in decomposing human remains. Aust J Forensic Sci 2016;48(2):171–85.

[32] Bugelli V, Forni D, Bassi LA, Di Paolo M, Marra D, Lenzi S, Toni C, Giusiani M, Domenici R, Gherardi M, Vanin S. Forensic entomology and the estimation of the minimum time since death in indoor cases. J Forensic Sci 2015;60(2):525–31.

[33] Byrd JH, Castner JL. Insects of forensic importance. In: Byrd JH, Castner JL, editors. Forensic entomology: the utility of arthropods in legal investigations. 2nd ed. Boca Raton: CRC Press; 2010. p. 287–302.

[34] Huntington T, Higley L. Collection and analysis of climatological data. In: Williams RE, Haskell HN, editors. Entomology & death: a procedural guide; 2008. p. 144–59.

[35] Vidoli GM. Expanding on total body score with use of geographic information systems (GIS). Final Report to National Institute of Justice. 2019 (in press).

[36] Kenyhercz MW, Steadman DW, Gundel AC, Vidoli GM. A new approach to estimating accumulated degree days (ADD): using binary observations from various regions of the body with random forest modeling (RFM) and geographic information systems (GIS). In: Paper presented at the 69th annual meeting of the American Academy of forensic Sciences, February 17, 2017, New Orleans, Louisiana; 2017.

[37] Wilson-Taylor RJ, Dautartas AM. Time since death estimation and bone weathering the postmortem interval. Forensic Anthropol 2017:273.

[38] Fink A. Estimating postmortem intervals of human remains recovered from mid-western waterways in various water temperatures [MA thesis]. University of Tennessee; 2017. Read abstract and discussion.

[39] Heaton V, Lagden A, Moffatt C, Simmons T. Predicting the postmortem submersion interval for human remains recovered from UK waterways. J Forensic Sci 2010;55(2):302–7.

[40] Anderson GS, Hobischak NR. Decomposition of carrion in the marine environment in British Columbia, Canada. Int J Leg Med 2004;118(4):206–9.

[41] Milligan C, Bartelink E. Modeling the fluvial transport of human remains in the sacramento river of California. In: Paper presented at the 71st annual meeting of the American Academy of forensic Sciences, Baltimore, MD, February 21, 2019; 2019.

Index

Note: 'Page numbers followed by "f" indicate figures, "t" indicates tables'.

Q

R

S

T

U

V

W

FSC
www.fsc.org
MIX
Papier | Fördert
gute Waldnutzung
FSC® C083411

Kolibri 360 GmbH
Ferdinand-Jühlke-Straße 7
99095 Erfurt, Deutschland
produktsicherheit@kolibri360.de